ALL YOU CAN BE

A soldier's reflections on
service in the greatest Army
the world has ever seen.

Address inquiries to:

David Kay
P.O. Box 10357
Spokane, WA 99209

ISBN 0-9703625-0-1

This edition printed by:
Valley Press
207 West Stewart
Puyallup, WA 98371

Cover design by Carrington, Ink!

Printed in U.S.A.

First Edition October 2000

This book is dedicated to Army spouses
and especially one in particular:

Irene

**A portion of the proceeds from this book
will go to the Combined Federal Campaign**

Acknowledgements

When one is not a writer by profession, it is always good to get a little help from family and friends more familiar with the written word. First and foremost, my wife Irene has provided invaluable assistance at every stage of this task. She has been the grammar beneath my wings.

My four children were of great help as well. But for them this book would remain only an idea.

I especially want to extend my heartfelt thanks to the following very special people who provided constructive critique, editing, comments and guidance along the way: Sandy Riddle, Rick Blondo, Fred Ruprecht and Mike Stake. Their "green light" helped me go for it.

The comments and suggestions of many others helped polish the final product. These outstanding Americans include Jamie Osborne, Amy Gillette, Audie Pressley, Chaplain (LTC) George Bearden (USA), LTC Dale Ziesmer (USAF Ret), CPT Cory Costello (USA), 1LT Mark Dedmon (USA Ret), 2LT Alex Morales (USA), SGM Charles Spencer (USA Ret), and SFC Reynaldo Toledo (USA).

I thank the patients, students and staff that visited my Army world, chuckled at the tales, gave me some great memories and inspired some of the philosophy. Without them and the tens of thousands of other soldiers and family members I have known, it would have been impossible for this book to be all it can.

David Kay

Table of Contents

Acronym Glossary

1LT	First Lieutenant		DF	Disposition Form
1SG	First Sergeant		DITY	Do-It-Yourself Move
4WD	Four-wheel Drive		DMZ	Demilitarized Zone
AAFES	Army & Air Force Exchange Service		DNA	Deoxyribonucleic Acid
AAR	After Action Report		DOA	Dead on Arrival
ACLS	Acute Cardiac Life Support		DOD	Department of Defense
ACR	Armored Cavalry Regiment		DOR	Date of Rank
ADHD	Attention Deficit Hyperactivity Disorder		DRE	Digital Rectal Examination
AFN	Armed Forces Network		DRF	Division Ready Force
AIDS	Acquired Immune Deficiency Syndrome		DROS	Date expected to Rotate from Overseas
AIT	Advanced Individual Training		DX	Direct Exchange
AMC	Air Mobility Command		EDCEN	Education Center
AO	Area of Operations		EFMB	Expert Field Medical Badge
APC	Armored Personnel Carrier		EIB	Expert Infantryman Badge
AR	Armor		ER	Emergency Room
ARNG	Army National Guard		ETS	End of Term in Service
ARPERCEN	Army Personnel Center		F	Fahrenheit
ASAP	As Soon As Possible		FA	Field Artillery
AVN	Aviation		FO	Forward Observer
AWOL	Absent Without Leave		FSB	Forward Support Battalion
BCGs	Birth Control Glasses		FTX	Field Training Exercise
BCT	Basic Combat Training		FYI	For Your Information
BDU	Battle Dress Uniform		G	Gravity
BMO	Battalion Maintenance Officer		GI	Government Issue / Gastrointestinal
BMW	Barvarian Motor Works		GMC	General Motors Corporation
BO	Body Odor		GP	General Purpose
BOQ	Bachelor Officer's Quarters		GPA	Grade Point Average
CAV	Cavalry		GPS	Global Positioning System
CEO	Chief Executive Officer		GS	General Schedule
CIA	Central Intelligence Agency		GTR	Government Transportation Request
CIF	Central Issue Facility		HMO	Health Maintenance Organization
CNN	Cable News Network		HUMMV	High Utility Multipurpose Military Vehicle
CO	Commanding Officer		IAW	In Accordance With
COLA	Cost of Living Allowance		IBN	International Business Machines
CPL	Corporal		ID	Identification
CPR	Cardiopulmonary Resuscitation		IG	Inspector General
CPT	Captain		IN	Infantry
CQ	Charge of Quarters		IOU	I Owe You
CT	Comp Time / Computerized Tomography		IP	Instructor Pilot
CZ	Combat Zone		IQ	Intelligence Quotient
DA	Department of the Army		IV	Intravenous
DAPAM	Department of the Army Pamphlet		JRTC	Joint Readiness Training Center
DCCS	Deputy Commander for Clinical Services		K	Kilometer
DD Form	Department of Defense Form		KIA	Killed in Action
DENTAC	Dental Activity		KIS	Keep It Simple

Acronym Glossary

LCE	Loadbearing Combat Equipment	PMCS	Preventive Maintenance Checks &Services
LES	Leave and Earnings Statement	POC	Point of Contact
LTC	Lieutenant Colonel	POL	Petroleum, Oil, and Lubricants
MBA	Motorbike Accident	POV	Privately Owned Vehicle
MAJ	Major	POW	Prisoner of War
MARS	Military Affiliate Radio Station	PT	Physical Training
MD	Medical Doctor	PW	Prisoner of War
MEDDAC	Medical Activity	PX	Post Exchange
MEDEVAC	Medical Evacuation (Aircraft)	R&R	Rest and Relaxation
MEPS	Military Entrance Processing Station	RA	Regular Army
MILES	Multi-Integrat. Laser Engagement System	REFORGER	Reinforce Germany
MO	Medical Officer	RLO	Real Live Officer
MOS	Military Occupational Specialty	RPM	Revolutions Per Minute
MP	Military Police	ROTC	Reserve Officer Training Corps
MRE	Meals, Ready to Eat	SAPA	Society of Army Physician Assistants
MSB	Main Support Battalion	SD	Special Duty
MSR	Main Supply Route	SFC	Sergeant First Class
MTF	Medical Treatment Facility	SGM	Sergeant Major
MTOE	Modification Table of Organization Equip.	SGT	Sergeant
NATO	North Atlantic Treaty Organization	SIGO	Signal Officer
NCO	Non-Commissioned Officer	SIR	Serious Incident Report
NCOIC	Non-Commissioned Officer in Charge	SM	Service Member
NOE	Nap-of-the-Earth	SOP	Standard Operating Procedure
NPD	No Pay Due	SPC	Specialist
NST	Not Sooner Than	SSG	Staff Sergeant
NTC	National Training Center	TA	Tactical Assemblage
NVG	Night Vision Goggles	TACSOP	Tactical Standard Operating Procedure
OBE	Overcome by Events	TDHGD	Travel Dependents Household Goods Auth
OC	Observer Controller	TDY	Temporary Duty
OCONUS	Outside Continental United States	TNG	Training
OD	Olive Drab	TO&E	Table of Organization and Equipment
OIC	Officer In Charge	TR	Transportation Request
OP	Observation Post	UCMJ	Uniform Code of Military Justice
OPFOR	Opposing Force	UH	Utility Helicopter
OPM	Office of the Program Manager	UK	United Kingdom
PA	Physician Assistant	UN	United Nations
PAC	Personnel Administration Center	USA	United States of America (or Army)
PACOM	Pacific Command	USAR	United States Army Reserve
PBO	Property Book Officer	USAREUR	United States Army Europe
PC	Personal Computer	USS	United States Ship
PCS	Permanent Change of Station	VA	Veterans Administration
PE	Physical Examination	VIP	Very Important Person
PERSCOM	Personnel Command	WIA	Wounded in Action
PFC	Private First Class	XO	Executive Officer
PLF	Parachute Landing Fall	YMCA	Young Men's Christian Association
PLT	Platoon		

The Long, Green Line

"When you put down the good things you ought to have done, and leave out
the bad ones you did do—well, that's memoirs."
Will Rogers

This book about the United States Army is a compilation of the
thoughts, memories, and the opinions of one man. It is somewhat
autobiographical, because it pieces together the personal experiences of a
twenty-year Army veteran. The intent, though, is to describe Army life, to
capture the people and some of the essence of what it meant to have served
in the greatest Army the world has ever seen. It is an organization with a
very human face. It is also a military machine fully capable of dominating
the world if left in the wrong hands. What a wonder that providence
entrusted such power to a democracy, a country instrumental in the *Pax
Americana* of the late 20th century!

The journey has been varied and worldwide. Few are afforded the
experience of meeting and working with so many great Americans, literally
tens of thousands. This is a picture of the Army anchored in sublime bits of
wisdom harvested from history, philosophy, religion and life in general. The
overriding theme is that there is a lesson in all we do, especially with people
who serve others.

Old soldiers have tales. Through this book may the lessons, mistakes,
and victories described educate future soldiers and Americans in general
about what their tax dollar buys. And may these stories, in some small way,
bring meaning and guidance to those soldiers currently in the service.

The tincture of time will cover over many details of our lives. Much
will be forgotten unless it is written down. The stories that follow offer some
unofficial humor, thoughts and details about the United States Army for
general consumption that otherwise would have been forgotten.

Behind the long, gray line that begins at West Point lies the all
important and much, much longer green line. It is a line made up of soldiers,
punctuated by officers, but held together by non-commissioned officers who
are like the vowels found in every word, making sense of it all. Together
they all make things happen. They make the Army.

Every citizen of our Republic would do well to honor the service and
sacrifice of the men and women of their Armed Forces. Nothing can be
nobler than to voluntarily serve. There is no greater privilege than to be a
part of that long green line.

American soldiers have been, and will continue to be, all that they can
possibly be.

Imprinting

"...all believe that the source of all power and goodness
is in the sky, and they believe very firmly that I,
with these ships and people, came from the sky..."
Christopher Columbus

Something influences every recruit who enters military service. The U.S. Army spends millions of dollars each year trying to entice young people to join up. Through advertisements, recruiters and incentives, the "all volunteer" military competes with the private sector in raising the necessary manpower to do the job at hand. There are even people who dedicate their entire professional careers to studying what things influence people the most in joining the military.

Every soldier probably can recall what motivated him or her to join the service. Ironically, many were not influenced so much by the slick Madison-Avenue ads on television or in magazines. Most were motivated to join by something deeper. For many it was some experience, often traceable to some incidental event in their childhood.

One of my earliest memories in life involved the Army. I was a small three or four year-old boy playing in the backyard of my house in the mountains of North Carolina. The day would have been just like any other, except for the sudden noise and arrival of fifteen or twenty U.S. Army helicopters in the sky right overhead. Flying low, the formation of attack and transport helicopters brought terror and fear into my heart. Paralyzed by it all, I stared in amazement as these noisy, man-made, wasp-like creatures entered my innocent world for the first time. Some of the pilots and crews must have sensed my fear, for I saw their friendly waves as they passed overhead. My fear transformed instantly into excitement as I realized there were people inside those flying monsters, and they seemed friendly!

In a few moments, they were gone, disappearing over the forest near my home. I stood for a long time listening to the chop-chop sound fade in the distance. "Oh, please come back!" I said out loud.

Later, when my dad came home from work, I excitedly told him of the marvelous event. He knowingly smiled and made it a point to take me down near the French Broad River where those helicopters had landed. There the huge, dark green helicopters sat in neat rows, their crews standing around in sharp flight suits. What an experience that was for me!

You ask, what makes a person join the military? Many things, I am sure. For one man, it was an inspiring childhood imprint from ships and people who came from the sky.

Fools

"Hain't we got all the fools in town on our side?
And ain't that a big enough majority in any town?"
Mark Twain

"You've done what?" How many times I heard that response from school buddies and friends when they learned about me joining the Army. The puzzled looks were followed by the kind of treatment one receives when there has been a death in the family. They displayed sympathetic mannerisms, hushed voices, concerned looks, and poor eye contact. In the longhaired group of high school and college friends of my life, no one entertained the notion of joining the service in the late 1970s. Even my wife, Irene, had her reservations. But for better or worse, she was going to be there for me. "We" had joined the Army. It was our decision.

Despite an education there were no jobs to be had. It didn't help that my college work was in something near to underwater basket weaving. Sure, there was regular work at a local snack cake factory, but it wasn't enough. Too confining. Making snack cakes was something for other people, not my idea of making a mark in life. A kid who played with toy Army men would one day want to be a real Army man. See the world. It had to be my destiny. Other people could work the factories.

As the clock ticked away during my three-month delayed entry program for the Army, my brain wondered whether it was indeed a foolish mistake to join up. My brain and my heart debated the issue back and forth. The brain thought that maybe it wasn't such a good idea after all. Then again, my heart said maybe it was. In the end, the heart would win.

The great adventure began just after my 23rd birthday in July 1979. The Kay's began a road less traveled as our friends moved on in their self-chosen civilian careers. In any path of life there is a high road and a low road. Starting out as a Private First Class may seem to many like a low road, but it is a road that does get higher if you stick with it.

Years later at class reunions, the paths of friends and classmates would cross ours again. Some folks were fairly successful and well to do. Most were not. Many seemed to "live lives of quiet desperation." It was as if they felt something was missing.

Not the Kays. Though not well to do, we did well. My wife often comments how seldom we experienced a dull moment in the Army. What some may have thought a foolish choice, turned out just fine. The stories ahead are an after action report.

The bottom line up front is the fools were a "go" at this station.

3

The Haircut

"Experience is a comb given to a man when he is bald."
Irish Proverb

Fewer and fewer Americans experience the induction process into the military. An all-volunteer Army and a downsized defense force leave many without the opportunity to experience military life.

For civilians who enter the military, one of the more dramatic initial experiences is the famous Army haircut. For males at least, one size and type fits all. Our first day in the induction center at Fort Leonard Wood, Missouri, included a stop at the barber. A forty-man platoon and five barber chairs—we were all done in fifteen minutes. The barbers, all elderly men, seemed to show a special joy at converting all these "hippies" into bald-headed recruits. Their daily experiences at sheering humans would without a doubt be the subject of an incredibly interesting book.

I especially recall a fellow recruit from New York State in the chair next to me whose hair was longer than my red mop. The barber asked him, "Well, how would you like your hair cut?" The New Yorker replied, "Take what you have to, but try to leave me something to comb." The barber, displaying a slightly fiendish grin in the mirror before us, proceeded to cut his hair the same as everyone else. The resulting quarter-inch stubble would need no comb.

As the hair fell into neat piles on the floor one could feel a new chill to the scalp's skin, so long accustomed to a warm blanket of hair. We learned to sympathize with sheep. Back in the 1970s a lot of hair was the "in thing" and some folks' scalps had probably not seen the light of day since birth. Those people had especially large piles of hair next to the chairs of the very efficient barbers.

Within a minute or so it was all over, the head now naked and the barber calling for the "next victim." As we assembled outside, one could barely recognize the shorn creatures exiting the building. Each of us would at first have sheepish looks of worry. What have they done to me? Then the laughs would come, something humans often do when faced with small tragedies. We would all laugh at our predicament. In truth there were also some watery eyes.

The haircut was an ordeal we would not soon forget and an experience that told us the bridge to the military had been crossed. To turn back was to go back bald-headed to the land of the hairy. No, we would go on, to share an ordeal that would forever change us on the inside, mostly for the good, with or without a comb.

Blood

"There is wonderful power in the blood."
Lewis E. Jones

For the new recruit into the military there are many new and interesting experiences that begin right on day number one. At any one of the military basic training facilities across the country new recruits get haircuts, are issued uniforms, fill out forms, and pass through a blur of stations and paperwork. Eventually they undergo what is probably the most memorable induction event after the loss of their hair: the medical processing station.

The military medical processing ordeal includes shots, physical examinations, dental x-rays, a hearing test, creating a medical record, and getting a DNA test. Everything gets checked. A first for most recruits is the discovery of their individual blood type. With it comes the realization that this military business is potentially very serious stuff.

After the soldier's name and social security number, there come two more items engraved on those brand new dog tags that could only mean bad news if they are ever required—the blood type for the medics and your religious preference for the chaplain. The medics and the chaplain need to know these things if you can't speak for yourself, which would mean that you are very wounded or, even worse, they need the tags to tell them who you once were.

People who enter the service come from all walks of life. The military takes all colors, Northerners, Southerners, Easterners, Westerners, accents, languages, religions, educational backgrounds and genders. The mutual experience blends them into soldiers first and individuals second. As they become soldiers there is a special power about this blood business. These varied people who are fast becoming a team realize that they are all cut from a similar cloth. They are not so different after all.

Blood symbolizes life. It is a powerful thing that someone else's blood, be it Irish-American, African-American, American Indian, Asian American, Hispanic American or whatever-American, can save the lives of people not of the same ethnic or racial background.

Nothing can be more powerfully democratic to soldiers than the idea that we are all for one and one for all. We are indeed all created equal. We are all made from a common pattern. We do not need uniforms to bind us together. A glance at the blood type on their dog tags as they go through life in the Army reminds soldiers that they need each other. Yes, there is wonderful power in the blood.

Boot Camp

"The suspense is terrible. I hope it will last."
Oscar Wilde

We called them "cattle cars." At least that's what they looked like. These silver tractor-trailers built to haul people looked very similar to the ones you see hauling livestock on the highway, the ones that take animals to the slaughterhouse. We made our way in these cattle cars across Fort Leonard Wood, Missouri, to our waiting drill sergeants.

Silence gripped us all as we swayed and bounced in the trailers. We knew that some life-altering, serious experience was about to happen and the cattle car ride was not helping calm our nerves. Little did we realize then how much of our "civilian-ness" was about to be slaughtered.

The truck pulled up in front of two very stern looking staff sergeants in Smokey Bear hats. I just knew neither of them had ever smiled a day in his life. The doors opened, and we were sourly greeted with, "Well, what are you waiting for? Get off that truck!" As we made our way out the doors as best as civilians knew how, one of the sergeants snarled, "Well, ladies, any time will do." We cast nervous looks at each other. Our worst fears were coming true. It was going to be a difficult time ahead.

We were a sorry-looking lot, a motley crew in new fatigue uniforms. We were probably just like any other group of new trainees arriving at boot camp. The sergeants knew their business though, and over the next few weeks they would shape us into soldiers. We would overcome fear and expand our abilities. The Army would challenge us. We would be assimilated, or be on the next bus home.

Scrambling on the double to our barracks, the macabre scene is forever ingrained in my memory. Forty grown men-boys struggling with gear, luggage, wool Army blankets, sheets, and toilet paper rolls in a strung-out line reminiscent of some awful retreat. Items fell by the wayside. I saw bed sheets, a roll of toilet paper, and a helmet. But every discarded item was dutifully picked up by our vigilant drill sergeant rearguard. Each abandoned item would later be dearly paid for by the owner when a very thorough inventory by our tormentors discovered who was missing what.

The suspense of our basic training ordeal was terrible. We were glad it did not last forever. Other aspects did last, things that made us into better men. We were men who would have made our mothers proud. Men who knew how to fold socks, do laundry, make beds, dress sharp and otherwise do what they were told. The constant prayer of moms and drill sergeants is that these effects in particular will last.

Everything I Ever Needed to Know

"Knowledge is power."
Francis Bacon

Stupidity has many synonyms: a lapse of memory, temporary disorientation, or an idiot attack. Whatever name we give it, most of us will readily admit, at least in our more honest moments, that at some time or other stupidity has struck us too.

I like to think I was never more ignorant than when I joined the Army. Some enlightened person might point out that merely joining the Army begs the question. But that is not what I'm referring to. What I mean by ignorance is how little I knew about how the Army worked. Many things had to be learned quickly from this American sub-culture. Of all the lessons though, there was one important lesson only the very stupid failed to grasp.

Obedience without question is very difficult for most people. It goes against our natural instincts, especially when we feel the order is arbitrary and illogical. Ironically, it is when orders seem stupid that the really important learning begins. Do I obey, disobey, or grudgingly comply but find every opportunity to grumble and complain?

Robert Fulghum wrote a wonderful book entitled *All I Really Needed to Know, I Learned in Kindergarten.* His well-presented premise is that we learned at an early age some of the most important lessons of life. Some of these points to live by were remarkably simple. Play fair, don't hit people, put things back where you found them, clean up your own area, and flush.

Soldiers learn a great deal in the Army. Boot camp is the military's kindergarten for soldiers. They relearn Robert Fulghum's awesome rules. Play fair, don't hit people, put things back where you found them, and clean up your own mess. They also learn to flush. On top of all this, like it or not, soldiers learn how to obey, especially when every fiber in their souls screams, "Why? This is madness!"

The "why" involves a very simple but powerful principle. Trust. Learning to trust your leaders is a fundamental law of the military. At some point we might have to blindly obey, even if it goes against everything we feel. Mr. Fulghum would call this the "holding hands and sticking together" part. You cannot act like civilians and "quit." You are part of a team. You may not have all the information. You may not be able to do this alone.

In the Army, this trusting lesson is the most important thing you ever needed to know to survive what sometimes seems to be apparent madness. It is just as well, for war is madness anyway and your best chance to survive and win is to stick together when the shooting starts.

Mothballs

"You may break, you may shatter the vase, if you will,
but the scent of the roses will hang around it still."
Irish Melodies

No doubt like millions of soldiers who preceded me, and many more who will follow, the smell of mothballs reminds me of an Army equipment issue facility. The pungent smell of mothballs permeates these giant military warehouses where everything from socks to tents are stored. Whether arriving at a new assignment or before departing an old one, soldiers have to visit these special warehouses to pick up or turn in gear that bears this interesting scent.

No matter what your background, there is something very memorable about that very first visit to "Uncle Sam's" warehouse, or the Central Issue Facility (CIF). You've only been in the service a day or so. The sergeants march you over to these buildings that are almost always situated along some railroad track. Your first step through the door engages all the senses—the eyes feast on the massive interior, your ears hear the barking of orders—"Next!" or "What size?" The building is cold in the winter, hot in the summer. The new aroma that moths abhor wafts around the freshly shaved heads of soldiers as the blankets, canteens, boots, uniforms and hundreds of other things are handled and moved.

A shopping cart line forms as each recruit, or newly arrived soldier, lines up to get gear and uniforms issued. Vintage civilian Government Service (GS) workers man each station as the long line winds through rows of new and interesting clothing, equipment, and gadgets. What looks like underwear is "drawers, men's brief, brown." A hat is a "cap, garrison olive green." What you think might be socks are really "socks, wool cushion sole." A small mountain of new clothes and camping gear with funny accessories is here. You can have it in any color, as long as it is green.

There's no cash register, just some kindly civilian with a strong desire for your signature. If you're smart, you'll check to make sure everything is present and accounted for before you sign. Otherwise, you will pay later for missing stuff.

The papers are duly signed and you pack the gear up in duffel bags and backpacks. Loaded to the gills with equipment, the ever-present and concerned sergeants march you back to the barracks. A small fortune in government-issue (GI) things are yours to use, some to even keep. You're for sure in the Army now. As the aroma of mothballs lingers in the goods carried on your back and in your arms, even you begin to smell like a GI item too, GI.

8

Birth Control

"People only see what they are prepared to see."
Ralph Waldo Emerson

Many people who join the Army discover that for the first time in their lives they need to wear glasses. In that very thorough medical induction process, the defect is identified and glasses are ordered.

In due time, the glasses arrive and fellow basic trainees show up in formation with their new glasses and a new perspective on the world. The glasses also decidedly change a soldier's appearance to everyone else, especially since for years the Army purchased the same out of fashion glass frames. These hideous spectacles are affectionately known "BCGs," or birth control glasses.

Like the short military haircut, seeing people who wore BCGs was a good sign they were in the military. Shakespeare would have thought this too for he wrote, "the apparel oft proclaims the man." For a long time the BCGs, with their square, dark brown or black color, identified the wearer as perhaps a bit out of style as well. But the Army was by no means going to have troops wear the latest, cool, civilian variety of eyewear. No sir. Are you kidding?

Today, people with sight problems have the additional option of laser keratotomy, something the military will probably take a long time deciding before offering it to soldiers. No, the Army no doubt has motives for basically sticking to BCGs over other more stylish or expensive options of contacts or surgery. BCGs are inexpensive, easy to replace, and maybe some decision-maker in high places felt it important to minimize a fashionable look in soldiers. No need to heat things up between the sexes for example.

If I could ever be elected to national public office, I would address this BCG issue. It would top our nation's legislative agenda, for seldom does Washington have time to think about recruitment. Soldiers should look cool, not nerdy. Maybe the reason for the persistence of BCGs is that the factory that produces them lies in some powerful representative's district.

Though not forced to wear them myself, I am sympathetic to the plight of soldiers adorned with these spectacles. My heart especially goes out to those especially brave souls who augment the BCGs with an attached "RRC," or rubber restraint cord to help keep the glasses on their head during the rigors of Army training. Yes, there ought to be a law against forcing soldiers to wear these things. Sharp soldiers deserve better. Surely the buyers and wearers of these BCGs can see that.

9

Mascot

"The frog's life is most jolly, my lads."
Theocritus

Kermit the Frog and I are kindred spirits. In the swamp of life, we both have had to dress in green to get ahead: Kermit as a Muppet character, and I as a soldier. It sometimes isn't easy being green, as Kermit often sings, but for some of us you have to be green to earn a living.

The official mascot of the United States Army is a mule. Have you ever wondered how in the world the Army came up with a mule? The old Army, you might say, an Army that depended on mules to get things done. Horses were not strong enough and donkeys had a bad habit of not obeying orders. Mules were strong enough and obeyed orders, a good combination of the breeding of horses with donkeys.

But we stopped using mules a long time ago. About the only one left on active duty is at West Point, used as a mascot for football games. I say the Army ought to update its mascot to something more current. Now see here, the Army uses trucks now, not mules.

I would like to suggest the Army take a serious look at Kermit the Frog as the new mascot. Here is an animal that everyone recognizes and enjoys. He is accustomed to living in the mud, being on the road, trying to take charge and do good, and truly wants to be a success someday. A lot of soldiers would be able to identify with this frog. He is even the right color. Why, Kermit would not even have to change his wardrobe.

Mules may be strong and part of that fine Army tradition, but give me a break; there is nothing glamourous about an animal with the ears of a horse and the face of a donkey. No sir, we need to recruit Kermit. Kermit would not need a cadet with a shovel following him around either.

Kermit has some great things going for him. He would have no trouble with the Army's weight control standards. He'd not be difficult to feed while on field maneuvers, and he'd definitely keep the bugs down. He's a likable character and always means well too, despite the blooming idiots he has to deal with on a daily basis. Yes, he'd be right at home in the Army. He has charm, wit, and class. He also doesn't come with much baggage, except for that pesky plump pink pig that is always after him.

Yes sir, the Army needs to step up to some fresh material in its mascot. I say if beer companies can sell their products by using frogs, then folks, this should be a no-brainer.

Kermit, in the Army you'll find yourself right at home. Many soldiers would agree: it isn't easy being green.

The Game

"When the One Great Scorer comes to write against your name –
He marks—not that you won or lost—but how you played the game."
Grantland Rice

It is a scene repeated over and over again in basic training: a drill instructor providing that special one-on-one close attention to some misinformed or forgetful recruit. With so many new military things inundating the brand new soldier, the sergeants are kept pretty busy with on-the-spot guidance in that uniquely military flavor. The drill sergeants give everyone personal attention, like bees sucking nectar from flowers.

Maybe I moved in formation, mumbled something under my breath, or looked at him the wrong way. Whatever I did, he was on me like a stinger missile. "You're not going to be a problem for me, trainee!" he snarled, barely inches from me, where I stood in the front row of our platoon. His piercing brown eyes complimented the trademark drill instructor's hat. His crisp, spit-less words bounced off my face.

Any hint of defiance quickly evaporated within me. "Uh oh," I thought, "maybe I should apologize." "I'm sorry…" He cut me short; "I didn't give you permission to speak. By the time I'm done with you, you'll be asking me for permission to breathe. Anyway, I already know you're sorry. The whole lot of you civilians is sorry. You might even be sorry you joined the Army," he continued, "but when I'm done with you, you will be a soldier. Is that clear, trainee?"

At this point I wasn't sure if I was supposed to talk. A bit hesitant, I nearly whispered, "Yes, sir." "What did you say?" he asked. This time a bit louder I said, "Yes, sir!"

The sergeant went on: "Allow me to make something clear to you, mister nothing-for-brains. I work for a living. I am not a 'sir.' I am a sergeant. And to you miserable excuses for human beings I am a drill sergeant." Backing away from me and glancing at the entire formation he added, "Have I made myself clear?"

Without hesitation, like the Mormon Tabernacle Choir at its finest, we all resounded in unison, "Yes, drill sergeant!"

And so ended my first spiritual bloodletting at boot camp. The bleedings would continue each day, some days more than others. Eventually we all caught on and played the game right. Why, by the end of our training I actually liked it! What I thought were involuntary donations of my spirit were actually transfusions of the spirit of the military into me. Some might call this process indoctrination. I call it learning to play and enjoy the game.

11

FYI

"Life is a foreign language: all men mispronounce it."
Christopher Morley

It is imperative that new soldiers entering BCT learn the language of the USA ASAP. This is RA SOP. DA unfortunately does little to prepare people for this acronym ordeal, things like FTX, PMCS, and how to wear LCE being more important. To get on top of things fast soldiers struggle with some AR or DAPAM to learn the lingo.

Perhaps soldiers can consider this a sort of MFR. First you have to report to the nearest MEPS, maybe by POV or with a TR. You get a PE, MOS, and BASD there. Now, you are in the Army and you're off to BCT and AIT, often via a GTR, since TDHGA is not authorized and you will not be able to use your POV there. After all this initial TNG, you PCS to that first assignment, maybe a FA, IN, AVN, CAV, or ACR unit. Some will go to a MSB, FSB, MEDDAC, or sexy places like ARPERCEN. Some even get a chance to go back home because they are ARNG or USAR.

Some SMs will DROS via AMC to an OCONUS unit in USAREUR or PACOM. The new assignment is a trip. Part of your BII includes a whole new group of codes and letters to learn, all IAW your unit's TACSOP and your place on the MTOE. The PLT LDR and PLT SGT should take care of you but you can see the 1SG or the CO if you have questions. I wouldn't recommend going too high up though, unless you're contemplating AWOL or being on a SIR.

Eventually you'll get TA-50 and go on a FTX. They'll give you MREs to eat, maybe you'll sleep in a GP tent, and you'll hang out at an AO. You can't get over the number of officers in the unit too, including the SIGO, BMO, PBO, FO, XO, MO, and, of course, the CDR. Before too long, you're back on that MSR in an APC after that last AAR heading back to garrison. There you follow SOP in getting the unit in a DRF status and your APC PMCS'd and topped off at the POL point. Maybe you get some R&R but then again, you may get CQ or get sent off SD.

Eventually you get a DOR and hopefully never a NPD. Whatever you do, you'll still get a LES, time to see the PX, and maybe some TDY out of the deal. Anything is better than a CZ and running the risk of becoming a PW, WIA, or worse, KIA.

Four or five FTXs down the road and that ETS comes into view. You go to PAC to pick up your 201 file and clearing papers. NST a week or two you clear through CIF, the MTF, DENTAC, SIDPERS, and EDCEN. That day finally arrives when you hang up the BDUs knowing you faithfully did your duty for the US of A.

Group Therapy

"We must, indeed, all hang together or,
most assuredly, we shall all hang separately."
Benjamin Franklin

A couple of weeks into basic training our platoon of forty men was abruptly awakened at two o'clock in the morning by the now familiar yells of one of our drill sergeants. Using language many would consider very rude, he ordered us out of our beds and out of the building on the double.

Hurrying through the barracks, most of us were still in our underwear as we headed out the door. We formed up outside the building in four half-naked squads. We waited and waited, shivering in our Army drawers, our faces illuminated by a light bulb on the side of the barracks.

Our drill sergeant deliberately took his time making his way to where we stood. We must have been a comical sight to him, but as he appeared before us there was no grin on his face as he sternly barked, "Get in the front leaning rest, trainees!"

Like conditioned laboratory rats we instantly dropped on all fours to the push-up starting position. There we remained for a few moments until the sergeant spoke up. "Someone has been smoking in my barracks," he said. "Which one of you left a cigarette butt in my latrine? You want to burn down my barracks?"

Silence. No one moved. A couple of folks quietly groaned, especially the non-smokers who were once again participating in group therapy for a smoker's misdemeanor. It wasn't too long before someone blurted out, "Whoever you are, turn yourself in!" Again, there was no response.

"Fine," our tormentor said, "you all can remain in this position for awhile longer." With that he turned around and went back into the barracks. We heard him getting some coffee as we continued our unnatural position.

After a small, painful eternity our drill sergeant returned, coffee mug in hand. He was ready to question us further. Every muscle in our bodies cried out for relief. The guilty one or ones remained silent though, in spite of further interrogation. Obviously frustrated, our leader finally said, "Okay, no problem. You folks can forget about a pass for the next two weeks." With that we were ordered to get up and go back to bed.

I believe some of our platoon members decided then and there to quit smoking. Others did not. I have no doubt that one or two nameless soldiers in our platoon, those who failed to fess up, quit under coercion from their fellow trainees. Somebody knew who the perpetrators were, for if everyone gets hung together, you can be sure that someone will hang separately.

Khaki

"I was born modest; not all over, but in spots."
Mark Twain

One of the strongest attractions to military service has got to be the sharp uniforms you get to wear. Whether it is the Air Force blue, Army green, Navy white or Marine Corps tan and green, all seem to serve as part of the allure of military service. There is something about wearing that uniform, regardless of your rank, that tugs at most of us who join.

Even within each branch of the service people have a uniform they prefer. Some feel best in their battle dress uniform, others in dress blues. Some cast longing eyes towards the uniforms of their sister services. How often I've heard, "Now why can't the Army fix us up with sharp dress uniforms like the Marines?"

For me, the all-time favorite military outfit has got to be the khaki uniform, something I am for sure going to bring back if I ever get to be the Commander in Chief. In my humble opinion, nothing was sharper, easier to get around in and maintain, than the tan Khaki uniforms the Army phased out in the early 1980s. Wearing it was like wearing a well-fitted pair of slacks and a polo shirt. Cool in hot weather and really comfortable to wear, this uniform had to be real close to perfect clothing.

Girls seemed to like how we looked too, especially with a sharp haircut and all our badges, awards, and stripes on a freshly cleaned and starched uniform. No, wearing a nice pair of Khaki's out on the town was not for modest types—that outfit was meant for those who were proud to strut their stuff and looking for action, like a rooster in a hen house.

I never knew why the Army got rid of the Khaki uniform. It is always interesting how popular things can sometimes disappear without the consent of what surely is a majority opinion to the contrary. Olive green fatigues were phased out too. Times always seem to be "a-changing."

Regardless of the changes, though, there will always be that appeal a uniform has on people. Wearing a uniform makes us a visible symbol, an ambassador for our country wherever we go. You can feel the pride inside as that freshly cleaned, pressed and decorated uniform is put on.

Even old soldiers will proudly dig a uniform out of the closet to wear on special occasions like Veteran's Day. It will most likely be the one they enjoyed wearing the most too. What fond memories that must conjure up! And some old timers, who make no pretense to modesty, proudly remember heading out on payday weekend with one cool set of Khakis on.

Little Bitty

"At the end of the game both the king and the pawn
go back into the same box."
Italian Proverb

If you really want to know how it feels to be on the bottom of a totem pole, then spend some time as a private in the Army. You are basically at the ground floor of the Army's two rank systems: enlisted and officer, not counting those warrant officers who lie somewhere between the two systems. As a private, E-1, anyone with any rank outranks you.

Rank has its privileges, they say. In addition to modest pay raises, a promotion brings with it some prestige. Private E-2s with their mosquito-wing stripes are one up on Private E-1s, for example. Therefore, every new soldier in the Army looks forward to getting their first rank to wear, even if it is single stripes. Something is better than nothing, even if it isn't much.

Alan Jackson sings a great song about it being all right to be "little bitty." In the U.S. Army, it is not all right to be "little bitty" for long. You either move up in rank, or eventually they kick you out. We therefore breed a culture that is forever looking to the next higher rank. It becomes not only a matter of more pay but of survival too. You have to get higher in rank to be "all right."

Sometimes I think the Army has too much rank. I once met a corporal in the British Army with twenty-four years of service. He was happy where he was, and the British military had no problem with that. You would rarely if ever see this in the American Army. If you did, then somewhere along the way the soldier messed up, was demoted, and is likely now on his way out.

One general I worked for once referred to most of his subordinates as just highly paid privates. Perhaps he was right. I bet there was someone else up the chain of command that thought of the general as a highly paid private too. There will always be someone who outranks us, but it is nice to be able to take some of this subordinate stuff to the bank once in awhile.

Whether we begin our Army career as a cadet or private, we should never forget that deep inside we are all formed of the same material. Though increased rank tempts everyone to get the "big head," we do well to remember that as mortals we will all end in similar circumstances at the end.

"To realize the value of the U.S. Army, ask the most junior man in the system," I once heard a senior Army sergeant say. Indeed, the very life of the Army begins with privates. And in the great game called military life it is indeed all right to be little bitty, at least for a little bitty while.

Briefs

"Drawers, Men's Brief, Brown"
U.S. Army Underwear Label

Nomenclature. Everything in the Department of Defense that is movable and inanimate has a nomenclature. Imprinted, labeled, stamped or tattooed on the item or the package is a terse, matter-of-fact description of what the object truly is. Coat, hot weather, woodland; insert, glove, hand; boot, leather, black; bayonet, sharp, dangerous.

The most personally relevant item the United States government purchases for issue to soldiers is a good, clean pair of underpants. Near and dear to everyone's private parts, underclothing forms the very start of at least 77 pieces and 110 pounds of various items of government issued accouterments a soldier going into combat will carry or wear.

It is intriguing that the quartermaster or acquisition folks chose "drawers" to describe such an important clothing item. Can you imagine the committee meeting that decided upon this archaic term? There are so many other synonyms to choose from, like underpants, undershorts, briefs, bloomers, boxers, BVDs, Hanes, or Fruit of the Loom. No, "drawers" was the big winner here, etched on rear elastic band labels all around the Army.

Now, brown is an okay color. Not my choice for briefs, but I wasn't asked either. The imagination can run wild as to why this color was chosen. Even though most equivalent civilian underclothing for men is white, the Army chose brown.

Some might say brown drawers need to match brown Army tee shirts. Yes, but Army socks are black and Air Force tee shirts are black. Yes, tis true, but brown better matches the dirt and grime of field duty, and if the Air Force has black, well, the Army has to be different. And as far as white is concerned, why, everyone knows that, use for use, white requires laundering more often than brown. Brown also hides a multitude of stains, sort of an undercover-up.

The underwear debate will go on and on. You'll never find a solution that fits everyone. It does not really matter anyway, since historians assure us that military history reveals no instances where underwear was a decisive factor in the outcome of any engagement or war. No, the presence or absence of drawers has not determined matters of great import. What seems to always make a difference in a battle's outcome, however, has been "man, one each, naked, black, white or brown." It takes hunks of living protoplasm to win a war; anything else is merely an accessory. U.S. Army drawers will probably change and be changed, hopefully on a regular basis. Soldiers, however, are forever.

Army Boots

"Boots—boots—boots—boots—movin' up
and down again. There's no discharge in the war."
Rudyard Kipling

Soldiers spend ninety-five percent of their time in the Army in a pair of boots. Wearing boots is a new experience for many people coming out of civilian life where trade name running shoes or patent leather are the norm. One thing is certain, if you join the Army you must wear boots, especially for those long marches everyone will do sooner or later.

Army boots are part of a soldier's uniform that gets a great deal of attention, probably more than any other. There is, of course, the need to keep the black-leather of the boots shined. You also work hard to keep them clean and dry to maximize their useful life.

Uncle Sam gives a soldier his or her first two pairs of boots. From then on, new boots come out of your own pocket, although enlisted folks do get an annual clothing allowance. Sometimes you get bonus boots if the Army sends you off to exotic places: jungle boots for the tropics or brown boots for the desert. Otherwise, when the boots wear out, you're off to the military clothing sales store to get new ones with your own money.

Despite the emphasis on uniformity with all other parts of the U.S. Army, over the years there has evolved an interesting array of boots apparently allowed by Army leadership. There are the standard issue boots—sturdy and durable but rather plain. The Cochran or "jump boots" are quite popular for their sharp look and firm support. Of late are the black jungle-type boots, desired for their comfort. There are dozens of other varieties too, differing in height, lacing patterns, lining, soles, and price.

Boots, in the end, are issued for two primary reasons: to protect the feet and for marching. Despite the variety, the primary end use of the product is for walking. And long walks if necessary. No matter what type of boot it is, most feet will ache anyway after a good march.

Too bad there aren't as many choices for military socks, which are, in the long run, as important as the boots. My guess is socks are perceived as less important as the boot. The truth is, a good pair of socks can make even lousy boots better.

It takes a soldier, serviceable boots, and a good pair of socks to make it all come together. The Army will constantly keep a sufficient quantity of each item on hand.

One thing is for certain, Army boots are made for walking, and in the Army that is certainly what they will do.

Getting Ahead

"There is no failure except in no longer trying."
Elbert Hubbard

Scattered around U.S. military installations are exercise courses designed to keep people in tip-top shape. Some courses are quite professionally laid out with sophisticated obstacles and permanent fixtures. Others seem as if haphazardly thrown together. Regardless of their appearance and attention to detail, I am convinced beyond any shadow of a doubt that their designers shared a common joy of inventing legitimate ways to torture soldiers.

You might think you are in great shape. You run, pump those weights, and go through those calisthenics on a regular basis. You might be all muscle and no body fat. All this is fine and good, but you never are truly in shape until you successfully tackle an Army obstacle course in full uniform with battle gear on.

They should make the military obstacle course one of the Olympic events, like a triathlon with its three trying ordeals of physical stamina. The military course adds even more drama when sergeants throw in simulated weapons firing. There are low walls and high walls, tunnels, ditches, beams to cross and ropes to swing on Tarzan-style. You face rope ladders, low crawls, mudholes, smoke, and barbed wire. You will get dirty, sweaty, wet, and very, very tired.

If the "coaches" don't like your performance during these sadistic exercises, then you get to do it all over again. Army sergeants seem to always monitor these places of pain closely, ever ready to correct the progress of the faithful during their very personal pilgrimage of perseverance and perspiration.

My all-time favorite obstacle on a military course is the barbed-wire low crawl, usually one of the final events before the finish line. Here is your chance to lie down and eat mud. Razor-sharp barbed wire lies inches above your head. All around are noisy sergeants popping smoke and firing weapons. I am so glad I missed the trench warfare of World War I.

Eventually you crawl through this manmade torture pit and come out the other side. You are totally exhausted and without a clean square inch anywhere on your body. Here is the secret of not having to do the course again—get as dirty as you possibly can, especially your face. The cadre often tag relatively clean soldiers to do the course all over again, so the pit is the perfect place to prevent this from happening. You need to fall on your face in order to get ahead. This is one time in the Army where you might not succeed with a clean face.

Police Call

"If the Army wanted someone to pick up after you,
you would have been issued a mother."
NCO Wisdom

I really don't know why they call it "police call." It has absolutely nothing to do with dialing 911 on the phone. It doesn't even involve policemen, unless one of these upholders of the law catches someone creating the need for a police call in the first place. You see, in the Army a police call means to pick up litter. It is lousy duty. Here you are in shiny boots and a freshly pressed, clean uniform. Through the luck of the draw or just by being in the wrong place at the wrong time, the Sergeant Major's dragnet picks you up for the picking up trash detail. They give you an orange reflective vest to wear and it isn't too long before the boots and uniform are dirty from all the walking, bending, and handling of other people's garbage.

Modern societies produce a lot of waste. From fast food boxes to plastic shopping bags, empty beer bottles to candy wrappers, you'll find our lifestyle produces a lot of temptation for normal, law-abiding citizens to become litterbugs, even on an Army base. Given the disposable income of folks, I guess the foreseeable future will continue to provide a fair crop of litter and thoughtless people too.

Most of the litter you find on Army posts is thrown from passing vehicles or flies out of the bed of some pick-up truck. I am always struck by how forgetful carmakers are. They continually avoid the obvious: why is there no garbage can inside a car? I mean, with nowhere to put their rubbish, people are tempted to roll down the window and let it fly.

Although it must be done, police call is without any glamour whatsoever. I can just see the Army doing a recruiting commercial: "Join the Army and get money for college," the announcer proclaims, "and help keep your country clean." Despite the challenge to be enthusiastic about this picking-up litter job, one can still appreciate how clean Army posts are kept, no matter where they are located. I've been stationed in some pretty dirty states, whose state flower ought to be paper or plastic.

I have often wanted to be a State Trooper and slam the folks I see throwing out litter. Not only would I hit them with a fine, I would provide opportunity for remedial training a couple of weekends a month for these fine citizens. They can don orange vests and get some hands-on training with picking up litter, just like soldiers doing police call. I would schedule these events especially on rainy days. I am sure every Sergeant Major in the Army would concur, along with a good many mothers.

Twinkies

"Would ye both eat your cake and have your cake?"
John Heywood

Basic combat training (BCT) is a tough experience. Time seems to stand still as you go through the rigorous routine of exercise, training, inspection and humiliation. Looking back, things seemed like a blur—like a difficult dream that went on and on. Over time it becomes harder to remember the details.

But some things about basic you will never forget. Tattooed into your brain are certain experiences, objects, habits, or people you cannot forget, even if you wanted to. One lasting memory for me was the *Twinkies*.

Given a stressful situation, some people reach for a bottle or a cigarette. These people found basic training especially hard; alcohol being forbidden and smoking seriously limited. Other people under stress will reach for other things. For me it became *Twinkies*, something the mess hall legitimately offered in significant quantity.

There is no doubting the fact that I have a sweet tooth. If there were a Sweet Tooth Anonymous Association, I'd need to be a card-carrying member. I had actually been a *Little Debbie* fan before the Army. I still am. To me, those nutty bars or oatmeal pies are right up there with the good things in life. But the Army mess hall at boot camp had only Twinkies and so circumstances forced me to expand my horizons a bit.

As suppertime rolled around each day, we would arrive at the dining facility very hungry. I can't remember the specifics, but the food was good. I do, however, remember those sweet two-packs of fluffy, yellow cake that surrounds a creamy white center. *Twinkies* were something to hold on to under the stress, and every suppertime, like a friend, they were there.

For the unfamiliar and the uninitiated, basic training offers very few pleasurable experiences. You live in close quarters, crawl out of bed at ungodly hours, have every minute of your life micro-managed, and discover new muscles you never thought existed before. You figure the whole experience is good for you and you make every effort to tell yourself so, but everyone needs an island of relief in the storm.

I've since gone back to *Little Debbie* over the years. This is not an endorsement, just a preference. Near where the *Little Debbie's* are in the grocery store sit those familiar yellow *Twinkies* two-packs. Each time I see them, they remind me of boot camp and the drill instructor's words of wisdom dispensed as we filed into the mess hall: "Take what you want, but eat what you take." If that's the case, I'll take dessert first.

Group Torture

"Nothing great was ever achieved without enthusiasm."
Ralph Waldo Emerson

It is five o'clock in the morning. A formation of over a thousand soldiers spreads out evenly spaced in an open field. In the early morning darkness, streetlights in the distance cast a hazy glow on the procession. You are half-awake in this dream-like, pre-dawn sacrificial service.

The Master Fitness Trainer mounts a wooden platform, located near the center of the mass of soldiers. It is time for physical fitness training, or PT. Through a megaphone the trainer's voice booms out, "Are you fired up?" A half-hearted crowd reply is given, "Fired up, drill sergeant, fired up."

The sergeant is not the least bit impressed. "I don't think you are awake enough. Maybe you didn't hear me. Are you fired up?" Once again, the tired trainees respond more in unison, "Fired up, drill sergeant, fired up."

Obviously not happy with the response, the troops are ordered into "front leaning rest," or the up position of a push-up exercise. He is trying to get their attention. As the minutes tick by, scattered groans begin as muscles ache from holding up the body's weight in this unnatural position. Drill sergeants hovering nearby provide verbal and emotional "encouragement" for those who groan or falter. Everyone is leaning to the front, but there is no rest from this position of dark torture surely developed for heretics.

Eventually the trainer on the platform thinks he has everyone's attention. The command "recover" brings the crowd to its feet again. The blood flows, partly out of the prolonged position and partly out of anger. There is no longer any thought about being tired, all are now wide-awake.

The trainer calls out again, "Are you fired up?" Like some massive war cry of heathens in the eerie morning light, a thousand angry voices rise up in unison, "Fired up drill sergeant, fired up!!" "Good," he says, "that's more like it." With that the sergeant leads them through exercises that torment the anatomy and try the soul, all the while, roaming drill sergeants make sure soldiers stay enthusiastic about the newfound pain. To protest only brings back the "front leaning rest." The faithful soon learn to do as they are told. The inquisitors bring the troops to the point where on a simple command, the crowd is fired up, enthusiastic and under one man's control. And what do the soldiers say when this daily ordeal is over? "More PT, drill sergeant, more PT."

With fiendish grins, the Master Fitness Trainer puts the exhausted back into the front leaning rest. "Now, let's do ten more for the Army!" he commands. Instantly the crowd responds in a chorus, "Hooaah!"

Asleep at My Post

"For some must watch, while some must sleep: so runs the world away."
Shakespeare

It was a hot summer in Missouri. Boot camp is tough any time of year, but the summer months bring the added stress of heat on an otherwise challenging training program. The heat of that summer in basic training would teach me an important lesson in vigilance.

Radio watch is boring duty, especially when radio traffic on the net is little to nonexistent. For safety purposes, Range Control, the agency responsible for Army training areas, requires a radio on-site during a field exercise and with someone to monitor it twenty-four hours a day. My turn at radio watch came while the rest of the unit took off to some distant range.

A hot day is bad enough already, but it is even hotter under a general-purpose (GP) medium tent out in an open field. Other than an occasional breeze, the heat wore on my ability to stay alert. Hours with no one to talk to, added to the absence of any radio traffic, only worsened the assaults of the Sandman. The faint static sound of the radio and the gentle flapping of canvas against a small breeze set me to daydreaming. A new private, only in the Army a few weeks, had a lot to think about—that next assignment, how the family was doing back home, wondering what's for dinner....

My next conscious moment found me looking up at an angry-looking lieutenant standing in front of me. He caught me red-handed, asleep at my post. I clumsily scrambled to attention as thoughts of remorse and impending doom raced through my mind. Gone were the visions about home, the heat, or my next assignment. I sensed a clear and present danger to my current military career. I even briefly wondered what the food would be like in an Army prison.

At parade rest in the heat, which was now unnoticed, the lieutenant, a veteran of Vietnam, gave me a short lecture on that unpopular war. It was a lesson on depending on people to do their job, on vigilance, on promises kept and duties performed.

Fail in your duty and people might die.

The rebuke was driven home with an admonishment to me about what punishment he could take against me. The lesson given, the lieutenant turned and left. I meekly saluted as the officer moved away. The adrenaline flowed freely inside me. No more rest for the wicked, despite the heat and the boredom. Yet, there was relief in knowing I had another chance, that there was this thing called grace, the Army's amazing grace. That alone was enough to keep anyone awake.

Toilet Training

"Cleaning toilets is one of life's most important lessons."
David Kay

Toilet cleaning duty has got to be the very bottom of any list that ranks occupations by glamour or prestige. During basic training it was my turn to clean toilets, the so-called "latrine queen." Eight dirty commodes stood ready for my attention and twenty-four hours of neglect by careless soldiers promised plenty of opportunity for me to excel.

Forty men can mess up a bathroom in short order. I found it interesting that despite the fact that each man had this prestigious duty before, the experience did not change their ability to aim straight or pick up after themselves. Perhaps it was only two or three culprits in the bunch. I don't know. What was clear was that the toilets, sinks, stalls, and the floors provided the opportunity for me to stay busy for several hours.

As the grime and mess are cleaned away you get time to wonder why in the world you joined the Army. You keep saying to yourself, "I didn't join the Army to clean toilets." Meanwhile, the latrine gradually begins to look and smell good. Toothpaste splashes on the mirrors are gone. The clean toilets stand at the ready. The floor shines. The place even smells good, too! Maybe there is a lesson in all this, you think?

Finally, you believe the latrine learning experience is done. The drill sergeant carefully inspects your work. If he isn't completely satisfied, then it's back to work correcting the missed spots. There is this "just so" look he wants. There always seems to be some flaw in your work that needs further adjustment, no matter how hard you try.

Cleaning toilets soiled by others is fundamentally a character building experience. When you are there scrubbing the sides of a commode you know it can only be up from there. If you're smart, you'll make the most of the work instead of getting an attitude.

I would guess there are very few highly successful people who didn't have to pull their hitch of latrine cleaning duty. The successful ones probably tackled dirty toilets much the same way they would tackle other unpleasant tasks life offers—especially as you move up the ladder. A "can do" spirit and doing the job right helps.

Others fail to learn the toilet-cleaning lesson and far too often end up repeating the failure over and over again in other unpleasant tasks in life. Perhaps they were too proud to learn the toilet lesson. If a job has to be done then you ought to learn something from it.

23

Benefits

"Government is, or ought to be, instituted for the common
benefit, protection, and security of the people, nation, or community."
George Mason

Every January the Army passes out to soldiers a summary of all pay and compensation they received the previous year. Included in this individualized report are items soldiers often take for granted. We normally don't put a dollar figure to things like Post Exchange and commissary privileges, untaxed allowances for food and housing, or medical and dental care. With these things considered, the higher total pay sometimes results in a figure some simple-minded soldiers might joke about.

Serious soldiers, especially those with families, have a deep appreciation for the fringe benefits, benefits you do not necessarily see on a regular pay statement. Thirty days paid vacation each year, training and Federal holidays, near unlimited sick leave, and various morale, welfare and recreation services are benefits that are no joking matter. Even free rides on Air Force transport planes, the so-called "hop," are a good deal for smart and patient soldiers and their families.

The birth of my first son cost $2,500.00. My second son cost $25.00. The difference between the two was more than just $2475.00. My first son, Nathan, was during a time when my wife and I were uninsured. Marlan, on the other hand, was born after dad made a significant commitment and joined the United States Army.

Medical and dental care rank near the top for most soldiers and their families. Often military medical and dental care get bum raps from the press. Unkind things are written or said. Fingers are pointed. Sure, the Army's health care system isn't perfect. Any system, including our government, is created and maintained by imperfect humans for an imperfect people.

The news is that civilian health care isn't perfect either. The press goes after these folks, too. More unkind things are said. More fingers are pointed. But the sad part is the price tag. For paying customers, the price of civilian care sometimes only adds insult to injury.

If the price is right I don't mind waiting a bit longer, being a bit more tolerant and patient with some inconvenience. We got what we paid for with Nathan's birth in a civilian hospital. The care was very good, but not perfect. Marlan's birth at Landstuhl Army Medical Center in Germany was very good but also not perfect. Given the price tag, clearly Army health care was the better option. In return for my service to our country, that's a government entitlement our family has especially appreciated.

Lifer Advice

"Some folks are wise and some are otherwise."
Tobias Smollett

He probably never read any great works on human philosophy, but he was very smart nonetheless. My drill sergeant's textbook was more experiential learning, namely life itself. Indeed, he was a "lifer," a career soldier. He also showed us our very first views of the Army far removed from TV ads.

It was over twenty years ago when he stood in front of our platoon. We were a brand new bunch of soldiers; most of us were still teenagers. In addition to daily administrative announcements, he would offer some advice before dismissing us for the day. The advice was simple and to the point. "You will find what you're looking for in the Army," he said. "If you're looking for trouble or success, you don't have far to look."

In time I too, became a "lifer." The drill sergeant was right. The Army experience was truly what I made of it. It is pretty easy to find trouble, somewhat more difficult to find success. One has to be patient and reliable for the success part. Work hard enough though and it will come.

Day by day back in boot camp we would receive some bit of Army wisdom and by transfer wisdom for life in general. One particularly interesting bit of advice was, "Don't ever volunteer for anything," a puzzling piece of advice from someone who often requested the services of volunteers. There was also the irony that with the draft now gone, every man in front of him was a volunteer. We all had willingly joined the Army.

Something paradoxical in life is the relationship between success and volunteering. Weighed in the balance, missions I volunteered for seemed to expedite the success part and, more importantly, the feeling of self-worth and satisfaction that came from unpleasant jobs well done. Over time I have often pondered this "don't volunteer" advice of my first Army mentor. The answer I found stemmed from the background of my Vietnam war-tested drill instructor. "*In combat*, don't volunteer for anything" was the answer I came to. The result of such unforced choices were often fatal, hence the advice. In that context, it was good advice, except for fools or heroes.

On the other hand, the peacetime equivalent of going beyond the call is to volunteer. It is also far less apt to be fatal, except to selfishness. To see an opportunity and seize the chance is to step out of our comfort zone. This opportunity stuff, when properly recognized, is a chance to get ahead. A successful "lifer" is someone who has seen the chance and made the move. These people will find the success they have been looking for all along.

25

Liar, Liar?

"I do not mind lying, but I hate inaccuracy."
Samuel Butler

Over the years I've told myself that the Staff Sergeant at the recruiting station in Chattanooga, Tennessee, was just inaccurate. Surely he didn't lie to me. Sometimes I've had doubts though, as I met other folks like myself who were drawn to the Army by promises of everything but heaven's pearly gates, only to learn too late it just isn't so.

The crux of my personal experience with misinformation involved my enlistment in 1979 for location of choice. My wife, of German ancestry, still had family in Munich, Germany. Entering the Army right out of civilian life, I didn't fully understand the difference between location of choice and unit of choice. All I knew was that Munich was where the Army should send me. The good sergeant said the 8th Infantry Division had its headquarters in Bavaria, the capital of which was Munich. From there, it couldn't be far, right? Sure.

I signed the papers for the 8th Infantry Division and into the Army I came. Completing basic combat training (BCT) and advanced individual training (AIT), I made my way to the 21st Replacement Detachment in Frankfurt, Germany. Imagine my shock when upon my arrival I was told that the 8th Division was not in Bavaria, but in a completely different area of Germany. Instead of Munich, that teeming cultural center of southern Germany, I was to be posted to Baumholder, Germany, affectionately referred to by the Germans as *Das Ende der Erde*, or the end of the earth. My meek protest was met with the answer, "You signed up for the 8th."

A deal is a deal.

Sometimes I wish I could find that sergeant and give him a piece of my mind. A lie is a lie, but if he didn't have the right answer, he should have confessed his ignorance and seen to it that I was assigned to the correct division, the 3rd Infantry Division. Maybe a three and an eight looked similar and it was an honest mistake. I hope so.

After that inauspicious start to my experience, it's a wonder I made a career out of the Army. Despite that setback, though, I had a truly great career, even if it began at the end of the earth and a six-hour car trip to Munich. Over time, I learned that the Army can be good to people, but there would be a few more liars along the way. One needs to watch out.

There will always be encounters with people who think they know, but who really don't have a clue. There have been times when I have numbered among the dumb and inaccurate ones too.

Lead

"Noblesse oblige."
Gaston Pierre Marc (Translation: "Rank has its obligations")

Where ever two or more people are gathered together, you will also find a hierarchy. Civilian hierarchies are more complicated than the military because ranking is at first difficult to figure out. Civilians do not normally wear their status on their collars, but given enough time through trial and error most of us can eventually figure out the pecking order.

The U.S. Army makes it easy to learn who is who. Its rank system is prominently displayed on every uniform. New recruits may need some time to recognize the unfamiliar symbols, but soon enough they get the hang of it. Often they require the help of on-the-spot corrections by higher-ranking impromptu mentors and usually in a very public fashion. For example, a Sergeant Major will gladly remedy errant soldiers who mistake a Sergeant Major for a First Sergeant, a subtle but important difference. My rule is, when in doubt think higher. At the worst your error will flatter them.

The down side of this rank business in the military is that many people associate ability with rank; the more rank the more ability. Right? One would hope this is the case, but it is often not true. Rank and ability are not synonymous. Though most people gravitate toward those of ability, everyone dreads those obligatory occasions where we have to grip and grin with rascals who hold rank but lack ability.

There are good colonels and bad colonels, good sergeants and those who need improvement. The challenge is to find those best able to lead. Common soldiers do not make such decisions. It is left up to impartial boards to review paper evaluations and a photograph in deciding who will lead this great nation's soldiers tomorrow.

The process of selecting leaders is not perfect. A great deal of subjectivity is involved. It works well enough in peacetime, but if history is any lesson, the crucible of war will cull out many of the fair weather commanders. Promotions for ability come quickly. Napoleon Bonaparte skyrocketed from captain to emperor in seven years; Ulysses S. Grant rose from obscurity to commanding general in four years; Dwight D. Eisenhower soared from major to five-star general in six years.

Where do you stand in the pecking order? You most likely occupy a position where patience and politics place you during peacetime. Where you really belong depends on what you would do in a crisis or in combat. Regardless of the rank you hold, combat will oblige you to lead, follow, get out of the way, get run over, or run. Now, if only selection boards knew ahead of time what you would do.

27

Telling Time

"You can ask me for anything you like,
except time."
Napoleon Bonaparte

It took me awhile to get the hang of telling time back in grammar school. For an attention deficit hyperactive disorder (ADHD) kid, figuring out what the big and little hands on the clock meant took some patience from my teachers and persistence on my part. By the third grade, it all began to make sense, but little did I realize then that learning to tell time was only just beginning. There is the right way and the Army way.

Army life will introduce you to two new ways to tell time. That civilian stuff of a.m. and p.m. is just not good enough. For instance, if you say ten o'clock, is that a.m. or p.m.? To further clarify things the Army uses military time and for the very intelligent, the ever-popular Zulu time.

Even after twenty years in the service I still get a mental block with military time. Now what is 2200? For some reason 1800 for six p.m. or 2100 for nine p.m. were never a problem. And 1700 was always easy, for this was the end of the normal duty day. With clocks measuring up to 2400 though, I've always had to think twice about 2200.

In the Army, plain military time is not enough. You need Zulu time, but I don't think it has anything to do with Africa or Rorke's Drift. No, Zulu time is something entirely different from all other times.

When people travel real fast, say across several time zones in a few hours, then it is important to have folks reading off the same clock. Say you want Air Force B-52s to bomb the dickens out of somebody near you, but the bombers have to fly across three time zones to get to where you are. You want to make very sure they drop their payload not only at the right place, but also at the right time. So, you give the flyboys a delivery time in Zulu, or Greenwich Mean Time. Now, if that is not already hard enough to figure out, throw in the complication of daylight savings time. Now, is Zulu time five or six hours ahead of U.S. Central Standard Time zone?

Complicated, isn't it? Many things in the military seem complicated. Sometimes I think you need a degree in time management just to keep up with what time it is. We can take comfort in the thought that if we can confuse our own soldiers then we've probably bewildered the enemy too.

Does anybody really know what time it is?

Perhaps it is fortunate we haven't attacked the moon. We could theoretically seize and hold terrain on the moon, particularly if it is not a blue moon. But the big question is at what local time would you want the Army to do it?

The Duffel Bag

"An empty bag cannot stand upright."
Benjamin Franklin

When you travel, the world offers so many different types of baggage. Look at any airport luggage carousel and you will see all colors, styles, shapes, and sizes. From the petite toiletry bag of the finely dressed lady to the backpack of the shabbily clad college student touring the world, their precious belongings are transported in containers as varied as their owners.

In the Army, variety is heresy. True to form, the Army procurement people try to standardize the luggage of soldiers. From what seems like time immemorial, the mainstay of military luggage has been the duffel bag, that tubular green canvas bag with "U.S." stamped on the side.

The first duffel bag I ever saw up close was when my older half-brother returned home on leave from basic training in the Air Force. The image of a servicemember toting one of these giant sausage-shaped bags is familiar to most Americans. In his blue Air Force uniform, my brother was no exception. He mesmerized his younger protégé with the stories of the Air Force and eventually that bag would be opened for show and tell.

I always marveled how much stuff could be packed into a duffel bag. Heavy items in first, then lighter stuff on top, followed by packing and pushing. Bouncing the bag up and down in the upright position provided even more space for worldly possessions. The end result is one heavy bag.

The day came when I was old enough to join up and in time, two duffel bags became mine too. Though cool to have at first, over the years the novelty of the bags wore off and the duffel bag became relegated to home storage missions somewhere in the attic or basement. My personal choice for luggage became the suit carrier bag or the small pull-luggage you can take directly on the plane. It is nice to arrive with clothes that do not look like they've been shot with a double-barreled wrinkle gun.

The Army still issues those duffel bags. I see them now and again in luggage claim areas and I know a service member is nearby, probably one who is still new to the military. Sure enough, often someone with a uniquely military haircut appears and claims the bag. There is that familiar grunt as they lift the tightly packed bag over their shoulders and move out smartly. Most old veterans knowingly look on, content in the knowledge that their back pain is noticeably less since those bags were retired. They are nevertheless proud of that time when, with the help of a duffle bag, they were able to stand tall as a soldier, sailor, airman, or marine.

Trousers

"As for clothing…perhaps we are led oftener by love of novelty
and a regard for the opinions of men, in procuring it, than by a true utility."
Henry David Thoreau

Before the advent of the camouflaged battle dress uniform (BDU) in the early 1980s, U.S. Army troops wore olive drab fatigues. Around the world, in all sorts of weather, the common thread worn by all troops for many years were the fatigues.

Fatigues were an excellent uniform for the milder climates and hot places, like the American South or Vietnam. Made from lightweight material, the uniform was easy to maintain and did not stick to the skin. Get a good starch into a set of fatigues and one could look pretty darn sharp, too.

The weather of central Europe, Korea or Alaska is cold at least six months out of each year and troops arriving in their starched fatigues during the colder seasons received a rude awakening. I remember arriving at the replacement detachment in Frankfurt Germany during October from Charleston Air Force Base in South Carolina. After a warm eighty-two degrees I was greeted with freezing temperatures and a piercing wind.

Early my first morning in Germany about two hundred of us stood before the large German-style barracks. We looked sharp standing there in our accountability formation. As the sergeants took their time getting the count and doing administrative business, I began to regret that I had not found a spot deeper in the formation. Standing in an outside row of soldiers, I was buffeted by the cold winds and quickly experienced what wind chill was. The light fatigue pants were no match for the Teutonic wind. My buttocks and lower legs began to sting as the wind whipped away. A good coat and gloves protected my chest and hands, but this southern boy was literally shivering in his boots by the end of the formation.

Although fatigues were very comfortable in the heated indoors, outside it was a different matter, especially with the pants. It did not take long to figure out that a good pair of thermal underwear bottoms would make a world of difference in keeping my backside warm.

Later on, BDUs fixed all that. Now soldiers had some pants that could hold back at least most of the German wind. Though we now looked like walking trees, at least we were warmer. Looking back, I definitely prefer certain things about each uniform the other didn't offer. Overall though, my vote would be for the BDUs. However, I would change the meaning of the acronym and would suggest BDF for **b**attle **d**ress **f**atigues, or, a bit closer to our anatomy, **b**utt **d**oesn't **f**reeze.

Times

"It was the best of times, it was the worst of times..."
Charles Dickens

In the fall of 1979 the United States Army was in bad shape. The Vietnam debacle and the poorly executed postwar draw down demoralized and decimated Army leadership and the soldier rank and file alike. Money and good morale were both in short supply. Into this sorry state of affairs I began my career, enlisting as a Private First Class on my way to being a medic, full of hope and idealism.

As already mentioned, my first assignment was to a forsaken place called Baumholder, in what was then West Germany. Located at least an hour's drive away from any European civilization, Baumholder held the bulk of the 8th Infantry Division, where soldiers out-numbered the few local civilians thirty to one.

My first unit was interesting, to say the least. Some leaders in my unit were chain-smokers, overweight, and rumor had it that they had previous UCMJ actions against them. That would explain why, even with 14 to 15 years in service, they were still E-5s (Specialist Fifth Class). Other leaders were alcoholics and the officers and NCOs could not stand each other. To keep peace within the ranks, NCOs were forced to segregate racial groups into squads of whites, blacks, Hispanics, or Pacific Islanders. Sprinkled through all this was near epidemic drug use.

Within minutes of arriving in the unit, a fellow medic informed me that he knew how to fix me up with some dope if I wanted some. Thanks for nothing. Just what I needed to get off to a good start. It was going to be a long tour. Some have made the now famous statement, "I smoked but never inhaled." Allow me to coin the phrase, "I never smoked but I did inhale." You couldn't help it if you lived in the barracks.

Over time, things did improve. The Army finally retired or rehabilitated our alcoholic leaders. Bad sergeants were quietly sent home, some for being overweight and others for additional UCMJ recognitions. Mandatory and credible urine drug screening began to cut down on the drug culture. More money in the training budget kept us out of mischief and actually preparing to fight our nation's real or cold wars. Racial groups were integrated and it worked. Finally, officers and NCOs began to work together.

As my first enlistment neared its end, a guy by the name of Ronald Reagan gave us an eighteen percent pay raise. For a Specialist Fifth Class that was a nice sum of money. A better U.S. Army was emerging all around me. What began as the worst of times was fast becoming something much better.

Payday

"They say that in the Army the pay is mighty fine.
They give you a hundred dollars and take back ninety-nine."
Army Cadence

One of the few times a soldier salutes while indoors is when he reports to a pay officer. In an era of direct deposits and automatic teller machines, one does not encounter pay officers much anymore. But not too long ago it was the main way soldiers got paid. In fact, once upon a time payday activities revolved around paying a visit to a heavily guarded pay officer holding about a half-million dollars in cold cash. Getting cash from this particular officer was the right way to start a payday weekend.

Being paid in those days was a public ordeal. You stood in line with hundreds of other soldiers and, interestingly enough, things were remarkably quiet. Money was serious business. It was therefore no problem to overhear the pay officer as he paid each soldier in twenty-dollar bills: "That'll be $680.00. Twenty, forty, sixty, eighty, one-hundred, twenty, forty..." Getting cash was not a private matter.

For married soldiers getting paid could be a bit uncomfortable, as their pay was significantly higher due to quarter's allowance, separate rations, and COLA. So, when the pay out came single soldiers in line would gasp and crack jokes, as the pay officer would say: "$1,350.00. Twenty, forty, sixty..." Then, while the single guys would head off to party, we married soldiers would make our way home or off to the commissary with the family. There were bills to pay too. Payday activity was family time.

Before dawn on Monday morning, completely broke soldiers, married or single, would reassemble for duty. While gathering together for the morning formation and for the First Sergeant to arrive, we would swap stories from the weekend. Laughs would erupt as single soldiers filled us in on their exploits and adventures. The married ones were quieter. Helping the wife with things around the house or playing with the kids could not evoke the same level of merriment, though we were just as content.

Easy come. Easy go. The big bucks of payday were gone and a new monthly cycle had begun. We lived from check to check. Despite being broke, we all had something to show for the ninety-nine that was "taken back." The single soldiers had their tales and trinkets and the married guys had their treasures and some trinkets too.

Each of us had what we wanted…and that was mighty fine.

The Volksmarch

"I have fought a good fight, I have finished my course,
I have kept the faith."
2 Timothy 4:7

My military career always blessed me with the unusual privilege of
having Army chaplains nearby who were actually clergy in my own
denomination. Most service members have clergy turned-chaplains from
their particular denomination or faiths, be it Catholic, Baptist, Adventist,
Presbyterian, Jewish or whatever. Whether it was Don Troyer at Fort Hood,
Steve Torgeson in San Antonio, Ed Bowen in Hawaii, or Gary Councell at
Fort Lewis, each assignment seemed to put me in the parish of one of the
active duty chaplains of my faith. When I remember the chaplains from my
denomination, the first one that comes to my mind will always be a great
American, Chaplain (LTC) Ralph Workman.

Baumholder as a first assignment in the Army was inauspicious. A
hillside stacked full of American troops in a backwater locale of Europe
could present a twenty-three year old some morale difficulties. I was just a
face among ten thousand other faces and didn't know a soul. Thank God that
my first duty station included Ralph Workman who, out of all those strange
faces, was one face representing an outpost of my faith far from home. In a
way, he would be like a father to me.

Even though Chaplain Workman had his hands full taking care of all
soldiers, as is the duty of an Army chaplain, he also took a special interest in
the small flock from his own denomination. My chance to get to know
Chaplain Workman was when he invited me to join him on a *Volksmarch*.

It was my very first Volksmarch or people's march. While our wives
made a leisurely hike over the scenic hills near Kaiserslautern, Germany, the
Chaplain thought I would be interested in a more strenuous outing over the
ten-kilometer route. How do you say no to a machine twenty-five years your
senior? As our wives had a great time visiting, we were off on the double.

My maiden march became a forced march. Huffing and puffing, it
was all I could do to keep up with this most fit man of the cloth, the most in
shape chaplain I would ever know. The "march" wore me out, but LTC
Workman was ready to do another ten Ks. "I'll pass," I politely said.

They say first impressions are lasting ones. Whenever I remember a
German Volksmarch I recall Chaplain Workman and our forced march.
Between breaths I managed to get to know a jewel of a man, a jock of the
Rock, a keeper of the faith, and an example of endurance and strength that
enabled me to survive many hardships that would later come in my faith and
my military career.

Short People

"Less is more."
Robert Browning

"If you are shorter than the person in front," the sergeant ordered, "move to the front." Obediently, the vertically challenged soldiers of the hundred-or-so man formation moved to the front of the group. Eventually, after a fair amount of jostling, the taller troops were in the rear. After a facing movement and a further order to do the same again, the shortest soldier found a place in the front left corner of our formation and the tallest one in the back right position.

Not by choice, but by genes, I stood next to the shortest chap, an Italian guy from New Jersey. I was number two in our phalanx of troops.

Once again stature, or the lack thereof, would provide some of the taller soldiers fodder for some fresh jokes: "Hey Kay, stand up," someone would crack. "He is standing up already," another would respond, followed by chuckles from everyone. It was another ration of jokes at short people's expense, jokes that those of us closer to the ground come to accept as a part of life. I discovered that if I laugh along the perpetrators shut up faster. It is a trick garnered from years of ribbing. Reacting otherwise only intensified their desire to follow-up the thrust with another.

The virtues of short men are often overlooked in an American society that worships height in males. Tall, dark and handsome, is what we hear the ladies are looking for, not the short, fair-haired, and common men. The tall men are automatically given first attention and interest. Just look at the evidence: are not most Presidents, CEOs and State Troopers tall in general?

Now add to this short stature handicap the fact that you are redheaded, as I am, and you can find yourself in some serious trouble. But in this survival of the fittest world, you learn to improvise, adapt, and overcome. You do more with what you have. You do more with less. Those dark-haired hunks with their slow-moving, deliberate manner provide avenues of opportunity for us fast, quick-witted, hyperactive, short, redheaded men. Personal energy and audacity, not necessarily stature, will make any environment target rich.

Some of my closest friends are quite tall. I get weather reports from them regularly. Seriously though, the strengths of a man lie not with what appearance, genetics, and chance may have given him. No, the real strength of a man is in his substance, what he accomplishes with his God-given gifts. Here is where the playing field of life gets more level, or maybe even lower, much to the advantage of short people.

Less can indeed be more.

Weekends

"The problem with a weekend is that the Army
puts a Monday on the end of it."
Anonymous

"Fall in," the First Sergeant calls out, "Receive the report." Platoon sergeants do an about face and receive the accountability reports given by each squad leader. Everyone is quiet and still. The sooner this is over the better. It is late Friday and the last formation of the week is underway.

Reports are passed on to the First Sergeant, or "Top" as these great leaders are affectionately called in the Army. Top quickly runs through some items of business for his 120-man company. Sometimes administrative housekeeping can consume a lot of time, but fortunately not today.

Finally, those sweet words to every soldier are said, "Fall out!" Instantly we are all temporary civilians again. We hurry off in a hundred different directions on this a spring day in Idar-Oberstein, Germany. I take off down the hill from our post at Strassburg Kaserne. My wife would have picked me up in the car, but I choose to enjoy the three-mile hike home. As my heavy boots pound the cobblestone sidewalk, the Army drifts away.

There is the teasing, sweet smell of a German bakery in the air. There is also the scent of flowers from window boxes and a kind smile from a German lady out sweeping the sidewalk. A couple of carefree German school kids giggle as this soldier marches by.

Soon, the climb up the big hill to my apartment begins. My wife and two young sons are there waiting for me. Though I am truly a nobody in the Army, to my sons I'm a general and Santa combined. And to my wife I am everything she wants, even without the stars of a general.

I climb the stairs and my young men greet me with open arms, like Rome celebrating the return of Caesar. Instead of slaves and gold, my rucksack contains German pastries and a couple of essentials my wife wanted from the commissary. The boys are ecstatic and a kiss from my wife is far better than any Caesar could have received. For the next sixty hours I have a small taste of freedom with the most beautiful woman in the world and two very above average children. But too soon it ends. It is o'dark thirty Monday morning and we are back in formation. There is the smell of old German beer on someone in front of me. Someone else puts a silent scent into the air and there are muffled groans. Someone probably ate too much German sausage. About this time Top strides to the front of the formation.

The period at the end of each weekend's story is that old, familiar phrase, "Fall in! Receive the report."

Mister Mom

"God could not be everywhere
so He therefore made mothers."
Jewish Proverb

Once my Army unit sponsored a "Mothers' Day Out" event. Married soldiers were allowed the day off to take care of the kids while their wives joined other spouses for a day of activities. "Piece of cake," I thought. "I get the day off and get to play with my sons." Right. My wife was excited. Courtesy of the U.S. Army, she was off to a day of shopping and activities with other ladies at our small Army post in Germany.

The day began well enough. We had a good breakfast. My ten-month-old especially enjoyed the new food I gave him. It was food mother would not ever allow him to have. After breakfast I got out the baby carriage and my boys and I headed out for a long walk. We'd clean up the house later. Our journey took us to the great out-of-doors, complete with fresh air and herds of sheep nearby. Everything was going so well until my youngest decided it was time for his daily business. It would be big business this time.

I don't know how many diapers other soldiers have changed in their lives, but I'd say I have been through a fair share. Of the hundreds, maybe even thousands I have handled, fate would have it that my second son would deliver the mother of all dirty diapers on our walk that day, thanks to the novel breakfast food he had enjoyed.

It took me awhile to figure out something was up, or out. There was that familiar odor in the air as I pushed the buggy along. My cargo was also beginning to squirm and show signs of discomfort. Soon his crying and my forgetting to bring a spare diaper along would force me to retreat home over the protests of my older, hyperactive first son, who wanted to press on.

Back home is where I discovered the full extent of the disaster. There was more than just a dirty diaper by this time. Clothes, carriage, baby, everything anywhere near my second son was now soiled. It would take me several hours to get everything cleaned up and restored to normal. In the end I was exhausted and looking forward to going back to my regular job.

My wife returned from her outing refreshed and happy. She found Mr. Mom recuperating from the diaper-changing ordeal, the house much the way she had left it. She was a bit frustrated at my apparent laziness, but I eventually filled her in on all the dirty details.

The boys have long since been potty-trained, and it's been years since I've changed a diaper. I am glad my wife understood what I had been through, for I had a much better appreciation of what moms do for us all, diapers included.

Powerful Queens

"We are the boys that fear no noise
Where the thundering cannon roars."
Oliver Goldsmith

In the distance, there is periodic rumbling, like thunder from a summer storm. But these sounds are different. They are shorter, sharper, and seem closer together in an artificial manner, far different than the random sounds of a thunderstorm. There is also the gentle shaking of the ground and rattling of window glass, as if some giant is walking about on the earth. Instead of a treading giant, these are the sounds of the Queen of Battle, the United States Army Field Artillery.

Live on or near an Army post and you become familiar with this man-made noise in the distance. At night, the far horizon will flash, like lightning bolts striking the earth. The sky will also shine in an eerie glow as parachute flares slowly descend out of the sky, giving light to targets in the artillery impact zone below. The lights and nighttime noise have the aura of some primitive rock concert bringing incredible power and destructive potential almost to your very doorstep.

Army folks, soldiers and civilians alike, grow accustomed to the noise of big guns firing in the distance. We humans have an amazing ability to adapt, to accept certain things that are totally bizarre to the uninitiated. The noise isn't weird at all. It is training.

I sat in my "Gamma Goat" ambulance through the cold, dreary night in the Baumholder maneuver area. It was my first real field training exercise in the Army, and I was supporting a field artillery unit. Just to the front of me were six large, self-propelled howitzers, each nestled under its own huge camouflage netting. The big 155mm guns were pointed in the opposite direction at some range in the distance. There would be no sleep for me, as I was unaccustomed to the incredibly loud, random firing of each gun, launching its nearly one hundred pound projectile into the darkness. Thirty miles away, the round impacts with a "womp-like" sound, and fifty square meters of some unseen place is instantly transformed into smoking, plowed chaos.

Soldiers learn not to fear the sound of the guns. They are often your friends. Soldiers only pray that they will never have to be on the receiving end of such horrendous power from the sky, a power that comes from any direction in any type of weather. This power is a life-altering present delivered by the unseen queen of the battlefield, field artillery.

37

On Time

"Better late than never."
Livy

For people cursed with a type A personality, an especially trying experience is to be late. You have a busy schedule but some unforeseen delay occurs. A traffic jam. A longer than normal appointment. A personal emergency. The end result is you're late. Like the rabbit in *Alice in Wonderland*, you rush like mad to get where you should already be.

Being late ordinarily is a minor inconvenience. However, the Army has a unique way of making the situation even worse. It is called a formation. 120 people form up at least twice each day. If you are not there, or "out of ranks," it is publicly reported. You are by name unaccounted for. Instead of one or two people knowing you are late, suddenly an entire company knows. Not only is it embarrassing, it can also cost you money in fines and extra duty time.

Your heart is racing. The palms of your hands are sweaty. The mind races through the possible scenarios you could face when you finally get to work. You are late. You do your best to hurry but despite your best efforts, the clock is against you. There is that familiar lump in your throat, or a tightness in the chest and a tremble in your hand, made all the worse because you have no valid excuse for being tardy. The temptation to lie is strong.

You finally arrive at work and discover the First Sergeant canceled the formation. It didn't matter that you were late. A wave of relief comes over you as the fear of embarrassment and potential punishment evaporates. The heart rate lowers, your breathing slows down and you get a hold of yourself as you head off to work breathing a sigh of thanksgiving.

Though grace saved your hide this once, junior NCO leaders will ensure you not quickly forget this important lesson that all civilian employers appreciate when they hire veterans. Soldiers become hard-wired for being on time. A person always late will find it an expensive habit.

Everybody hates hassle. Maybe showing up is eighty percent of life. If so, then being late can be eighty percent of life's hassles. Most of us are conditioned to show up. We see what happens to those who don't show up on time or have experienced first hand what happens to the tardy in the Army. Unlike school where being late is merely a mark on the report card, the Army can make it a mark on your bank statement.

Many soldiers show up early for mandatory troop formations. They have learned that showing up is eighty percent of staying out of trouble, at least with life in the United States Army.

Angels and Roots

"Fear gave wings to his feet."
Vergil

My oldest son, Nathan, is now fully-grown and deep into college. He is following a path that is leading him into the sky. He is studying to be a pilot. It is a noble pursuit and one he began when just a toddler.

An exciting part of Army life is all the traveling you can potentially do. Now don't get me wrong, there are some pretty out of the way, lousy places to be assigned to, but even bad assignments offer opportunities to at least get away on trips to some neat places nearby. With my first major assignment in Germany, off duty time became a great opportunity for my wife and I, with our small one-year old son Nathan in tow, to climb into our tiny car and take off to see the sights. Volksmarches, shopping, food, museums, scenery, and castles were everywhere to be had, whether you are wealthy or broke. And we fit into the broke category most of the time.

Irene and I prided ourselves on not letting our small children hinder our efforts to get out and be in life. To help haul Nathan around we bought a small child carrier pack. One day, with Nathan tucked into the special yellow backpack, we began the vigorous climb to the top of a mountainside cliff where a castle stood. As we neared the summit, Nathan pushed and squirmed, something he did on a regular basis when determined to be free of that child carrier. He had had enough of this riding business. Daddy was tired too, so Nathan was lifted out of the carrier and allowed to walk a bit. He proceeded to make a beeline to the edge of the walkway we were on, where the guardrail was built for adults and not for small children.

To our utter horror, Nathan slipped under the guardrail and fell down the steep slope on the other side. Instinctively, I dove after him, thoughtless of the consequences. The built-up side of the walkway gave way to a sharp decline to the cliff's edge where it was a good three hundred foot drop to the rocky bottom. I grabbed Nathan and we tumbled to the edge as my wife collapsed in pure terror, about to lose both men in her life.

God had other plans for Nathan and I, though. Just before the edge, the now empty yellow child carrier on my back snagged on a root just before the deadly drop-off. Nathan, oblivious to the danger, giggled as our tumble ended. I recall him saying, "Let's do that again, daddy."

Throughout life, you remember things for which you are eternally grateful—an answered prayer, a stroke of good fortune, a golden opportunity not missed. My wife is especially thankful for the day when a root kept her two falling angels from prematurely winging their way into eternity.

Hooaah!

"Let us have the faith that right makes might, and in that faith
let us to the end dare to do our duty as we understand it."
Abraham Lincoln

Attitude is important. It is more important than schooling, uniforms or whom you know. It is probably the most important thing in a successful Army career. A "can do" frame of mind will led to success.

Nothing in military jargon epitomizes a can do attitude better than the term "Hooaah!" Hooaah can mean anything but no. Most often it means I understand what you want and it will be done. Hooaah is the NCO war cry in leading soldiers. It is a message that says, "We make things happen."

Those with an attitude problem think Hooaah means something else. Maybe something you step into when in a farmyard. They forget that the tone of the voice or the facial expression will reveal the true meaning of their brand of hooaah. It has been said, "a bad attitude is like a flat tire. You are not going anywhere until you fix it." True Hooaah is not flat or fake.

A great day in the Army is when good things happen. Exceptional things happen when there is a good plan. Ideally, after listening to their NCOs and evaluating all the data, officers make a good plan. NCOs then make that plan happen. Without a plan, you might as well plan on failing.

Many factors come together to make a good soldier who is having a great day. Starting with a sharp uniform, exceptional soldiers have proper military bearing, respect for those of superior rank and a genuine concern for those inferior in rank. They are ready to go to work, not just to stand there all day and look pretty. These people understand the business at hand and are obviously taking care of business, whether it is police call or developing a plan of attack. Whatever a good soldier is doing you can be sure of finding some "Hooaah" mixed in.

Hooaah is a uniquely military term. From time to time I've caught myself saying this term in the presence of civilians unfamiliar with the military. Their puzzled looks warranted an explanation. The explanation is simple: a can-do attitude, the power to have a good day.

When the time comes to do some really unpleasant things, Hooaah is what it will take. Hooaah is what will get you through those terrible days that come. Indeed, the day will come when great people will have to die for this wonderful nation once again. Freedom is not free. Like the rebel yell of the American Civil War or the war hoop of the plains Indians, Hooaah will be that soldier's battle cry. When everyone else turns and runs, those with genuine Hooaah will do their duty.

The Dubious Honor

"Sometimes when nature calls, you need call waiting."
David Kay

An unforgettable memory for me occurred not long after I arrived in my first line unit. Energetic and full of "hooaah," I was ever ready to prove myself to my leaders that here was an extraordinary soldier.

We were in a night convoy movement of perhaps thirty or so vehicles. Short handed, I found myself the driver and sole occupant of a Gamma Goat ambulance. Our objective was a Rhine River crossing, near Mainz, Germany. The German Army, called the *Bundeswehr*, would ferry our convoy to an assembly point somewhere across the river.

The road trip began quickly and I didn't think about the need to relieve myself until about an hour into the journey. That cup of hot chocolate and the bumping of the Gamma Goat hurried the filtration ability of my kidneys and before long, "I had to go."

There would be no relief however. The convoy, already behind schedule, was not going to stop for anything. For the next three hours, the pressure became ever stronger, to the point where I felt like I was about to pop. Every bump in the road, every shift in the tight driver's space, brought me ever closer to the point of answering nature's urgent call.

With no radio, I could not ask anyone for permission to stop. Being the last vehicle in the column, stopping would result in getting lost, since I didn't know where we were or where we were going. In short, the situation was desperate, and wetting my pants was becoming a distinct possibility.

After five hours of hard driving and even harder holding, we arrived at the ferry point, stopping only after the ever-efficient *Bundeswehr* rapidly loaded our vehicles onto the ferry. Shutting the engine off and applying the emergency brake, I hurriedly made for the side of the ferry to release a brake of a different sort. In the early morning darkness, as the world slept and the ferryboat began its journey across the Rhine, I found incredible relief in answering nature's call on that dark river under a cold, starry sky.

Finishing my urgent business, I discovered that the ferry had completed the crossing of that wide river. A sergeant was yelling at me to get back into my truck. Settling back into the cramped, cold compartment of my ambulance, I felt very exquisite relief at finally ending the pain of my bloated bladder. It came, however, with the dubious honor at having been without doubt the first individual to go number one the entire breadth of the Rhine River.

Top

"Laugh, and the world laughs with you; weep, and you weep alone."
Ella Wheeler Wilcox

It had been a typical winter day in Germany—rainy and cold. Preceded by an untold number of additional wet days, the ground at Baumholder's maneuver training area was a boggy morass, with small lava-like flows of mud heading for low-lying areas. Created by years and years of maneuver training, first with Hitler's armies and now with GIs, the mud was an especially gooey variety.

Our First Sergeant was an exceptional man. He was a go-getter, a fast track enlisted soldier spawned in the Vietnam War. He was also genuinely concerned about his soldiers and the occasional stranger from some other American or Allied unit who found himself in our midst. His creed was taking care of soldiers.

In looking after his troops, Top believed chow was a number one priority in the field. He had my vote on that count. For our First Sergeant, a rainy, cold German day lent even more urgency to making sure his troops received hot food in an era before MREs or tray rations. He kept a special eye on the cooks, these budding chefs at making food from scratch.

This day was a special day, despite the horribly depressing weather. The aroma of steak and baked potatoes with onions drew us all to the cooks' converted two-and-a-half ton truck. In no time, an eager, hungry line of troops had formed. We were like flies to…well, you know what I mean.

Top would always be the last through line. "My men eat first," he always said. The cooks knew it too and I have no doubt that our clever staff sergeant cook set aside a choice serving for our beloved First Sergeant.

Satisfied that his soldiers were fed, Top made his way through the chow line. With his plate in one hand stacked with three or four thousand calories and a huge coffee mug in the other, he began to negotiate the muddy, downhill path back to his Jeep. I stared in horror as he lost his footing and landed face down in the mud with food and coffee splattering in the muck. After muttering some exceptionally unique French words, he began to laugh. Recovering from our shock, the dozen or so of us who witnessed the fall laughed as well.

Composing himself, the First Sergeant made his way back to the chow truck, restocked a new plate and ate it then and there, muddy as a pig. As we watched, we knew why he was a fast track kind of soldier. He was undaunted. Top rose above misfortune by laughing at himself and to this day he probably still laughs about that fall.

Tantrum Management

"Train up a child in the way he should go:
and when he is old, he will not depart from it."
Proverbs 22:6

Some people have a difficult time taking no for an answer. They cannot understand any version of no they hear. "No" is just simply not a part of their vocabulary. In response to a negative answer, some will weasel their way up the chain of leadership until somebody somewhere says yes, the leader not realizing how an affirmative decision undermines the credibility of junior leaders the petitioner circumvented.

I think this "can't take no for an answer" problem begins very early in life. I have seen parents struggling with toddlers in the store, especially on the candy aisle. "No, Billy! I will not buy you candy!" a parent will firmly say. Billy persists and persists, doggedly trying to wear down mom or dad's resistance until finally the parent says, "No, and that's final!" Billy, out of desperation, resorts to the time-tested tactic of pitching a fit right there in the supermarket. Embarrassed, the parents either give in to shut him up, or resort to some dramatic draconian disciplinary demonstrations, all likely to be of an uncivilized nature.

My wife is the wonderful mother of four Army brats. Irene has taught me a great deal on leadership, especially in the handling of our three boys. The Army should write manuals based on the leadership abilities of good mothers and teach it to commanders and general officers. My wife's style and technique should be the centerpiece of the discipline instructional block of the Command and General Staff College or Army War College.

When Irene says no, she means it. It is a Supreme Court decision. If our kids can't make their case the first time, then too bad. Even appeals to the father are like taking the case back to a lower court—Mother's decisions always stick. Dad knows better, for he has learned over the years.

Irene had a superb tactic for dealing with fledgling temper tantrums in public places, too. When my boys first tried some noisy demonstration, Irene would proceed to quietly hold their shoulder with one hand. She exerted a subtle, nonverbal, but definitely physical control by applying pressure similar to *Star Trek's* Mr. Spock's Vulcan nerve pinch. Not very painful, but enough to get the boy's attention and squelch any fit.

But pressure points were a last resort, and rarely used. Irene mostly led with carrots, even in influencing her devoted husband. No is sometimes the answer to life's desires, but in the end it is carrots, the rewards in life, which make the world go around. After so much training, it is all so clear to me now...and to my boys, too.

Water

"Water is the great necessity of the soldier."
Napoleon Bonaparte

A field training exercise is typically a long, somewhat boring time punctuated by periods of intense work and excitement. The Army trains in all types of weather, and it seems that commanders know when the rain is coming, for it is often during rain that we train.

Sitting inside at home, one can appreciate the need for some rain. It helps the farmers. It waters the grass. It fills the creeks and rivers. It refreshes the out of doors. On the other hand, being out in the rain day in and day out is a different matter. This is a perspective most Americans have never experienced, unless they are avid campers, hunters, or fishermen.

Soldiers train in the mud and every now and again the training can actually be fun. One of the great pleasures in the rain is playing in mud. For instance, take driving tactical vehicles through mud holes and mud pits. The tanks, trucks, or Jeeps make quite a splash, or splat, whichever the case may be. The gaping marks in the mud are impressive, but only temporary.

After such driving escapades, a thick layer of mud sticks to the tank or truck. Day after day during the FTX, new layers of mud are added. If the rain clears and it becomes sunny and warm, the mud hardens to the vehicle's sides, almost becoming a part of it, hiding the original paint underneath.

But when all the training ends, the final event is the wash rack. This Army version of a car wash is not anything like the civilian one. It is designed for heavy duty, like tanks that carry a couple hundred extra pounds of dirt, grime and mud that need clearing off. You need three things to get those tanks clean again—water, high-pressure spray and elbow grease.

Soldiers tackle this job with gusto, usually because they know that as soon as the vehicles and equipment are clean, they'll be heading home. The water flies as the metal monsters wait patiently for their drivers and crews to give them a bath. Large chunks of mud and dirt come off the wheel wells, sprockets, and tracks. Occasionally, tank crews will have water fights in honor of this festive occasion, much to the irritation of other soldiers patiently waiting in line for a chance to wash their tanks and trucks too. In the end, everyone and everything comes out cleaner.

In time, the vehicles are parked in their allotted spaces in the motor pool, all clean and ready for the next use. The water has a way of renewing all things, whether it falls from the sky, flows from a hose, or provides that steamy massage in a hot tub after two weeks in the field. Wherever it comes from, it is a great necessity of soldiers still.

Audacity

"Sometimes audacity pays."
David Kay

While I was stationed in Germany, my wife and I took a vacation to Italy—one of the most interesting countries in the world. It was in Italy that a bit of boldness gave us an experience we will long cherish and remember.

Capri is a beautiful island, lying off the southern coast of Italy near Naples. One can reach Capri via ferries departing from the port at Naples. We had a wonderful day trip to the island and were returning by ferry to the city. As we arrived, we noticed to our left a large submarine docked at an Italian naval base. The Stars and Stripes was flying at its stern.

Thinking what a treat it would be to tour one of our American submarines, I said to my wife, "Let's see if we can visit that submarine." Always ready for an adventure, my wife quickly agreed, and we headed with high hopes to the Italian naval base where the sub lay at anchor.

There was a rather interesting and brief encounter with three Italian guards at the gate. We were nervous as we approached the gate in our small car, not knowing any Italian. Sometimes not knowing the language can be helpful though. We drove up to the gate, stopped and waved our passports, saying out our window "Americano." Without a further word said, the gate promptly went up and the guards with their sub-machine guns and smiles waved us through.

After a maze of turns we finally reached the dock. The sun had set, and the sleek, dark submarine was silhouetted against the lights of Naples across the harbor. The duty officer, an ensign, was in the coning tower. I asked from the dock if we could visit the ship. After a short wait and a couple of calls below deck for clearance, he welcomed us aboard after checking our military ID cards.

The attack submarine U.S.S. Birmingham was quite a vessel. With half of her crew on shore leave, an amicable petty officer guided us throughout the ship and we met its skeleton crew. From the galley to the engine room, from the officer's stateroom to the bridge, the Navy did an excellent job of impressing two land-locked Army folks. We saw everything, save a couple of classified areas where the missiles were. I especially enjoyed seeing distant objects through the "million dollar periscope."

The submarine tour was the highlight of our trip to Italy, more memorable than just seeing another castle or ruin. The tour was also a good example of how audacity can really payoff for a couple of "Americano" tourists.

Victory

"Better is the end of a thing than the beginning..."
Ecclesiastes 7:8

The warm Italian day was almost heavenly. A brilliant sun bathed the countryside. A slight breeze blew in from the Mediterranean Sea, and the picturesque landscape belied the fact that once this was a bloody battlefield. Anzio held strong memories for Fred Ruprecht, my German father-in-law. It was here he saw action against American and British Forces during World War II.

Fred was one of the bad guys. He was an eighteen year-old draftee in the Wehrmacht, serving as an artilleryman with the Herman Göring Division. After boot camp in Holland and a quick train ride to Italy, Anzio would be his first serious fight of the war, the first of many more to come. The battery of Nebelwerfer rocket-guns he was assigned to man had plenty of work to do on the target rich beachhead full of Allied troops and equipment.

The pristine military cemetery lay just by the roadside, a good place for a stop after our light lunch of fruit, bread and pasta. Fred also wanted to stop, have a look around, and take a peaceful stroll during our holiday.

The grounds were the final resting-places for British soldiers who fell at Anzio. Each white marker, neatly spaced in row after row, displayed the name and rank of the soldier, as well as his unique regimental crest that was prominently displayed at the top. Occasionally, a Star of David interrupted the rows of crosses.

The markers fascinated me. One could identify units engaged in the battle by noting the crest on every marker, each with exquisite carvings. I turned to Fred, pointing out to him a particularly interesting regimental crest. I stopped in mid-sentence when the glistening tear rolling down his cheek caught my eye. It suddenly dawned on me that the crests meant nothing to Fred. He had noticed the sad tale each individual marker told.

"David," he said, "the thought chills me that I probably killed some of these men. I was here when they were killed." He paused, lowering his head, "Who would have thought," he continued, choking slightly, "that each of my three daughters would one day marry the enemy."

Pausing, I said, "Yes, Fred, but I personally am glad it turned out that way. Sad, certainly, that each of these men fell, but glad because their cause was ultimately victorious in more ways than one," as I deliberately nodded in the direction of his beautiful daughter Irene, who was now my wife.

Sleeping Bag Heaven

"As a well-spent day brings happy sleep,
so life well used brings happy death."
Leonardo da Vinci

Someday I would like to meet the inventor of the military's cold weather sleeping bag. That outstanding individual deserves a heartfelt expression of thanks from every soldier who has experienced that warm, cozy cocoon of pleasure in the midst of bitter cold field training conditions. I truly hope the Army paid this person well. With this procurement the Army for once bought a truly useful piece of gear from a genius. And, unlike infamous Air Force toilet seats, the Army probably did not pay an exorbitant price for them either.

Field training exercises are busy times in the U.S. Army. Fatigue, grime, noise, boredom and fumes are just a few of the unpleasant things soldiers face. Frankly speaking, these exercises are tough any time of the year, but winter conditions impose another factor that intensifies the experience: being cold.

It is immaterial what gear or clothing a soldier wears. If he stays outside long enough, he will get cold. Layered clothing is not enough. The *Gortex* eventually allows some cold in, those $200 boots will fail to keep the toes in contact with the body's heater, and that pair of gloves will not keep the fingers warm. But no matter how bad things are there is always that wonderful sleeping bag where you truly can have a warm place to stay awhile, a warm oasis from the bone chilling, freezing weather.

As soldiers run to and fro each frigid day, they try to stay ahead of the cold with warm drinks, tent stoves, vehicle heaters, and good chow. In the back of their mind, however, is that pleasurable thought of finding some time to crawl into that warm sleeping bag heaven and escape the cold and the sometimes-frantic pace while on maneuvers. I am convinced that every soldier shares this thought, from the newest private to the big guy with four stars, all of whom sleep in the same type of sack.

When that moment of rest finally arrives, it can truly be one of supreme contentment. Things you look forward to can always be so. To snuggle into that lair and hibernate for a few hours is rejuvenating.

You don't have much when you're in the field—gear, food, maybe a radio or a book. Of all the things you have in the cold no doubt that sleeping bag is enjoyed the most. It can be how you define contentment as a soldier during your duty in a cold, frozen world. That sleeping bag is something you have and can enjoy, a happy sleep in the dead of winter.

47

Army Wives

"Who can find a virtuous woman? For her price is far above rubies."
Proverbs 31:10

My wife met me at the door after I returned from maneuvers after thirty days. She looked beautiful in her new dress, freshly done hair, and a smile that said, "welcome home, soldier." A whiff of her light perfume filled my nostrils as she gave me a warm embrace. Behind her, each child began to arrive from different parts of the house—"It's daddy!" they yelled.

The strongest women in the entire world are Army wives. These ladies follow their husbands around the world trying to make do with what time and circumstances give them. The experience makes or breaks them. Those who survive are stronger in spirit than the mightiest soldier. Like the coveted Ranger tab on soldiers' sleeves, Army wives should have a tab too.

Try as much as I like, fully understanding what these wives have gone through evades me. How can I know? We soldiers are always gone. We often have to stay late at work and the fatigue at the end of a day leaves little desire left to empathize. Unless you walk a mile in their shoes, to paraphrase an old Indian bit of wisdom, you will never understand them.

The duties and responsibilities of an Army wife are many. A psychiatrist, chef, sanitation engineer, educator, interior designer, judge, accountant and human resources manager are just a few careers that color any description of what an Army wife is and does. She has to be a bit of all these and more. Those who do it well will become, what the Presbyterian minister Peter Marshall called, "Keepers of the springs."

These women, like their Army sisters before them, very often make do without their man. Over a twenty-year Army career, their husband will be gone on TDY, deployments, FTXs, to war or school anywhere from three to ten years total time. For some it is even longer. Their ladies learn to be independent and expert at patience in order to survive.

Men learn to accept their women as the Army experience changes them over the years. From the young, innocent, novice wife and mother at the start of his career, in time she becomes a seasoned manager of home, offspring and husband. They make the quarters a home, the children into "Army Brats," and the husband into a human being. And they do it very well, as few civilian spouses can imagine, thank you very much.

The subculture of the Army is very much like the small, imaginary community of Garrison Keilor's *Lake Woebegone*. Maybe all the men are not handsome, but it is a place where all the women are beautiful in their own special way. The women are what hold it all together. They are the jewels of the Army.

Deterrents

"The heights by men reached and kept were not attained by sudden flight,
But they, while their companions slept, were toiling upward in the night."
Henry Wadsworth Longfellow

It is early in the morning. Very early. Outside the window it is still pitch black. Most of the world is asleep when the post siren blares out or the telephone rings. Everyone is awakened from his or her deep, peaceful sleep. Another day in the Army begins, a bit earlier than normal for it's "alert time."

From the largest barracks to the smallest family quarters, soldiers moan as they look at the clocks by their beds: 2:30 a.m. "Tell me it isn't so," they mumble. Slowly they rise out of their warm beds and grope in the darkness for gear and uniforms as their spouses roll over and go back to sleep. Everyone is groggy and a few have hangovers. Gradually, these soldiers put themselves together and make their way to unit sign-in desks to report ready for duty.

Still half asleep, the reporting soldiers learn the alert is a drill. Like phantoms of the night, they quickly disappear to various locations, but always stay near a telephone to await any further instructions. Some go to the motor pool, others to their offices or ready rooms. Though it may be just a drill, the preparations for a move out continue. The drill is far from over.

By dawn, everything is ready. Weapons and equipment are issued to every soldier. Military vehicles are lined up and equipment loaded and prepared for departure on a moment's notice. Reports come in to headquarters informing commanders of each unit's readiness status. Tick marks are made on unit status boards and woe to the unit that is not ready.

As the normal world awakens to a rising sun, the Army has been at work for hours already. The shadows of the night were soldiers preparing for a duty they pray they will never have to perform—going to war. As Douglas MacArthur once said, "It is the soldier who prays most for peace. For it is he who stands to lose the most if peace fails us."

Civilians can rest easy. Around the clock and around the world, men and women are on duty. From lonely arctic outposts to hot carrier decks in the Arabian Gulf, soldiers, sailors, airmen, marines and Coast Guardsmen keep the watch. These shadows of the night are ready for the fight by dawn, a conflict that paradoxically never comes, partially because they are ready.

While those who wear no military uniform sleep on through the night, there will always be service members toiling upward in the night. This is the best way to keep the light of readiness and peace burning bright.

First In, Last Out

"I am Alpha and Omega,
the beginning and the end, the first and the last."
Revelation 22:13

Send troops anywhere in the world, and there will always be a small group of soldiers known as the advance party who go there first. The usually NCO dominated advance party prepares the way for the main body that will soon follow. Whether it is an airfield, a seaport, or a rail depot, you will find a group of busy people setting things up ahead of time.

It really does not matter if the main body is 500 men or an army of 500,000; the advance party's task is essentially the same. When all the warm bodies of the main force get there, how are we going to feed, house, and supply them? Advance troops handle important details such as enemy and environmental threats, communications, storage depots, loading and unloading facilities, and dozens of other issues.

As the first troops of the main force arrive, they discover that someone has gone before them. The parachute drop zone is marked or there is hot food waiting for the travel-weary troops. Somewhere nearby is a cluster of soldiers who made it all happen ahead of time.

Eventually, the deployment ends, or the post shuts down. Everyone is excited about going home. The Army begins to disengage, to break contact, to pack up and go home. The last group out is the rear guard, another NCO-heavy group of soldiers who police up the last pieces of equipment, do the final checks, close out hand receipts, or lock the last door or gate.

Visit any U.S. military cemetery where a major battle was fought and you will be struck by how many non-commissioned officers fell in the battle. There are officers' graves, too, but the proportion of NCO tombstones is striking. These people led from the front and died doing it.

Join paratroopers jumping out of planes into combat, and more often than not the first and last man out the door and into hell are NCOs. The breakthrough of a rescue force will most likely have an NCO in front. The first people to die for this great country are often NCOs. They are the engines that drive the Army train, right up in front. They are also in the caboose, there to encourage the stragglers to join in all that fun up front.

The alpha and the omega of each branch of the U.S. military are more than likely people with several stripes on their sleeves or collar. Everyone else lies somewhere in between.

NCOs are the first and the last, the backbone of the United States Army.

Patriotism

"No one loves his country for its size or eminence,
but because it is his own."
Seneca

The United States of America is a unique nation among nations. America's experiment in democracy, begun in the late 18th century, has survived war, politics, economic collapse, political break-ins and sexual scandal. It is a land of freedom, a freedom that allows for good or bad, rich or poor, brilliance or stupidity. America is truly a unique country in history.

Such a country as the United States breeds a remarkable people. Instead of following some genetic or social pattern, one encounters folk best described as a patchwork of personalities and races, languages and religions, opinions and incomes, creeds and ethics. Diversity and tolerance for diversity is the theme. Here you'll find a people brought together in pursuit of life, liberty and happiness with true gusto.

Each generation of Americans produces citizens who rise to serve the whole. Whether faced with danger from within or without, thousands of Americans stand the generational guard duty. These are the ones who have entered into the military service of this great country.

Ask most Americans and they will understand what the statement "I've joined the service" means. They have a deep and abiding respect for those who serve in America's armed forces, who wear the uniform, who are there to defend this unique nation against all enemies, foreign or domestic.

I stood in a formation of soldiers at a public ceremony. As the minutes ticked by, the heat of the day bore down upon us. But we stood firm. Standing like evenly spaced small trees, there was no movement, no talking, and almost no sign of life at all. We were a forest of soldiers.

As I stood there, my mind reflected on many things. While the boring speeches went on, I thought it remarkable that every person standing next to me volunteered. All were in the Army for different reasons, but all by free choice. I searched for common denominators, something that each shared other than having "joined up." Education, travel, medical care, and money came to mind, but I concluded the universal thread among us was patriotism.

Like the civilian citizens of the United States, each soldier has economic, social and spiritual differences. But within the soul of everyone who wears a uniform lies something else, something that makes them very different from a civilian. Each soldier may describe his or her motivation differently, but all of us have a common thread. We love the United States of America, enough to die for her if necessary.

Everybody Doesn't Like Something...

"Let them eat cake."
Attributed to Marie Antoinette by Rousseau

Some places are as close to heaven as you can get. Though everyone may differ on what these places are, heaven for many smells good, looks great, and tastes divinely delicious. For soldiers assigned to Germany, a *Bäckerei* is an outpost of heaven on earth and provides a fresh daily offering of what food from the Tree of Life must be like.

Quite frankly, German bakers are geniuses. The real number one product of German industry does not come in a bottle, nor does it have four wheels and a brand with the letters BMW. No, the real deal is made with dough, sugar, and stimulates the taste buds like nothing else can.

Whether it is the firm German bread or finely prepared pastries, the mouth-watering *Brötchen* or the sinfully delicious cream-filled truffles, these people have perfected manna. Soldiers who praise German beer up and down are way off target. The real gold medal of praise goes to those culinary artists of the Bäckerei, the creators of things almost better than sex.

Take the sense of smell, for instance. Drink a beer, and you stink. Visit a German bakery, and you leave smelling like you've been in the Promised Land, a land flowing with milk and honey and coated with chocolate. The wonderful scent of a German bakery hypnotizes anyone with even the beginnings of an appetite, causing serious spasms of the salivary glands and mobilization of the digestive system.

It is somewhat disappointing to return home to the offerings of the American baking industry. The soft, substance-lacking bread and the mass-produced cakes do not hold a candle to the German masterpieces. Oh, that the U.S. Army could add German bakery goods to MREs!

My father-in-law tells me that in the German Army during WWII, each battalion had a couple of bakers assigned for duty. Daily fresh bread, even in the dead of winter on the Russian front, made men willing to die for their country, or at least for bread.

Perhaps the U.S. Army could take a lesson here. The nomenclature for this new TO&E position would have to be "Baker, German, one each, capable of exquisite creations such as *Apfelstrudle, Bienenstich, Berliners, Brötchen*, and *Pflaumenkuchen*." Yes sir, build some ovens on the back of a five-ton Army truck and you can have your cake and eat it too!

A bit of heaven on earth does a body good. Everyone has a definition of what that may be. But nobody doesn't like a *Bäckerei*!

Books

"Where is human nature so weak as in the bookstore?"
Henry W. Beecher

They are one of the most ubiquitous pieces of equipment you'll find in the U.S. Army. Wherever you find soldiers, you'll encounter some of these items, lying on a table, stuffed in a rucksack, bulging the cargo pocket of a uniform, or occupying the seat of a some military vehicle. What is this item you may ask? A paperback book.

Soldiers seem to be voracious readers. Goodness knows the Army provides lots of reading opportunities given all the hurry up times that are followed by long waits. Many soldiers learn to fill the time gaps by reading snatches from their favorite paperback books. Brand new or tattered and torn, it doesn't matter. A paperback is standard equipment.

The military's store system, known as the Army and Air Force Exchange System (or AAFES), provides for this fundamental need to read. Whether it is a huge post exchange or a trailer that pulls up out in the remote desert, AAFES will usually offer a fair number of the latest paperback books: westerns, science fiction, detective stories, romance novels, nonfiction, war stories, self-help guides. For the price of a matinee movie ticket, you get hours and hours away from the Army while still in the Army.

On paydays it seems you can hardly find a spot to stand in front of an AAFES magazine or bookrack. Some soldiers probably read half the book there before heading to the cashier. I marvel at how the hustle and bustle of the store recedes into the background in the bookstore area. Despite the crowd, it is very quiet—just the gentle swish of flipping pages.

I would wager that the paperbacks of soldiers have been to some very unusual places—with paratroopers jumping out of planes, special operations troops in remote intelligence gathering operations, or under the seat of an Apache attack helicopter. I even found one once on a "POW" I searched at the Joint Readiness Training Center. Since the book contained no important intelligence information, I let him keep it for the long wait ahead of him in a POW camp.

Aldous Huxley once wrote, "Every man who knows how to read has in his power to magnify himself, to multiply the ways in which he exists, to make his life full, significant and interesting." Soldiers know how to read and enjoy it. Those who read are one up on those who don't, whether they are a general officer or a private. Reading improves us. It enlightens us. Reading can make us into someone far more valuable to all concerned. If reading is a weakness, then I think we could all use more of it.

Tanks

"What is the passing strange force contained
in these passing strange steeds?"
Nikolai Gogol

Riding on top of a tank down a public highway has got to be one of the most exhilarating human experiences. It is right up there with roller coasters, parachuting, or receiving an Academy Award.

Imagine seventy tons of man-made machine and metal underneath you. The behemoth moves forward at 35-40 mph. The slight vibration of rubber track pads against the pavement is the only disturbance to what is a surprisingly smooth ride. You sit at nearly twelve feet above the pavement and from that perch, you have a tank's eye view of things.

What is very interesting is the response of the more humble vehicles and their drivers on the streets and roads, even the massive tractor-trailer trucks. The tank, because of its unique shape and solid size, commands immediate respect and attention. Cars pull completely off the road, trucks come to a complete stop, and motorcycles, well, they don't stop for anybody.

The most remarkable thing is the attention people give to this giant symbol of national power on land. Often, the noise of a tank's engine, that whirring of turbines, brings people to their feet. Then come the stares and looks of surprise or fear. Next come the nervous waves, and then, after we wave back, there are smiles. People scramble to the roadside to get a look at the mechanical monster, this battleship of the land. You can see them calling or waving to family or friends to come and have a look too. And to children, we are god-like marvels.

Even powerful things are vulnerable, though. Tanks do break down. I remember a long convoy of tanks held up in a German town because one tank lost its track-guiding sprocket and came to a dead halt, blocking the only road through town.

When a tank breaks down it is still one heck of a pillbox that traditional wrecker trucks are helpless to move. So, how do you move a broken tank? You use another road-monster, an M-88 or tank recovery vehicle. This slightly longer vehicle, minus the gun barrel, is of the strength and size to handle even an armored mammoth in trouble. Within its metal hull is some serious horsepower.

Whether stationary or on the move, tanks are impressive. They are military marvels that offer a great ride. Whatever you do, never pass up a chance to hitch a ride on these awesome steeds!

Scrounging

"Antiques are junk that had a second chance and took advantage of it."
Anonymous

They say one man's junk is another's treasure. This saying is especially true in Germany where class-conscious Germans have a day every spring and fall when they discard unwanted large items from their homes. Driving down the street, you see old appliances, furniture, and other odds and ends laid out curbside, much of it with only minor damage. Germans will readily throw away some serviceable things to make room for the new, given the limited storage space they have in smaller homes and apartments.

Among American service members stationed in Germany, there are some who eagerly look forward to the times when Germans jettison their unwanted household baggage. These enterprising folks go "junking," meaning they drive around in their cars and trucks trolling the streets looking for potentially valuable items. Often they find treasure, maybe a bit tarnished or scratched, but valuable to them nonetheless.

I once met a fellow soldier who furnished practically his entire apartment from junking forays. It was a major hobby for him. I was impressed with his various finds and the stories he related behind each piece. "All this antique table needed was a new leg," he'd say, or "This washing machine works fine after I adjusted some wires." Nothing in his home matched, of course, but hey, the price was right, and it all had character.

I indulged in junking once, though I must confess it was a half-hearted, even half-embarrassed effort. It was early in the morning, but I must have started late, for the good stuff was already gone, if there was any to be had to begin with. Most of what I saw was indeed junk, though I was hesitant to really dig deep into the piles. The early ones made off with the keepsakes, I thought, and so I had to settle for a few consolation pieces.

An old carpet and a bookshelf found their way to my office. A couple of other things lay around my house for a while, but eventually they found a place curbside once again. My repairing abilities and motivation were lacking. It takes talent to turn trash into treasure, and a master pillager has to be a master repairman too.

Someone once said it is better to pillage first before you burn. All in all, pillaging can be good deal. It is especially good if you are not too proud to accept hand-me-down stuff. Some are gifted with the know-how to see beauty in the dross and rust too. I admire these people, for they epitomize the spirit of recycling. They lead the way. They remind us to always pillage before we burn, throw away, or buy.

The Promotion Board

"Knowledge comes, but wisdom lingers."
Alfred, Lord Tennyson

There are a lot of very smart people out there. They are what one would call a quick study. They have a keen ability to memorize and retain information. Their abilities are very impressive. Sometimes we might fancy ourselves one of them.

Twice in my military career I went before a promotion board of five senior non-commissioned officers. Their task was to evaluate my abilities, knowledge, and performance to determine if I was made out of the right stuff to become a non-commissioned officer. To prepare for this ordeal I had to study hard and drill into memory hundreds of details about the U.S. Army. Hours and hours of study on myriad topics: What is the muzzle velocity of a round fired from an M-16? How do you treat nerve agent poisoning? Who is the Command Sergeant Major of the Army? What is in the news today? Which Army regulation governs the proper wear of the uniform?

On both occasions, the group of Vietnam hardened veteran NCOs considered me the right stuff to advance in enlisted rank. I was a quick study. I received the maximum score they could give, even though I didn't know the answer to all their questions. I was rightly proud of my performance, but the best answer for why I did so well was the help and advice I received from a veteran staff sergeant who took me under his wing in preparing me for the boards. Most of my success was due to his sage advice.

He was not a highly learned man and not very eloquent either. But those things did not matter. He had experience and that was and is the most important credential any sergeant owns. In his simple manner he told me, "Specialist Kay, if they ask you a question you don't know the answer to, then just plain tell them you don't know. Don't tap dance or lie, but make sure you tell them you'll get the answer before the day's over." It was good advice then and still is to this day.

I cannot recall what I memorized for those boards. I have forgotten the maximum effective range of an M-16 or what regulation governs drill and ceremony. Though most of the knowledge has left me, some things remain. One thing that stuck was the advice that sergeant gave me and how wise he was. Do not fake the answer. Find it instead. You cannot know everything, but wise soldiers know they find any answer later if they have the will to look for it.

56

Real Readiness

"By different methods different men excel,
but where is he who does all things well?"
Charles Churchill

As a lower enlisted soldier, you are never quite sure if you'll have the coming weekend off. Until that final Friday formation is finished and you are released, you always remain fair game to sergeants trying to plug gaps in weekend duty rosters. It seems someone on the duty roster always gets sick, has to go on emergency leave, or is AWOL. The result is ruined plans for some unlucky "volunteer."

To keep the military running twenty-four hours a day, seven days a week, you have guard duty, people to answer telephones, drivers, medics on duty, and dozens of other important jobs. Duty rosters are used to plan personnel to fill these positions around the clock. If your name is not on the roster, then prospects for time off are good, but there is no guarantee.

We stood in formation that Friday afternoon. The First Sergeant called out to our platoon sergeant, "See to it that you get two volunteers for the funeral detail this weekend." Our formation of thirty men nervously stood fast. "I need two people to volunteer for this funeral detail," the platoon sergeant announced. "Would anyone like to volunteer?" No one moved or made a sound. No hands were raised. Everyone had plans. The fear of potential loss now loomed before us and the tension was palpable.

"All right," he said, "I'll have to choose some volunteers." Now comes the moment when you hope you remembered to be in proper uniform. Through a uniform inspection the sergeant culls two less than perfect specimens to offer in sacrifice to the First Sergeant. A systematic check for correct dog tags, military identification cards, proper military belt or any of a dozen other things usually singles out "volunteers" in short order. Forgetting to be in proper uniform would cost them their weekend.

New guys are especially vulnerable to "volunteering," but they learn fast. You need only to lose a weekend once in order to imprint this lesson on readiness. Over time, soldiers become hard-wired for being ready in the ways that really count. Uniform inspections, battle drills, pre-combat checks, equipment layouts or room inspections are all well and good, but even if folding your socks a certain silly way will save a weekend or forestall hassle, then so be it. Being prepared is a matter of survival, whether in combat or at the start of a weekend. Soldiers are never flawless, but sometimes there are distinct benefits to being more perfect than others.

Take a Break

"Too much rest itself becomes a pain."
Homer

Everybody deserves a break once in a while. Everybody that is except "shammers." You might wonder what a shammer is. This is a person who is on break as much as possible. You probably know someone like this. When not under the watchful eye of a supervisor, this person will more than likely slack off doing anything that even remotely hints of real work.

Every work area, every office, every squad has at least someone bringing up the rear with regards to productivity. These *Dagwood Bumsteads* might be likable sorts of people, even capable of arousing our sympathies, but chances are someone else has to pull the weight that was meant for them.

Just like the poor, I suppose shammers will always be with us. I remember an episode involving lazy people back in Baumholder, Germany. The post Sergeant Major did an unannounced check of the Post Exchange at about ten o'clock one weekday morning. His visitation captured about twenty-five hapless soldiers playing hooky. Instead of being at their appointed place of duty, they were hanging out at the snack bar, checking out the latest music, or lingering by the bookstore or magazine rack. Their "official errands" were about as solid as cotton candy and it would cost them. But believe me this group was only the tip of an iceberg.

Productivity makes the world go around. Although everyone may be created equal, productivity makes some of us more equal than others. There are truly hard workers out there and sadly, supervisors will shovel off the undone work of shammers onto the hard workers to meet deadlines and quotas. They ignore the slackers. They hang their hard workers up to dry when they should be hanging their good-for-nothings by the neck.

But taking care of shammers is hard, sometimes distasteful work. It is the stuff ulcers are made of. As a supervisor you have to have your ducks in order, build that paperwork trail, constantly check on them, and finally confront them face to face when they are not pulling their fair share. It is work for the supervisor to do this, but hey, it is their job.

Oh what a joy it is when the slacker goes up in smoke! The freeloader gets caught and has to do the payback. For those who perform and perspire on a regular basis, it warms the heart to know that once in awhile a leader is not shamming. They do their job too. They police up the *Thornapples*, *Bumsteads*, and *Sad Sacks*. For those who really do work for a living, it's the best break of all.

Hot Chocolate

"Success is getting what you want:
Happiness is wanting what you get."
Anonymous

They produce at least one small hint of heaven in Kansas City, Missouri. It is found in every field ration package, or Meal Ready to Eat, in the U.S. Army. That very special delight is hot cocoa powder, or as the military would term it, "Cocoa Beverage Powder."

The First Sergeant rouses everyone out of his or her deep slumber long before dawn. It is time to "stand to." You reluctantly crawl out of that warm Army sleeping bag into the icy cold outdoors. The cold of winter assaults you from every angle, and your exhaled breath produces a white cloud of ice crystals.

Only half-awake, you shiver and struggle into cold clothes and cold boots as your exposed skin screams out in protest against the chill. You manage to get dressed without collapsing into hypothermia, but your next thought is to find something that warms the soul.

Before long, the creative genius of soldiers produces a fire. Ice is melted or unfrozen water is found and soon you have hot water. Then out come those wonderful packets of instant coffee or cocoa. For the non-coffee drinkers, and for those who brew a field version of cappuccino, the cocoa is a godsend. Now, my friends, is when a real basic human need finds marvelous satisfaction. The Army version of a breakfast drink is born.

You husband the precious hot water, usually held in the fairly large military aluminum canteen cup. Tearing open the small green packet of military cocoa, you gingerly mix the contents into the piping hot water. The brown powder soon produces a tan liquid and a sweet chocolate aroma that mocks the bitter cold. You savor the steam and cuddle the warmth of the cup clasped in your bare hands.

The first sip of the hot fluid is savored as if it were a fine French wine. You hold it on your tongue and swish it around your mouth. Conquer the cold! Relish the taste! The merciful warmth bathes your throat and chest as each swallow goes down. Here, my friends, is pure delight.

By the rising of the winter sun in the bitter cold of a German morning, an Army day is nearly half over. What better way to conquer its cold beginning than jump-starting the day with a chocolate delicacy? For once in the Army, exactly what you want and exactly what you get come together in perfect harmony.

The Gamma Goat

"Let us be thankful for the fools.
But for them the rest of us could not succeed."
Mark Twain

Somewhere within the retired ranks of the Department of Defense is that person (or persons) responsible for the purchase of the Gamma Goat. This peculiar vehicle found its way into the Army's inventory in the 1970s. I am convinced it was an Army genetic malformation of the Vietnam era.

The Gamma Goat was designed as a light, 1 ¼ ton cargo vehicle. In its perfect state, it was supposedly capable of floating across small bodies of water. Of course several dozen seals and functioning parts had to be in optimal condition for it to swim. Unfortunately, I never saw a Gamma Goat float and you would be hard pressed to find someone who did.

Appearing more like a cross between an ant and a Pekinese dog, the Gamma Goat definitely was unconventional. There were three sections or compartments; each supported by two wheels—the driver and cargo areas separated by another with the engine. Its anatomy lent itself well to generating lots of noise and attracting every piece of mud and dust a field exercise had to offer. It was also a nightmare to maintain, with dozens of lubrication points for starters. In short, this vehicle had all the things a driver could hate.

Something you hate a lot can bring you down, or it can build character. I decided it would be the latter when it became one of my first Army responsibilities to be a Gamma Goat Ambulance (M792) driver. Noisy, drafty, leaky, and bumpy were just four names I could give this mechanical dwarf. It could never be kept clean and fixing one thing would only seem to break another. I don't even recall ever being able to haul patients in it, preferring instead to send our casualties in our Jeep or Dodge truck ambulances.

You keep at something long enough and time will be on your side. My battle with the Goat ended in a draw with my PCS. Later, a blessing of the Reagan years arrived, the HUMMV ambulance. Slowly, the Gamma Goat disappeared—thank the Lord (and U.S. taxpayers)!

Not too far from where I now write this story, a Gamma Goat ambulance is on display. Still a curiously funny looking vehicle, it now serves as a monument. The Army keeps it painted and looking sharp, but I bet it still cannot float. This vehicle has got to be the *Studebaker* or *Yugo* of military transportation, at least to those of us fools who had to drive it.

The Urine Test

"The man who has never been flogged has never been taught."
Menander

The ringing telephone jerks you out of a wonderful night's rest. You grope for the receiver in the dark and mumble a groggy "Hello." On the other end, the CQ informs you that you have been selected to participate in a urine drug-screening test in progress that morning. "Congratulations! Report to the Company Orderly Room to give up a sample!"

Since the late 1970s the U.S. Army has aggressively screened for drug abuse in the troops. Unannounced tests catch those who yield to the temptation to smoke dope, shoot heroin, or snort cocaine. For everyone else who tries to live a clean life, the mandatory urine dragnet is a necessary inconvenience, a periodic flogging.

I always tried hard not to go to the bathroom the morning of the test. As a result I would arrive at the orderly room "needing to go really bad." Invariably there would almost always be a long line. For those of us all ready to go, waiting in line was an ordeal, since most of the time there were only one or two escorts. Hanging out at a water fountain or soda machine nearby would be ten or twenty soldiers trying to build up enough to fill the plastic specimen cup with the required amount of urine. Others merely had stage fright, for many normal people do not like someone watching you go.

The process of collecting these samples from troops is quite sophisticated, the result of years of experience with cunning and devious troops and lawyers. You show up at a desk where a sergeant asks for your ID card. It does not matter if he knows who you are either. No ID card, no test. No test, big trouble. He closely scrutinizes the card to make sure it is yours. A small plastic bottle is then produced with a label, upon which your name and social security number are written. An escort takes you to the latrine. He must physically watch you pee into the cup. Now, some people just can't go when they're being watched. But I know one thing: watching people's private parts pee all morning has got to be right up there with the most lousy jobs in the world.

After dutifully producing the fluid, you wash your hands and carry it back to the desk sergeant, the escort never taking his eyes off you. At the desk, you have to initial a roster and the bottle itself, acknowledging the specimen is indeed yours. They always seem determined to make sure the urine is yours. I once had a sergeant ask me, "Is this your specimen?" Picking up the bottle, I deliberately paused to look at it closely. Carefully unscrewing the cap, I took a sniff of its contents and replied, "Yep. It's mine."

Taking Responsibility

"The Buck stops here."
Sign on President Harry Truman's Desk

One of the most difficult things to do in life is to take responsibility for our actions. Denial, shifting the blame, searching for a scapegoat, or otherwise trying to evade our responsibility seems to come naturally, an aspect of human nature that almost seems imprinted from childhood. "It wasn't my fault," could be our motto.

It is a hard thing to accept responsibility for the negative things that occur. Sure, it is easy to stand up and be counted when praises are handed out, but what about those times when criticism and blame are to be had? My bet is that most of us would rather shy away from the negative.

She stood in front of me, obviously not in a happy mood. The Nurse Corps Captain was upset with me, one of the medics working in her emergency room. She felt I had a bad attitude—and you know what? I did. As she lectured me in her office behind closed doors, I stood there respectfully at parade rest. I hadn't been at 100% performance.

I was tired of Army life. There was room for improvement. My lame excuses didn't hold water, either. That Nurse Corps officer gave this medic buck sergeant a wake up call, and I needed to learn the hard lesson of taking responsibility for my actions.

Twelve years later, the same Nurse Corps Captain was a Colonel and I was a Captain when our paths crossed again. She was still as dynamic as ever, always the take charge kind of person, maybe now with a few more gray hairs. Though I did not work directly for her again, my job as an infantry division staff officer necessitated frequent contacts between us on various medical readiness issues.

The day finally came when things between the hospital and our infantry division caused some tension. I had dropped the ball on an immunization readiness issue and she was concerned. As division liaison officer, I stood in her office taking the heat, and there was this familiar déjà vu. But this time, I found it noticeably easier. Yes, once again my erstwhile mentor was right. I needed to pocket the blame buck and take corrective action. "Yes, ma'am, you are correct," I said. "It won't happen again."

The Army teaches many lessons. Some are easy to learn and others we'd rather avoid and forget. One important lesson is learning to take responsibility for your actions. Learning where the buck stops as soon as possible can save you some headaches and maybe even some bucks too.

The Brave

"O'er the land of the free and the home of the brave."
Francis Scott Key, U.S. National Anthem

Grafenwöhr holds no meaning for most Americans. For soldiers who have done tours of duty in Germany, or who come over temporarily from the United States as part of training exercises, "Graf" conjures up memories of gunnery exercises, mud and dust, field training, of being away from home and missing the family.

Graf is a former Nazi Germany military training area taken over by American occupation forces after World War II. Measuring some 25 x 15 miles, it provides ample room to test and train the finest, most modern army in the world. There are things you can do on this training reservation with tanks and guns that you just cannot do anywhere else in Europe.

Units rotating through the facilities at Graf stay busy around the clock, seven days a week. Opportunities to rest and relax during the usual one-month stay at Graf are rare.

One of the few amenities available to soldiers when they do have some free time is a small movie theater, located in the middle of the contonement, or troop housing area. One of the most important memories for many soldiers about Graf has got to be the playing of the national anthem before viewing one of the second-run films usually shown at that theater.

The movie house is often quite full of soldiers from various units in their speckled green battle dress uniforms. Without any verbal command, the soldiers automatically rise to attention as the image of an American flag soundlessly waves on the movie screen. There is not a murmur or sound from them as that familiar tune begins to play with the words they all treasure, though never completely memorized. It puts chills up and down your spine to experience such a moment in a room crowded with patriots.

These soldiers are not conscripts. They are volunteers. Each soldier has his or her own opinion about the Army or the great country they serve. Each one grapples with their special set of problems. Each has a pot of gripes somewhere. Each soldier is unique. But as that flag waves and the music plays, the spirits of all become one for a brief, patriotic moment.

What is done at Graf is done for America, that sweet land of liberty. The training and the soldiers are there to be ready like no other nation on earth should be. As long as the U.S. Army trains at Graf, it will remain a home away from home for those from the land of the free and home of the brave.

The Weapon

"...for want of a shoe the horse is lost..."
George Herbert

Spend any amount of time in the Army and you learn what "sensitive" items are. Examples include weapons, ammunition, night vision goggles, and classified documents. Lose any one of these items and a sophisticated command reporting system kicks in, informing higher authorities that the item is unaccounted for and a search is in progress. Higher commanders tend to react quickly to these reports, hence the adjective "sensitive."

While training in Hohenfels, Germany, a member of our Command misplaced his M-16 rifle. You would think that the sky would fall only on that one unlucky individual, but no, it falls on the entire unit. Forget those showers and hot meals you were looking forward to after two weeks in the field. No, you, along with five hundred other men in the battalion, stay in the field and embark on a massive hunt for the weapon. Commander's orders.

True to military efficiency, the entire training area is divided up and a careful search is made of every suspect place, much like a police search for forensic evidence. Side by side at arm length, troops walk the fields and roads, nooks and crannies looking for the lost weapon. With each passing hour, tempers rise, and some with less self-control are close to the point of lynching the irresponsible soldier. Many fall short of actual violence. Instead, flowered language is conjured up to express their anger.

After two sweaty, dirty days, we found the weapon, mistakenly left on a refueling truck rack, where it luckily remained the whole time, despite miles and miles of bumpy roads. 1,400 man-hours were expended looking for that $1400 rifle. Incidentally, two previously lost sensitive items from other units, a bayonet and a pistol, were found as well.

Reports are sent higher that the weapon is found. The gods of command are appeased and their anger abates, allowing us to return to garrison and finally wash our now even dirtier bodies, though our souls are forever stained by the group punishment. Seldom is there a thank you.

Perhaps someday the Army will acknowledge that soldiers are sensitive items, too. Group hunting sessions for lost weapons or ammunition is not material for recruiting posters or television commercials, but it is part of the Army experience, especially for lower enlisted soldiers.

My bet is that good soldiers have left the Army because of group punishment. For the want of a sensitive item, the soldier is lost....

The Chewing Out

"Anger is a weed; hate is the tree."
Saint Augustine

I suppose that in order to have truly outstanding days one has to have a despondent day every now and again. We all get one of these thrown at us from time to time. Try as we might, lousy days still come our way. Nothing can make for an awful day more than being chewed out for something you didn't do. My bawling out came from a superior when I found myself as the wrong person, in the wrong place, at the wrong time.

My first really serious dressing down occurred when I was a buck sergeant. I happened to be the nearest NCO available, as the battalion executive officer, a major, apparently wasn't having a good day at all. Some minor infraction had occurred and the good major needed to lash out at the nearest junior leader available. I had the misfortune of standing within the kill zone of his anger burst.

I respectfully stood there at parade rest as the major lashed out at me for something I didn't do, nor for which I was responsible. He wouldn't even allow me to speak. So, as the frustration boiled inside me, I had to silently take what seemed like an unwanted dose of castor oil. Perhaps it made him feel better to vent, but for the half-dozen or so onlookers, and for me, it was a good example of how not to lead.

The whole episode tore a hole in me. There never was an apology and it took me a long time to try and make some good out of that ugly display of misguided authority. Even now as I write about the affair, the old pent-up feelings return. I still wish I could give the good officer a piece of my mind, though by now he is probably a general officer somewhere. But I need to let it go and writing about it has helped.

Sometimes leaders give you excellent examples on how not to lead. In my case the major taught me a couple of things that helped me throughout my remaining Army career when time and circumstance allowed me to lead soldiers. First, there is no need to loose your cool if you lead people. Even if there's an emergency or lives are at risk, the last thing you need is to loose your composure. Second, one person's lack of self-control is their problem—not yours. Like rain on a duck's back, just let it roll off.

As General Colin Powell once said, "Get angry, but get over it." If you let it get to you, then you will wind up a few fries short of a happy meal.

The Laundromat

"A lot can be learned from lingering near loose lips in the laundry."
David Kay

Moving around in the Army forces people to make do without things. During the transition time between assignments, household goods and large possessions are shipped. As a result, Army families make do without many conviences while the moving company does its job.

During all these moves one thing everybody misses is their washer and dryer. You never fully appreciate these appliances until you have to go without them. But the Army understands this and provides a thriving business in laundry facilities on or near post. These public washing places are among the best locations to get all the intelligence you'll ever need about the local area and the Army in general.

My wife is a soft-spoken person with a streak of shyness as well. But she had a genuine interest in getting to know people, especially when the Army moved us to new places. No matter where we were stationed, Irene made new friends and acquaintances quickly, often jump-starting the process with visits to the local laundry facility.

Coin-operated laundry areas are hotbeds of information. You have several groups of people mingling—those who are leaving, those who are arriving, and, especially overseas, lonely spouses and soldiers ready to talk about anything. The shared chore of sorting and folding clothes sets the stage for socialization and information gathering.

Irene always seemed to get fresh and accurate information long before I did. The ladies she would meet would fill her in on dozens of important details unavailable in your standard Army welcome information packet soldiers receive. She'd know where the best places to shop were, what places to avoid, from whom you could get more information, or what recreational activities there were to do. Though it was a pain to carry the laundry off to some public place, the payoff was more than just clean underwear. Laundromat intelligence saved us a lot of time and money too.

The things washing machines have heard! I am convinced that if you want the real scoop on what is going on in the Army, hang out at the local laundromat. Whether it is the hottest gossip or troop movements, you are bound to get the latest without waiting too long. Indeed, there are two welcome centers on post. Both provide useful information on a variety of things that interest soldiers and their families. There is the official welcome center staffed with smiling people and dated welcome packets. And then there is another one equipped with washers, dryers and the latest scoop.

To Fly

"No limits but the sky."
Cervantes

It was in the spring of 1982 that I saw my very first UH-60 Blackhawk helicopter, or should I say helicopters. On the way to lunch one day from my job as a medic in an armored battalion at Fort Stewart, Georgia, a formation of six U.S. Army Blackhawk helicopters landed in a large field next to where I was walking.

The helicopters came in low, just over the treetops. You saw them before they could be heard, like dark, monstrous birds of prey rapidly swooping down on the unsuspecting. One behind the other, they did a deliberate but graceful banking U-turn to the left and then landed in a straight line, one behind the other, all right in front of me. It was an air show with me acting as spectator and reviewer all at once.

The follow-on noise was tremendous. The wind created by the large turning rotor blades only added to the effect, with old, brown leaves blowing past me as in a hurricane. The whole synchronous maneuver was over in no more than a minute, but it became frozen forever in my memory.

The helicopters paused on the ground only a few moments, like giant, dark green wasps crouching, ready to pounce on some prey. The engines of the six machines made a tremendous noise, driving the rotor blades above each aircraft like controlled whirling dervishes. It was an awesome display of manmade power.

Gradually, the aircraft, despite their large size, began to become lighter on their three small wheels. Then suddenly, all in unison, they came to a low hover, maybe ten feet off the ground. Next came a slight shift in the noise pitch of the engines as each aircraft tilted forward, slowly rising into the sky and passing directly overhead and out of sight.

That moment further reinforced my longing to fly, to soar above our sometimes-mundane existence below, to be what so few dare to become. It would be nearly five years later, as a young warrant officer, that I would begin that journey of learning to fly a helicopter. To defy gravity and do the dance of the sky is one of the greatest privileges of mankind and a great opportunity offered by the United States Army.

It would take some time, some patience on the part of my flight instructor, and hours of practice on my part before I would get the hang of flying a helicopter. Those who dare shall fly like an eagle.

Eventually I did fly. What a glorious moment it was when that hover button on my helicopter was finally located!

Undaunted

"I was never afraid of failure;
for I would sooner fail than not be among the greatest."
John Keats

Watch a toddler and you can learn some things. My oldest son, Nathan, wanted to walk as quickly as possible. This crawling stuff wasn't for him. Always pushing the walking envelope, he fell many, many times. Falling hardly bothered him, however, and even with tears on his cheeks, he'd be back at it until he had it. Eventually, that coveted mobility of being on his own two legs was his own. Mother and I had to re-look at the house sooner than expected to keep our precocious walker from hurting himself.

One method to grow excellence in a group or an individual is to set goals and try to reach them. Successful people are the ones who are always ready to try again. To reach goals they set for themselves, those who really succeed keep on trying. Each time they do just a little better than before.

A meaningful life, in or out of the military, can be had by anyone. Far too many people, though, fail in their quest to find lasting satisfaction at what they do. Their goals are unclear or unrealistic. Their spirit fades away and they settle for much less than their true potential. Many quit.

The road of life is littered with failures that people make. But many people who fail often are ultimately successful. The difference with this group compared to those who quit trying is what they do with their failure. They learn to fall forward when they fall.

Take Thomas Edison for instance. He did not perfect a working light bulb until he had thousands failures under his belt. That is a lot of failures. Another example is that of Abraham Lincoln. He failed miserably at numerous attempts to enter public office before becoming the best President the United States ever had.

In a "zero defects" Army, we create a world unwilling to recognize failure as a learning opportunity. Instead, error is looked upon as a discriminator between those who move ahead and those left behind. In this type of environment soldiers learn to fear failure. This fear prevents them from taking risks that expand their abilities. Or their integrity is in question because of hiding their "mistakes." You cannot grow leaders without some margin for error. Leaders learn from their shortcomings. They hate to make them as much as anyone else. Yet, the paving stones of a successful person's path are made out of clay fired in the kiln of life's failures.

Butts

"A cigarette has a fire at one end,
a fool at the other, and a bit of tobacco in between."
Anonymous

I never took up smoking. Oh, I did my patriotic duty as a youngster born and raised in North Carolina. I took a puff or two on a cigarette and a toke on a cigar, but that was as far as my loyalty went. How people can stand to smoke will forever escape me, even though everyone else in my family smokes like chimneys.

The glamorous life of smoking passed me by. Just watch a classic movie, say *Casablanca,* and it seems everyone who is anyone has something hanging out of their mouth. To get that lucky strike you had to be cool.

Though I never smoked, I have inhaled. Don't like to, but growing up around smokers made it a fact of life. I've also joined smokers and nonsmokers alike in the never-ending process of keeping Army posts clean, a fundamental part of which was picking up cigarette butts.

You could write a small book on cigarette butts. They come in all varieties. There's the half-smoked cigarette, for instance. The owner either got caught smoking when they weren't supposed to or maybe they simply lit up to be a part of the crowd. Then there are the filterless butts out there, although there are fewer—the owners meeting their end sooner than others.

It is rare, but you can even find self-made cigarette butts from time to time. I remember my dad, also a smoker, rolling his own nicotine fix using *Prince Albert* tobacco from a little red can. The tobacco had a nice smell as I recall. You have to be careful with self-made cigarettes today, especially those grown in the wild that sometimes find their way onto Army posts.

Most of the of cigarette butts out there have the cotton packed filters. Some filters have teeth marks on them, perhaps from a tense or angry owner. Others have lipstick, a good bet some woman has come a long way, baby, but probably doesn't have much further to go. A generic brand marking probably connotes someone making every dollar stretch as far as possible.

Check out the end of a cigarette butt filter and you can gauge the puffing ability of the owner. A colorless end reveals a patient person or someone with emphysema so bad they can hardly pull air in anymore. A dark brown filter end indicates an impatient, nicotine-starved soul, taking long, deep drags on that cigarette as often as possible.

I shall never join the camaraderie of a designated smoking area. Let other people pay those taxes. No sir, I want to draw that retirement pension as long as possible. No need to have all that hard work picking up cigarette butts go up in smoke.

Break in Service

"...an' ye sometimes have t'roam afore
ye really 'preciate the things ye lef' behind."
Edgar Albert Guest

Many career soldiers have had a 'break in service,' known as a period of time when they left the Army and later came back. For whatever reasons, they decided the Army was not for them and they ETS. After trying out civilian life for a bit, they learn that the Army might be a better deal after all.

I once had a break in service, too. My first three years in the Army were sometimes such a pain that it is a wonder I ever came back. Having done my time, I was hopeful to finish up college work and get a civilian job.

I always wanted to teach history. Time flew as coursework led to a degree and an earnest search for a job. But teaching jobs were not to be had back in 1982. The paltry few that were available paid less than what a married, lower-enlisted soldier made in the Army. In a near, self-inflicted panic, I had to figure out something soon before my scholarship money ran out, seeing that I had Irene and two growing boys to provide for.

There were options. Though accepted for postgraduate work in history at Vanderbilt University, the professors there cautioned that even with advanced degrees, job prospects were dismal. I toyed with law school. It is noble to defend the innocent, but I've always been uncomfortable with the thought of defending liars. And then I could have waited for a last-minute high school teacher vacancy, but the pay and prospects were lousy.

Gradually it all dawned on me. I had taken a wrong turn in my education. Although you may intensely love to do something, the bottom line is food on the table and hope for your family.

I thought of retraining in medicine. My years as an Army medic stimulated my interest in this field, far removed from the liberal arts. But there was no way my family or finances would survive medical school. It was at this point that I remembered the Army's scholarship program for physician assistants. I had worked closely with a couple of PAs while on active duty, people like Mike Priest, Don Huggard, George Libby, and Lou Smith. The work these people did in the Army was pretty cool, and with my education and background I had a good shot at the scholarship.

In the end, the grass was greener back in the Army. Security and opportunity are incredible magnets, both of which the Army had in ample supply. My flirtation with civilian life ended with a much deeper appreciation for what the U.S. Army offered. There is absolutely no doubt that in parting, I learned to appreciate.

Merry Old Souls

"Old King Cole
Was a merry old soul,
And a merry old soul was he.
He called for his pipe,
And he called for his bowl,
And he called for his fiddlers three."
Old King Cole Nursery Rhyme

"I want to be an Airborne Ranger, living a life of..." And so the cadence continues. As long as there are soldiers, there will always be marching formations and merry little chants. Certainly the best time-tested manner to move large groups of people by foot in a uniform fashion from point to point is to march them in an organized group. Cadences help keep people in step so that they do not stumble on each other. Calls and chants also keep the mind focused, preventing us from drifting into a daydream and thereby getting out of step with everyone else.

Entire books are written on cadences. Some are clever, others are lurid, many are patriotic, and all are interesting. There are cadences for marching and faster ones for running. There's a cadence that describes just about every thing in the Army.

Find old soldiers and give them part of a cadence from many years' back and they'll be able to finish it for you. "They say that in the Army, the biscuits are mighty fine. One rolled off the table and..." These calls bonded soldiers together like memorized scripture bonds Christians together. "Jody calls" are indeed ties that bind, passed on through generations of soldiers.

I was never very good at calling cadence, but I sure could sound off. Visit an Army post and watch troops marching and you are likely to hear some really great cadence callers. Some sergeants really perfect this art of leading soldiers in verse. And how much sounding off you will hear!

"Old King Cole" was a favorite for the sergeants in my earlier Army days. Interesting how a nursery rhyme became a cadence and how loud we would respond to the sergeant's cadence call! One particular sergeant would reserve the Old King Cole call for only good times—keeping everyone in a merry step as we marched back from the motor pool at the end of the day or taking people to the pay officer on a payday. Like Disney dwarfs, how we sang our military version of *"heigh-ho, heigh-ho, it's home from work we go!"*

Yes, Old King Cole was indeed a merry old soul...and so were we.

71

Photo ID

"A picture is worth a thousand words."
Fred R. Barnard

A sure sign you are in the Army is when they issue you your first military identification card. This small laminated document is proof positive that, at least until the expiration date, the taxpayers own you. The information on it, along with your photo, is your ticket to important fringe benefits like the commissary, medical and dental care, and the Post Exchange. You might dress like a soldier, have a sharp haircut and talk the talk, but without the green identification card, you are, as they say in the Army, "out of uniform."

I went through at least nine ID cards while on active duty, one for each promotion. Each one was important, but to the very last card the picture always left something to be desired. Despite my best efforts, the photos never came out well. Perhaps they were trying to tell me something. Maybe the cameras that take military ID photos are pre-set on the ugly mode. Even my last portrait made me look like a roughed-up POW.

The ID card has a lot of information on it, more than most soldiers realize. Name, rank, signature, social security number, and the expiration date are the common items. But the card also holds vital personal and Geneva Convention information. Newer cards have bar codes and electronic data strips with even more details. Even the fingerprint of earlier ID cards is replaced with a bar code print of who you are.

Soldiers that leave the Army for a while often have a unique appreciation of the benefits that come from military service. That appreciation begins as soon as the last ID card expires. Sometimes you don't fully appreciate something until it's gone. My short break in service was enough to give me a better perspective on the Army Experience. The benefits I took for granted before became things that would sustain me when I came back into the Army, especially when difficult times came again. The medical benefits, thirty days paid vacation each year, tangible advancement opportunities, untaxed allowances for rations and housing were just a few of the good things from military service I now appreciated even more.

My military ID card photo in particular reminded me of things to appreciate. Now, if only the Army could fix those cameras so that we can appreciate the photo too! We could all benefit from a good photo of ourselves, especially one on such an important document like an ID card that is seen by so many people. It is a picture that is worth at least a thousand benefits.

Extra Duty

"Punishment brings wisdom. It is the healing part of wickedness."
Plato

In every U.S. Army unit there is a bulletin board, normally mounted in some prominent public place. Upon this board are posted duty rosters, command policy letters, announcements, and official results of disciplinary actions taken against soldiers. Article 15. Every soldier knows what this term means. It refers to the Uniform Code of Military Justice (UCMJ) and the section authorizing non-judicial punishment of what civilians might refer to as misdemeanors. Article 15s come in two flavors: company grade and field grade. The main differences between the two are in the rank of the officer administering the justice and the severity of the punishment.

Violation of stated rules and policies is often found out quickly within the controlled, closely monitored world of the military. Disrespect to a superior, drinking alcohol while on duty, being late or petty theft are examples of sins handled by Article 15. The big boys—those who kill, rape, pillage, and burn go to court martial. Here the big-time judicial punishments are dished out, including those long, working vacations to Leavenworth, Kansas. When convicted in a court martial, the soldier, or now perhaps former soldier, is also technically a felon, guilty of a federal crime.

Often a key component of an Article 15 punishment is 'extra duty.' "Sergeant so and so is found guilty of petty larceny. He is to forfeit $400 in pay, receive a reduction of one grade in rank, and perform thirty days extra duty."

Visit any Army post and you will see the extra-duty personnel out doing penance. Mowing grass, painting rocks, picking up trash, or otherwise maintaining the sharp appearance of Army posts. Whatever the duty, it is extra, often dirty, and done when the guiltless have gone home.

Make no mistake, to do well in life you have to obey. Fail to catch on to this basic rule quickly, and it can cost you. Penalties come in various forms: a speeding ticket from some state trooper, failing health because of some nasty habit, or a lost relationship because of some stupid indiscretion.

My platoon once lost a day off because we didn't keep a part of our barracks clean. The First Sergeant declared a "GI party" in honor of our platoon. Instead of getting time off like everyone else, we went to our 'party' to scrub, sweep, mop, and paint. The party's punchbowl was a mop bucket and everyone had a turn to dance with the mop. We grumbled and griped, but we also learned. We learned to do the job right the first time during normal duty hours. That was all the extra duty I ever needed.

Tempers

"The female of the species is more deadly than the male."
Rudyard Kipling

There are times when medical providers see conditions in patients that stand out in their professional experiences. It might be the distinct odor of a patient with gangrene, the ill patient who suddenly dies and you were the last person they talked to, or the patient with a fishhook stuck in his throat, eternally grateful for the skillful removal of the ectopic object.

A patient I will never forget was a gentleman I saw when I was a medic in the Madigan Army Medical Center's emergency room. He casually walked into the emergency room late one evening and calmly stated, "My wife has stabbed me." The big sergeant had returned home from being in the field on maneuvers. During the inevitable adjustment period with his family, he found himself in a war of words over some silly issue with his tiny, temperamental wife. Things eventually got so out of hand that his wife grabbed the closest thing she could find to vent her fury—an ice pick.

The sergeant had a small puncture wound on the lower right anterior neck, just over the carotid artery. There was hardly any blood to speak of, just a small patch on the front of his shirt. The triage nurse asked him to have a seat on a treatment room bed while I began to take his vital signs. Within moments of sitting down, the sergeant asked, "I feel a little tired. Do you mind if I laid down?" Within seconds after lying down he quickly lost consciousness. The nurse preparing his chart yelled at me to get the trauma team on the double.

Sad to say, despite the patient "crashing" right in the emergency department and the quick intervention of the trauma team and major surgery, within the hour he was dead from massive internal bleeding due to a laceration of the carotid artery. It was a sobering experience for all involved, but especially for his unfortunate wife, who, by the time she was told of his untimely demise, was in a total state of shock. I heard later that she had to undergo long-term, in-patient psychiatric care.

Since that episode I have always thought twice when my wife and I have had our rare disagreements. Though my wife is the epitome of peaceful methods when it comes to conflict resolution, I cannot help but think about what befell that hapless sergeant. My counsel to argumentive soldiers or those married to temperamental spouses:

'Tis wiser to be known as a peacemaker,
than to need the services of an undertaker.

74

The Azimuth

"Nothing succeeds like success."
Alexander Dumas the Elder

"Specialist Kay, do you know how to shoot an azimuth?" the instructor asked. Embarrassed and red-faced, I mumbled a negative response. Up until the class on how to use a compass, the word was as foreign to me as Chinese. Pronounced "aazz-muth," it sounded like some cleverly concocted Harvard cuss word. And to shoot one, do you shoot it with a weapon?

The Army has special skill badges for qualified infantrymen and medics called the Expert Infantryman Badge (EIB) and the Expert Field Medical Badge (EFMB) respectively. These awards are given to soldiers who successfully pass a number of combat-related skills tests, one of the more difficult tasks being how to cross any type of terrain, day or night, using a compass. Not knowing what an azimuth was definitely put me behind the power curve at this point in my training.

For those who may not know, the Department of Defense has maps of every square inch of the earth's surface. They are unique maps, far different than your average road map. They come in all sorts of sizes and depict terrain features and man made objects. Even your house is on a map somewhere.

Learning to use these maps, over-printed with lines into "grids," is a critical skill every soldier needs to learn. Having a map and compass is extremely important if you want to get from point A to point B, especially if there are no roads involved. Without the tools and knowledge on how to use them a person is as good as lost.

Which brings me back to this azimuth business. An azimuth is synonymous with direction—an area you wish to get to. Hold a compass a certain way, aim it at the place you wish to get to, note the degree marking on the compass and, viola! You have shot an azimuth!

Big deal. Yes, it is a big deal. Stay on that mark through thick and thin and you will reach your objective, day or night, rain or shine. You can even find some tiny course stake with a number on top of it out in the middle of nowhere, a key step in passing the EIB or EFMB compass courses.

Direction. It is something you will need if you wish to go places. Little did I realize then, but shooting the azimuth of life was something I had already been doing. Sometimes I was a little off, but I was getting better at it.

What we can become is the map of life. The azimuth is the direction or the goal we wish to reach. Stay faithful to the direction you choose and put one foot in front of the other. You will get there. But to start down that path to success you have to shoot an azimuth first.

75

The Roadmarch

"It is a rough road that leads to heights of greatness."
Seneca

The Army's Expert Field Medical Badge (EFMB) is a coveted award within the Army Medical Department. It is not an easy badge to earn. Many attempt the dozens of tests required to get it, but only 10-15% pass and receive the badge. The others fail at least one of the different military and medical tasks, all designed to test expert medical knowledge and ability.

Many find the twelve-mile forced road march one of the most challenging of all the tests involved with the EFMB. Usually the march is scheduled as the last ordeal before the awards ceremony, that final event where the coveted badges are handed out. Often beginning at dawn in any type of weather, the march must be completed within three hours while each candidate carries a specific amount of equipment.

For most participants there is no way to complete the distance within time allowed without some running. For short people, the EFMB road march requires even more running. Legs that are only so long can cover just so much distance with each step. Those blessed with shorter legs who walk at a normal pace waste precious time. To make up for the shortfall—no pun intended—vertically challenged soldiers like myself have to run a great deal.

The first hour goes well, though fatigue begins to set in and those awful blisters flare up. The second hour is serious work as you maintain the necessary speed. The initial chatter between marchers ends. The periodic bursts of jogging with a pack on begin to remind you that you are not infallible and that you must bear this cross all alone. The third hour is a blur. The body's memory mercifully forgets this traumatic time. Extreme fatigue combined with the sense of urgency to get to the finish line cause each participant to press doggedly ahead, with little or no pauses. Making it to the finish line is everything.

Some fall by the wayside and are picked up by ambulances that trail behind the marchers like buzzards with red crosses. Most soldiers drive on no matter what the cost. For those who do push on in a timely manner, the finish line comes and they cross it successfully. The ordeal is over. They have succeeded.

After the march there is a big ceremony. Words are said, hands are shaken and the victorious go home achy, sore, and happy. They are proud of that small, new silver piece of metal now on their uniforms. They are among the few to get the badge. It is a badge of greatness that includes a rough road.

76

The Ranger

"Fall seven times, stand up eight."
Japanese Proverb

To continue with the previous story, any way you look at it, the Expert Field Medical Badge road march is tough. Twelve grueling miles in three hours will try most folks. Add a rucksack with gear, a humid day, and some evolving foot blisters and you have something near what the torment of the wicked will be.

Army Rangers are extraordinary people. Tough, motivated and totally dedicated, these volunteers are trained for the difficult jobs the Army has for them from time to time. Jobs like securing hostile airfields, blowing up bridges, operating behind enemy lines, or cracking some particularly difficult obstacle. This day a Ranger medic was tackling the EFMB road march ordeal along with a hundred or so other non-ranger medics.

I knew that keeping pace with this guy would assure me a successful road march. Nowhere near in as good of shape as he, it was a challenge for me to just keep up with him—even though he deliberately carried twice the amount of gear required for the march. The first hour he jogged. I ran too but gradually began to drift behind. I still kept him within sight despite slipping and stumbling on the road gravel or the periodic mud hole. It was going to take some "hooaah" just to keep up with this guy.

The second and third hours passed in a slow-motion daze. Surely death was about to overtake me, the pain and aches were so great. Drenched in sweat and smarting from scrapes during several falls, I pressed on, limping because of the blisters. The Ranger medic, still within sight, confidently strode on as if on a Sunday Volksmarch.

Eventually the finish line came into sight. Composing myself, I pushed hard to close the gap. Crossing that line a few minutes behind the Ranger, I collapsed onto the ground a few feet from where he still stood.

After a few moments, I looked up to see the Ranger's medical officer, a PA by the name of Steve Brick, come up to him. The medic greeted him enthusiastically. "Sir," he said, "I did the march in record time!" "Fine," Mr. Brick replied, "now get into the front leaning rest for failing to salute an officer." After enthusiastically knocking out ten push-ups with his rucksack still on, the Ranger requested permission to get up. Mr. Brick, chuckling but gruff as ever, said, "Recover. I'm proud of you." Through my exhausted and fallen state, I was impressed. Truly, at least in spirit if not in body, I was ready to stand up again and follow one of these remarkable Rangers.

Rangers will always lead the way.

Movers and Shakers

"If we didn't have ordinary men, how could we tell the great ones?"
Japanese Proverb

Adorning the front of the uniforms of many soldiers are special-skills qualification badges. Located on or above the left breast pocket, you may find up to five of these emblems, affectionately referred to as "Merit Badges." Though there is never a 100% guarantee, it is a fairly good bet that a soldier with a fair number of these patches or pins is a go-getter.

There are badges for airborne training, flight school, infantry or medic skills, scuba diving, pathfinder, and air assault school. Each symbol signifies successful completion in some rigorous school, or that its wearer saw service in combat. A gold star on the parachute badge, for instance, signifies its wearer did a parachute drop in a hostile area. A wreath around the infantryman's badge denotes combat service with the infantry.

My first merit badge in the Army was the Expert Field Medical Badge. How proud I was to sport that special pin on my uniform! When 370 people set out to get that award and only 42 pass, one can be justly proud to be among the few and perhaps, to some extent, the lucky.

What people will do for a piece of metal! It all starts at a young age, when in Sunday or Sabbath School we strive for gold stars next to our name for successfully learning memory verses. Or maybe we sought after treats from our parents for getting good grades. From there it is only a small step to memorizing battle procedures and successfully passing cleverly designed ordeals or feats of physical endurance.

It is good that the Army has these merit badge carrots out there for the hyperactive types. There is a good chance that some of these hyperactive soldiers grow into movers and shakers later on. That is, they become people that make big things happen.

In an organization as large as the U.S. Army, it is good to have some of these go-getters in our midst. They stir things up and get things moving, much to the dismay of the passive ones. They look for opportunity and take advantage of it. They make things better. And even bigger things happen when movers and shakers get stars on their collars, in addition to their four or five merit badges.

Some people will rest on their laurels. Success will make some of us content. There comes a time when we move and shake less. Those persistent movers and shakers however, irritate those of us slowing down. They just keep going and going, especially the ones that wear stars on their collar.

The Morgue

"The fear of death is more to be dreaded than death itself."
Pubilius Syrus

The first time I had ever seen a morgue up close was at Madigan Army Medical Center. Assigned as a medic to the emergency room of the busy hospital, most shifts included some unfortunate soul brought to the ER who could not be saved.

The death of a loved one is a very traumatic thing for people to go through. It takes very special people to help break the news and minister to the initial shock of grieving family members. While the docs and chaplains helped the family, the medics usually took care of the remains.

It is a bit chilling to handle a dead body. Very mixed feelings—fear, revulsion, sadness, and emotional detachment blend together into a knot I do not much care for. But the job has to be done and, usually with another medic, we get busy at this necessary but unpleasant task.

First you position and clean the body. Wrists are lightly bound together over the abdomen and the ankles tied together. Tubes and catheters are cut, but not removed. That will be done at the autopsy. One particularly chilling thing to do is taping the often-open eyelids closed.

Finally, nametags are tied to the right great toe and left wrist, then the body is wrapped up in linen. When moving the corpse to a gurney, certain gases may be released and a fleeting fear grabs you like a visit from Freddie Kruger. Could he still be alive?

The work of transporting the dead becomes even more frightening as you move down the quiet, semi-lit long corridors of the old hospital all alone in the middle of the night, pushing the remains in front of you. There's material for Steven King in that experience, let me tell you.

Entering the morgue you see the special refrigerators where the bodies are kept. You see a frightening reflection of yourself and the remains off the large, square, stainless steel doors. Quickly, the body is loaded onto special trays that slide out of the refrigerator. I could never do this alone—hard on the back I'd say then. But really it was the terror of the other bodies hidden inside that dark, gruesome icebox that made me long for company. Fear always enjoys company.

Soon the unpleasant task is done and we scurry back to the world of the living, comforted by the fact that the duty is done. "Next time somebody else will do this job," you mumble to yourself. God bless those who do this for a living, this handling of the dead. I for one was glad when the task was ended. Leave it to the brave to tuck the dead into their long sleep.

MREs

"I am convinced that digestion is the great secret of life."
Sydney Smith

The food given to troops in the field changed in the early 1980s. The Department of Defense phased out the old "C" rations in cardboard boxes and began using the MRE, or Meal, Ready to Eat. Gone were the cans and "P-38" can openers of the long-used C-rations, and in came the plastic blister packs and dehydrated food items.

The MREs were widely accepted. In fact, they were a hit with the troops. Containing a mixture of the old and new food items, the meals were lighter, tastier, and had more variety. When it comes to food, new is generally better, at least for those enduring the same old fare.

Over time, however, a few imperfections with the MRE emerged, or should I say, developed. The dehydrated components needed attention before eating and woe to the impatient soldier who partook before proper reconstitution with water. Bloating and gas were his fate. Others would consume the meals too quickly and get a serious case of indigestion. Still others partook too often and experienced prolonged delays in their bowel movements.

Many soldiers have found creative ways to make the MRE contents into as many different culinary varieties as possible—from "Ranger Stew," where every edible part of an MRE is mixed together before eating, to selective combinations such as the field Reese's Cup when the peanut butter and chocolate components are eaten together. Leave it to soldiers to make things even better, these sons and daughters of the American mother of invention.

There is a place near Boston, Massachusetts, where the Department of Defense does dietary research on what troops will be eating tomorrow. Food experts, some with doctoral degrees in nutrition, pore over food items and preservation systems that will meet the dietary needs of soldiers in any worldwide environment, from the arctic cold to the tropical heat.

It is the prayer of all soldiers that these Army dietary experts, in their warm and dry research offices and labs not far from Harvard, will remember to reach the goal so long desired by all soldiers forced to consume their creations. Please give us the four basic food groups: cheeseburgers, pizza, submarine sandwiches and tacos. These are food groups that, I would wager, many of these experts will likely have for their own lunch there in Boston.

The troops are always ready to eat. Give them not just Meals Ready to Eat, but Meals Really Expected.

Pooper Scoopers

"And though hard be the task, 'keep a stiff upper lip.'"
Phoebe Cary

I cannot recall his name, this Specialist Fifth Class medic who was my intermediate supervisor at Madigan Army Medical Center emergency room. Although he was moderately egotistical, we worked well together and I was very glad to get ER duty as a medic.

This fellow had his act together. He dressed immaculately; even in the Army whites they gave us to wear. Sharp haircut and good-looking features, this guy was never far from a mirror either. He knew his stuff, too. He understood that emergency room from top to bottom. It was when I worked with him that I was to become very acquainted with the bottom part.

It was an evening shift. Most of us always seemed to get evening shifts, since it tends to be the busiest time of the day for emergency rooms. When the favorite TV show ends, the full moon is out, or the weather changes, you can count on the ER visitation numbers to rise.

The numbers were up this particular evening. We were working hard. On top of the busy pace, in comes a patient from an MBA—motorbike accident. He was in bad shape. He had broken both femurs and sustained abrasion injuries all over his back and buttocks. Fortunately, he had his helmet on, otherwise it could have been much worse. On top of all these injuries, he had defecated on himself, as we readily discovered while removing his clothing.

Now I don't know whoever got the idea that the nurses clean patients up. They certainly didn't do it in our ER. No sir, the medics on each shift did the menial tasks, including that very unpleasant job of cleaning up bodily secretions emanating from the nether regions of the GI tract.

Which brings me back to the suave medic and me. Orders were orders, and we moved in to get the guy ready for the operating room, which included splints, IVs, and pain medications in place. It was a two-man job. Surgical masks on, we got to work. Hurrying to get the job done and get out of there, I bent over to pick up something, and as I came up I hit my head on a protruding shelf. The next moment found me lying flat on my back looking up into the faces of four or five fellow ER staff members.

"Are you okay?" someone asked. Well, I wasn't sure. "Was it the stink or a bump that brought me down?" I thought to myself. In the end I became a patient too, getting knocked out from a head injury. My mentor, the suave one, had to finish the poop detail alone. I don't know where he is today, but I'm sure he'll always remember the title, "Pooper Scooper."

81

Placebos

"As to diseases make a habit of two things –
to help, or at least, to do no harm."
Hippocrates

Over the years, I have seen thousands of America's finest soldiers, and some of her not-so-fine soldiers, on military sick call. Every morning the lobbies of my various aid stations and clinics have held any number of troops hopefully awaiting the best medical care the Army could give. From those who only thought they were sick to those with grave medical conditions, the daily task before me was to sort it all out and do the right thing for each one.

Year after year, experienced military medical personnel begin to understand sick call more clearly. They learn that there are three basic groups of soldiers who report for medical attention: those who will get better no matter what you do, those who improve with what you offer, and those who will worsen no matter what you do. If only the high-tech medical equipment inventors could create a gadget or meter to identify who is which, the job would be so much easier.

Many people think they are sick when they are probably healthier than the medical officer they see. What they desire, maybe, is merely attention. They need the assurance that someone cares. They gain comfort from the knowledge that if something is truly wrong, then "doc" will square me away. Like a mother who soothes the aches of an injured or sick child, the medical officer uses various medicines, treatments, tricks and perhaps a profile to make them "well" again. With young troops, healing will pretty much occur without a lot of help.

For the really sick soldiers a small amount of attention will not be sufficient. Often these soldiers are the ones who rarely use medical services. When they get sick, then you can figure on a serious bug involved. The placebo does not work for these patients. Anything short of the right medical care and these troops see right through to the quack trying to fix something they know little about.

Our government needs to understand that at times the whole Army can get sick. It is rare, but it does happen. Just reflect back on the late 1970s for example. When the military is sick, the last thing we need is an elected representative who acts like a quack with the purse strings that can keep the military alive. We will always need civilian leaders who can be like a good doctor and make all the difference in the world. A quick fix will not do, nor will the placebo.

Is there a good doctor in the house?

Cut Short

"A dirge for the most lovely dead that ever died so young."
Edgar Allen Poe

"Base, this is Med One," the ER's radio crackled, "we are en route to your location with a thirteen year-old female struck by a pickup truck while getting off a school bus." The staff of the Madigan Army Medical Center emergency department sprang into action. The large trauma room, always kept in readiness, was rechecked. Equipment turned on. Packages opened. Each team member, from the newest medic to the most experienced staff physician, knew his or her place on the trauma team. One person would be in charge. Another would start an intravenous infusion line. Someone else would manage the airway or record everything we did in trying to save the life of the girl on the way to us that very moment.

The ambulance pulled up and the back doors swung open. The paramedic was already doing CPR, not a good sign. Quickly we moved into the trauma room and placed her on the main stretcher. I noticed how pretty her uninjured face was.

Orders were barked out. Everywhere there was organized commotion. We were going to do everything we could to save her. At least twelve staff members were dedicated to this desperate endeavor.

Her body was bruised across the chest. The left arm and right lower leg were twisted and obviously broken. Large abrasions were all over her body where her delicate soft skin had made contact with the road. Expertly, we did everything we could for her: airway, breathing, and circulation. Still no spontaneous heart beat. For nearly two hours we worked, though we knew that with each passing minute our chances of success grew less and our hope for her survival grew dimmer.

She died. It was such a tragic, needless loss. For his stupidity the drunk driver of the pickup went to jail, but that was no consolation to her family. Theirs was a crushing loss every parent prays they will never have to face. And though we did not know her, the sadness of this tragedy was almost overwhelming for every staff member, after having tried so hard and so long to save her.

The last thing I did that day was go home and quietly check on my own sleeping children. They were safe and sound. Someone else's terrible loss became another chance for me to be grateful for the treasures I do have. The death of one renewed the seeds of appreciation for those in my life I held close and dear.

Children

"The best thing to spend on your children is your time."
Unknown

Our legacies to the future,

Are our children of today.

Through them we touch tomorrow

Even though we pass away.

Forget not these young couriers,

Now busy in their play,

For they are the messengers

Of who we are today.

They are the precious jewels

Our pride and our joy,

Each with a wonderful value

Be they girl or boy.

Tombstones inspire only a few,

And graveyards are lonely places.

My epitaph to unborn men,

Lies on my children's faces.

David Kay

Sweat and Blood

"Respect was mingled with surprise,
and the stern joy which warriors feel in foemen worthy of their steel."
Sir Walter Scott

The U.S. invasion of Grenada in 1984 ended in a decisive victory for the forces involved and the administration of then President Ronald Reagan. The lightning strikes by Army Rangers and Navy Seals prepared the way for follow-on airborne troops to secure the island. Communist forces, staging a brief but fierce resistance, were quickly brushed aside.

The long, dark-green Army bus with large red crosses on its sides pulled up outside the Madigan Army Medical Center emergency room. Eleven wounded soldiers of the 2nd Ranger battalion were on board. They were the wounded from that early morning airborne assault on the main airfield of Grenada. They had sustained amputations, broken bones, gunshot and fragment wounds.

One by one we brought them into the ER for admission to the hospital. Six patients were on litters and another five walking. There were other casualties, the seriously wounded soldiers too unstable to move back to their base at Fort Lewis, Washington. These were hospitalized in facilities closer to the Caribbean. There were other casualties, and thankfully only a few, who numbered among those who lost their lives in the operation.

Family and friends were waiting nearby to see these wounded men, so we worked quickly getting them ready. It was a great privilege to take care of them, back from such an important mission and assigned to the best of the best, the Rangers.

Visit any Army post where U.S. Army Rangers are and you'll likely see them training. Often you can see them on the roadside marching, complete with full battle gear. They stay in constant physical, mental, and emotional readiness. What they do is a down payment on the costs of combat. When the balloon goes up and they go in, that is the time where all the sweat pays off. The drills and teamwork, the knowledge of each other's job and the courage to get it done, all come together to do some nasty, but critically important jobs.

Most Americans go about their days in a fine suit or set of work clothes. They flourish in a society of freedom. They benefit from an idea made possible by the sacrifice of those who came before. The toughest of the tough, the most capable of the capable, are the United States Army Rangers. When America is faced with a tough nut to crack, these sweaty, tough, prepared and motivated warriors are the nutcrackers. Hooaah!

Tee Shirts

"What he hath scanted men in hair,
he hath given them in wit."
Shakespeare

Irene once wondered why I always wore my brown Army tee shirts backwards. It was a valid concern; after all, a reversed tee shirt looks a bit dorky. The answer lies across the expanse of history when there arose a race of human beings that learned to survive and prosper in the cold and wet climates of northern Europe. In the dense forests, lonely moors, and majestic highlands of what is now Scotland, a people arose who were short in stature, full of spirit, and fair-skinned. Their women had some of the most beautiful hair in the world and their men folk were among the hairiest of humankind.

The Romans called these tribal clans barbarians. These brave people of the northern reaches of the British Isles were so fierce they could not be subdued. Instead, the Romans built a wall, Hadrian's Wall, to keep the red-heads away from an empire of the civilized. The modern descendants of these barbarians are now more cultured, especially the males who serve in the U.S. military. The kilts and beards are gone, replaced by a nondescript camouflaged tartan and clean-shaven faces.

What in the world does this have to do with tee shirts? Well, the males of Scottish descent carry in their genes and chests the persistent marks of a highlander—an abundance of chest hair that presents itself above the standard neckline of an Army-issue tee shirt. Repeated washings and the rigors of Army life also exacerbate the exposure of chest hair because the neckline elastic tends to stretch and droop, further showing one's manliness.

Spend any amount of time as an enlisted soldier and you will face an "in-ranks inspection." During this ordeal an officer or NCO walks down each line of soldiers, looking each man over, carefully searching for defects, or "gigs." Haircuts, boots, loose strings, and dozens of other trivial details receive their attention. For the short, stout soldiers blessed with an abundance of body hair, the scrutinizers sometimes take exception to the hair peeking out above the tee shirt.

Historically Scots have not had an underwear problem. They simply didn't wear any. Their American soldier descendants, however, do not have the go-without-underwear option, at least not with the undershirt. Some shave the protruding chest hair. Others of us are too proud to mutilate ourselves so. Given defective tee shirts we improvise by turning them around, thus providing a higher neckline. Let the world know that we have been there, done that, and wore our tee shirt backwards.

86

Of Buffers and People

"Let your light so shine before men,
that they may see your good works..."
Matthew 5:16

A striking feature that greets visitors to military buildings is shiny flooring. If there is no carpet, the floor is buffed so that you can see yourself in it. We often give little thought to how these floors get that way.

The trick to creating floors that look like you can eat off them is time tested. Generations of non-commissioned officers passed the recipe on to the next—a recipe of wax and elbow grease—a recipe most CQ runners in the Army have been intimately involved in. For it is in the wee hours of every morning that CQ runners buff floors all over the Army.

Thank heaven for the electric buffer. Once a novice learns the fine art of controlling the rotating disc, what took hours before becomes a job done in a fraction of the time. Before the introduction of the electric buffer, the hands and knees approach, combined with elbow grease, was the main way to shine those floors.

Learning to control a buffer is a lot like learning to lead people. There is a lot of potential energy and good that can come from both buffers and people. Both are difficult to move without power. Without direction, both are worthless. You need only give power and direction to make things happen. Lack of attention or gentle control will result in bumps, scratches, an irregular pattern, and a poor outcome. Gentle pressure and attention, combined with a slight forward motion, brings both buffers and people to productive results. It produces a shine everyone is proud of.

The last time I operated a buffer was a few days before I left for school to become a warrant officer. The last floor I buffed kept its shine only a short time. The next day, pedestrian traffic, spills, and moving objects across the floors marred that shine. But life goes on. The following night another soldier tackled the job of re-shining the floors in a dance with that electric buffer.

As my military career progressed, I found myself responsible for leading more and more people. All needed daily attention from me. Their ability to shine as soldiers was directly related to how much support and direction they received from this leader appointed over them.

One cannot lead without getting out onto the floor. You have to walk the hall. Check the shine. The skillful application of power and direction makes things happen that all of us can be proud of. Jobs well performed become things that benefit everyone. It's a shine everyone can see themselves in.

Boot Ornaments

"Now for good luck, cast an old shoe after me."
John Heywood

The regimented world of the military is legendary and the U.S. Army is certainly no exception. Streets, buildings, vehicles, and soldiers all look alike to the average layperson. As one takes in all this uniformity, look carefully and you might see one glaring exception. It might just be the Army's version of a graffiti problem: a pair of leather boots dangling from a power line.

Civilians who visit Army posts are often humored by an interesting but unofficial custom passed down (or up) from soldiers departing the service. As some soldiers prepare to leave, they take their last pair of Army boots, tie the long laces together, and then fling the pair up into some prominent tree, telephone pole or power line, anywhere that is difficult to reach but easy to see.

This semi-defiant act is, of course, done clandestinely, usually in total darkness with no one watching. The resulting outdoor ornament is their parting shot, sort of like the "Kilroy was here" graffiti of World War II Europe.

Some of these "boot hanging" servicemembers display quite a creative streak in painting or otherwise decorating their footwear. Their freelance works must of necessity be incognito, as powerful post Commanders and Sergeant Majors generally frown upon such budding artists. Over the years the custom of boot hanging waxes and wanes. The expressions of artistic soldiers will vary and levels of resistance from the establishment will differ.

In a world that seems to swallow up individuality automatically, perhaps these errant boots symbolize much more than some last act of rebellion. Each of us has an innate desire to leave our mark—to not be forgotten—to know that we have made a difference. Maybe those boots, hanging outside, like some bizarre rearview mirror air freshener, are a memorial misdemeanor to those who were otherwise unable to leave their mark, their touch, or like wild animals, their scent (pun fully intended).

Whatever motivates these "boot hangers," my guess is that commanders will forever have to deal with the sometimes-tricky removal of these boots. The waters of the military will inevitably close in around these leather pebbles thrown into the proverbial lake of uniformity. But it does not really matter. The boot hanger's point is made and will be made in some creative way by others who will follow. Kilroy was here, and always will be.

Chemistry

"It is only the ignorant who despise education."
Pubilius Syrus

During our first months in the Army's PA school at Fort Sam Houston, Texas, we were deluged with chemistry courses. Many a day was spent sitting in class, bombarded with organic chemistry at the Army's Academy of Health Sciences. Barely in school a few weeks, the material was coming at us hot and heavy. As one veteran PA once told me, "It was like drinking from a fire hose."

Mr. Emmett Foulds was a superb chemistry teacher. He knew the material and he also knew the nature of his class. He had trained many Army PAs in the complexities of chemistry. His work was cut out for him once again with another class. We were all former enlisted soldiers, now wearing Warrant Officer Candidate insignia and going to college.

Mr. Foulds knew that chemistry would be one of our more difficult courses in school. Many PA students failed the school because of chemistry. Therefore, he had refined the course carefully so that even the "rocks" among us could learn it, if you applied yourself. He'd start with simple concepts. Easy stuff. "This is an atom. Add one electron and one neutron and you have..." Through the skillful use of military similes and comparisons, he drove home each principle, each procedure, and each necessary component. Slowly it all began to make sense.

Despite making things as simple as possible some of us still struggled with the material. A particularly difficult hurdle for some was the detailed description of the chemical processes involved in the digestion of a typical cheeseburger. Combining several concepts already presented, we were now to bring to paper, in a logical format, an essay tying together every chemical step concerned with the complete digestion, from the mouth to the anus, of the standard American cheeseburger. The formidable essay question, requiring at least a six-page answer, loomed before us.

We studied hard and Mr. Foulds worked with us. More and more it all began to come together. We drilled each other and practiced like soldiers going through pre-combat checks and drills. In time, we all caught on.

Years later I would meet former classmates at PA conferences. We would reminisce about school and particularly Organic Chemistry under Mr. Foulds. We all admired him deeply and appreciated the education he imparted to soldiers not accustomed to the world of chemistry, but who were willing to hang around long enough to catch on. Years later his cheeseburger test in particular was fondly remembered by all. Everyone still agrees it was a whopper.

Talking the Talk

"Humility is modesty of the soul
and the antidote to pride."
Voltaire

As a surgeon he must have been pretty good in his field. He was very knowledgeable with plenty of anecdotes and illustrations. He was older, an Army Colonel, and assigned to duty training U.S. Army physician assistants. His task was to teach us the fine and not so definite art of recognizing surgical problems in the thousands of cases we would encounter in our forthcoming medical careers.

I didn't get along well with him. Maybe it was because I found him somewhat intimidating. Perhaps it was his somewhat gruff manner. It was difficult to put a finger on it, but part of it had to be the important non-surgical lesson he taught me.

The lectures and classes for PA students in the Army's school lasted eight hours a day, Monday through Friday. There was none of the Monday-Wednesday-Friday or Tuesday-Thursday typical civilian college schedule for our classes. A four-hour block of surgery lectures could be trying and it was a challenge keeping the interest up, especially after lunch.

I talk too much. I've always known it. If things are particularly boring or if I get nervous, then my tendency to talk is even greater. It did not help that my speech at that time came with a distinct southern accent.

To keep awake I would ask questions at opportune times during class. Maybe they were good questions, but in hindsight probably too many questions. This particular day found me asking a question to our surgeon about cancer of the larynx, a word pronounced in my best southern drawl as, "Larry-nix." With a look that expressed obvious disdain, the perturbed surgeon responded to my inquiry in his finest New Jersey tone, "Mr. Kay, could you please repeat your question?"

Now singled out and uncertain, I hesitatingly repeated the question exactly as before, ignorant of the trap. "You see, ladies and gentlemen," he said, "it is extremely important to communicate clearly. Everyone should understand that what Mr. Kay has said is not "larry-nix," but properly pronounced "Larn-ix." Are there any more questions?"

There were no further questions. Embarrassed, there would also be no more questions from me. The lesson was learned. I realized that to succeed you have to not only understand but also correctly speak the language. Sometimes it is important to keep your mouth shut, at least until you know how to talk the talk.

Binds

"Science and art belong to the whole world,
and the barriers of nationality vanish before them."
Goethe

They say he had been a distinguished physician before he died. Upon his death, he willed his remains for the use of the United States Army's Academy of Health Sciences. His final resting place was in an anatomy lab. Of the several cadavers available in the lab, his was the only one sort of personalized. We knew him simply as "Doc."

"Doc" was my first serious contact with the dead. No need for some séance to bring someone back, Doc was there to stay in living color. Lift the remains up out of the formaldehyde storage tank and you had a three dimensional anatomy textbook: muscles, bones, organs, tendons—certainly everything you ever wanted to know about human anatomy but were afraid to ask about, look at, or smell.

Though we were initially squeamish about this gross anatomy business, the lectures, required assignments and the examinations helped us, or maybe forced us, to overcome our fears. One natural fear was the simple task of handling the dead, something we would have to do again and again in our careers.

For the uninitiated, a human anatomy lab packs the powerful smell of formaldehyde and other chemicals, far more than the frog lab of your average high school biology class. To this day the scent of formaldehyde will always remind me of Doc and what he taught us, even though he could no longer move or speak. Like the incense of some ancient religious ceremony, growing accustomed to the smell of Doc was a rite of passage for our study of medicine and a reminder that we are all indeed mortal.

Doc's gift, and that of tens of thousands of special people like him, allows students of medicine to really get into science, even up to their elbows. Though donating one's remains to science is a strange thought to many lay people, it is nevertheless indispensable for the training of new physicians and physician assistants.

Unlike other professions, science can bind people together in unique ways, as seen by our experience with Doc. The long hours we spent with him saw my classmates and I grow in our knowledge and especially our confidence in medicine. His was truly one of those good gifts that kept on giving—binding us together in that noblest of all pursuits—the care of the sick and injured.

May God bless all the people like "Doc" in the world!

Master Teachers

"A teacher affects eternity;
he can never tell where his influence stops."
Henry Brooks Adams

It is after lunch—a large meal of pizza and soda. The warm afternoon drags on as you sit in some Army course classroom listening to lectures from some so-called subject matter expert. The monotone voice of the instructor reading directly from his or her notes hits you like a big dose of Valium. Your well-fed living organism begins brief flirtations with the process of hibernation. Each boring word brings on new attacks of narcolepsy. You are bored to tears and falling asleep at the same time.

What makes a master teacher? Is it someone who can keep your interest and involvement despite the subject? Or is it a person who does not put you to sleep by reading their notes to the class?

Many things make up what an expert instructor is. Depending on your background, each person would answer these questions differently. Perhaps a master teacher knows the subject very well and also knows how to make it simple to the uninitiated.

Teachers hate ignorance but love the ignorant.

Great instructors are patient, know their own limitations, and have not allowed titles, honor, rank, or superior knowledge to rob them of genuine humility. They know that, yes, even students might know something they have not pondered before.

The best teachers also live under the philosophy that there is no such thing as a stupid question. They encourage questions. There may be a dumb question for not paying attention, but it is still never stupid to ask it. The answer might very well save a life someday.

Though certainly not qualified to be a master evaluator of who is and who is not the best teacher, I feel the very best instructors are those who make the material interesting. Regardless of the subject, they can deliver the stuff with enthusiasm, unexpected twists, and always in a wrapper that gets and keeps your attention. You can't fall asleep. You don't want to fall asleep. Every word is like a fresh dose of caffeine.

William Arthur Ward once wrote, "The mediocre teacher tells. The good teacher explains. The superior teacher demonstrates. The great teacher inspires." To paraphrase, I would add that the mediocre teacher puts students to sleep, the good teacher makes them doze, a superior teacher keeps them awake, and the great teacher makes students willingly go for days without sleep.

Inspiration

"So it is that the gods do not give all men gifts of grace –
neither good looks nor intelligence nor eloquence."
Homer

There are some very smart people in the world. You run into them all over the place. A photographic memory, 4.0 grade point average, or a high IQ—these people seem to know everything about anything. Walking encyclopedias. One cannot help but be grudgingly impressed with them, especially when your level of intelligence is somewhat less than theirs.

These smarty-pants types often bother most of us regular folks. They study for an hour and have it. We take three hours and still are not sure if we know the material. Academic challenge is a piece of cake for them.

But smart people have their problems too, especially when they are a know it all. A "know it all" is a term used for someone who may indeed be very smart, but they have an attitude problem. They have allowed their superior intelligence to create an ego that, quite frankly, makes them into something synonymous with a donkey. Their exceptional brains cause them to ignore common sense. A good attitude with a superior intelligence can take you places, but a lousy attitude, no matter how smart you may be, will get you nowhere in the end.

I've never met one, but I've heard that there are people in life with PhDs who are working for minimum wage because they cannot find better work. Imagine, eighteen to twenty years of school, only to find you working at some burger joint. You can be smart and unsuccessful at the same time.

The really intelligent people are the ones who are inspired to use what they know for good purposes. They think before they act. But act they do. They make a difference and it shows. They do not have an attitude problem either. Instead, the successful, knowledgeable people understand that they can never know everything and that even the dumbest person might know something they do not. Everyone has a perspective, an angle from which they see things that others might not see.

Imagination can inspire us. Inspiration gives our knowledge a direction, a goal. Without a goal you're headed nowhere. You might as well line up for that permanent duty minimum wage job. On the other hand, to have a goal and be smart enough to achieve it is a great thing. The really smart people figure this out soon enough in life to make a difference with their God-given abilities. What these people are then capable of doing cannot help but inspire the imagination of all.

Shots

"Nothing in life is so exhilarating as to be shot at without result."
Sir Winston Churchill

At 5'6" you might say I'm below center of mass. Nothing reminds me more of this than when I am on a basketball court. Though it is a great game, and a good workout, personal physical limitations passed on from my genetic forebear's affect my scoring ability. No Michael Jordan potential lurking within me. My scoring stats stink. In short, I'm short.

Despite the limitations of gravity and genetics, I still get out on the court from time to time when they let me. You know who I am, the little guy chosen last, the one nobody ever passes the ball to. I mean, why waste the shot? Give the ball to the taller guy. The one with style, with the $150.00 shoes, but not the one whose growth plates closed too soon.

Well, that's okay. You learn to make do. Among all the B-17 hotshot bombers on the court, you become that pesky little fighter that messes with their lay-ups. You cut in and out quickly, often with a chance to steal the ball. You make up for an inability to slam-dunk the ball with that perfected low strike maneuver. Apply yourself and the basketball court can develop your weak areas, both emotionally and physically, a skill useful in any successful civilian or military career.

Randy Newman wrote a funny song once entitled *Short People*. The subtle humor in the song taught me that in a sense we are all "short people." You might be short in stature, brains, looks, social graces, finances, or any number of other things. The important thing is to improve your shortcomings. Keep at it. Find your niche. Find your strengths and exploit the competition's weaknesses. Deliver the unexpected to your unaware and overconfident opponent. Always remember that each of us is 5'6" in some aspect of our lives and careers. Use that shortness to your advantage.

Helen Keller was a remarkable woman with serious handicaps. Deaf and blind, she pushed on in her personal development and accomplishments to set an example that inspired the world. She overcame huge barriers and told us all that "can't" does not count. She took every shot she could.

Failures to exploit your own weaknesses are the shots in life you did not take. You're guaranteed to miss all of them. Many soldiers are sadly content to put down their strengths and magnify their shortcomings and apparent inabilities. Seldom do they think to use them to their advantage.

Go on, take the shots. Sure, you will miss a lot of them. You might even look stupid at first, but keep at it. You will get better—not physically taller necessarily, but definitely better. It's a shot worth taking.

The Salute

"Hail, Emperor, we who are about to die salute you."
Suetonius

The military has an interesting custom when it comes to saluting newly commissioned officers. The very first person the brand new officer returns a salute to becomes the proud owner of a silver dollar. You can imagine the looks of surprise when some soldier salutes yet another second lieutenant or brand new warrant officer and discovers to his or her surprise that they get a shiny dollar for the effort.

I have often wished I could go back and find the Marine Corps gunnery sergeant that first saluted me back in 1985. I was a new warrant officer, complete with that distinctive black stripe down the side of my green dress uniform pants. There was a silver dollar in my pocket. My classmates and I had just pinned on our new rank and moved on to a reception in our honor, all indoors.

Caught up in all the excitement of the special moment, I suddenly remembered an appointment I had at city hall downtown to pick up an important document before we left town. Bidding a hurried farewell to my friends, all newly minted officers, I exited stage left to my car, but for the want of an enlisted soldier missed any chance to return my first salute en route to the parking lot.

City traffic in San Antonio was the usual mess. It was a hot day and I had my car windows down as I stopped in heavy traffic at a red light near a pedestrian crosswalk. At first I did not notice the Marine walking up from a side street to my right. As he arrived there was just enough time for him to snap a sharp salute at me and state with vigor, "Isn't it a fine, hot day, sir?" Caught off guard, I nodded and fumbled behind the wheel with my first return salute.

The traffic light immediately turned green and the cars behind me forced me to move on. I circled the block to find him, but he was gone. His sharp uniform was nowhere to be seen, that trademark Marine white hat, tan shirt, and blue pants with the red stripes down each leg, all clothing your typically near zero-percent body fat Marine wears.

I'd sure like to meet that man someday. I owe him a silver dollar. My enlisted days had passed on with that first formal salute, confirmed by an honored custom rendered by an American service member, a Marine.

From the halls of Montezuma to the shores of Tripoli, would that I could find that United States Marine!

Friends

"A friend is one who forgives you when you have overtaken him
professionally and financially."
Eugene E. Brussell

The playing field is level when you start out in the Army. Whether
you are a private at basic training or a plebe at West Point, all soldiers start
out equal. Over time, however, we begin to spread out based on personal
abilities, the needs of the Army, or just by being at the right place at the right
time. Leadership positions, schools, promotion below the zone of those
considered, or early school selections are ways that spread people out in
differing rank.

I was a brand new warrant officer—a so-called "wobbly one." A shiny
silver bar with a single black dot in the middle adorned each shoulder of my
uniform. One morning I was walking down the hallway of Womack Army
Hospital at Fort Bragg, North Carolina. Suddenly, a voice from behind me
called out, "Hey, Kay!" Turning around, I recognized one of my buddies
from basic training some six years earlier. Seeing my new rank he hesitated
and said, "Oh, sorry, sir!" Embarrassed, I said while vigorously shaking his
hand, "Hey, that's okay, Bill, how are you? You're a staff Sergeant
already?" I asked.

Taking no notice of how far he too had come, he profusely
congratulated me on being a warrant officer. I was touched by how
sincerely happy he was for me. His response to my success was a lesson I
only then began to understand.

Through the years I have met folks who advanced faster than me. I've
had to work for supervisors who were younger than me, with much less time
and experience in service. There is a fast track and then there is a faster
track. Sometimes you wonder if you are even on any sort of track at all.
Every now and again the rank system serves you humble pie, an often-
difficult thing to accept. Humility is so hard to eat especially when you
honestly know how to do the job better than those "greenhorns" appointed
over you.

I have often reflected on that chance meeting with my old friend from
boot camp. There will always be someone faster than me, smarter than me,
more successful than me, or better than me. In the race of life there will
always be someone ahead of us. We have to accept the success of others as
a fact of life. If we can be at peace with the success of others, as my friend
so ably demonstrated towards me, then we can bring enduring internal
success to ourselves, regardless of our rank or bank account balance. To do
this well is to truly succeed.

Autopsy

"The life so short, the art long, opportunity fleeting,
experiment treacherous, judgement difficult."
Hippocrates

There is an experience that would give any normal person the heeby
jeebees. For medical people, a critical part of their clinical training includes
participation in an autopsy, the examination of a deceased human being. It is
a rite of passage. It is here that all the neat anatomy pictures and diagrams
come alive in a most frighteningly three-dimensional way.

We gathered in the mortuary, a large, cold, formaldehyde scented
room. Unlike our studies of "Doc" back at the Academy of Health
Sciences, we were about to view fresh material. A stainless steel table with
raised edges stood in the middle of the room with a draped corpse lying on
it. Bright surgical lights hanging from the ceiling above illuminated
everything, like stage spotlights on the main attraction. The room was
otherwise sparsely furnished with only a medicine cabinet, a bookshelf, a
table, and some chairs.

A short, rather plump pathologist in wire-rimmed glasses and white
lab coat joined us. He was older, slightly stooped and balding. All he
lacked was a thick foreign accent and the last name of Frankenstein and our
foreboding and fear would have been complete. He was good-natured and
readily allowed us three PA students to watch as he did the dissection.

With German-like efficiency, the pathologist opened up the chest and
abdomen of the deceased, who was a male about sixty-five years old. He
spoke in a quick fashion, pointing out key organs, bones and tissues, all the
while preparing specimens of various organs and tissues for analysis. We
watched in astonished wonder as the parts of the body came into view in
living color. Soon, the cause of his death was apparent. Heart attack.

Early on, a queasiness overcame me with that familiar ringing in my
ears, accompanied by a slight nausea and a closing darkness in my
peripheral vision. The voice of our mentor became sharper and more
pronounced. I knew I was about to faint. Quickly squatting down, blood
was forced up to my brain, a brain not unlike the one now exposed on the
table before us. I narrowly escaped passing out.

Our fantastic voyage into the wondrous human body ended with the
doctor placing the final staples in the abdomen of the deceased. We had
seen and learned a great deal. For our sake, the gentleman had not died in
vain. We had learned so much in so little time about this noble craft of
healing.

Morning Report

"Everybody is ignorant, only on different subjects."
Will Rogers

We had a busy night in the internal medicine service. Our three-person team was on duty: a third-year family practice resident, a first-year resident, and myself, a physician assistant intern. Our 36-hour shift would be without any sleep, as nine seriously ill patients would be admitted to the hospital and numerous other patients would be seen in the emergency room. We would also have one death on a ward during the night.

Morning report and rounds come at 0700 hours even after such an eventful night. This daily gathering of usually ten or twenty doctors is more an ordeal than a report. Duty medical officers come together and present the new admission cases over the last twenty-four hours. After the admitting medical officer makes the presentation of a particular patient, the floor is open for questions concerning the case. It goes without saying that in hospitals, especially teaching hospitals, some senior MDs make certain that a point or question is found which exposes the frontier of the presenter's knowledge.

We study hard, preparing our cases to present so that we do not look like fools. Each admission is different and some, like a diabetic with high blood pressure and kidney failure, can be complicated. Bleary eyed, our turn to present comes and we put forth our best effort. Our well-rested colleagues sit patiently as we speak.

We feel good about our cases and by how well prepared we are. The history, physical examination, special laboratory and x-ray studies are thoroughly covered. We think we have the diagnosis and treatment nailed down tight on each one. But about the time we feel we just might get through this thing unscathed, someone says, "Did you think about…?" or "What about the influence of…?" "Why did you choose…?" or "Have you read the latest article…?"

Finally, the senior doctor delivers the humiliating blow. Having seen through our initial information blitz, he or she has the leisure to carefully probe for a weakness in each of our cases, perhaps something we have yet to learn. Inevitably, gaps are found and the penetrating questions are asked—"What would you do if such and such happened?"

No one on the team will know the answer. Red faces show. The experienced MD is afforded the opportunity to teach us something new to drive a point home. Once again we humbly learn. Eventually we learn the most important lesson of all: you can never know everything.

Surrogate Family

"If you take care of the Army, then the Army will take care of you."
NCO Wisdom

I was pretty scared and excited at the same time. This would be the very first baby I would deliver. The obstetric nurses of Womack Army Hospital helped get the patient all ready to go, for she was fully dilated and the baby was crowning. That baby was coming out, ready or not.

We worked quickly and soon my patient was delivered of a six pound, five ounce baby boy. What a rush it is to help bring a new child into the world! Mom does the bulk of the work, but it is really good to help out.

By now that baby boy is old enough to join the Army. Life for him began pretty tough, though he would not realize it for a while. Though his delivery went well, as the nurse held the baby up for mom to see, the mother said, "Please don't show me the baby. I don't want it."

The unwed mother had chosen not to keep the baby. For whatever reasons, she felt it best that this child find hope in another home other than her own. One can only imagine the pain the mother and that child, now a man, must feel. The cost is immense, hopefully offset in some measure by the special people who help out by adopting these unwanted children. There are a lot of surrogate families in the world.

In a way the Army becomes a family for many people. It is a strange type of family for sure, but there are people who take care of you. And you know what? You even get an "old man."

I once met a soldier and in our discussion I asked him if he had a family. 'Well, sort of, sir," he said, "I don't know who my mom and dad were, but I've got a family now. My family is the Army."

I once heard a joke that went something like this: "Yeah, I tried joining the military once, but they wouldn't accept me when they found out I had parents." Thank goodness the Army does not require people to have parents before they can join up.

Families, any type of family, form the foundation of a strong society. We simply cannot do this thing called life very well without some sort of group to belong to. The Army family is a part of our society's foundation.

The next generation of soldiers are children today. Most of these future soldiers are not born with a silver spoon. The military will indeed become a type of family for many of these Americans. The Army will take care of its own. I have no doubt that the Army family will continue to help give people meaning and purpose for years to come. It is a family that will always "leave the porch light on" in many people's lives.

The Penny

"Pay attention to detail."
Drill Sergeant Wisdom

One of the best physicians I have ever worked with was a gastroenterologist at Womack Army Hospital. While doing my physician assistant internship rotation through his clinic, something occurred that has become one of the most important lessons I've ever learned. It was a lesson that has been reinforced daily thereafter by the military routine of inspections, procedures, checks, and double-checks.

We saw an eight-year old handicapped child who was having repeated coughing, bouts of bronchial infections and the occasional case of pneumonia. After ruling out serious conditions such as cystic fibrosis and asthma, we suspected a tracheal-esophageal fistula, or an abnormal connection between the trachea, the body's air tube to the lungs, and the esophagus, where food is transported from the mouth to the stomach. Further testing confirmed our suspicions and we proceeded to admit the patient to the hospital for corrective surgery involving the insertion of special tubes into the trachea and esophagus, identifying the defect and repairing it surgically.

As hoped, the procedure went well. The child recovered very fast and was discharged from the hospital. The child's cough was gone and the parents were very happy.

As we completed all the paperwork related to the admission, my responsibility was to obtain and review all the laboratory and x-ray studies on this particular case. I had not seen the admission chest x-ray before, but now it sat on the x-ray viewbox in front of me. There, clear as day, was the penny lodged in the esophagus, just below where we made the repair.

A quick check with the gastroenterologist confirmed my fear that we had not removed the penny. A flawless procedure suddenly became a significant embarrassment for us all as we called the child's parents, explained our oversight, and had the child brought back to the hospital.

In no time we went back into the child's esophagus by endoscopy, recovered the errant penny and presented the mother with the change we had forgotten. The mother was grateful and forgiving. We in turn, who are sometimes overly proud and confident, were humbled by it all and very grateful. It was an important lesson for each medical officer on our team. A dose of humility was indicated.

We never stood taller than when we stooped to pick up that penny.

Change

"There is nothing permanent except change."
Heraclitus

A common Army acronym is PCS—Permanent Change of Station. It ought to mean permanently changing stations, for most career soldiers seem to be moving all the time. Sitting in the living room of your home, you are given the day off. There will be no time to relax though, since it is moving day and everything within the house is in chaos. The movers have arrived and the smell of sweat, cardboard and tape is in the air. Boxes are everywhere. The possessions of your life lie all about in organized disarray.

A squad of strangers is busy wrapping, padding, lifting and boxing every movable object in the house. You pray they are careful and trustworthy as they expertly tackle the task of handling every inanimate object you hold dear in life. The packers are quick and efficient, as if driven by some unseen force. Indeed, it is the force of time equals money.

Each household and personal item is packed into a brown box or wrapped in brown paper. Liberal amounts of packing tape hold it all together. A bright number label is affixed to the outside of the box or wrapping and the number corresponds to a master list prepared by the packers of everything you own. The list becomes the sum total of your material life.

The boxes and packets are neatly stacked into huge wooden crates outside on the moving truck. Each large crate could hold a Volkswagen standing on its front bumper. The movers skillfully pack the crates so that every cubic foot of space is used. Their trained eyes can spot that needed box or wrapped piece that completes the packing puzzle inside each crate.

Gradually the house is emptied. The walls are bare and the carpets have only imprints of where furniture once stood. The sounds of your children echo through a house that was a home. The echo of memories is there too, like the distant trumpet call of a rearguard. Only the briefcase remains, standing forlorn in a corner, repeatedly saved from being packed throughout the day. It contains the papers your immediate future will require: orders, passports, checkbook.

In the end, the moving truck holds practically every material possession you ever owned, those keepsakes and the memories. The kids wonder if they will see their toys again. They will in two months or so.

Each move is a chapter in a soldier's life. You either move up or move out. In either case you move. A soldier's world is turned upside down and changed. The change is permanent, but not the station.

Homesick

"Be it ever so humble, there's no place like home."
John Howard Payne

Moving can be difficult for most people. The familiar surroundings of home give way to change and strange places. For my third son Brian, my transfer with the Army to Germany was his first real move and quite a traumatic event at the tender age of twenty months. He was old enough to realize something was happening, but too young to fully understand what moving was all about. He was also not ready to appreciate the location of our family vacation en route to Europe—a stop at Cape Canaveral, Florida.

Despite excited encouragement from his two older brothers, Brian didn't want to see space ships. Space was just another place that wasn't home. He didn't like the hotel or the food either.

As everyone hurriedly got ready for our big, exciting day at the Space Center, Brian came toddling into the hotel bathroom where I stood at the sink shaving. "I don't like it," he said all teary-eyed, "I want to go home."

Glistening tears made their way down each of his red cheeks. He stood there with those sad, deep, brown eyes and a look that said, "Daddy, please make it all better." Putting down my razor, I sat on the toilet seat lid and I lifted him up onto my lap. It was high time to give him some needed sympathy and attention, even with shaving cream still on my face and a full day ahead.

"Brian," I said, "home is where we all are. Home is not a house," I continued, "but your mom, your brothers and me. Right now we don't have a house, but we have each other." He looked incredulous. I went on to describe what moving was all about and that we'd get another house soon. Continued whimpering told me that he still was not totally convinced.

Finally, I resorted to a tactic most fathers are guilty of: the time-tested technique of simple bribery.

"You miss your toys, don't you?" I asked. "Yes, daddy. My cars." He said. "Well," I responded, "we're going to have to get you some more cars then. Today." With that, he brightened up and though still sobbing a bit, another crisis was averted.

Our family laughs about that episode with Brian and the move. And Brian, much older now, blushes and laughs too. The experience taught Brian and the rest of our family that very important lesson: home is not a place; it's the people who occupy it.

But I'll be the first to admit that some toys can help too.

The Best House

"The home of everyone is to him his castle and fortress."
Sir Edward Coke

Our family arrived in Fulda, Germany, on a cold, rainy October day. I was grateful that the Army allowed us concurrent travel, that is, we all could travel to Europe together as a family. Often, the service member has to go on ahead, with his or her family following later after housing is arranged.

Naturally, we were worried about where we would be living for the next three or four years. It is always unsettling to move, even more so when you move to a foreign country. Fortunately, the Army had a fair amount of family housing available in the greater Fulda area, some of it on post and some down in the city, "on the economy" as it was called.

The first housing areas we saw were the "beehives" located right on Down's Barracks, where all the units were based. "Beehives" were three or four-story apartment complexes that provided adequate and convenient housing, but were a bit too small and crowded for our tastes. Not that we thought we had much of a choice in the matter, for often the choices are simply what is available when you arrive.

I was pretty tense as I showed up at the U.S. Army family housing office that first Monday morning. A real friendly lady greeted me and sat me down to fill out the necessary forms. After some small talk, we got to the business at hand. "How many children do you have?" "Three," I said, "and a fourth due in four or five weeks." "Wow!" she exclaimed. "A four-bedroom requirement and your wife is due so soon. Let me see…" My hopes began to rise as she thumbed through index cards in a box on her desk.

She gave me the address of a house "on the economy" and told me to go check it out. With the family in tow, including my very pregnant Irene, we negotiated the local bus system as best we could, since our car had not yet arrived. Soon we were making our way down quaint German residential streets. I could just hear the comments of local Germans as we marched by: "Doesn't anyone ever teach these Americans about birth control?"

But that didn't matter, for we were about to see our big house for the next four years, 3A Geisaer Strasse. My wife took a deep breath, as she was the first to see the modern townhouse. "Dear, are you sure you have the right address?" She asked. "Yes, this is it," I responded.

There before us was a beautiful and large German townhouse on a quiet cul-de-sac street, far from the hustle and bustle of crowds. It even had a garage. It would be the very best government castle we ever lived in.

Seeing is Believing

"I am from Missouri. You have got to show me."
Willard D. Vandiver

Irene and I have four children, an unusual number for an average American family at the close of the 20th century. It is also an unusual number of children for an Army family. My wife could have had six children; she loves them so much. We had four instead, and now Irene makes up the shortfall with even more children in her third grade classroom.

I've always wanted children too, boys or girls, it didn't matter. But any father is tickled to have a son. Irene and I were blessed with three sons in a row. My three sons. Despite the healthy, active boys, though, Irene naturally wanted a girl. "It would be nice," she said, "to have someone I can especially relate to." In my male Neanderthal way, I agreed, and so in due time we conceived our fourth child and hoped for a girl.

The pregnancy progressed splendidly and our visits to the Army hospital included an ultrasound where, just for the asking, we could know for sure if it was a boy or a girl. We chose the suspense of not knowing.

We pored over names. A boy's name was easy, since with three boys already we were so experienced at it by then. Nathan, Marlan, and Brian— the fourth would be Justin. A girl's name was a different matter. We struggled with it. Julie and Lisa were nice names. In the end we decided upon Stephanie.

My wife was seven and a half months pregnant when we made our move back to Germany. We would move together as a family, my lovely wife insisted. Irene would have nothing of staying in the States and having the baby alone—not with three rambunctious boys to look after, too. No sir, dad was not going to get off that easy.

The stress of the move brought Irene's delivery a bit closer than scheduled. Her water broke the morning we were to sign for that lovely German townhouse. I rushed back to the German hospital by taxi after hurriedly signing for our quarters. Meanwhile, Irene fought a delaying action with the contractions. Immediately after my arrival, she delivered.

Without her glasses on, Irene was skeptical when I announced my excited findings, to include the observation that our new girl had red hair, too. "It's another boy, I just know it is," she moaned. I gingerly lifted Stephanie out of the arms of the German midwife and moved to Irene's head. "See," I said while prominently displaying Stephanie's gender to my nearsighted wife, "It's a girl."

Blessed are those who see and believe.

Spit and Shine

"Work is the yeast that raises the dough."
Irish Digest

The official smell of the United States Army should be Kiwi boot polish. Somewhere, in every soldier's day, is an encounter with this stuff, whose odor becomes synonymous with getting ready to go to work. Unlike the smell of coffee, which is a close second as an official Army smell, Kiwi polish finds its way into everyone's day, coffee drinker or not.

Black shoe polish stains on the hands are a basic soldier issue item, especially the more junior in rank you are. Some pay to have their footgear polished, but many forgo such luxury. So most of us spend many hours over the years conforming to this daily group ritual of preparing shiny boots.

Some folks are very devoted to the process of polishing their boots. Elbow grease and spit, along with a good dose of their off-duty time and Kiwi polish, go into making one sharp pair of boots. You can almost see yourself reflected in color from such a shine as theirs.

In my experience, I only wish some of the soldiers' dedication to sharp looking boots would spill over into their dedication to the job at hand, especially dirty jobs. I remember one of my first squad leaders, a Specialist Fifth Class. This man epitomized the image of a sharp soldier. His tight haircut, pressed uniform, military bearing, cardboard-cuffed pant leggings and perfect boots were of the highest standard. He looked good and would have made a good poster boy, but he detested any work that might make him dirty. He avoided it at all costs. He would lead from the front only if it promised to be a clean job.

I guess he wanted to stay sharp looking. In a platoon with work to do and not many hands to do it, it wasn't long before the good sergeant's impeccable uniform and image among the men didn't mean very much. To us he was a loser in a cute package.

The smell of Kiwi still reminds me of that sergeant. A First Sergeant once told me, "A sergeant with fresh, dirty boots is a leader." In a world involving work, and very often dirty work, the first lesson of leadership is to lead by example. Get in there and get dirty.

Wars do not come to us behind a computer terminal in some air-conditioned cubicle. The stuff of war is quite dirty. So also is the getting ready for war part. The aroma of get in there and get dirty with the troops is much stronger and more enduring than Kiwi polish. Nothing smells like a job well done. The shine left by experience and success lasts so much longer too.

God Bless the USA

"Don't spread patriotism too thin."
Theodore Roosevelt

For many soldiers the best re-enlistment pitch the U.S. Army can make is to let them visit home. This was certainly true for me when a trip back home to the mountains of western North Carolina would reinforce the reasons that drew me into the military years ago.

Growing up in the mountains, a young man is given few golden opportunities that beat a path to his front door. Opportunity is something you had to go out and find. No one owed you anything. You had to go out and make that living.

If your family was well off, then you had a better chance. Most of us were not well off. If you were smart and determined to study towards a particular career, then colleges and universities offered a bright future. Again, a goodly number of us were not brilliant and certainly weren't exactly sure of what we wanted to do. Jobs, good paying jobs, were scarce too. Sure, there were construction jobs, some factory jobs, and loads of minimum wage positions, but what kind of future was that? You get to work thirty-plus years and have a foreman constantly over you to boot.

No, the sharp uniforms, the chance to travel, and the intense honor and respect these mountain people had for service members were strong incentives to join up and stay in. Once in the service then, going home was like going to the sidelines in a football game. You're there to rest a while, but you'd better get back out into the game. That's where you belonged and the crowd, those folks back home, would make sure you knew it.

Seeing the stalled, mediocre lives of old schoolmates is another strong plus for a military career. While they jump from job to job and go through the ever-present risk of layoffs, the military gives you ample opportunity for change while doing good jobs. You also have relatively little fear of involuntary lay-offs.

The Smoky Mountains are beautiful. The land is rich in tradition and family. The unique southern accent of the people of the hills sounds oh so familiar after being away for so many years. But the Army became home with the opportunities the uniform afforded. There is a deep pride in serving and there is always good work to be done. Yes sir, that was where I belonged. The old folks back home speak about me "having made good." All this and more were strong medicine that kept me in the service. I believe it is a medicine that will be strong enough to make others willing to stand up and defend this great land tomorrow too.

Spurs

"Allons, Allons, the Pride of Cavalry…"
Regimental Cavalry Song

My first assignment as a medical officer was to the 11th Armored Cavalry Regiment in Fulda, Germany. The four years I would spend with this regiment on the then East/West German border were the best of my Army career. The mission, location, people, and equipment all came together in a truly fantastic Army assignment.

U.S. cavalry units have a unique spirit and ritual very different from other Army units. Much of spunk had its origins in the American Indian Wars of the late 19th century and the introduction of the tank on the battlefields of the 20th century. The advent of infantry fighting vehicles and attack helicopters has made modern cavalry even more formidable.

Highly mobile cavalry units, especially armored cavalry, are the most lethal land forces on the face of the planet. The power, esprit de corps and priority for training dollars attract some of the best officers and men to U.S. cavalry units today. If the Army ever gets into some serious fighting, armored cavalry will likely be there in the thick of it. In land warfare armored cavalry is king.

"If you ain't cavalry, you ain't," so the saying goes. New officers to a cavalry unit learn real fast that you "ain't a real officer" in the cavalry until you earn those coveted cavalry spurs. Even the chaplain and "doc" have to earn them or suffer ridicule and jest.

So, in the dead of night after a regular duty day, I head out on a "spur ride." The goal is to pass nine special stations, hidden all over the countryside—some precariously near the East German border. Each station covered key skills officers in cavalry needed to know, starting with how to read a map and use a compass at night to find the stations.

I learned many new things that night: how to get lost and find myself again, how to determine if a bridge could hold the weight of an Abrams tank, how to set up and use a military radio from scratch, and how to call artillery fire in on a target. These and more were all new and strange tasks to a medical officer.

Just before dawn, this sleepy-eyed physician assistant found and passed the last station. The spurs were mine. It felt good. The only drawback was that a new duty day was dawning and the usual 25-30 patients would be waiting back at the aid station for my services.

There would be no rest for the wicked, but that was okay, because I knew that I was now cavalry. Allons!

Finance

"How's my driving?"
Tractor-Trailer Sign

For the novice driver or for foreigners traveling in North America for the first time, encounters with the large tractor-trailer rigs on the highway can be stressful. The stress is even more intense when the driver of the rig is rude or erratic. Perhaps to cut down on errant truck drivers and prevent accidents, some companies have ingeniously posted on the rear trailer doors a clever sign that says, "How's my driving? Please call 1-800…."

In an era of greater sensitivity, it is becoming more and more difficult to be rude or misbehave and get away with it. Whether it is a concerned citizen with a cell phone, an auditor, or a surveillance camera, somebody is watching you.

Some of my most frustrating moments in the Army have been with finances. After the gold medal for Army Personnel, the silver medal for inflicted anguish in my life goes to the United States Army Finance Department. Whether it was a NPD (no pay due), an erroneous deduction or a prolonged delay in some back pay, it seemed that at any given moment of my career the Army Finance Department was developing my patience.

Once my patience with finance completely ran out. These people promised to pay me and when I showed up for the third time to get paid, they said that I'd have to return the next day. "Fine," I said and then proceeded to vent my frustrations on the shocked Specialist who delivered me the bad news. Essentially, I lost it. I shot the messenger. But I was fed up with the special forms, suspense dates, and particular times when forms would be accepted or money could be picked up. In short, the system was not user-friendly in an especially sensitive area, my pocketbook.

It felt good to get things off my chest as the years of frustration were delivered to the stunned Specialist. I dumped a pretty big load of pent-up grief into her lap. Relieved, I returned to work.

An hour later, a call came in from the Squadron XO. "Doc," he said, "did you give some Specialist over at Finance a hard time?" "Well, sir…" I said and it wasn't long until I was back on the phone apologizing to the finance Specialist. It wasn't her fault. I had been out of hand.

How's my driving? Well, it's better than before, thanks to some constructive assistance from my bosses over the years. As far as U.S. Army Finance is concerned, however, I was frequently frustrated. Their driving record has often left me wanting to know their toll-free number.

Winning and Losing

"Not in the clamor of the crowded street,
Not in the shouts and plaudits of the throng,
But in ourselves, are triumph and defeat."
Henry Wadsworth Longfellow

Sometimes it can't be helped. Try as you might, the deck is already stacked against you. The outcome has already been determined, but circumstances still require that you put forth an effort.

My medical platoon was broken. No standard operating procedures (SOPs), no load plans for vehicles, and no one knew when combat medical drills were done the last time. Leadership abilities of my predecessor had either been nonexistent, apathetic, or didn't focus on these things. I've often wanted to run into those guys who preceded me and ask them what in the world they did with all the time they had.

Despite the lousy state of affairs, the regiment required us to participate in a medical platoon competition, some very high visibility stuff. They wanted to see who was the best. I was certainly prepared to share with those regimental medical training planners which platoon was likely the worst.

With only a few weeks to get ready, we got to work. A couple of dead weight sergeants received new jobs elsewhere and fresh junior leaders were brought in. Slowly, equipment and plans came together. A few days before the exercise, we were finally able to drill and train as a team. Despite being far short of competitive, the platoon was much better than before.

The big day came and our medical platoon did their best. The competition, however, was significantly better. Whether finding locations on a map, talking on the radio or setting up the aid station, we were better than before, but not as good as the other guys.

After a full day of exercises, we lined up at regimental headquarters for the awards ceremony. Seven or eight trophies were given out—our platoon didn't receive even one. Like the grand prize in a cereal box, the message we got was, "sorry, you're not a winner—please try again."

As we began packing up our gear to go home, our squadron commander came over to us. Instead of being disappointed, he was in good spirits. "You men did great," he said. "I know how far you've come and I am very impressed. Next year you'll do better. Keep at it."

The next year did come and the Old Man was right, we did very well. The way I look at it now, we were winners both years in a row, though it was nice the second time around to bring home some trophies.

Convoy Follows

"...let us hasten to retrace our steps and to regain the road alone
which leads to peace, liberty, and safety."
Thomas Jefferson

Being a convoy commander has got to be one of the most difficult
duties in the U.S. Army. Few people volunteer for this thankless task, even
though the concept is fairly straightforward: simply move twenty-five or so
military vehicles loaded with men and materiel from point A to point B.
Those who master this skill are the ones we should pick to lead our armies.

The real proving ground for convoy commanders is in Germany, the
land of the famous *Autobahn*. It is in this unlimited speed playground,
where the famous German *Fahrvergnügen* and finely crafted automobile
technology come face to face with the lumbering, tightly packed nature of
U.S. Army convoys. Here you have the ingredients of disaster with troops
who want to drive like the Germans, and Germans who wish they did.

The textbook convoy discipline so firmly enjoined by the novice
convoy commander in his safety briefing to his drivers always gets severely
tested on the autobahn. Mercedes and BMW sports cars maneuvering for
passing rights soon create large gaps between Army vehicles. A breakdown
or two, always as certain as Murphy's Law, creates further holes in the long
line of Army trucks. Pass through a congested area or roads under
construction, and someone in the convoy will miss a turn and get lost. In no
time, the commander is left with only a handful of vehicles behind him.

When a convoy begins to fragment, the smart leader pulls off the road
and regroups. A little patience pays off handsomely at this point. The
inexperienced or incompetent commander presses on towards the goal, only
exacerbating the problem. In either case, the leader of this military
movement is frazzled and worried, much like a mother hen counting
chickens that were supposed to be following her. These commanders
eventually resign themselves to the fact that not all will make it to the end
destination as part of an intact group.

The fortunate convoy commander doesn't get lost, and his crews
sustain no accidents en route. They know that breakdowns and lost sheep
will eventually make it back to the fold. The Germans breathe a sigh of
relief as the tail vehicle of the convoy exits the autobahn. That would be the
one with "Convoy Ahead" sign on the rear end.

They should rename the stenciled yellow or white "Convoy Follows"
sign that hangs on the front of a convoy commander's vehicle. I believe
every commander and every German would agree it should read, "Trouble
Follows."

Top Guns

"If you can't bite, don't show your teeth."
Old Saying

It is called Tank Table VIII, and the Army always uses Roman numerals for the VIII part. For U.S. Army tankers, Table VIII is an annual ordeal where tank crews demonstrate their expertise to maneuver and fire the Abrams main battle tank. Starting with simple tasks in Table I, four-man crews advance to ever-more-complicated maneuvers and firing situations that culminate in the final test, Tank Table VIII.

The best tank crews, the top guns, score 1000 points on Table VIII. In the 11th Armored Cavalry Regiment, they were referred to as "thousand-point crews." Though the task of scoring this well is difficult, the rewards are often tangible: medals for each crewmember, promotions, days off, bragging rights, and sometimes even some extra cash. Commanders make every effort to give their forty or so tank crews every opportunity and motivation to max their score during tank gunnery exercises.

One commander I had led our squadron with a flare I shall never forget. One of the most unforgettable times I saw him was when I was inspecting one of our unit's ambulance crews manning a Tank Table VIII range at Germany's Grafenwöhr training area. The Colonel was just returning in his command tank from completing the Table VIII gunnery test. Riding high atop his 72-ton beast, he had the look of a triumphant warrior.

The squadron's staff officers near the range tower had set up quite a reception for his return, for the Colonel's tank crew had achieved the coveted "thousand-point score." There was food and cake to be had, courtesy of the squadron cooks. The unit's signal officer had been busy too, erecting an elaborate system of large stereo speakers so that as the Old Man came up the dusty road from the range he could hear triumphant music—the theme song from the movie *Top Gun, Highway to the Danger Zone*.

There was some serious wattage of sound output from four or so loudspeakers as the familiar 1980s tune blasted downrange. I believe people could hear the music for miles around, so well did the SIGO set up the musical tribute to our commander. Every time I hear that song, I am reminded of that great commander, a truly top gun leader. Under his skillful attention and that of other capable commanders who followed him, we were always ready to go down that highway to the danger zone. We never had to draw our guns on our watch during the Cold War, but you can be sure that thanks to commanders like the ones we had, we would have shot straight had the need arisen.

The Punch Bowl

"First the man takes a drink.
Then the drink takes a drink.
Then the drink takes the man."
Edward Rowland Sill

Formal gatherings of cavalry soldiers will frequently include the brewing of a regimental or squadron punch. A large punch bowl is placed in a prominent place in the room. Usually starting with the most junior officer, a sequence of selected officers recite the history of the cavalry unit. Along with the recitation comes the pouring of a select variety of alcoholic beverages into the punchbowl.

For example, while the history of service during the Vietnam War is read aloud, an officer pours a bottle of rice wine into the punchbowl. A service record in Germany would add a fine German wine to the brew, or a stint of unit history fighting Indians out west would call for adding a bottle of whiskey to the concoction. The longer the history, the more varied the brew.

Eventually, ten or twelve different varieties of spirits come together in what is definitely some awfully powerful firewater. Believe me, you can smell this punch from afar.

Some units add a dramatic flare to this much-anticipated event of "brewing the punch." Using a serviceable cavalry saber and elaborate ceremony, an officer lops off the top of each bottle before pouring its contents into the bowl. No need to unscrew the cap or pop the cork. The resulting mix might also include a few glass fragments that settle on the bottom for added flavor.

In the end, some individual, not normally the commander of course, will be the first to taste the mixture. You can hear a pin drop as everyone watches the taster. The facial features of the person sampling this stuff should go on the cover of *Life Magazine*. After a brief recovery period, during which, I have on good authority, their entire insides feel like they're on fire, the taster solemnly pronounces in a strained voice that the potion is fit for human consumption. Sure, whatever you say.

United States Army cavalry units still attract people with a bit of flare, a touch of audacity, and an appreciation for horses and those of the opposite gender. Once you've been in the cavalry, you can never truly leave. It stays with you. Once you taste the powerful spirit of the cavalry, it is a drink that takes hold of you and never lets go.

Dining In

"A host is like a General: it takes a mishap to reveal his genius."
Horace

Our regiment held its annual "dining in" at some very fancy German locations. This particular year it was held in the large banqueting hall of a prominent chateau near the city of Fulda. Opening ceremonies included an honor guard and horse cavalry, all in their finest costume. Brewing of the regimental punch and other preliminaries came next. And then the feast was brought out. The sumptuous five-course repast left everyone feeling like they got their fifteen dollars worth of chow.

Next came the show, an hour and a half of impromptu entertainment for all. Jokes and skits pitted squadron against squadron. In time the grand finale arrived, a "chariot race" competition between the five squadron commanders. The Regimental Commander, like a Roman Procurator, sat in the most prominent spot of the hall as each of the lieutenant colonels entered the arena especially created in the central floor. A track had been laid out, a mock-up in miniature of the major annual tank gunnery exercise the Army has for tank crews, Tank Table VIII. Each commander would ride a tricycle and attempt to hit as many targets as possible in the shortest time packing a fully loaded squirt gun.

I stood next to our Corps Commander, a three-star general, as the race began. He was truly enjoying himself as the grown men, some more grown than others, struggled to move about on their tricycles and "engage" the targets. The task was more difficult because of incoming fire, simulated by officers hiding in the crowd who threw water balloons at the commanders.

Suddenly, one projectile overshot its mark, bounced off my left shoulder and splattered all over the General, dressed in his finest dress-blue uniform, complete with ribbons and medals. His aide, a captain standing on the other side of him, yelled, "The General has been hit!"

The tricycles came to a halt. Silence fell over the room as the roars of laughter abruptly stopped and all eyes focused on the General. Recovering himself, he chuckled and yelled, "I'm not bleeding. On with the games!" With that everyone let out a hearty laugh and returned to the hilarious show, much to the relief, no doubt, of our Regimental Commander.

I've admired many of the Army generals I came to know. They knew how to focus on what was important. Crashing the good times of a party because their finest uniform got wet was not important. Their genius was in knowing that everyone enjoys a laugh, even at their own expense.

113

Tincture of Time

*"The art of medicine consists of amusing the patient
while nature cures the patient."*
Voltaire

"So, what brings you to sick call today?" I asked my twentieth patient of the morning, and it is not yet eight o'clock. "Sir, I have back pain," my young patient replied.

Back pain. The number one workman's compensation claim in the U.S. civilian sector is also a major medical problem in the military. I am convinced low back pain is issued to soldiers during basic training and, like some herpetic condition, is characterized by periodic flare-ups followed by latent phases.

It is extremely difficult to successfully treat most cases of back pain. Our medical arsenal includes many things for back pain, from medications to a neurosurgeon's knife. The trick is to find that treatment or combination of therapies that make the patient healthy and happy. Sometimes the cheapest things will work.

The most interesting back pain case of all time for me had to be a patient I repeatedly saw. It seemed as if nothing worked, but he faithfully kept coming back to see me. Physical therapy, ibuprofen, exercises, work limitations, braces, x-rays, a new mattress: all were in vain. Even an orthopedic evaluation and a chiropractor couldn't help. After using almost every option available, my patient sat before me again. "My back hurts."

He had been on at least five or six different medicines over the last year, none of which seemed to work. Sick call was extremely busy that day, so in order to buy time, I hurriedly gave him a short duty limitation profile and some orange-coated aspirin tablets. I fully expected him to return.

As the days passed, he did not come back. After a couple of weeks, I chanced meeting him in the motor pool. As he saw me, a huge grin filled his face. "Doc, those orange pills worked a miracle. My pain is all gone." Skeptical but happy, I accepted his profuse thanks for "curing" him.

To this day I'm not sure what happened. How could a seventy-five cent bottle of coated aspirin cure something that other more expensive things could not? The answer was probably time, or what we refer to in the medical field as the *tincture of time*. Time for the body itself to do the work of healing. Meanwhile, a satisfied customer thinks I walk on water, and those orange pills a miracle cure.

114

Radio Talk

"Don't talk unless you can improve the silence."
Vermont Proverb

It is during the height of the Cold War in Central Europe. Our armored cavalry squadron is on maneuvers east of Kassel, Germany, with over 250 vehicles scattered over the countryside. To help control them is a complicated network of several hundred vehicle-mounted radios.

In the early morning light, there is a cold drizzle outside, quite typical for winter weather in central Germany. A soft static can be heard from the radio in our vehicle. In the dawning of a new day, the radio gradually comes alive as members of the squadron wake up and check into the net control station—the main field radio base station for the squadron.

"Bengal base this is Bengal four alpha, radio check, over." A different voice quickly responds, "Bengal four alpha, this is base. Roger, out." Along with check-ins come short housekeeping messages on various topics—food and fuel deliveries or finding the location of some meeting.

Talking on military radios is like learning an entirely new language. Personal names are not used. Instead, units use letter or animal names in combination with numbers. For instance, Bengal Six is the squadron commander. Letters and numbers are pronounced differently as well—three is pronounced "tree" and the letter "B" is "bravo."

Soldiers also learn to be very, very brief in their radio transmissions. It is an important lesson, for the enemy can hone in on prolonged radio transmissions and determine your location. Once they know where you are, there's a good chance you'll get shot at.

Traffic picks up on the radio net as the morning progresses. At times, many folks seem to want to talk at the same time. A couple of winded talkers tie down the radio frequency, prompting a rare transmission from the squadron XO, who always seems to be listening in.

"Clear the net. Clear the net," the XO says in that gruff, familiar voice. "This is Bengal five. Break. There is too much chatter on the net. Keep your traffic to a minimum. Out."

The radio goes quiet. The XO's terse rebuke abruptly ends a couple of conversations not yet completed. The welcome quiet is short lived, however, as the silence is interrupted by someone who apparently didn't hear the XO's message. Further XO attention snuffs out this late arrival too.

All is finally quiet on the radio front. Though I need to talk to the chaplain, I'll just drive over and speak with him face to face instead of over the radio. Let's allow the XO some peace and quiet.

Home

"Where thou art, that, is Home."
Emily Dickinson

You've been on maneuver training exercises for two weeks. Crisscrossing the German countryside, there never was a chance to get a shower or a sit-down meal. Day and night you've been living in your HUMMV. Now, the war games are over and you're heading home.

Despite being tired, hungry and smelly, the excitement builds as you near home. She is there waiting for you in the doorway. Boy, does she look good! You, on the other hand, need some work. But to her, it doesn't matter what you look or smell like. She's just awfully glad you're home. She gingerly gives you a kiss on that stubble face to welcome you and then whispers in your ear, "There'll be more later after you've had a shower."

The children are ecstatic to see you and, boy, do they ever have so much to tell you. Politely listening to all of them inevitably talking at once, you manage to pull out a few trinkets from the past two weeks—some chewing gum, an MRE, a chemical light or a small toy. It's Christmas all over again for them, for daddy is home.

Soon thereafter you retreat to a real bathroom. There is serious long-delayed business to take care of here. As the uniform comes off and the hot shower begins, you feel as if it's all a dream. The grime and dust come off. Slowly, the residue of the field training exercise flows down the shower drain. You begin to feel like a human being once again.

The smell of freshly baked bread fills the air. There is a hearty home-made meal of fresh potato soup, cold milk, and delicious cinnamon rolls packed with raisins and nuts. Surrounded by your children, they have tons of stuff to tell you, and eagerly listen to your every word. They almost worship your presence. You forget that some day they will be teenagers and all this will be history.

The day ends with baths and bedtime stories for the kids. With prayers said, they are off to bed. That special person tucks you into bed, too, and crawls in next to you. It has been a long and exciting day. But the excitement of the day is far from over. Now it's your time together.

You're tired, but not too tired.

The day is about as close to heaven as one can possibly get. Home is the real reason you wear the uniform. Never ever forget that. It's good to finally be back home again. The worry and concerns of tomorrow will have to wait because there is no place like home.

Army Trucks

"In the Army there are three classes of travel.
Up front, in the back, and on foot."
David Kay

The canvas rhythmically flapped against the wooden banister behind me. Periodically small puffs of dust would rise up between the canvas and the side of the Army truck seat. More choking dust came in through the ever-present holes or tears in the canvas. With the back flap also down, we had hoped to keep the dust out of the back of the troop cargo area, but our hopes were in vain. The twelve of us, six on each side facing each other in the dimly lit interior, suffered on in silence with only the occasional cough or gasp from the dust. The thought of walking instead of riding did cross my mind.

Up front, "Mario Andretti" was making it a point to explore every pothole in the road. Surely truck drivers know how to avoid bumps and holes in the road. Talk to anyone who has ridden in the back of an Army truck, and they would testify that all Army truck drivers conspire to make every ride as bumpy as possible. Perhaps they have forgotten how hard the wooden troop seats are in back, compared to the driver's cushioned seat with spring shocks up front. With loud curses, some of the soldiers seek to remind the driver of his poor performance, but it usually falls on deaf ears.

Every few minutes we bounced over some hump in the road. In time, our butts got very sore from all this. Shifting in your seat doesn't help much either and sleep is absolutely impossible. You long for the trip to be over, and you realize now why officers and senior NCOs ride up front in the cab or in HUMMVs. Riding in the back of an Army truck is a no-frills experience; essentially a dump truck loaded with human flesh and gear.

I find it interesting that Army recruiting commercials never show what it is like to ride in the back of five-ton truck. Instead, you see cool spots featuring troops jumping from helicopters or exiting armored vehicles. Though it is true you just might get to ride in some of the sleeker stuff, the truth of the matter is most soldiers ride in the back of trucks complete with flapping flaps, dusty dust, stone-hard seats, noisy noise, and bumpy bumps.

Most troops will make the best of any situation. Shared hardships or inconveniences bond people together, the so-called "we've been through this and you haven't" mentality. Riding in the back of Army trucks is one such bonding experience. Indeed, it is a good bet that the reason Army truck drivers have locks on their cab doors is to keep their rattled cargo from inflicting bodily harm at the end of the journey.

117

Maneuver Damage

"The crisis of yesterday is the joke of tomorrow."
Herbert G. Wells

In the summer of 1987 we bade farewell to a truly great cavalry squadron commander. Well loved by his men, the Old Man took care of troops and led from the front.

A farewell dinner in the Army can be a hilarious affair, especially if the commander is well liked and doesn't mind giving his men a chance to poke fun. Our dinner was in a German *Gasthaus,* or hotel-restaurant. Many kind and humorous tributes were given to our remarkable Colonel, but the best remembrance was rendered by our very talented executive officer and was about an occurrence that at the time was deadly serious.

During the winter of 1986-87 our Squadron was involved in war game maneuvers in the then West Germany. We were the "Russians" attacking units brought over from the United States participating in REFORGER (Reinforce Germany). The game was played with relish by our command, creating a fair amount of maneuver damage "attacking" the Americans with our tanks and Bradley fighting vehicles marked with red stars. As was his habit, the Old Man was up front with the main effort riding in his Bradley.

There came a point in the "fight" when the squadron was in hot pursuit of "enemy" units falling back. German traffic was about the only thing that hindered our pressing the attack. The traffic would cause the Old Man to get caught between two train crossing barriers and an on-coming train. Thinking quickly, the Colonel decided upon the option of taking out one of the train crossing barriers rather than fighting the train. His chances with the train, having no live ammunition, were of course, not too good. The driver instantly responded to his command and the U.S. Government bought about $18,000 worth of railroad safety equipment.

The dinner had gone very well. The XO rose to make a toast and to present the squadron's gift. All eyes were focused on the covered plaque in his hand as he eloquently described the heroic actions of our commander that fateful winter day, as half-suppressed snickering and giggling reverberated through the room. In the end, the plaque was unveiled and everyone could see a beautifully carved piece of wood with a model train railroad crossing affixed to it. One of the two road barriers was destroyed and Bradley track marks were painted on the road identifying the perpetrator. Below the toy was an engraved plate that read something like:

For heroism and gallantry while being attacked by a train.

Doomsday Gunners

"Theirs not to make reply.
Theirs not to reason why.
Theirs but to do and die."
Alfred, Lord Tennyson

Eighteen artillerymen in our squadron of 850 soldiers had a very special extra duty. In addition to their normal daily jobs, they carried a responsibility given to only a few, a job that required very sophisticated and careful training. Theirs, in fact, was the most important job in all of Central Europe at the height of the Cold War. Though other units in Europe also had men in this special duty, these men, assigned to the 1st Squadron, 11th Armored Cavalry Regiment, positioned in the middle of the Fulda Gap, would be the ones most likely to begin Armageddon. Their mission, the job, was to handle, deploy, and detonate tactical nuclear weapons.

The allied battle plan in the 70s and 80s clearly reserved the option to use tactical nuclear weapons, had the Soviet-led Warsaw Pact attacked Western Europe. Heavily outnumbered, the Allies counted on superior tactics, air power and equipment to stop the Russians. Plan "B", the insurance plan, would be nuclear weapons should conventional measures fail, as everyone fully expected in a determined Soviet attack.

Nuclear weapons handlers had to be the most emotionally stable, problem-free soldiers you could find. Frequent inspections and drills from the Army and DOD Agencies made sure that only the very best men would be involved in this obviously sensitive work. No history of drug use, no financial problems, no family troubles—each man was thoroughly investigated. Once chosen, they had to continue walking the straight and narrow, with even the slightest misdemeanor being grounds for dismissal.

In the plan of defense, sophisticated though it may have been, no one doubted that Western leaders would have relied on these personnel to stop the Russians. Bottle-up the Soviet massed armored forces in specific areas and then nuke 'em. A chilling thought now, given how easy it would have been to escalate such an option to air, land, and sea launched missiles.

As things turned out, the nuclear business was a good deterrent. Why step across the line into Western Europe when the price was exorbitantly high? No, the Russians would rattle their sabers from time to time, but that was all. The attack against NATO's thin conventional forces never came, in part because of the power a few men could deliver from an artillery piece.

These unsung artillerymen who handled the keys to doomsday number among the best of those who won the Cold War. Never in history was so much prevented by so few.

Flight Suits

"Clothes make the man.
Naked people have little or no influence in society."
Mark Twain

There we all stood, some forty medical officers, all of us attending the U.S. Army's flight surgeon course. The Army was going to teach us how to fly, but first we had to dress for the occasion. For that, the supply folks at Fort Rucker, Alabama gave us our first fire-retardant nylon flight suits.

Like roosters in a barnyard, we strutted around in our new, olive drab green flight suits, the same suits worn by fighter pilots and astronauts. Noticeably absent were our silver wings. We would have to earn those in the coming weeks. For now we would have to settle for crowing, but not flying.

The one-piece flight suits fit very well. Quick to put on and take off, they were also very comfortable to wear. I marveled at the large number of zippered pockets—two on each leg, two in front, and even one on the upper left arm. Missing were rear pockets over each buttock. Strapped into an aircraft seat for long hours would make rear pockets and their contents a pain in the butt I suppose.

Though the nylon suits were comfortable to wear, they were not too complimentary to the rather rotund members of our group. Unlike the blips and bulges that BDUs can mask, the relatively snug fit of a flight suit reveals every body contour, every extra ounce of mother's pie that managed to hang around. I have to admit, though, that the ladies in our group looked especially nice in their flying attire.

Like birds of a feather, we flocked together in our new suits. We envied the pilots and crewmembers that already had the silver aviation wings on their chest. Our chests were devoid of wings. For now, the novelty of our new clothing would have to do.

"It is not only fine feathers that make fine birds."
Aesop's Fables

Aesop was right. Our flying suits were one thing, but the wings were another. We now had to learn to fly. That would take some work, but it would not be too long before we'd get our wings.

With the wings on our new flight suits we were finally no longer naked. We became flight medical officers with some influence in the society of Army aviation.

Hover Button

"Oh! for a horse with wings!"
Shakespeare

Long ago, in a place far away, the Army taught me how to fly. On a sunny autumn Monday morning at Fort Rucker, Alabama an instructor pilot (IP) and I made our way down a neat row of small, orange helicopters at Shell Army Airfield. There were dozens of these TH-55 training helicopters, each looking the same, and all were snugly tied down with ropes and chains.

We began by carefully checking our chosen aircraft out. The IP left no detail untouched. Key components and parts were inspected. Fluid levels checked. Equipment properly stowed. We carefully walked around the helicopter, looking it over. I had little idea what we were looking for, but the IP knew and religiously went over every part of what is known as "pre-flight checks." Nothing is left to chance with flying for you cannot pull over to the side at three thousand feet to check things out should something go wrong.

Soon we were sitting in the aircraft's two seats under the bubble-like canopy of the cockpit. There were dozens of switches, buttons and gauges. The IP began explaining them to me, but soon I would just nod. Information overload had long since kicked in! In time, I would memorize them all. For now I patiently listened to him, who, like all pilots, did things by the book, checklist in hand. Inside I was itching to get that baby cranked up and into the air.

Finally, we put our radio headsets on and my instructor turned the ignition switch. The engine came to life and the rotor blades started to turn. Soon those blades were spinning like the fine hair of a beautiful woman, waving in unison with the wind.

Lesson number one was learning to hover. Three things control helicopter flight: pedals, cyclic, and collective. Mastering these controls takes time, determination, and patience, especially on the part of an IP. If you can't walk, talk, jump and chew gum at the same time, then you probably should not fly a helicopter.

Sooner than I expected, the IP had me on the controls. Flying lessons usually begin in the deep end of the pool, so to speak. The aircraft yawed and swung in an erratic, intoxicated manner as I struggled with the controls. The IP grinned but prevented any mishap through the expert use of his own set of controls. The look on my face betrayed my lack of confidence, for the IP said, "Don't worry kid, you'll find the hover button soon enough."

He was right. I found that imaginary button, though it would take me some time. The metal horse would actually fly, despite a donkey at the controls.

Fear of Water

"Lord, Lord! Me thought what pain it was to drown:
what dreadful noise of water in mine ears!"
Shakespeare

The aviator water training facility at the Jacksonville, Florida, Naval Air Station is the largest indoor swimming pool I have ever seen. It looks different though, with various pieces of training equipment, towers, and divers' gear located all around it. This swimming hole was clearly not built for recreation.

Our group of flight surgeon trainees huddled around the Navy instructors as they explained the various portions of our water survival training. We were all nervous, especially those among us who had a fear of the water, particularly the two poor souls who didn't even know how to swim. I reflected on how thankful I was for those Boy Scout swimming lessons I had years ago in my hometown YMCA pool.

The Navy put us through several skill and confidence-building exercises. We leaped from high towers into the water, learned how to float for extended periods of time, and dealt with trying to swim with boots and flight gear on. Each task upped the ante concerning risk and fear.

The most difficult portion of the training was the dunking machine. This contraption looked like the compartment of a Huey helicopter with all the windows removed. Positioned on a ramp next to the pool, the instructors would strap four of us in it at a time. On the signal from divers watching out for us in the pool, the device was released and we forcefully slid down a ramp into the pool. The compartment then flipped upside down and quickly filled with water, simulating what happens to helicopters in deep water.

Our instructions were to stay put, hold your breath, keep oriented to where the exits were and then release our seatbelts only after the rolling and commotion ended. In a real accident, not staying in our seats, even with the water rising, could lead to bodily harm from turning rotator blades or G-forces flinging us around the inside of the aircraft. It was a terrifying experience, especially when they blindfolded us to simulate a nighttime crash. In addition to blindfolding, the trainers required us to exit from one particular exit of the "doomed" aircraft. The disorientation and tossing about had all of us involuntarily take a drink or two of pool water. Some of us came near to drowning and required the help of a diver.

In the end, we all passed this critical training. Some had to endure the ordeal a few extra times to get it right, but ultimately a feeling of confidence replaced everyone's natural fear of emergencies in the water. It was as close to drowning as I care to go.

Autorotation

"Be nice to people on your way up
because you'll need them on your way down."
Wilson Mizner

The best way to describe initial helicopter training is "pushing the envelope." Day by day the novice aviator sweats behind the controls of the aircraft as the IP provides ever-challenging learning experiences. As soon as the trainee gets comfortable with one flying procedure the IP ratchets up the stress level by introducing something new.

My IP was a competent, capable pilot, seasoned from multiple tours of duty flying Cobra attack helicopters in the Republic of Vietnam. He was also an entertaining individual to fly with. His war stories and humor helped keep my stress level down while going through all the tasks necessary for me to become solo proficient in flying a helicopter.

Hour by hour, day by day, we progressed from one flying skill to another. Practice and coaching began to pay off, and I was beginning to get the hang of this unique way of flying. The point came in my training where the IP was hardly ever on the helicopter controls any more. "You've done well so far, Mr. Kay," he said one morning as we started up the aircraft. "Today," he continued, "is pucker-factor day." I knew immediately what he meant. Today I would learn how to autorotate the aircraft.

The concept of autorotation is pretty straightforward. Losing the driving force of the engine turning the large rotator blades, you trade altitude for rotator blade rpm's. The tricky part comes just before you hit the ground. Timing things just right, you elevate the collective when you are fifty or so feet off the ground, and trade rotor blade rpm's for a braking effect. In theory at least, the impact of the aircraft with the ground is dramatically cushioned if you get it right.

Experienced aviators do an autorotation like its no big deal. For the new guys, it is one of the most terrifying of life's experiences. Suddenly the IP, whose controls override the trainee's, reduces the engine power to almost zero, and you begin falling out of the sky like a rock. The adrenaline flows, and every sphincter in your body tightens. Watching the altitude and the ground, you stabilize the turning of the aircraft by applying pedal pressure. Then you pick that key moment to elevate the collective and add more pedal pressure. Get it right, and you land as soft as a feather. Yeah. Right!

In the inevitable falls of life, I hope I get the landing right. A good landing is one you can walk away from. An even better landing is one in which you can reuse the aircraft of life to fly again.

A Happy Drunk

"Not drunk is he who from the floor
Can rise alone and still drink more.
But drunk is he who prostrate lies
Without the power to drink or rise."
Thomas Love Peacock

One part of our flight surgeon training included a 'ride' in an altitude chamber. Even though the eight of us would physically not move anywhere, the pressure inside the chamber would go up and therefore test our ability to function at extremely high altitudes.

The test was quite simple. We were to sit comfortably facing one another in two rows. As attending technicians in oxygen masks raised the altitude within the small chamber, the oxygen concentration would drop accordingly. Meanwhile, the attendants would observe us, and upon their signal, we were to begin some tests, all without supplemental oxygen.

Some people were given paper and pencil, and were to begin subtracting sevens from one hundred. Others were given a deck of cards, with which they were to play a card game with the person sitting across from them. I was to do simple addition problems. It was really easy addition, so easy I laughed. I mean, come on! Two plus two is four. Three plus seven is ten, and six plus three is ... Six plus three is... I know this, come on Dave, six plus three....

"Are you okay, sir?" the altitude chamber technician asked. I was lying on the floor looking up at the ceiling. Three or four concerned faces looked down at me. I was now breathing through a rubber mask on my face. They had masks on too, and the sound of their voices through the primitive voice transmitters sounded hilarious. I had to laugh.

In a few moments they lifted me back up and sat me on my seat. I noticed everyone else already had masks on, too. We were quite 'high' by then, a simulated 20,000 feet or so, as I recall. The test was already finished and we had begun the slow process of coming back down.

I have never taken a fancy to alcohol. My father left me an orphan at a young age as a result of alcohol in his life. I have often wondered how it would feel, how I would act, if by some chance I became drunk. I asked my partners what I was like during my 'blacked out' time in the chamber. They all assured me I was a riot, laughing and cracking jokes all the time. In short, I was a happy drunk. They began to get worried when I collapsed on the floor and couldn't get up again. Funny, I cannot remember a thing, but I'll take their word for it.

Milk

"Thank you, pretty cow, that made pleasant milk to soak my bread."
Ann Taylor

Milk and I go way back. Breast-fed babies tend to have an abiding fondness for milk, reluctantly adjusting their mammalian preference after weaning to the cold, cow-type right from the refrigerator. Efforts of my father to convert me at a tender age to the benefits of buttermilk failed miserably. My favorite variety of cow juice remains 2% and there is no close second, for 1% is too thin and whole milk is, well, too whole.

I have a theory that soldiers who were breast-fed as babies have a particularly difficult time when the Army sends them to exotic, fresh milk-less locations. Prolonged periods of deployment or field training exercises cause withdrawal symptoms such as depressed mood and blank stares, especially exacerbated by consuming dry desserts. All these things are symptoms of a craving for that familiar, frigid flavor of fresh milk.

Try as they might, researchers have not yet perfected real milk with a long shelf life, capable of surviving the rigors of your typical Army camping trip. In all fairness, they have come close, but, in my humble opinion, their product is nowhere near as good to the palate as the real thing.

The Army buys these small, rectangular shaped long-life milk products for the troops in the field. This "what used to be milk" requires no refrigeration and so therefore it is often served warm. Strike one. The process the manufacturers use to kill off the bugs and preserve the milk leaves it with a funny taste, something you reluctantly grow accustomed to. Strike two. Finally, here you have these mean looking warriors in the field, walking around in full military gear, carrying automatic weapons, sipping from tiny, delicate six-inch straws that come attached to the small, usually baby-blue milk cartons. Come on people, if we're going to use straws in the field they ought to be manly ones! Strike three.

Most soldiers have primarily one thing on their mind when they return from a prolonged period away from the comforts of the modern grocery store. As soon as possible they go looking for that tall, cold one to quench a desire long deprived through absences from civilization.

I waddle into my wife's kitchen, newly arrived at home and still in my field gear. I am careful not to get dirt on anything. Those familiar yellow Tupperware containers on the counter are always stocked with oatmeal or peanut butter cookies. I pillage a couple and they disappear quickly into my mouth. Now comes that supreme moment when desire finds satisfaction as I reach for a tall, cold one from the refrigerator. Yes, I've got milk!

Better Sleeping Through Chemistry

"Sleep 'tis the current coin that purchases all the pleasures of the world
cheap; and the balance that sets the king and the shepherd,
the fool and the wise man even."
Cervantes (*Don Quixote*)

Travel to Europe from North America and you will jump forward in time anywhere from six to nine hours, depending on which time zone you departed from. The time change sets your biological clock in turmoil. Your daily routine of sleeping at a certain time will cause you to be tired during the European daytime and wide-awake late at night and into the wee hours of the morning. This malady is commonly known as "jet lag."

I had never taken sleeping pills before, but this time, a trip back to Europe loomed before me and I didn't want to arrive all tired and useless the first few days back home. The goal was to arrive well rested and ready to go. So, I settled upon the recommended prescription sleep aid *Temazepam*.

My flight was from Atlanta, Georgia to Frankfurt, Germany. Departing Atlanta at seven p.m., I would arrive in Frankfurt at nine a.m. the next day after flying eight hours and losing another six to the earth's normal rotation. The plan was to take the Tamazepam capsule before boarding and hopefully fall asleep quickly, arriving in Germany all rested.

I don't have much personal history of alcohol or drug use. The example of an alcoholic father kept me voluntarily away from the legal stuff, and the drug scene thankfully passed me by. This didn't cross my mind when I dutifully followed the flight surgeon's guidance to take the 30mg capsule just before boarding. Within minutes after popping the pill, I began signing off the air.

I cannot recall getting on the plane. I vaguely remember a tray of airplane food before me as I shifted in my cramped second-class seat somewhere over the Atlantic Ocean. The effects of my first serious elective use of drugs began to wear off as we were on final approach to Frankfurt. I was so drugged during the flight that I didn't even need to bring my seat back forward or replace the tray table before me.

It was a great sleep. I was ready and rarin' to go. The Temazepam rewound my clock and there was no jet lag. But I wonder to this day how I got on that plane. Perhaps the gate personnel had pity on the tardy "drunk" with the boarding pass in the waiting area, the last to heed the boarding call. I only hope I didn't drool on those angels of mercy as they helped me to my seat.

Portraits

"A missing picture is worth a thousand words too."
David Kay

Visit any U.S. Army unit and you are likely to find on some hallway wall a group of framed photographs. Normally you see about ten or twelve in a row, mounted at eye level, each in an 8 x 10 inch individual frame. Pictured are smiling and unsmiling people, some in Army uniforms and others in fine suits. You see a pictorial representation of the military's chain of command. It starts with the most junior officer, normally a captain serving as the current company commander, and ends with the President.

The individuals depicted in these portraits are what we would call a successful group of people. You'd think they'd all be smiling, given the honor, attention, and extra pay they get. But invariably two or three of these characters look like they just might bite your head off, especially those wearing a uniform. Their stern visage suggests that they apparently forgot to take their "kinder, gentler pill" the day of the photo session.

I always marveled at how seldom units could keep their chain of command photos current. You'd look down the row and invariably one photo would be missing. Instead of some sharp individual's image, there frequently was the terse statement, "Photo not available."

One can wonder if the "Photo not available" means there is a break in the chain of command. We comfort ourselves with the thought that someone is filling that spot, and it is merely a photo distribution problem.

But a picture in the frame does not guarantee the leader is available either. Oh, they may have an 'open door' policy in the lower levels, but just try to drop in to visit the President or the Secretary of Defense. They should have a caption below those photos, "Accessible to a select few."

So there it is. The ideal, of course, whether a picture is there or not, is that a leader does make himself or herself available and accessible. My mental image of the best leaders was far superior to any portrait hanging on some wall. They were available and accessible. They listened. They were good blockers of the dung that so often rolls downhill in the military. They were not afraid to make tough choices.

I didn't always agree with the decisions of my leaders, but I always knew that their choices were in everybody's best interest. I especially admired their tendency to take the blame where appropriate. They were also liberal about giving away credit. I do not need a picture to remind me of these All-Americans. Their memory is readily accessible, even if the photo is missing.

127

Perfumed Letters

"Friendship is the great chain of human society and
the intercourse of letters is one of the chiefest links of that chain."
James Howell

One busy morning during sick call the squadron mail clerk paid a visit to the aid station. Slung over his shoulder Santa Claus fashion was a U.S. mailbag. In it were hundreds of letters from people all over the United States, each one addressed to "Any soldier, Iron Curtain, Germany."

I cannot recall if it was *Dear Abby* or *Ann Landers* who started it all, but the gist of this deluge of mail towards lonely soldiers far from home one Christmas season was an appeal from one of these syndicated columnists to her readers. She discussed the important work U.S. cavalry soldiers were doing along the Iron Curtain and thought it would be a nice gesture to write those soldiers and thank them for the important work they were doing on "the frontier of freedom." Her appeal resulted in tens of thousands of letters; many from ladies back home, all sent to some of the loneliest soldiers in the world (if my medics were any indication).

The platoon sergeant divided up the contents of the bag. There were a couple of small packages too. The packets received instant communal attention, as they contained cookies and candy that quickly disappeared in a small feeding frenzy. Next came the letters, several of which were noted by the sergeant as possessing an attractive perfume. He saw to it that the single medics received these.

My stack of letters contained one from a veteran of World War II, thanking me for the great work we continued to do. Another had a crayon drawing from a second grader also praising our duty along the border between East and West Germany. There was one amorous letter from a college girl that I promptly handed off to the nearest single medic. I could just see Irene getting hold of that one. The remaining letters were mostly from elderly ladies all over the country, praising our patriotic duty.

One of the medics who landed a perfumed letter took up a lively correspondence with a rather attractive lady from the Northeast. Two lonely people had found each other in a most unorthodox fashion. The newfound pen pal relationship flourished and six or so months later I understand they were married when he returned to the United States.

There is something about perfume that mesmerizes a man. Not too much, but just enough to grab and hold his attention. Those letters, with or without perfume, did just that. What a great country to serve whose people would think of bringing happiness to their soldiers.

Frontiers

"I know nothing except the fact of my ignorance."
Socrates

The medical profession is constantly changing. New research and treatments force everyone in this occupational field to learn something new practically everyday. Stop learning and soon you'll end up high and dry on the beach of ignorance.

It is both refreshing and rewarding to teach eager, young soldiers medical information they have never seen before. No need to unlearn anything. Everything is brand new to them.

There is a neat device out there which lends itself well to on-the-spot learning. I like to call this device a "brain box." Based on one I had seen in Germany, I had my father-in-law build one for me.

The brain box consists of a small, rectangular box that stands upright or can be mounted on a wall. The front facing of the box has slots into which three by five index cards fit. Beside each card slot are four buttons, one for each potential answer to a multiple-choice question. A green light is placed in the upper left corner of the box's front, a red light on the upper right side, and an electronic buzzer midway between the two lights. Inside the box are various moveable wires that connect everything together so that, when a soldier presses a button to answer a question written on an index card, either a red or green light comes on. A red light also triggers the buzzer, indicating an incorrect answer. The whole system is powered from a small, six-volt battery inside the box.

To entertain and educate my medics, I installed the brain box just outside my office door where I saw patients. Every few days a new set of four multiple-choice questions on medical subjects would be mounted on the box. As soon as the new questions were up, my medics would queue up to test how much they did or didn't know. I was always impressed by their eagerness to learn.

Over time an unwritten, peer-enforced custom developed among the corpsmen. If the red light and buzzer went off, then that medic was obliged to do ten push-ups. The patients in my office would marvel when, outside my door, they would hear a buzzer go off, often followed by a cuss word. Then, without any prompting or ridicule, the sound of straining and counting could be heard as the medic did the requisite push-ups. Some of my medics did push-ups more often than others.

What better way to push back the frontier of ignorance than with push-ups? Hooaah!

Stars and Bars

"Two men look out through the same bars:
one sees the mud, and one the stars."
Frederick Langbridge

For sickness of the body or the spirit, soldiers go on sick call. A young soldier sat before me with a chief complaint of having a cold. My medics would normally take care of soldiers with a simple cold, but this soldier's medic asked me to have a look at him, for he didn't seem quite right. Something was amiss.

The soldier's eardrums were normal and his sinuses were non-tender. The throat was clear, the neck supple, and there was no nasal congestion or drainage. The heart and lung examinations were also unremarkable. In short, he was quite healthy. He didn't even have a cold.

"Are you sure something else is not bothering you?" I queried. He shifted in his seat and then big tears began to well up in his eyes. "Sir, I can't stand the Army. It's the pressure. I can't take it. I want out," he said, the tears now freely flowing down the sides of his face.

My patient had only been in the Army nine months. After basic and AIT, he was posted to Germany, his first time away from home. He was eighteen years old and a good soldier, but Army life was fast becoming a trap for him, with its daily dose of control and regimentation. It was only a matter of time before he would run off. Go AWOL.

A phone call to the chaplain and the First Sergeant set my patient up to get some help. Try as they might, there was no helping him stay in the Army. He wanted to be free and every day in a uniform was only making it worse. After a few weeks, he was back to see me for a chapter physical exam. The Army would be sending him home for good.

What is it about people where some can thrive in a regimented world and others go crazy? There are those who feel secure in an environment where rules and schedules manage every moment of their lives. But others find heartache and a crushing of the spirit at the same time.

Two men join the same Army: one sees oppression, and the other opportunity. Would that we could know the difference before they joined. I suppose we will never be able to tell the difference ahead of time. These matters of the heart are so difficult to understand.

One thing is for certain: in the Army you will see bars, mud, and stars.

Tellin' Stories

"A lie is something that can handle the present but has no future."
Anonymous

I would often get into some sort of mischief back home as a boy. Though nothing of a criminal nature, it certainly was enough to warrant the notice of my dear mother. She'd confront me about the deed—a missing piece of cake, not being where I was supposed to be, or a fresh rip in that new pair of pants. I'd hem and haw and often tell a lie to avoid her wrath.

My mother could smell a lie about as easy as you can smell a skunk roadkill on the highway. She'd point her finger at me, and in that uniquely feminine version of the North Carolina mountain dialect, she'd say, "Now David, don't you go tellin' me any stories."

This tendency to speak less than the truth and to need corrective attention from authority continued into my grade-school years. Whether it was pulling pins from hallway bulletin boards, blessing the class with my fledgling attempts at some cuss word, or talking when I was supposed to be quiet, each sin was met with a spanking, washing my mouth out with soapy water, or writing five hundred sentences: "I will not talk in class." I would, of course, try to maintain my innocence throughout any interrogation by lying wherever appropriate. But my lying seldom worked out in my favor.

Along about the ninth grade or so, something began to click inside. Maybe the remedial training took effect. I began to realize that trying to fib my way out of things might not be the best course of action. Cussing, telling lies, and otherwise being some sort of nuisance just didn't pay—too much hassle. Maybe it was a hormonal thing, this sudden conversion in my behavior. If they can ever figure this one out, then they should add it to our water, especially the Army's water.

That's right, the Army has a fair number of mischief-makers and liars. Nothing really felonious, mind you, just enough to be a nuisance. I soon discovered that I had become the mom, the teacher, or the principal in confronting the minor misdeeds of my subordinates. Instead of spanking or washing their mouths out with soap, I would train with counseling statements, extra-duty details, or Article 15s. They'd stand at parade rest before me, caught red-handed in some misdeed. Avoiding eye contact when their turn to speak came, they'd come up with some incredible story to cover their tracks. All of their effort was no more than a smoke screen made from burning the truth. Remembering my mother, I'd say in a masculine version of the North Carolina mountain dialect, "Now soldier, don't you go tellin' me any stories."

131

Hip Pocket Lessons

"Knowledge is of two kinds: We know a subject ourselves, or we know
where we can find information about it."
NCO Wisdom

In the Army they call it "hip pocket training." I first heard this catchy
phrase as a young soldier during the U.S. Army buildup in the early Reagan
years. As more money for training was made available, generals would push
their particular training agendas. One was the idea that all leaders should be
prepared to teach anytime, anywhere, in any manner, and on short notice.
The class could be on anything: how to put on a gas mask, search a prisoner,
stop the bleeding—the lesson plan drawn from memory or pocket notes.

There are PhD types out there, the ones who seldom stand before a
class anymore, who will tell you that a really good lesson plan needs this,
that, and the other. Maybe. But for leaders who do not hold sophisticated
teaching credentials and have not spent the time to get those degrees to hang
on their walls, you have to make do with the next-best thing, especially since
there are not enough professors to go around in the Army.

Army sick call provides plenty of opportunity for hip-pocket training,
much to the discomfort of soldiers on sick call. Maybe it is an unusual rash,
some strange physical defect, or a seldom seen illness. Whatever the
condition, chances are I'd get the soldier's permission to show it to all my
medics working sick call. Five or six medics would gather around and see
some on-the-spot training, something they had never seen before.

Oh, it is nice to have a full-service research library and the services of
the Internet. But I'm here to tell you that these things will often not be
available. Teaching cannot always be in front of a comfortably seated class
in a climate-controlled environment with all the books and sexy audiovisual
gadgetry at your fingertips. No, more often than not, teaching in the Army
will occur out in the boonies somewhere. It may be cold or hot, noisy or
quiet, dry or wet, light or dark, and you may even get shot at.

Your classroom is often the great out-of-doors, where the class is
comprised of people whose very lives depend on the applicability of your
lessons. A quick lesson on mines and minefields, for example, takes on new
meaning when these devils in the dirt are a very real threat to you, such as in
places like Bosnia, Cambodia, or the Sinai desert.

On-the-spot training is a good thing, especially when given in very
applicable circumstances. Such training could keep you out of hot water or
save your rear end (including hip pocket) from an untimely death. I can
think of no stronger incentive to learn or to teach.

The Ice Cream God

"Whoever obeys the gods, to him they particularly listen."
Homer

In the ancient world, gods were beings viewed by men as deciding their fate. Good or bad, man's destiny was tied to the choices and input these gods had in their lives. Most modern people do not believe in the gods of the ancient Greeks and Romans anymore. Other gods have entered our lives. There are, however, people and organizations that, if we are not careful, can assume roles in our world not far removed from divine worship.

Take for example a world full of rank and status, like the military. The pomp and prestige of high rank can almost assume demigod status, complete with worshipers and sacrificial offerings. Nothing illustrates this worship business more than to spend some time walking around with a high-ranking Army general. Here is a human being, not too dissimilar from other mortals, who never wants for attention and acclaim. Just follow a general as he or she enters a troop area for an inspection. All present assume the position of attention, the legitimate military posture to render respect. Key subordinate leaders quickly come forward and after shallow pleasantries, escort the general through the area, often prepared specially for his arrival, the so-called "dog and pony show." The whole ceremony is not far removed from religious pageantry.

Salutes and short questions punctuate the visit of the "gods" to the modern soldier. There might be a speech, a sermon to the faithful who especially pray it will be a short one. Perhaps some individual is singled out for attention, "Where are you from, soldier?" Or perhaps, "Are they feeding you well here?" Under the watchful eye of his immediate leaders, you can be assured that answers to the general's questions will be politically correct.

Once, a senior general officer visited Observation Post Alpha, a border post along the Iron Curtain near the German hamlet of Rasdorf. The general asked a private if the Army could do anything to make life better there. "Ice cream, sir. We don't have ice cream."

The divine visitation ended and the general was whisked off in his special helicopter along with his entourage. The very next day, as soldiers returned for supper after their daily patrols along the Iron Curtain, the "gods" had answered their prayers: a state-of-the-art soft ice cream machine was up and running.

The gods sometimes listen to mere mortals. For years modern American soldiers at OP Alpha would sing the praises of one in particular.

133

Small Town

"A town is a place where you are known
by your first name and last scandal."
Anonymous

I never could put a finger on this fondness I have for the smaller posts. It probably goes hand in hand with a personal desire to stay away from large cities. Oh, the big places are nice to visit, but let me hang my hat in a small town or small military installation. Life seems a bit simpler there.

Smaller posts have fewer problems and less competition. They are easier to figure out when you first arrive too, not so many days wasted just trying to find your way around. You grow closer to people. You can see the results of your contributions to society much more easily in a small place and it seems you can get to know everybody faster too.

Now getting to know people better in small places can have its downside. People will know everything about you in short order. It's difficult to hide anything, especially if you have rascal propensities. Whether it's a speeding ticket, a problem child, or some other dirty laundry, chances are word will get out, and before you know it, everyone knows it.

As a small Army community medical officer, I thoroughly enjoyed taking care of people. Like a small-town family doctor, I made a difference in people's lives, especially when posted overseas where you are about all the "Doc" they have. People come to depend on you and go out of their way to say "Hi," or otherwise be friendly in a world often cold and indifferent.

Sometimes this small-town stuff can be embarrassing. There was the guy who asked me about his chances for a vasectomy in a crowded post office, or the grateful lady in the Cub Scout meeting who praised me for curing her urinary tract infection.

But the real prize for embarrassment goes to the lady who saw me going through the commissary checkout line. She said in a strong voice, "Hey, Doc Kay! How are you today?" "Fine," I responded, "How are you?" "Okay," then, feeling at ease with herself she asked, "Did you get the results of my last Pap smear in yet?"

Pausing, I glanced around and sure enough, five or six ladies also in line, some of whom saw me for their exams as well, immediately honed in on what "Doc" was about to say. "Yes," I nearly whispered, "come by and see me at the office tomorrow."

Yep, nothing beats the openness of a small town. It is here that Doc is known by name and last office visit.

Leaks

" 'Tis healthy to be sick sometimes."
Henry David Thoreau

We were proud of the work we had accomplished that day. Our fourteen vehicles were clean from all the scrubbing and attention we had given them. The preventive maintenance checks were done and all the necessary forms completed. The vehicles stood side by side, looking sharp in the squadron motor pool. The commander would be proud.

A phone call came through to me from the squadron sergeant major, "Sir," he said, "where are your vehicle drip pans?" The drip pans? Of course, despite our best efforts we had forgotten to place the drip pans, those little metal oil and fuel catchers placed on the pavement under the engines.

Despite all the work you do on Army vehicles, they almost always seem to leak. A leak is probably standard issue, especially for tactical vehicles. If a new vehicle does not have a leak, then we issue it a driver and some challenging terrain and the leak will develop. Leaks are so common that the Army mandates the drip pans for environmental protection and also as something to gig people for.

There are three types of leaks in the Army: seepage that does not drip, ground stains with no visible dripping, and the classic drip that is dripping. Good preventive maintenance is supposed to stop all leaks, but the rigors of Army life necessitate allowing a small amount of leakage—hence drip pans.

Sometimes people leak too. The wear and tear of our day to day military experiences make leaks a personal standard Army issue too from time to time. Irritability, being down, low productivity, trouble at home or work are examples of personal leaks. Some personal problems seep, others are dripping. Preventive personal maintenance can help stop the leaks. Rest, a listening ear, or fixing a pay or personnel problem are ways to stop the leaks from destroying our personal engines.

Drip pans are okay, but they do not take away the problem. At some point every vehicle and every soldier will break down or need maintenance. They need more attention than a drip pan offers. Too often we focus on the drip pan and not the problem.

Successful organizations and leaders have preventive maintenance for people as well as equipment. Everyone has problems. There is a leak somewhere. Like vehicles, you may not be able to get rid of every concern or problem, especially with normal wear and tear. You fix what you can and get them help from higher up. Until then, a drip pan will have to do.

Hummer Hum Dinger

"The power of a man is his present means
to obtain some future apparent good."
Thomas Hobbes

In 1987 our unit received the first HUMMVs to replace our aging
fleet of jeeps. Much wider and larger than our beloved jeeps, it took the
troops a while to get accustomed to the new vehicles. But it didn't take
long to appreciate the power and mobility of the HUMMV. This puppy
could go places that you wouldn't dare go in a jeep!

The maintenance officer for our squadron was in charge of the
distribution of our seventy-two new "Hummers." Late one afternoon, he
dropped by my aid station there in the Grafenwöhr training area. "Doc," he
said, "have you been in the new Hummer yet?" "No," I replied, "but I'm
sure looking forward to it." "Good, let's go try one out!" He said.

And so we were off in my initial orientation to this wide-bodied
marvel of the American automotive industry. The seats were relatively
small and the seat belts snug as I got settled and began to survey the
interior. The new paint smell and olive drab green color greeted me. All
new Army vehicles seem to have every nick and cranny painted.

The takeoff was smooth as the 230-horse power engine kicked up, the
automatic transmission shifting smoothly as we gained speed. The traction
tires hummed against the pavement and the new diesel engine purred like a
kitten. There was that thrill of a great machine as we careened down the
road, pushing the vehicle's power to show how marvelous the new toy was.

"Now," he said over the engine's noise, "let me show you what she
really can do." For the next half-hour, we crossed terrain, inclines and bush
you would never try with a jeep. The grand finale was "getting stuck." We
literally plowed into a deep mud puddle, so deep that mud was oozing in
through the edges of our canvas doors at waist height. Honest.

"We're stuck now," I said. He chuckled, "Watch this." Skillfully
using the power of the transmission and the engine, he gently rocked the
vehicle back and forth and on the third or fourth attempt, we slowly began
moving forward over the mud. In no time we were back out on the road.

Every now and again the government does some smart purchasing.
Though we loved our jeeps, the new HUMMV with its power and ample
interior space was a huge hit. For cavalry soldiers long accustomed to
sleeping next to their iron horses, we could easily get there and even have a
roomier sleep inside these hum dingers. What could be better than that?

The Business Card

"We make war that we may live in peace."
Aristotle

Business cards are important little pieces of paper, especially when you need some of the vital information contained on them. Generally there is a name, address, and phone number. There may also be other information such as a fax number or an e-mail address. For anyone taking care of business, it is a good idea to carry business cards.

You might find it strange if I told you I once belonged to an Army unit that had a business card. Why would a U.S. Army cavalry squadron want a business card? Well, in the big business of defending Western Europe from communist aggression during the Cold War, having the squadron business card went hand in hand with the flare and audacity so characteristic of cavalry outfits.

Upon the calling card of the First Squadron, Eleventh Armored Cavalry Regiment was a tiny outline of a map of West Germany. Along the top of the card was this quotation, "Lo, I beheld a pale rider astride a black horse, and the rider's name was Death."

A giant pointing finger indicated a spot near our maneuver area on the map of Germany, accompanied by the large words, "YOU DIED HERE." Then, "Reforger '88" indicated the training exercise during which the recipient "died." Along the bottom of the card was the note, "Compliments of First Squadron, 11th ACR, IRONHORSE!" Finally, to give the business card even more authenticity, in the bottom right-hand corner of the card was the red ink stamp depicting the head of a roaring grizzly bear, the trademark of our squadron commander.

We were the bad guys during that REFORGER exercise back in 1988. We handed out a lot of cards to units we overran and "destroyed." You can imagine the looks on our opponent's faces as the umpires declared a "kill" and some cocky cavalry troopers dropped by to present the losers with their "calling card."

The war games would eventually end. Sometimes we won and sometimes we'd grudgingly allow the other guys to win. All would say it was "good training." Our tactics, techniques, and procedures would get looked at again, improvements made and through it all, we would be better prepared to keep the peace in Europe.

I have carried many business cards over the years. None of them, however, topped the battlefield calling cards of the Blackhorse!

The Selection List

"For many are called, but few are chosen."
Matthew 22:14

Every year in the United States Army hundreds of boards convene. From selecting who will be in the next class at West Point to who will wear the next stars as a general officer, people anxiously await the results of these various selection boards, commonly published as "lists."

Getting on a list is generally a good thing, and it is a great feeling. Of the many looked at, you are chosen. I remember receiving a phone call from a staff sergeant on duty in Kuwait, anxious to know the results of a newly released PA school selection board. Out of hundreds of applicants considered, was she on that final list? I could sense the tension on the phone line as, halfway around the world, I sat at my computer terminal to pull up the board results.

"Staff Sergeant Schaaf," I paused deliberately, "It looks like you're going to PA school next April." Ten thousand miles away, I could hear the scream of joy over the phone. "Thank you sir! Thank you!" she said, as if I had anything to do with it. What a warm feeling it brings when you get to pass good news on.

There is the other duty, which falls to people who have to pass on bad news about selection results. Take, for example, officers who are not selected for promotion. The day prior to the release of a promotion list, commanders around the Army seek out the non-select officers to give them the bad news—something the Army requires to be done before official officer promotion lists are released. This is a somber time when you will see grown men cry.

There is much weeping and gnashing of teeth when the Army fails to put you on the list for advanced schools too. Nearly everyone will taste this disappointment at some time in their careers; a time when you feel left behind, overlooked, or as they say in the Army, "passed over."

But it doesn't do us any good to linger on the thought of being passed over. You cope. You regroup. "There is always next year, coach."

Like all human organizations, the Army is a pyramid. Only a few will get to the very top. Somewhere along the way some finally fail to make the cutoff, miss that "magical timing," or get left behind with the group that was "also-considered." That's life. What is important is that in the end let it be said of us that though a few were indeed chosen, we always did our very best. That is a list everyone can be on.

Six

"The charismatic leader gains and maintains authority
solely by providing his strength in life."
Max Weber

It is strange that the Army's field radio system call sign for
commanders is associated with the number six. Every commander on the
radio is known by the number six. But "Raider Six" or "Blackjack Six" just
does not sound as powerful as "Raider One" or "Blackjack One." Reason
dictates that the top of the pile should be the number one. I'm sure there was
a reason six was chosen, but just the same, numero uno sounds better.

One is known as the loneliest number. Not in the Army. Six is the
loneliest number and anyone who has commanded anything understands
this. Many factors make this a somewhat forlorn job. One of the most
significant factors is, unlike their CEO counterparts in the civilian sector, the
time may come when military commanders have to send people to an almost
certain death. Though CEOs are powerful too, they get sued or go to jail if
they hurt or kill people.

Much to the consternation of my wife, I have always enjoyed war
movies. Irene prefers non-violent drama. I, on the other hand, favor war
films like *Private York* or *Kelly's Heroes.* I have appreciated Hollywood's
efforts to portray the Army, even if it is often inaccurate. One Hollywood
exception may be *Saving Private Ryan*, produced by Steven Spielberg.
Combat veterans of World War II say the film came very close to portraying
the uniqueness of combat command. I agree, though I have never seen the
elephant. For once, Hollywood superbly portrayed the emotion and pressure
commanders feel, especially regarding those life and death decisions they
face in combat. Indeed, these decisions are probably the most difficult part
of military command. It has to be done. Maybe if one dies we can save ten.
But sometimes ten have to die to save one.

There are other things about command that make it a lonely job. At
times you have to be the judge and jury. Sometimes people have to be yelled
out, corrected, or otherwise "motivated," especially when lives are at stake.
Unlike movie stars, you are not necessarily going to win a popularity
contest, especially when you make a mistake, which, by the way, comes
with the turf. All commanders make mistakes.

One is not the loneliest number. Six is. On the playing field of the
military, watch out for number six. The Old Man always seems to be
listening in on the radio and seems to know everything. The commander has
the leading role, even if it ain't the movies.

A Little Night Music

"Without music life would be a mistake."
Friedrich Nietzsche

The lights are out and you settle into a good night's rest. It's been a long, hard day, but you feel good about how much you've accomplished. The body and spirit are tired but content. You have earned your pay. The sweet caress of slumber comes over you as every muscle in your body relaxes. You slowly fade away into a blissful sleep.

Nearby, in the darkness, the rude breathing noises of a fellow soldier pull you back into reality. The rhythmic respirations are punctuated by clearly audible sounds, further amplified by the general quiet of the room. You notice two other snoring soldiers sleeping nearby in the open bay-type barracks. Like the croaking of bullfrogs with frogs stuck in their throats, the trio of fellow soldiers, already deep in their own sweet slumber, now have you wide-awake. The nocturnal concert begins and you reluctantly have a front row seat.

You marvel at the varied noises. Yes, there's a tenor, a bass and a baritone. The regular, almost inhuman sounds are periodically interrupted by pauses, some quite long. You wonder if you should render first aid, fearing they have forgotten to breathe. But fears of respiratory arrest end when the irritating guttural noises begin again, as strong as ever.

In time, the god of rest mercifully causes some members of the trio to shift in their sleep and the serenade becomes a duet or a solo, albeit for only a short while. The absence of other snoring members intensifies the remaining performance and the concert goes on unabated.

But enough is enough. After what seems like an eternity, you finally sit up in bed, wondering what strategy to employ that will guarantee the return of your hard-earned repose. A pillow over the head is too uncomfortable, for you must breathe, too. Though the urge is strong, throwing things at the performers would be too rude. Maybe I should intubate them? No, better not. Further patience is pointless, too, since the concert shows no sign of ending.

In the end, you resort to those blessed foam earplugs. Though uncomfortable at first, these simple marvels of modern industry block out nearly the entire audible world, to include the unwanted serenade. With earplugs in place, it isn't long before you finally slip off into that world where upwards to a third of our lives is spent.

Later, as rumor from other concert attendees would have it, the trio became a quartet.

A Monkish Brew

"It is a kindness to lead the sober; a duty to lead the drunk."
W.S. Landor

In the U.S. Army a formal party without dates is called a "dining in." These are almost always interesting affairs, especially with cavalry units. Everyone dresses up in their finest dress blue uniforms with all their awards and decorations prominently displayed on their tunics. Cavalry units have the added flare of Stetson hats, cavalry spurs, and a good dose of rowdiness.

There is a monastery near Wildflecken, Germany that is renowned for the beer brewed there by an illustrious group of monks. Devoted to the cause of religion, they augment their dedication to the cloth by sharing their brew for a fee. I am not a drinker, but I have it from many diverse sources that this beer is about the best you'll ever find. It is also very potent stuff, not like the watered down beers of other lands. Certainly, the dedication of my squadron to this brand was helped by the close proximity of the monastery. It was only a matter of time before our unit would gather there, complete with liberal offerings from this fine Catholic establishment.

U.S. cavalry units work and train hard. They do the same when it comes to having a party. Espirit de corps is very high. Mix this tendency with German beer and the fun begins, at least for a time.

The Old Man was in a good mood that evening. The rising stars of regimental headquarters were either leaving him alone or his "Old Man" must have given him some good news. In either case, the Colonel was having a good time. Funny jokes and skits organized by the squadron executive officer were the best. The food was delicious and the beer flowed freely. Finally, without any doubt, our squadron commander was drunk.

By necessity, the "doc" is always close to the commander, just like the executive officer and the Sergeant Major. The only problem that evening was that like their commander, the XO and Sergeant Major were similarly drunk. In that Little Big Horn of the drinking world, I was one of the last left standing—at least without a stagger in my gait. It was therefore my self-appointed duty to see to it that the Old Man, the XO and the Sergeant Major got home.

From the perspective of some fellow cavalrymen, I was definitely a few drinks behind. But for that I was able to keep three important drunks ahead, faithfully seeing them home where their lovely spouses knowingly sent them off to bed. All, including a teetotaler, had a good time. I will long remember the time, the men, and the events. I took care of those temporary rascals, as I knew they would always take care of me.

Paris

"Liberty, equality, fraternity."
Benjamin Franklin

When I was a platoon leader in Germany, there were several medics in the platoon who were what we call barrack's rats. Basically good soldiers, they refused to get out and see the world, content to just hang around the barracks every weekend or holiday. It was a shame to let them miss the dozens of European travel opportunities all around them.

Over time I was determined to give them a chance to expand their horizons. Talking with the platoon sergeant, we hit on the idea of taking them to Paris, an eight-hour drive away. To our surprise, most of the seven or so barrack's rats greeted the suggestion with enthusiasm, glad for the chance to get away with buddies instead of in some impersonal tour group.

Borrowing an old Volkswagen van, nine of us loaded up and were off to Paris one Memorial Day weekend. Nine Americans in Paris. It was my fourth trip to one of the world's most famous cities. For everyone else it was their first trip. The sights, sounds, smells and tastes were all new and exciting for them. Things I had seen and done before came alive again, my soldiers' enthusiasm being contagious.

We eventually found a reasonably priced hotel near the Eiffel Tower and not too far from the Champs Élysées. For the next three days, my troops saw the sights, sampled the food, tasted the wine, took in some shows and no doubt the women too, though I have no firm confirmation of the latter. There certainly were a number of amorous types on the street interested in the sons of the GIs who liberated this great city from the grasp of a Nazi dark age.

All in all, my medics had a blast. On our way back to Germany, the tales of their adventures entertained us all for hours. Each had a unique and memorable time. Every story, every experience was followed by another and another. Getting lost, seeing famous places, discovering French toilets, trying to speak French, haggling over prices, sampling the expensive food, or chasing beautiful women filled the hours of driving back to our unit.

Of all the cultural experiences each had seen, one common thread, or should I say paper, united them all. Though they enjoyed the trip, they looked forward to getting back to good old American toilet paper. My barrack's rats especially missed the soft kind stocked in ample quantity in Army latrines.

For them France would forever remain the land of great wine, food, interesting people, and terrible toilet paper.

Bottom Line Up Front

"A prostitute is someone who is footloose and fanny free."
Anonymous

The wonder and marvels of Paris lay before us. We had three days to see and do as much as we could. My group of eight medics and I made our way down narrow avenues near the Eiffel Tower looking for a hotel, before tackling all the sights. One had to walk carefully, maneuvering around the typically over-parked cars up on the sidewalk and the somewhat frequent piles of canine fertilizer left by local four-legged French friends.

Suddenly our small group halted. One of our more dedicated smokers had smoked his last and could we possibly stop to replenish his supply? "No problem," I said, and we headed into the nearest, typical looking Parisian hotel to see if cigarettes could be found. It wasn't a first-class hotel, but this wasn't an upscale part of town either.

Rather than linger outside while my nicotine addict medic found solace in French tobacco, we all seemed interested to follow him inside. Maybe we all wanted to escape the street noise or just stick together, after all it was easy to get lost. But probably we were just curious.

It was indeed a hotel of sorts. The rather plain exterior hid an exquisite interior fully laid out in the finest French styles. Thick, red Persian carpets covered the floor. Lavish draperies and fine lace adorned each window. As my sight adjusted to the dimly lit room, I could make out beautiful chandeliers and elaborate wallpaper adorning the walls. Around the lobby were fancy, velvet-cushioned love seats and couches. Upon these sat six or eight rather scantily clad ladies in high heels.

The ladies immediately stood as we entered and proceeded to make their way towards our group. We stood there in surprised shock as the near-naked ladies approached us. Their amorous intentions were immediately made known to us by their visual, verbal, and non-verbal gestures.

Nine Americans in Paris had walked themselves right into a brothel. Ooh la la, what to do? Clearly, some of my single soldiers thought we had stumbled upon El Dorado. Maybe so, but we had other things to do and some of us, though tempted to appreciate the beauty of these French ladies of the evening, remembered our spouses back home.

We bid a hasty, rather nervous adieu to the lingerie ladies. The need for cigarettes was forgotten. I assembled my troops outside to continue the mission to get a hotel before dark. I have no doubt that some of my men noted the grid coordinates of this establishment and later came back for a reconnaissance in force of those bottoms lined up front.

143

The Great Leveler

"Disease generally begins that equality which death completes."
Samuel Johnson

A profession that will never want for work is the medical field, especially in the military. Regardless of what Army units are doing, there is always someone who is sick or injured. Given time and opportunity, everyone will eventually need medical services, from the newest private to the highest general. Military medical personnel care for even the President of the United States and his family.

By far one of the best jobs in the Army is to be a battalion or squadron medical officer. Looking after a group of 500-800 officers and men provides plenty of opportunity to conserve the fighting strength, especially at six o'clock in the morning when sick call lines up outside the office door.

Volumes can be written about military sick call. Each morning in the early dawn light, all over the Army, thousands of soldiers make their way to treatment posts, aid stations, and troop medical clinics to be triaged, treated, turned back to duty or "turfed" to a specialist at a supporting hospital. You see all kinds: those who are sick, those who think they are sick, those who want to be sick, those you wish were sick, and those who are not sick at all. Somehow, the doctors, PAs and medics get them processed and cared for appropriately. They work hard and fast, doing the best for each soldier, but from time to time, they get sick too.

Healthcare providers must have strong immune systems. Bugs lurk everywhere everyday. Healthcare facilities are where these bugs can concentrate. You are splattered, touched, coughed and sneezed upon. You put your hands in awful places and confront some very memorable, unpleasant smells. If one sticks with the job, it is only a matter of time before a bug sticks you.

Illness is part of being human. So is healing. Taking care of the sick, regardless of rank, is incredibly rewarding work. That is why most of these healthcare folk get back at it every day even though they know that it is only a matter of time before some bacteria or virus gets through their defenses. Their war on disease will never know peace, only temporary cease-fires.

Woody Allen once said, "I don't want to achieve immortality through my work. I want to achieve it through not dying." Right. I wish it could be so. Most of us will have to settle with achieving immortality through those we touch with healing hands and the faith we carry in our hearts, for all will eventually succumb to the great levelers, disease and injury.

Executioner

"We live in deeds, not years;
in thoughts, not breaths,
in feelings, not figures on a dial."
Gamaliel Bailey

It began as any other squadron staff meeting. All the company commanders, the Sergeant Major, and all the staff officers were seated around the large oak table. They were a good group of leaders, educated, proactive and resourceful. They led the best unit in the Army' Fifth Corps.

The commander arrived and we all rose to our feet. Normally a likeable commander, we were shocked as he crisply snapped, "Take your seats." A sudden chill came across the room as his stern words betrayed anger and frustration.

The Old Man was obviously not happy with a meeting he'd had with his boss, the Regimental Commander. The chewing out he received there now was rolling downhill. Stuff rolls downhill in the Army. Our commander now was to vent his frustration upon his surprised and unprepared officers.

First came the lecture for all to hear. Our performance and readiness had slipped. We were no longer the best. He then proceeded down one side of the staff table and, by name, singled out each officer present, identifying some defect, some shortcoming the officer was responsible for.

Like awaiting our execution, we sat paralyzed as the attention of our commander shifted from officer to officer around the table. People shifted in their seats. A cool sweat broke out on every brow. I nervously tapped my fingers on the book in my lap.

The chaplain and I were at the end of the table. As the Old Man's eye came to us, imagine our relief when he said, "Doc, I'll spare you and the chaplain for now, but I may think of something later."

That was as close to a public execution as I ever came. It was more like a stay of execution. But no need to celebrate our good fortune. Instead of boasting about how the Old Man had spared us, the chaplain and I redoubled our efforts in doing our best in helping our fellow staff officers to succeed as well. They were the best the Army had. We were a team.

The Old Man was upset, but he got over it. He apologized at the start of our next meeting. But the message was received; all the more so because he was rarely mad about anything. He was right though, we were too proud, resting on our laurels. His rebuke shocked us into realizing that there was room for improvement. We needed to find ourselves further along tomorrow than where we were today.

Caring People

"No one is useless in this world who lightens the burdens of another."
Charles Dickens

Mike Pankratz was the best Medical Service Corps officer with whom I ever worked. A nurse by training but an administrator at heart, Mike passed up a career in nursing to follow paths in leadership. That path brought him to the 11th Armored Cavalry Regiment in Fulda, Germany— one of the best places on earth to learn how to lead.

As unit medical officer I was glad to have Mike come on board. Taking care of the medical needs of 850 men plus a medical platoon was a bit too much for one officer. It was a great relief to have Mike take over the day-to-day management of the forty-two man medical platoon and fourteen vehicles.

In the two years I worked with Mike I never saw him in a down mood. He always seemed positive about work, the mission, and life in general. He made it a point as a leader to be noticeably upbeat about the people who worked for him too.

Mike would get to know every soldier in the platoon and find out something that motivated him. He would then use this information to influence and help them. You could tell Mike got a kick out of making people happy with the things he'd go out of his way to do.

Our squadron spent a great deal of time each year away from home station—maneuvers, border patrol, and tank gunnery kept us on the road five or six months out of each year. It was hard on the families we left behind each time we rolled out of Down's Barracks on some great Army adventure, and the separations wore on the soldiers as well.

To be honest, I missed my family terribly from time to time. A beautiful, young wife and several children can keep a guy distracted, always wondering if they were okay. I would try to keep up a good front, but Mike would see through it. He latched onto my love for Ritter Sport chocolate bars as a way to keep "Doc" happy. Sure enough, during some blue spell, I would find a subtly deposited Ritter Sport candy bar on my field desk, cot, or my HUMMV seat. Mike had struck again.

The message was always crystal clear: you are not alone and you'll be all right. Mike's actions on behalf of me and the other men in our platoon to keep morale up was one of the finest lessons on leadership I ever learned. It is because of Americans like him that we won the Cold War.

146

Burgers

"You are what you eat."
Anonymous

The food group I can earliest remember as a child is the cheeseburger. A trip to a burger joint when I was about three or four years old imprinted me at a tender age that manna came with cheese on it and from places with golden arches out front. Ever since then, my favorite American food remains the cheeseburger, despite the negative cardiovascular publicity it receives and the bit of body fat it brings.

All cheeseburgers are good. It is incredibly difficult to botch the preparation of this delightful sandwich. However, when it comes to excellent cheeseburgers there are some truly great ones to be had. The famous *Coffee Burger* in Caldwell, Nebraska or a *Fuddrucker's* burger are right up there near the top. But the all time best cheeseburger I've ever had was the "Kenny Burger," a self-styled name for a culinary delight prepared by one of the best U.S. Army medics who ever worked for me.

Sergeant Kenny Molbert was from Louisiana. A Southerner from Creole country, Sergeant Molbert knew how to make one heck of a hamburger. It didn't matter where we were on maneuvers, he was always prepared to pull out a small grill and charcoal from his HUMMV, add some fresh Army beef and his secret formula, and we were in business.

Sergeant Molbert carefully prepared each Cajun-style burger to be truly phenomenal. His recipe was a protected secret, carefully hidden in his mind. We knew the patties had salt, pepper and Tabasco sauce added, but he also had an unmarked spice bottle in his pocket, the so-called "secret recipe."

Try as we might, we could never pry the unwritten recipe out of Sergeant Molbert. When asked for the code, he would respond in that fine Andy Griffith southern drawl, "Naw, can't do that." We had to content ourselves with the momentary enjoyment of his preparations that marvelously transformed Army chow.

Years later, I still remember those Kenny burgers. They were an important quality of life issue while stationed in Germany and on maneuvers. I often wonder where Sergeant Molbert is now. I hope he has opened a restaurant, maybe down in Louisiana somewhere. Burger franchises should hunt this guy down and add his secret to their menus.

They say the way to a soldier's heart is through his stomach. Maybe so. One thing I do know, the Kenny Burger was the very best Army food that ever became a part of me.

Spies

"Two roads diverged in a wood and I—I took the one less traveled by,
and that has made all the difference."
Robert Frost

A large map with its multicolored plastic overlay dominated one side of the large field tent. The squadron's fifty-five officers were seated in front of it as our commander briefed us on the coming "fight."

To the west of our location lay the city of Dortmund, Germany and several key bridges across the Rhine River. To the east were "Warsaw Pact" forces, played by a brigade of tanks from the 3rd Armored Division, reinforced by a battalion of Canadian Leopard II tanks. Our squadron's screening and delaying mission would be against a force over five times our size. We had twenty-four hours to prepare.

As each officer briefed the commander on their piece of the fight, I noted from the map that we were basically defending three main roads, each in a long valley, through which the opposing force had to come. A German village lay along the main road at the far end of each valley near the enemy.

I leaned over to the squadron executive officer. "Sir," I said, "Let me take some men and hide them in those villages. They could use a local German phone and call the Old Man on his mobile phone every time the bad guys come up any one of the three valleys." "Doc," he said, "brilliant idea!"

Within a couple of hours I was off down each valley, hoping enemy reconnaissance forces didn't stop us. Six cavalrymen were in my HUMMV. Diplomatically using my very best German, I negotiated with local German families living on each main road. We carefully arranged for the soldiers to spend the next week as "spies" in their homes. A baker, a banker, and a lingerie shopkeeper were all excited to be a part of our operation against the "Russians." Everything went off without a hitch.

The war games began and the reports started coming in. Knowing in advance which valley the enemy's main effort was in, our commander was able to concentrate forces and stop the enemy cold. They would try again in another valley and there we were in force waiting for them. It was a turkey shoot and the "bad" guys did not have a clue about what was happening.

After the war games ended, the three German families, one on each road, received our squadron's coin and handsomely framed certificates of appreciation for their "patriotic" service. In addition, one of the six cavalrymen would eventually marry the baker's daughter!

Three roads diverged in Germany. We knew which one was most traveled by and that made all the difference.

Traffic Cop

"Seek responsibility and take responsibility for your actions."
Army Leadership Principle

As I reflect on the event years later, my heart still races. For me it was an exciting moment, a chance to be part of a real reenactment like the traffic jam scene portrayed in the movie *Patton*.

Our maneuver training exercises over the German countryside had ended. Scattered over a thirty-square kilometer area were hundreds of squadron vehicles—tanks, trucks, Bradley fighting vehicles and HUMMVs. The order went out over the radio net for all units to converge at selected rail depots for loading or convoy movement back to our home station in Fulda.

With my driver at the wheel of our HUMMV, we began to make our way to the rendezvous point. The warm spring afternoon and clear blue sky were a welcome sight as we drove through the picturesque German countryside. Before long, we began negotiating the narrow streets of a small town. Arriving at the town center from a side street, we met a huge traffic jam where four main roads converged.

What we encountered was a serious traffic problem caused by our tanks and trucks combined with increased German traffic at the end of the workday. Backed up on each road were dozens of military and civilian vehicles. A cluster of Germans and soldiers were trying to communicate at the crossroads where one of our tanks was involved in a small accident. The German *Politzei* or U.S. Army military police had not arrived yet. As each minute passed, the traffic continued to back up each road.

Impulsively, I stepped out of my HUMMV and walked up to the cluster of soldiers and Germans. One of the tank sergeants recognized me and asked for help. Speaking with the unfortunate owner of an Opel that dared tangle with an Abrams tank, I asked him in German to move the car out of the way. Step by step we began to restore some control to the situation and before too long I stood in the city center directing traffic.

Until the police arrived about fifteen minutes later, I had a great time. A small crowd of Germans had gathered to watch the show. Having never directed traffic before, I had to learn quickly. This one small man was directing this huge flow of trucks and tanks. Troops passing by would recognize me and yell, "Hey Doc, you a cop now?"

Eventually the Politzei and the MPs arrived and I was relieved of my newfound duty. It was fun while it lasted. For a moment I played George Patton, the star of the traffic jam.

Fire of the Army

"Fire is the best of servants; but what a master."
Thomas Carlyle

It was the middle of a bitter cold German winter and we were on maneuvers once again, or being "in the field" as most soldiers call it. The ground was frozen, the wind howled like some charging barbarian horde, and the blown snow pelted the sides of our burlap tent. Inside that tent was our squadron aid station. The rectangular ten-by-twenty foot tent was attached to the rear of an M577 medical command tracked vehicle. The "spacious" interior accommodated our medical equipment, personal gear of five people, and enough room to treat two patients at a time.

Despite the inhospitable circumstances outside, we lived with almost all the comforts of home. We had electricity, courtesy of our generator, lots of food, albeit Army field rations, unfrozen water from five-gallon cans, and beds made from litters and sleeping bags. Most importantly, we had heat.

I have developed a deep respect and admiration for the resourceful sergeants the Army has given me. The gold medal for resourcefulness in my book goes to Staff Sergeant Dean.

I do not know from where he procured the Canadian Yukon stove. I learned long before not to ask my resourceful NCOs too many questions. As its name would indicate, the little rectangular stove was designed for survival in the cold reaches of a Canadian winter. Somewhere, amongst all those NCO connections, SSG Dean once again demonstrated his keen eye for acquiring things of strategic importance. He was expert at maintaining this precious little metal box, measuring no more than one by two feet. At o-dark thirty he'd be up and stoking that wondrous invention up to the point that it glowed like a small Bessemer furnace. We would awake to the smell of coffee and so much warmth that we would break into a sweat.

The awesome warmth of our cozy little haven was so efficient that a one-foot gap would form around the ground edge of our tent where the radiant heat had melted the snow and ice. Needless to say, our aid station was a magnet to other cold souls in our unit with less resourceful NCOs. They would find some reason to visit and linger around, but we always knew why they stayed. Our heat was the envy of the squadron.

Whenever I enter a warm area from the cold I am reminded of SSG Dean and that Yukon stove. The resourcefulness of the non-commissioned officer is the fire that drives the United States Army. They are the masters of making good things happen. Their energy is what drives back the cold of winter, inactivity, indifference, or officer ignorance.

The Code

"Be Prepared."
Boy Scout Motto

For medical personnel nothing gets the adrenaline flowing faster than hearing the words, "We have a code. Someone is down." Wherever medical folks are, no matter what they are doing, everything is dropped and attention is focused on responding quickly to the scene of the emergency with the right equipment in hand. All the preparation, equipment and training of medical personnel are put to a life and death test, often in front of a crowd of onlookers.

Emergencies will occur in everyone's life. Some are minor. Others are major. When the big life or death emergency occurs though, lay people turn to the medical system for help. Being prepared for the times when emergencies occur is the name of the game for healthcare personnel.

To get ready, doctors, PAs, nurses and paramedics take some pretty tough courses. One of the most challenging is the Acute Cardiac Life Support (ACLS) course. This three-day experience trains providers in how to handle heart attacks and strokes. Going beyond what many people are taught in Basic Cardiac Life Support (or CPR), ACLS students have to learn many things. Some of these include how to read electrocardiographs, how to use a defibrillator to shock the heart, how to put breathing tubes into a victim's lungs and how to choose, dose and administer over twenty-five different medications for over a dozen conditions.

ACLS is not unlike a medical version of an Army gunnery exercise. The training is tough. The drills, always in front of fellow students and staff, are sometimes grueling and humbling. The end product, if you pass, is someone who knows what to do in an emergency and someone confident enough of their abilities to take charge.

There is no greater calling than to save life. The emergencies I've attended to in the Army were always scary, but also very rewarding. From stabilizing a German lady who slammed into one of our tanks on a highway to resuscitating a soldier who collapsed of a heart attack on a battalion run, I've put the training to the test.

On a moment's notice, you are plunged into an unforeseen emergency and the drill, the training, and the preparation pay off. As the patient, now stabilized as a result of your efforts, is sent off for more specialized care at a hospital, you are left exhausted but content. You made a difference and did your best. The high from that beats anything.

Prayer

"Prayer is a sermon to our own selves."
Emil G. Hirsch

"Let me take this moment to welcome everyone to our farewell dinner," our commander said. "Since the chaplain is not here, Doc, I was wondering if you might offer our prayer?" All eyes looked toward me. "Certainly, sir." I said nervously, "It would be an honor."

It was indeed an honor and a humbling experience to be asked to pray for such an outstanding group of officers. These men, who led the First Squadron, 11th Cavalry Regiment back in 1988, were among the best in the U.S. Army. It was sobering that they would pick me out from their number for the privilege of talking to God for the whole group.

I cannot recall what I prayed that evening, it all happened so suddenly. Words were probably offered to express our gratitude for the food, the fellowship, the fun, and for the great leadership we were blessed with, as well as the very important border guard mission for which we were responsible. I do recall thanking God for such a fine group of officers to work with, literally the cream of the crop.

The U.S. Army has several ways to grow officers: West Point, the Citadel, Virginia Military Institute, and the Reserve Officer Training Corps program in various universities and colleges. Our squadron had representatives from all these fine schools. There were also officers who had risen up from the ranks through the Officer Candidate School at Fort Benning, Georgia.

But the way to grow great officers, regardless of where they went to school, is to assign them to units with a serious, meaningful mission—a mission like that which the 11th Armored Cavalry Regiment had in central Europe during the 1980s. Such opportunities take the raw material of schools and produce leaders, many who would later become general officers: men like Starry, Kern, White, and Abrams.

Which brings me back to the prayer. Here I was barely an officer for two years, and a warrant officer at that. Only visited West Point, tried unsuccessfully to go to the Citadel, drove by VMI once, and ROTC was not offered at the college I attended. No, I was in the midst of working my way up through the ranks, taking the long road and still four years away from a real commission.

A man's rank did not matter to the Old Man. Ability was what counted. Not only did I belong with these commissioned officers, but these hard charging, rugged modern cavalry officers wanted me to pray for them too. I did and always will.

Kinderfreundlich

"Children have more need of models than of critics."
Joubert

While we were stationed in Germany my family seldom ate out. There were several reasons for this: expense, finicky eaters, and time. But the main reason was that we had four small children. Germany is a country that at the time we were there generally frowned upon having many children. One or two are okay, but four was a social concern. Even the German's have a saying that in public places they are not *Kinderfreundlich*. They just don't take children, and especially small children, out to eat in restaurants.

Despite this general background I want to say that the best restaurant my family ever ate at was in Germany. The irony has never been lost on Irene and I. There we were on vacation in Berchtesgarden, Germany, truly a "must see" place for any trip to Europe. The U.S. military has a couple of recreation services facilities there, including the General Walker Hotel, an old Nazi-era facility taken over by Americans after the war. Today it boasts a great sleep with a wonderful view and a superb restaurant.

Hunger hit us all one day and we were tired of sandwiches and fast food. With our four small children in tow we visited the General Walker Hotel restaurant for a sit-down meal. As we settled into our seats we immediately felt at home. The waitress was very friendly and there were no stares or subtle finger pointing from other patrons. The guests were mostly fellow American service members, some with their own children present. There were also a couple of *Kinderfreundlich* Americans, acknowledging with smiles Irene's great work of keeping us all on our best behavior.

All went well until the thunderstorm burst. In the mountains a storm rolls in rapidly. Flashes of lightning and sheets of pouring rain quickly knocked out the electricity and there we sat, in semidarkness late in the day, waiting for our food. The noise and commotion outside was too much for our kids. Nathan shifted in his seat, staying up on every detail. Marlan's head turned like Inspector Gadget as he counted the number of chandeliers on the ceiling. Brian played with a small bowl of olives on the table, entertaining himself by putting olives on the end of each finger. Stephanie, our youngest at eighteen months, looked to us for reassurance from her child seat, grinning and giggling when she saw that mom and dad were not afraid.

The power eventually came back on. The food arrived and we had a great time. People may say many negative things about Americans, but one thing is certain: we are *Kinderfreundlich*. On that count we are as a nation all above average.

Stars

"There is a smaller world which is the stage,
and that larger stage which is the world."
Isaac Goldberg

The city of Nijmegen, Holland hosts an annual road marching festival. For walking enthusiasts, it is as near to Nirvana as you can get. Nijmegen's main event involves four days of hiking over a different twenty-five mile route each day. Such an opportunity does not escape the attention of the commanders of NATO forces.

The United States Army Europe, or USAEUR, is heavily represented at this event, often with hundreds of troops drawn from units all over the continent. Divided into individual teams of fifteen or so soldiers, they compete for the best time with no loss of team members against teams from the armies of Holland, Germany, Britain, Norway, Italy and other countries.

Due to the size of U.S. forces participating, American medical support there is substantial. My job in the summer of 1988 was to run the base camp treatment areas. Located just across from the main beer tent, we set up two large tents, one for trauma and another for treating foot blisters. With a staff of gung-ho medics and lots of supplies, we were ready to work.

Road marching is hard on the feet with blisters being the most common problem. Normally, the best treatment is to stay off the feet and allow them to heal. Nijmegen, however, is a four-day event and marchers have to get back out on the road the next day. Based on past experience, we used a special plaster of cotton web roll and tincture of benzoin to cover and pad the blisters. Our secret weapon got soldiers back into the march.

On the first evening when the marchers came in for treatment, I saw him out of the corner of my eye. He looked familiar, but I couldn't place him initially. Followed by a camera and light crewmen it dawned on me, it was the news anchor guy from the Armed Forces Network (AFN). He was looking for a story and the commander sent him my way.

We were quite busy that first day. There were lots of patients. For the next few moments the news crew interviewed my busy medics and filmed what we were doing. Our trade secret to keep men marching would be a secret no longer. Though we never did get to see the TV film clip, when we returned to our home stations we were greeted by those who had.

My four young children saw me on TV too. Stars were in their eyes as they greeted their daddy/movie star. To them what daddy did in the field was obviously very important for it to be on TV. I marveled then, and still do, at the power of TV. The world is indeed a very large stage.

Beer and Blood

"There are bonds of all sorts in this world of ours,
fetters of friendship and ties of flowers…but there's never a bond,
old friend, like this, we have drunken from the same canteen."
Charles Graham Halpine

The odor of beer on someone's breath will forever remind me of the Nijmegen road marches. After hard marching each day, NATO soldiers would party each evening in specially erected beer tents. These canvas saloons boasted beers from all over Europe and America. Here both thirst and muscles could find temporary relief.

Among all the NATO troops at Nijmegen that year, the American and British soldiers had a particularly intense rivalry. This competitive spirit would come to a head in the evenings where the soldiers of these two great nations would demonstrate to all other allied soldiers how much booze they could hold. After a few beers, it wasn't long until a war of words began over politics or personal strength. The creative and not-so-creative insults would follow with darn Yank this and bloody Limy that.

One particular evening, the verbal skirmishing over political issues led to blows. Fists at first, then twelve-ounce cans of lager became opportunistic mortar rounds as these two great peoples, divided by a common brew, began bombing each other. Before long, blood was let and the heretofore-passive MPs took a more serious interest in the progressing international political squabble.

I was duty medical officer that evening when two of the "wounded" were brought to me for care by the MPs. Each arrived in a very intoxicated state, with minor lacerations and bruised egos. The former I could easily repair and the latter would be forgotten as the alcohol cleared their systems.

It was a struggle to gain the cooperation of the patients in allowing me to put them back together again. Things improved after segregating the combatants (one American and one British), and I duly went to work stitching together a cut cheek, an eyebrow and a couple of scalp wounds.

By the time the sewing jobs were done, my charges had mellowed to the point of peaceful coexistence, exchanging apologies and handshakes, allies once again. The MPs escorted the now singing, arm in arm, drunken soldiers off into the night. Their temporary strife chalked up as good training.

Blood and beer, what a strange combination, these timeless potions of mankind! It is the stuff of war and peace, politics and punching, at least among English speaking allies.

Surprise

"Your true pilot cares nothing about anything on earth but the river
and his pride in his occupation surpasses the pride of kings."
Mark Twain

It was a routine, uneventful air transfer of a patient to the U.S. Army
hospital in Nuremberg, Germany. A soldier had possibly broken his pelvis
from a fall off an Abrams tank. I rejoined the MEDEVAC helicopter crew
for the trip back to Grafenwöhr. I felt a little tired, so I settled back into my
crew seat, all snug and secure in the harness. The warm summer breeze
through the open sidedoors of the aircraft and the monotone chatter of the
crew over my headset soon lulled me into a power nap.

It wasn't too long before I abruptly awoke to the sharp turning and
maneuvering of the helicopter. At first I had to recall where I was. Then as I
became oriented, a fleeting worry crossed my mind: Is there something
amiss with the aircraft? We were flying quite low and fast, maybe 75 or 100
feet off the ground. The pilots were doing nap-of-the-earth (NOE) training,
that is, they were flying at tree and land contour level to maximize a
helicopter's ability to hide and move at the same time. For the uninitiated,
riding so low and fast can be scary.

I began to listen in on the pilots talking back and forth in the cockpit
up front. "Roger, I hear what you're saying," one of them stated. "Now up
here is a very interesting place. Yes, just along the left shore of this small
lake coming up. Pay close attention out the left side of the aircraft," the pilot
in command directed.

Everyone on board began to shift and look out of the left-hand side.
With the doors wide open, the crew chief, flight medic and I had a
panoramic view of the German countryside and forest passing quickly by.
You could see everything. There are few things more thrilling than hanging
at a 35 or 40-degree angle near an open helicopter door. Straps hold you
firmly in place and the warm wind is in your face. You enjoy a sense of
freedom and power few experience.

"There," the senior pilot exclaimed. "Bingo," the co-pilot joined in.
Flying in fast and at a low-level, we came in air-assault-style, swooping in
over a German nudist colony. Several dozen men, women, and children, all
in their birthday suits, starred up into the sky as we crashed their back to
nature party. They seemed momentarily startled, but some smiled and waved
at us and we waved back.

"Cool," the crew chief said. "Nice view," commented the flight
medic. "Yes, gentlemen," the senior pilot added with a sigh, "it is a tough
job, but somebody has to do it."

156

Expensive Lessons

"There are defeats more triumphant than victories."
Montaigne

The early morning fog obscured the German countryside at the Hohenfels training area. I sat inside a Leopard I German tank, Hauptmann (Captain) Jähnecke next to me. His company of tanks lay in wait for my units' tanks to attack him. He would be outnumbered four to one when the war game commenced.

The Germans, part of our Bundeswehr sister battalion, had joined our squadron for maneuver training exercises. The intent of the cross training was to learn how to do things better. The Germans were about to give the Americans a good lesson.

Setting up their defensive positions during the night, the Germans efficiently camouflaged each tank. They then carefully placed sheets of plastic about two meters to the front of every tank. Finally, they kept their engines off and were on complete radio silence. Like hunters waiting for the kill, their Teutonic forebears would have been proud.

It was the Army's battle of Kasserine Pass all over again. The tip of the spear of the Army's V Corps, my unit's tanks came noisily up the valley. The loud whir of the turbines and the clank of tracks came ever closer and closer. The Germans waited. My heart raced. More and more of our tanks kept coming. "Why don't they see the Germans?" I thought.

Suddenly, the Hauptmann radioed, *"Alle Einheiten, Feuer!"* Like claps of thunder and lightning, each Leopard tank spat noise and fire in rapid succession. The simulated blasts from the German tank gun barrels sent laser flashes down range instead of real tank rounds. One by one each American tank came to a halt as their laser tag system registered direct hits and the engines were disabled. Within moments, the skirmish was over. The Germans: 8. The Americans: 0. As my American buddies scrambled to make sense out of the mess they'd walked into, the German's cranked up their engines and pulled back into new positions, ready to strike again.

Later the key to the German victory was revealed to all. Our American tendency to depend only on thermal sights when in foggy situations was overcome by a ploy the Germans discovered—defeat a multi-million dollar system by hiding behind a ninety-nine cent sheet of plastic. The plastic had made the German tanks invisible for heat signature detection. The Americans would not fail that lesson again, especially not when something so cheap can become so expensive.

Working with the Best

"Do your best."
Cub Scout Motto

My only command of a company-sized element was in Fulda, Germany. The community needed a Cubmaster for its struggling pack of Cub Scouts. With two Cub Scout-aged boys at home, my wife asked me if I would be interested in leading out. At first hesitant, the idea sounded like a good one after some reflection and I consented.

For the next two years it seemed like every boy in the Fulda military community wanted to be a Cub Scout. Certainly not triggered by my charisma, the phenomenal growth from fifteen to ninety-two boys was caused by many factors. I think the most important was a strong group of ten super den leaders who were the greatest moms and dads a kid could ask for. They were simply the best.

From meetings, events, promotions and activities, I discovered many principles in Scouting remarkably similar to the Army. People are happy and work harder if they are kept busy and know they'll get promoted. If you're not on time, you miss out on some pretty important stuff. A successful organization takes many people, not just one or two. It is important to belong to something bigger than yourself.

During my tenure with Pack 166, we took the boys on many field trips. One was to a medieval castle in Coburg, Germany. We had a photo taken there with nearly the whole pack together—about a hundred people. Over the years it has become a very treasured photo and a reminder of great times working with great people.

Years later, while stationed at Fort Hood, Texas, I met one of the former den leaders while I sat in a dental chair under the drill of a dentist. She worked at the dental clinic as a dental hygienist. Unable to talk, I listened as she enthusiastically recounted those times with the Cub Scouts, times, she assured me, which had had a profound impact on the lives of so many future men. The gleam in her eyes and her expression of gratitude to me touched my heart and for the first time I realized those boys were now indeed men.

The tears in my eyes were not from the dentist's drill.

The road of life takes many turns. Sometimes we take the wrong path or paths that lead nowhere. Sometimes though, the turn is a good one. The day you say yes to leading a pack of wild boys, especially the sons of Army men and women, is one of your very best turns.

Travelers

"I traveled among unknown men, In lands beyond the sea:
Nor England! Did I know till then, What love I bore to thee."
William Wordsworth

I remember a long family vacation in Italy when our family finally arrived at Camp Darby, a U.S. armed forces recreation campground near Pisa. It warmed our hearts to see the Stars and Stripes waving from the camp's flagpole and to understand the language of people again. We quickly set up our camping gear, and in no time our children had sought out and made instant friends with the offspring of fellow American military travelers. You would have thought our children had known these other kids for years, the way they hit it off together.

It was not long before my wife and I made friends with fellow military travelers, too. Forgotten were the natural rivalries between the different services. Circumstances made the Navy and Air Force folks around us automatic friends, everyone being thirsty for the fellowship of other Americans. We'd share laughs about our common ordeals at getting around and communicating in the endemic confusion of Italian culture.

Individuals, who stateside would probably not care if you existed, seem to change their tune when posted overseas. Perhaps it is the culture shock, or maybe the natural expression of that xenophobic tendency in each of us. Whatever its source, it is clear that Americans tend to be more friendly towards fellow Americans when abroad.

For those soldiers who make their first journey outside of the United States, many are struck by a blast of loneliness as they step off that airplane onto foreign soil. Different sights, sounds, smells, and societies overload their senses. When they hear that familiar American accent over the babbling noise of a foreign crowd, lonely soldiers are more apt to reach out to that other American traveler.

Shakespeare once penned the now-famous lines, "Friends, Romans, countrymen, lend me your ears." It is clear to every traveler abroad that the familiar dress, manners, and speech of other Americans we see abroad cause us to lend an ear and be more likely to forge a shared experience where our paths cross, be it an airport waiting area or some exotic restaurant.

It is good to encounter known men
In our travels beyond the sea.
For they will remind us of our America
That sweet land of liberty.

Trabbies

"The main thing is still to make history, not to write it."
Otto von Bismarck

The German nation has undergone two unifications: one in the 1870s under the leadership of Otto von Bismarck, the Prussian who became known as the Iron Chancellor. The second unification came with the fall of the Iron Curtain, that national scar caused by the ineptitude of Adolf Hitler and the paranoia of Soviet Russia.

I can still remember the autumn of 1989 when, in the early morning hours, our regiment alerted for deployment to our border surveillance positions. We knew something was up and quickly learned this was no drill. We were briefed on the seriousness of what was happening in East Germany, where the populace was clamoring for freedom. The big question was what would the Russians do, the 8th Guards Army directly across the Iron Curtain from us.

The movement of our troops and equipment went like clockwork. We were nervous, but the work at hand kept us focused and surprisingly calm. Full combat loads of ammunition and gear were issued to every soldier, every vehicle readied for war. Even my medics received their war issue of narcotics and chemical warfare antidote sets. We prayed all would go well, but were not taking any chances since the Russians outnumbered us 30:1.

By dawn we were all in position watching over the no man's land between East and West Germany. As the morning progressed, the invasion did begin, only this time it was the East German people making history by tearing down that ugly metal curtain of hate. There was no invasion with massed infantry, concentrated artillery fire, or Soviet T-72 tanks. Instead, there came a hoard of pedestrians, blaring horns, and East German Trabants, or "Trabbies," those cheap yet coveted cardboard box-like cars produced in East Germany. Their objective was not to brush aside the American cavalry units in their way and push on to the Rhine River. No, they were heading to any West German bank they could find, cash in on their modest monetary gift from the West German government, and then concentrate their attack on the bountiful stores of West Germany as well as visit long lost friends and relatives.

As events unfolded, the American troops on the border were so proud to be there. America's longest war, fought against its largest enemy, at its greatest financial expense, was won without a shot fired. It warms my heart to reflect on it even now. Anyone can write about that experience, but nothing beats being part of it.

The Wall

"Before I built a wall I'd ask to know
What I was walling in or walling out,
And to whom I was like to give offense.
Something there is that doesn't love a wall,
That wants it down."
Robert Frost (*Mending Wall*)

The gray wall had stood in the midst of Berlin, Germany for three decades. That symbol of the Cold War divided the city in half, one part free and the other without liberty. In 1989, that would all come to an end, as *Glasnost* under Mikhail Gorbachev motivated the East German people to clammer for the wall to come down.

My uncle, a maintenance warrant officer, was stationed in Germany in 1961, just as I was starting grade school. He would see the wall go up. We came very close to war then. Years after he retired from the Army, I was also stationed in Germany with the Army as a medical warrant officer. I would see the wall torn down in 1989. We too, thought war might come again as the turbulent will of the people expressed itself. Luckily for everyone in Europe and around the world, war did not raise its ugly head.

You cannot but marvel at the folly of men. How can you permanently isolate a people from one another, especially people bound together by history, blood, and culture? It is only a matter of time before these divisions end and those walls of ignorance and hate come crashing down.

Check Point Charlie was a famous crossing point in Berlin for Westerners wishing to visit East Berlin during the Cold War. Over the years, a great deal of history swirled around this famous international gateway. The day before the final sections of the wall were to be removed from around the checkpoint, I had the great opportunity to remove a piece of the wall there. Sledgehammer in hand, I pounded away at the concrete, not far from where one of the last victims of the wall had been gunned down.

A chunk of the Berlin Wall, about the size of a football, now sits in my home, a reminder of that awful symbol of hate and paranoia. That concrete fragment also reminds me to be very careful about what types of walls or fences exist in my life, either real or symbolic. Sometimes the fences we build wall out or limit our opportunities.

Some fences make enemies. When a fence makes enemies, its only end is being torn down, either through the clash of arms, neglect or the will of the people. Good fences may make good neighbors, but only if there are unlocked doors in them too.

The Difficult Duty

"Do your duty, and leave the rest to heaven."
Pierre Corneille

No one had a clue he was suffering. Perhaps it was because of the momentous events unfolding all around us, the fall of the Berlin wall and the Iron Curtain. In our euphoria over those tremendous things we did not notice that one of the unit's key sergeants had some deep troubles.

He was an outstanding soldier. So exceptional was he that the squadron commander made him the NCOIC of the unit's border patrol operations. He flawlessly executed this critical duty, doing those important things NCOs do that hold the Army together. It was work made even more important by the unfolding events that would make the history books. And he had risen to the challenge. He was the sort of enlisted leader that makes the Army successful.

Not one to complain, he eagerly went about his work without telling anyone about his personal troubles. The job was his refuge from it all, those difficulties with money, marriage and drinking. It all ended, however, one Saturday night. There had been a fight with his young German wife. She left to stay with her mother in a nearby village and he turned to drink. Too much drink. In the early hours of Sunday morning, in a fit of apparent drunken depression, he leapt from the top floor of the four-story apartment building where he lived, meeting a horrible end headfirst on the cobblestone pavement below.

Early Sunday morning the Commander's phone call roused me from bed. It wasn't long before we arrived at the family home of this soldier's wife. It was the first time I joined a commander and a chaplain in the sad task of notifying the next-of-kin concerning the death of a soldier. I served as translator and, if needed, would render medical assistance. There was not a dry eye in the place after the terrible news was delivered. We all knew this exceptional soldier and felt the devastating loss, though not nearly as badly as his dear wife.

The Army requires that the news of a soldier's death be delivered to the next-of-kin in person, not by an impersonal telegram, phone call or letter. Those who do this work are called casualty officers. Casualty officer duty is one of the most heart-rending jobs in the world. The duty requires compassion, empathy, and a firmness of soul that can help give loved ones something to hold onto to during those tempestuous times of terrible tragedy. With such a difficult duty you try to do your best and leave the rest in God's capable hands.

The Cough

"A merry heart doeth good like a medicine."
Proverbs 17:22

To your average civilian it is a strange name to give a liquor store: the Class VI Store. Maybe class X or XX, but where does this VI come from? Like many other things in the military subculture, you have to study further or actually join the military to find the answer. Sometimes the Army can be weird. How the Army handles alcohol is no exception.

When it comes to supplies, the Army assigns numbers to the major types of things. Food is Class I and medicine is Class VIII. VI is the number given by logisticians for alcoholic beverages. This oftentimes-troublesome group of supplies requires separate handling and accounting, especially in a world of folks who have an especially fond taste for spirits of all types. Over time the Army even developed special stores to sell booze on base, from beer to wine to hard liquor. Hence the name Class VI Store, for want of any other name I suppose.

In medicine there are many products that contain varying amounts of alcohol. Couch medicines often contain alcohol due to the anti-tussive effects alcohol has on the human body. Whiskey and brandy in particular seem to have medicinal value in suppressing an irritant cough, but only when used properly of course.

I once kept a couple of small bottles of whiskey from the Class VI Store in my medical kit while on maneuvers. Sergeant Kenny Molbert, a medic who often served as my driver and assistant, would make it a point to cough a bit every time I opened my medical kit that contained the whiskey. We'd laugh out loud even though not a word was said, and our patients would wonder what was so funny.

Every autumn I often get a cold. The nuisance starts as a scratchy throat, progresses into a runny nose, and then works into a dry, irritating cough. The cough will keep my darling wife and I awake at night. Though I do not reach for whiskey, for the sake of a good night's sleep I do frequently resort to some form of cough medicine that has alcohol in it.

Each time I taste a couple of teaspoonfuls of that *fortified* cough syrup, I chuckle inside, vividly remembering Sergeant Molbert's faked coughs. I think the memory and the laugh alone are often enough to cure my cough and help me get back to sleep. If only we could bottle the humor of those moments, for medicinal purposes of course, and buy it at the Class VI store!

High-tech Soldiers

"The best victory is when the opponent surrenders of its own accord before there are any actual hostilities…It is best to win without fighting."
Sun-tzu

In a dark German forest, just north of Ulm, the two Soviet officer observers to the REFORGER exercise saw something that forever changed their view of military doctrine. For three weeks, they had traveled all over Central Europe, visited dozens of places, and seen practically everything in the NATO's field armies. The planes, tanks, briefings by generals, and VIP treatment were okay, but a Specialist Fourth Class would take the prize in impressing these Warsaw Pact officers.

The two large Bundeswehr helicopters carrying our entourage landed in a large clearing of the forest, the huge rotor blades kicking up snow and branches that January morning. It was bitter cold outside under a clear blue sky. The unit we were visiting, a 10th Mountain Division infantry battalion, had been out in this chill for over two weeks.

The mission of these light infantrymen was to deny passage of tank/armored forces through key roads in the forest. The terrain was ideal for light infantry—plenty of cover, narrow choke points, multiple defendable positions to choose from. The battalion commander skillfully briefed the Russians on all this and more. They visited soldiers in their defensive and attack positions, seeing their weaponry and tactics up close. It was all very impressive, how lethal foot soldiers can be in the middle of tank country.

But all that didn't take the prize. Passing through a tactical operations center, one of the Russian colonels noticed a soldier off to the side in front of a laptop computer. Intrigued, he went over to the soldier, and, of course, the crowd followed. Through an interpreter he began asking questions to this Specialist who was not part of the dog and pony show.

The impromptu visit caught the young soldier off guard, but he composed himself and began to explain what he did. At his fingertips was a computer programmed with three-dimensional maps of Germany, available in many different scales. He showed the colonel how he could, by simply using this notebook-sized computer out in the middle of nowhere, provide his commander exact locations and 3-D visuals of where to best position troops to block or attack the enemy.

The Russians were very interested in this high school graduate from Iowa. "Comrade," one of the Russians said with a somber look, "we cannot win a war against a people whose soldiers are so computer literate." For him this soldier was a greater deterrent than any expensive or sophisticated weapons system.

The Sergeants' Good-bye

" 'What are the bugles blowin' for?' Said Files-on-Parade.
'To turn you out, to turn you out,' the Color Sergeant said."
Rudyard Kipling

Sergeants have always been people I could identify with more than officers. Later as an officer, I couldn't hang out as much with the sergeants, the difference in rank and all. To be honest, though, I have always found myself closer to them in spirit, this being the curse for officers who were former enlisted soldiers. And so, I was truly touched when one day a group of my sergeants said good-bye to me, their supervising officer.

It was time to move on again. My most excellent tour in Germany was coming to an end. There were the usual orders, clearing papers and the moving day. Finally, you're down to the final days, living out of a suitcase.

There were nine sergeants in my platoon and every one of them was a good man. The platoon sergeant, Staff Sergeant Lindsey, grabbed my arm one afternoon and said, "Doc, you owe us some of your time. Bring your wife and be at the aid station at six p.m." Somewhat startled, I stammered out an, "Okay, what's up?" "You'll see," he said, betraying a slight smile.

Something definitely was up. My wife and I dutifully arrived at the appointed time with all nine of those outstanding sergeants there waiting for us: SSG Lindsey, SSG Dean, SSG Nicacio, SSG Haynes, SSG Gut, SGT Molbert, SGT Garcia, SGT Velez, and SGT Smith. Grinning from ear to ear, they proceeded to take my wife and I out to dinner.

Over some of the best steak I have ever eaten, I blushed as the sergeants regaled my wife with tales of our Army adventures together. She laughed and laughed. Masters at exaggeration and embellishment, their eloquent attention blessed my heart and deeply impressed my Irene.

Finally, SSG Lindsey cleared his throat and said in a voice as clear to me now as then. "Sir, we have really enjoyed working for you. You are one of a kind. We wish you all the best in your career. We will miss you." With that, he handed me a gift from the sergeants, wiping something from his eye as the other sergeants chuckled. A pewter plaque hangs in my office to this very day, and always will. On it is a simple inscription, so characteristic of my effective but unpretentious leaders:

"Thanks for your leadership and guidance."

Thank you, sergeants. The plaque has meant far more than medals, rank or diplomas. It has been one of the very best gifts the Army ever gave me.

Hot Mike

"Be not forgetful to entertain strangers…"
Hebrews 13: 2

In the Army a "hot mike" is not some chap by the name of Michael all excited from reading a men's magazine. No, a hot mike is when some inattentive person fails to release the talk button on a radio microphone. The end result is that no one else on that radio frequency can talk but everyone can hear any conversations the "hot mike" person may hold.

This hot mike business frustrates many people, particularly leaders trying to get the mission accomplished. Radio frequencies can usually handle only one call at a time. Someone inadvertently holding the transmission button down ties down the line and important business cannot occur. On the other hand, the whole affair can be quite entertaining as the hot mike guy continues on his or her merry talkative way, unaware that an unseen audience is laughing their heads off at their antics. Some budding stars even serenade us with merry little tunes, often in an off-key voice.

Normally troops are forbidden from using colorful language over military radio nets. But off line soldiers revert to their "mother tongue," which for many includes some words not necessarily found in the dictionary. Other poor souls spill their guts or express low opinions about some particular person, completely oblivious to the fact that the person in question is hearing every word.

Meanwhile, all communications on the often very important radio net come to a standstill. The important business of the unit stalls. Eventually the entertainment ends as an angry officer or NCO finally discovers who the culprit is, either through voice recognition or a systematic, physical check of every radio. The red-faced soldier normally gets a good talking to and a quick lesson on how to operate a military radio. He also realizes for the first time that he has made a fool of himself for all to hear. The lack of attention is embarrassing and others will make a point of reminding him of it later.

With fifty or so soldiers standing in the field chow line that evening, someone calls out to "Jones," the hot mike guy of the day, "Hey Jones, where did you learn how to sing?" There are chuckles and grins as everyone remembers Jones' earlier indiscretion. Jones is, of course, embarrassed and speechless by now.

Hot mike is a lesson many in the Army eventually learn the hard way. In a cocky moment, when we think we have this radio down pat, we make the careless mistake of leaving the mike on. I, too, have not been forgetful to entertain strangers over the FM airwaves.

Blackhorse

"A friend is a single soul dwelling in two bodies."
Aristotle

You can see one every now and again on the right shoulder of their uniforms—the 11th Armored Cavalry Regiment's Blackhorse patch. It is a rearing black horse silhouetted against the red and white colors of cavalry units. The soldier wearing the patch is someone who saw combat with the famous Blackhorse Regiment, either in Vietnam or as the follow on force during the Persian Gulf War.

Having spent nearly four years with the Blackhorse, I envy these soldiers who have the honor of always being able to wear that coveted piece of cloth. If I had only stayed with the Regiment another year, then that cool patch would have been permanently mine as well.

Each time I see one of these chaps, I go out of my way to recognize them—a handshake, a salute with the "Blackhorse" greeting, or a gentle tap on the patch with the comment "great unit." They beam with pride and we often strike up a conversation. Sometimes I even meet someone I once knew during the forty-four months when the Blackhorse patch adorned my uniforms.

Every soldier can identify with certain Army unit patches. Each unique patch fosters team spirit, loyalty, and camaraderie. Combat veterans say that it is the close-knit relationship between soldiers of the same unit that becomes the stuff that men die for in combat. They seldom die for abstract words on a piece of paper somewhere.

When heroes are asked why they performed such incredible feats on the battlefield, the answers are often surprising. Their sacrifice, the risks they took, were often not, we are told, out of loyalty to the flag, the President, their family or even our country. No, they did it for their buddies, the men in the trenches with them, men who wore the same patch, who are alive now because of what they did.

Leadership can accomplish things only to a certain extent. Money can buy things up to a point. But friendship fosters a loyalty that will put up with and accomplish far more. Camaraderie runs deeper than what leaders can motivate people to do or buy with money.

When your career in the service is over, the Army says good-bye to you with a pension and the friendship of fellow veterans. The pension provides a modest living and the memories of veterans help make life out of the Army worth living. The memories are the unseen right shoulder patch all soldiers wear. Blackhorse!

Improvise, Adapt, Overcome

"The mind is slow in unlearning what it has been long in learning."
Seneca

Stay in the Army long enough, and you will move. A permanent change in station, or PCS, is a chance to travel at government expense. The flip side to the excitement of a permanent change of station is the struggle one goes through adjusting to a new job.

Adjusting to a new job is of course not a phenomenon unique to the military. Everyone who draws a paycheck has seen this rite of passage. But in the military it occurs often. Over a twenty-year career, you can expect to move ten to fifteen times. Even if you stay put for any length of time, new bosses will rotate in every 18-24 months. My own experience included fourteen moves and sixteen changes of command.

It goes without saying that with all that turbulence going on, things tend to change. Every new place and every new boss has a different way of doing things. Sometimes it is only a minor change, but at other times one gets a complete overhaul. It is one of the ironies of military life that, despite the outward uniformity, there is an incredible amount of variation in how things get done.

It seems that with every new leader comes some sort of effort to stamp his or her individuality on things. Never mind that the old way just might be better. These people need something on their evaluation reports. You can't get a stellar evaluation if you just maintain the status quo. Oh no, let's stir things up a bit.

So, you have to be flexible when the periodic stirring comes. There are things you are comfortable with that become obsolete. Loadplans for vehicles, standards for CPR, standard operating procedures, changes to officer rating systems, or staff briefing style adjustments are a few examples of things that change over time.

"We used to do it this way," or "when I was in Germany we did it that way," does not matter. What matters is that you adapt. Hopefully, we are changing for the better.

Unlearning is a problem for most folks, especially when something really good is unlearned. Maybe that is what survival is all about. Adapt. Improvise. Overcome. But don't get too comfortable. The moment you think you've figured things out, someone changes things. As the saying goes, "as soon as you think you make the ends meet, someone moves the ends." Hey, welcome to life's lesson No. 1.

Good Advice

"We ask advice, but we mean approbation."
C.C. Colton

It was August 1991 and the United States Army was on the move. The build-up in the Persian Gulf had begun. President Bush was marshaling forces in the region to counter the aggression of Iraq against Kuwait. While most of the Army was in motion, I found myself in a quiet assignment with an infantry battalion posted in beautiful Hawaii. We were not going to the war; light infantry was the last thing the Army needed to fight the mostly mechanized Iraqi Army, especially with airborne troops already there.

Some of us could not enjoy the barbecue and pristine beaches while fellow soldiers were going without hot meals for weeks and eating sand. Despite living in paradise a few of us less sane individuals were itching to get into the coming fight.

Like Henry Fonda, who played the role of a frustrated officer in the movie "Mister Roberts," Mister Kay also wanted to see action. This and a curious blend of other factors caused me to explore volunteering. My wife, quite frankly, thought I was insane. But the battalion XO thought it was worth a shot, his opinion being the only official Army sanction I sought.

A short phone call to the PA assignment officer at the Department of the Army quickly increased my chances for seeing action. Within two days of that call a request for orders arrived at my division headquarters, orders that would assign me back to cavalry, the 3rd Armored Cavalry Regiment.

The day after the request arrived my name came up in the Division Commander's daily staff meeting. It is usually not a good sign when a company-grade officer's name comes up in a meeting of stars and colonels. The Commander, a two-star general, asked who this "Kay" was. After being told by my no-doubt-now embarrassed battalion commander, he proceeded to lecture the entire division staff and subordinate commanders about how he was not going to allow his command to evaporate before his very eyes with people wanting to get into the war.

Later, I was called on the carpet, unaware that the request had arrived or of the new guidance from the Division Commander. My commander had the request for orders in his hand. He asked for my side of the story, gave me a short lecture, followed by a "no" answer, and then dismissed me. Later, after learning all that had happened, I paused by the XO's office and said, "Sir, thanks for taking the heat for me." He knowingly nodded, gestured towards his backside, indicating the chewing out he had received, and then told me to "scram." Without hesitation, I readily complied. This time it was good advice.

Fathers

"The child is father to the man."
William Wordsworth

War veterans almost always have war stories to tell. Everyone has "war stories," but theirs are real. The crucible of combat leaves its mark on the soul. Each generation of new soldiers owes their knowledge and spirit to the mentorship of veterans, who have seen real combat, who have "seen the elephant."

The U.S. Army is incapable of bearing its own children. America must provide the raw materials that are shaped into soldiers. With each passing year, a subtle but constant process of transferring our military heritage and preparedness occurs. The handoff of information and experience from older soldiers puts a human face to lessons learned. It drives home a point which books and drill can only partially do. Done correctly, the torch of readiness is passed on to the future. Our "gunpowder" is kept dry.

Corporal Desmond Doss was nearly eighty years old when I met him. He served in the Pacific during World War II. He had been a combat medic and earned the Medal of Honor through single handedly saving the lives of at least seventy men. I had seen his picture in Able Hall at the Army's medic school at Fort Sam Houston, Texas. Now he stood in front of me.

I nervously shook his hand, and then fumbled a salute, realizing that the Medal of Honor on his chest required it of me. He looked sharp—still dressed in a World War II dress uniform with the famous Eisenhower jacket on. We exchanged a few words and then others had to meet him. In those brief moments a transfer had occurred for me. There was a palpable feeling that he was somehow a part of me now. His heroism, his extraordinary sacrifice and quiet demeanor became something I would want to emulate.

The soldier is a father to a recruit. Old soldiers must teach new ones. Watch me do one and then I'll watch you do the same, is the oldest of training principles. On the spot corrections, battle drills, remedial training—all are methods used to pass the trade on, methods developed because people died not knowing them.

The deepest, most lasting things one remembers, however, are the faces associated with the learning. The general who mingles with the troops, the one-on-one time a NCO spends with a soldier, or a World War II hero sharing a few words with a young officer. The *Geist*, or spirit, transfers. The idea now has a face. A child becomes capable of becoming a father to another soldier.

PT

"What does not destroy me, makes me strong."
Friedrich Nietzsche

Hawaii is a great assignment. If soldiers are given the chance, they should jump on this opportunity. Beautiful weather all year round and tons of stuff to do are two great reasons to go. You are located where millions of people pay big bucks to enjoy paradise for only a few days.

A highlight of my tour there was the large, spacious quarters the Army gave my family to live in. The house was located next to a gigantic parade field and my wife especially enjoyed the open, beautiful view from the living room. The five bedrooms were also ample for our four children.

An advantage of living in the Hawaiian Islands is how many family and friends finally take the time to come and visit. I mean, look, they even get to stay for free. During our three years there, dozens of guests stayed over with us and all had a wonderful time, except for one small detail.

For the uninitiated it is an eye opener—literally. The cool, breezy tropical evenings lull one into a deep sleep. The patter of rain from an occasional evening shower refreshes the earth and further contributes to a good rest. Long before sunrise, however, even in the rain, our guests would awake to sounds my wife and I had long grown accustomed to.

It would begin in the distance, that faint sound of strangely musical voices. Gradually, through the early morning darkness, the sounds would become more distinct. "Your left, your left. Your left, right, left. Your military left…" Our visitors would awaken to the sounds of "Whoooaahhh!" and "In cadence, exercise!" Instead of the sound of music, it was the sound of physical fitness training.

The PT ritual took place on the large parade field in front of our quarters. Thousands of soldiers, in huge formations, would be taken through various exercises and physical fitness drills. Like some massive outdoor prayer service, the lines of exercising soldiers would chant, "One, two, three, one. One, two, three, two. One, two, three, …."

Our guests would rise out of bed and make their way to our large living room window. They would marvel at the sight before them, these thousands of soldiers in unison jumping, pushing, or wallowing in the wet grass. They were impressed. It was something they had never seen nor imagined about the Army. Though inconvenienced by the noise, they were also proud. In a strange way one can sleep easier knowing that there are those who train while you are yet sleeping, even in paradise.

Combat Lifesavers

"The first virtue in a soldier is endurance of fatigue;
courage is only the second virtue."
Napolean Bonaparte

"First Sergeant," I said, "let's test some of your soldiers in starting an intravenous infusion." "Great," he said, "I've got just the platoon I want tested." We set off by foot through the lush Hawaiian tropical vegetation to where Bravo Company, 4th Battalion, 87th Infantry was training. As we neared the training site, we entered a network of interconnected trenches and bunkers. Ahead of us was the sound of gunfire and periodic explosions. Smoke drifted around us. A "fight" was in progress.

Bravo Company was engaged in infantry assault tactics. This tedious but important training involved maneuvering through obstacles and opposing force to capture key terrain and destroy or capture the opponent. The platoons had been in training all morning and the heat of the advancing day was beginning to slow down the overall effort. Eventually we found the platoon the First Sergeant had selected. The thirty or so men were in their "lane" of training, waiting in the long trenches for their next mission.

"Give me two of your combat lifesavers," the First Sergeant said to the platoon sergeant. Within minutes, two infantrymen fell back from their resting areas and appeared, dripping sweat, with uniforms dusted in that reddish hue unique to the volcanic soil of Hawaii. As they saw me standing there with two IV sets in hand, they immediately knew that "Doc" was here to test their combat lifesaver IV skills.

Over the next twenty minutes, the tired soldiers tackled the tricky task of starting IVs on two dehydrated "volunteers" the platoon sergeant had selected. Hands trembled slightly as they both carefully went through the seventeen or so steps involved in starting an IV. Of the many medical skills a combat lifesaver learns, the intravenous infusion task is the most difficult. As each finished the steps, both showed noticeable relief as the solution began to flow into their patient's arm. Despite the fatigue, dirt, smoke, heat and sweat, both of these infantrymen, without advance warning, properly started real IVs.

The First Sergeant and the platoon sergeant beamed. I, too, was impressed. The combat lifesaver training the soldiers had was paying off in conditions close to combat. Some day, their skills might very well help save a life. Meanwhile, the two soldiers, now with something different to talk about, rejoined their comrades in more combat "life-taker" training.

Listeners

"No man ever listened himself out of a job."
Calvin Coolidge

Army chaplains are a very important part of helping soldiers with day-to-day problems and the occasional personal crisis. In most Army units there are at least two people a soldier can turn to in confidence when confronted with a personal problem: the medical officer and the chaplain. It is the chaplain, though, who is especially qualified to handle difficulties of the heart and soul. He or she is a master listener.

Someone to turn to in troubling times is all well and good, but to whom do the chaplains turn? Certainly not their commanders, for this might call into question their ability to function. Other military chaplains might help, but these are people they technically compete with. No, more often than not it's the "Doc" to whom the padre comes to talk.

It took me a while to get accustomed to this need of the Army's clergy, but after a few bungled cases I finally caught on to why chaplains visited the aid station fairly frequently. One reason was that they needed someone to talk to, who, for a change, wasn't coming to him with problems. They were there to be listened to instead of to listen.

I owe a debt of gratitude to these Army chaplains who taught me the fine art of listening. One has to learn how to sit by and let others sound me out concerning their frustrations, how to sort out what's important in the "10,000-year scheme of things," to quote one of the Army chaplains I knew.

In this synergistic dialog with the chaplains, I learned how to keep my mouth shut. Sometimes you have to be quiet in order to be heard, especially if you are a person afflicted with chatter-itis like me. The eloquent message of these Army chaplains to me was loud and clear: "Doc, I respect your opinions and counsel. Can I use you as a sounding board?" That these officers, so expert at giving counsel to so many, would come to me for advice and counsel was both humbling and an honor. I am sure other medical officers around the Army have had the same experience with God's representatives to the troops.

Maybe I helped the chaplains. I certainly hope so, but I don't know for sure. On the edges of these "lending an ear" sessions I got a word or two in edgewise, but mostly I listened. My listening probably helped them more than what I had to say. One thing was for certain: those chaplains helped me. Their experiences, sympathy, common sense, and connection to God strengthened me and taught me how to listen. No doubt the Big Guy was listening too.

Quarters

"They that be whole need not a physician,
but they that are sick."
Matthew 9:12

It is called a DD Form 689, the Individual Sick Slip. The form is an important document in the day-to-day affairs of administratively handling soldiers during sick call. On it are written the orders from the medical officer to the sick or injured soldier's supervisors concerning his duty disposition. Return them to full work status with the "duty" block checked, or give them a work limitation "profile," say no lifting more than ten pounds for five days for example. You can also send the patient off to the hospital or home to bedrest, known all over the Army as "quarters."

The origin of this quarters term in the Army most likely goes way back. Probably referring to the lodging constructed for troops to live in, the actual word most likely originates in the occupying of one-fourth of something, say a room or building. Wherever the term came from, it usually means a day off from work for modern soldiers.

Getting time off for any reason is something every soldier wants, especially those who work for tough bosses. It is a good bet that a fever, infectious disease or a significant injury will buy you some time off. But there are hardheaded types out there who will keep on going no matter what.

I was pretty sick one day and really should not have been seeing patients at all. But there was no one else available to see them. I had a low-grade fever, a slight headache, and some nausea, but otherwise I was up and about tackling the usual quota of thirty or so patients. As the morning progressed, I joked to one of my medics that I ought to put myself on quarters. "You ought to, sir," he replied, having already appreciated my ill state of health. I pressed on though, in my stubborn way, probably spreading more disease than I cured.

Passing by my office between seeing patients, I noticed a white object lying on the seat of my desk chair. Checking it out, I saw two U.S. 25-cent pieces scotch-taped to a DD Form 689. One of my more creative and thoughtful medics had filled it out for me with an attached note:

"Sir, it's not legal for me to put you on quarters,
so here is the next best thing!"

The note was both humorous and humbling. I took the hint and promptly went home to heal myself.

Honor

"Act well your part: there all the honour lies."
Alexander Pope

We had been waiting for four days at Hickam Air Force Base, Hawaii. Our names were on a waiting list for space available seats on Air Force transport planes to the mainland United States. Weather, maintenance problems and poor timing contributed to our delay, but we had fun tooling around Oahu, seeing the sights.

Our big family of six was now at the top of the waiting list—numbers one through six for the next available seats, with at least two hundred other folks waiting behind us. Considering the cost of commercial air transportation, we were about to save a significant chunk of money for our three-week vacation, as flying space available is free for service personnel and their families who are patient enough.

The long awaited call came over the passenger terminal loudspeaker, "Those passengers seeking space available transportation to Travis Air Force Base, California, please report to counter number three." Within minutes a fair sized crowd gathered around the counter. After a few moments, an Airman stepped up with the now familiar waiting list and announced that there would be twenty-one seats available on this flight. My wife and I smiled at each other. Our chances looked really good.

There was a slight delay as an older gentleman quietly stepped by us and went up to the counter. We waited patiently as the Airman processed this stranger who was given the first available seat. After a few minutes, the Airman announced that there were now twenty seats available and began calling names off the top of the list, "Kay, family of six." "Here," I said, as the crowd behind us moaned, knowing that we had just filled nearly a third of the available seats. Our small platoon waddled up to the counter, bags in tow. As the Airman processed our paperwork, my curiosity got the best of me. "Who was that man who went ahead of us, since our names were at the top of the list?" Pausing, he smiled, "Medal of Honor winner."

Of course, I thought, what an excellent reason. We should gladly step aside and take a backseat for those who go beyond the call of duty and who live to tell the tale. I wish we could do something for those who did not live to see the glory of their ultimate personal sacrifice. Allowing these living heroes to go to the front of the line is the very least we can do for these people of honor.

In honoring our heroes, we also honor the America they have already done so much for.

Grunts

"I am a man; nothing human is alien to me."
Terence

The acronym "GI" has over the years evolved into an endearing term describing all U.S. military people in general. I do not know when the acronym came into common use, but it is derived from "Government Issue." General infantry form the keystone of all that the government issues.

The United States Army has many new occupational areas since World War II. The advent of sophisticated electronic equipment, helicopters, and communication capabilities spawned hundreds of new jobs. Each and every job in the Army needs a designation. For this a number and letter code developed over time. For example, 91B is a medic, 71L is a clerk, 98G is a linguist, and 65D is a physician assistant. But by far one of the most common jobs is still 11B—infantryman.

If they ever shut down the entire Army, someone will have to lock the door. That somebody will probably be an infantryman. Armies always need the services of infantry. In a way everybody, regardless of his or her Army job, holds the secondary occupation of infantryman. They'll give a rifle to anybody they can if we are ever in a pinch, but we'll be in some serious hot water when the medics have to start shooting too.

There is a special kinship, a brotherhood shared only by infantrymen. They are "grunts." But as mentioned above, circumstances may dictate that the fraternity of the grunt might rapidly expand its membership. It therefore behooves us to ponder the qualities of the infantry.

The grunt will go into the next battle carrying everything he needs to survive and do damage, normally about 110 pounds of food, ammunition, gadgets and gear. He is the most lethal item on the battlefield still. Give him a fifty-pound weapon system and he can take out a multimillion-dollar tank or plane. With a radio he can ruin your day. With his bare hands he can help someone else die for their country. It does not take much to keep him working either: a little food, some water, and a bath now and again. He learns to appreciate the little things everybody else takes for granted.

Getting infantry ready for war doesn't create as many civilian jobs as building helicopters and planes. Congress always seems to bite on the expensive, sexy, let's create jobs stuff. The big bucks bypass the grunt. The gee whiz, high dollar, obsolete tomorrow things will come and go, but the need for grunts will always remain. They'll always cost about the same too. The brotherhood of the grunt will never become obsolete or too expensive. Grunts will never be alien to the Army!

Stop Smoking 101

"With man, most of his misfortunes are occasioned by man."
Pliny the Elder

Moonlighting can be a beneficial experience. The extra money obviously helps, but for medical types, the cases you see and procedures one gets to perform can enhance knowledge, skills, and background. Indeed, working in a civilian emergency room during off-duty time can provide exposure to conditions and trauma very similar to what combat will produce.

Take the case of the hapless smoker. While moonlighting at a small emergency room in Hawaii, I was taking a small nap when the charge nurse awoke me at about 3:00 a.m. Arising from my slumber, I could hear the echo of groans down the hallway. As I came closer to the trauma room, a tearful voice cried out over and over, "How could I have been so stupid?"

A smell you will never forget is the smell of singed human hair and burned flesh. This aroma greeted me shortly before I arrived to where my unfortunate patient lay. He was in bad, very bad shape. From head to toe his entire front was covered with second and third degree burns.

We rapidly went to work. With all the screaming, his airway was certainly intact. I ordered an IV infusion, to be followed by IV morphine. Vital signs monitoring, a Foley catheter and moistened, sterile dressings for his burns followed. Meanwhile, I did a brief physical exam, called for air transfer and worked on getting some history from the ambulance crew.

My patient and his wife had had a heated argument over something quite trivial, money or bedroom activities. The war of words escalated to actions when his wife grabbed the nearest thing, a Mason jar full of Coleman fuel, and threw it at her husband. The loose lid came off in midair, drenching the front of my patient in this highly flammable fluid.

Shocked and disgusted by this act and the strong smell, the fight quickly ended and my patient went to take a shower. While waiting for the running water to heat up, he nervously reflected on the whole episode while thoughtlessly reaching for a cigarette, something he automatically did when under stress. A further attack of stupidity led to a flick of a cigarette lighter. It would be the last time he ever smoked again.

Twenty minutes and a large dose of morphine later, the evacuation helicopter landed and my patient was whisked away into the night to a burn center in Honolulu. Despite the interventions of all concerned, he would die two days later. His death was a tragic mistake and a lesson for all. It was one of the best stop-smoking lessons one could ever have.

Donors

"We be of one blood, ye and I."
Rudyard Kipling

If there is one group of people who know how to give blood, it is soldiers. I'm not referring just to the sacrifices made in blood on the battlefield, though Heaven has a good record of how enormous that donation has been. No, I refer to how liberal soldiers are in donating pints of precious blood and plasma on a regular basis through Department of Defense blood donation drives.

I have a deep admiration for these people, especially the frequent donors. They line up and roll up their sleeves. When most people are pretty squeamish about any kind of needle stick, these brave individuals get stuck with needles several times larger than those used for the usual vaccinations we all get. Those long 14- or 16-gauge needles used to draw blood are no piece of cake.

Getting jabbed with a needle is one thing, but the sight of blood for some is another challenge. There you are, all propped up in one of those comfortable chairs while a plastic tube carries your dark red lifeblood to a small plastic bag on a mixing device nearby. The sights, sounds, smells and drama of it all are not lost on first-time donors. Some take the opportunity to even pass out in honor of the occasion.

What impresses me most about folks who donate blood is that they often do it for free. Oh, their commanders may give them a few hours off, but in general the whole process is gratis. And some soldiers donate blood or plasma on a regular basis, once every six to eight weeks.

Modern mankind vainly attempts to artificially recreate blood. Researchers have come awfully close. Maybe someday they will produce a blood substitute fully capable of restoring volume, removing body wastes, and carrying life-sustaining oxygen, all with the same fluid that does not require refrigeration. Until that great discovery arrives, we will continue to need direct donations from people like you and me.

You would be hard-pressed to find a group of people more willing and able to give up their blood than soldiers. Whether it is on the battlefield or in the donation center, to me they are all heroes. When I see those massed formations of soldiers lining up to go to war or to donate blood, I remember that both in war and peace there are those who are prepared to willingly shed their blood. They do it for their fellow man, ye and I. That will always be a great cause.

Ranger Stew

"Tell me what you eat, and I shall tell you what you are."
Anthelme Brillat-Savarin

There is a coveted patch worn on the upper left sleeve of the U.S. Army uniform. The arch-shaped applique displays in black letters, "Ranger." This "Ranger Tab," as it is called, is not earned easily.

Candidates for Ranger school undergo a grueling sixteen weeks of intense, nearly sleepless training. Divided into three phases and located in as many different locations, candidates are forced to endure harassment, physical stress, minimal food, and extreme fatigue. All the while, they learn and execute tactical training missions in mountains, deserts, and swamps.

You lose a great deal of weight during this training. I remember a light infantry sergeant I sent off to Ranger school. This 190-pound muscleman returned four months later forty pounds lighter, but also with the coveted "tab." The reason soldiers lose so much weight is because they work hard and receive so little food. A fundamental part of the rigorous Ranger program is minimal food—one MRE per day when it's warm outside, and two if it's very cold. And if your group has trouble reading a map, you may not even get the MRE. That's when snakes, bugs, and anything else even remotely edible look inviting.

When Ranger trainees are lucky enough to get their MREs, they are forced to eat them quickly, all part of the training stress. Realizing their need to eat fast and the delay caused by taking each part of an MRE one portion at a time, many trainees simply mix every edible part of the MRE together in a single high-calorie mixture called Ranger Stew.

Quickly ripping open each small packet, the soldier adds them all together in the larger entrée pouch. The concoction might seem revolting, but it's better than grasshoppers or snake meat. To the main entrée, say corned beef or spaghetti, they add Tabasco sauce, the salt and pepper packets, the cheese spread, crackers, dessert bar, cocoa, instant coffee, and non-dairy creamer with some water. The mixture contains every calorie found in an MRE and is quickly gobbled up by the half-starved Ranger candidates, often in the early hours of the morning.

Rangers have a unique appreciation for food. In addition to the rigors of their physical and mental training, they cultivate a strong desire for food of any sort. How do you recognize a Ranger when he is out of uniform? More than likely, they're the ones who'll eat anything, hot or cold, burnt or raw, fresh or stale.

Rangers are also known to leave their plates clean, too.

179

The Great Escape

"The change...is forever."
U.S. Marines Recruiting Slogan

The dark, moonless Texas night surrounded us as we made our plans to evade the Marines sent out to find us. Their reputation and record were excellent. Seldom did anyone make it through their dragnet. The Marines were accustomed to the terrain and the job they had to do, so we had to be good, very good, to get by them. Our objective was four miles away—get there and we're home free. The odds, though, would be against us.

There were about seventy in our "POW" group of medical officers, all there at Camp Bullis, near San Antonio, to train in combat medical and tactical skills. It was a simulated POW breakout, and now was our chance to make our own "great escape."

The work for the Marines would be easy, for most of these officer escapees were unaccustomed to the rigors and tactics of combat drills and training. Within the first few hours of darkness, the bulk of the "POWs" were rounded up. A cakewalk for those Marines, except for the remaining six or so of us who took the game very seriously. Divided up into pairs, we moved only when absolutely necessary and always low and with lots of cover. The darkness was our friend. Not a word was spoken.

We worked our way forward, following terrain features well within the training area boundaries. We'd shadow our more noisy fellow escapees, and slip quietly forward in the wake of that moment when the Marines would ambush them, coordinating our moves with hand signals.

By the early morning hours, things became more difficult for us, as the Marines fell back closer to where our objective was. As we drew nearer, we had to force ourselves to be more patient and much quieter. The Marines were waiting. By four a.m. though, some of them must have dozed off. Others had to have that cigarette, shuffle their feet, or otherwise make their presence known. Ever so gently we moved on, step by step closer to the goal, taking advantage of every opportunity the few, the proud, gave us.

By dawn's early light, we were close enough for that final dash. Watching carefully, each of us found the moment for the last sprint forward. In response to our final move, the Marines sprang into action and we'd lose three more, but three would get through. The few, the proud, were not the Marines that day. No, it would be an Army doctor, a physician assistant, and a Medical Service Corps officer. We had succeeded in our great escape. The change was indeed forever—for those Marines and for us.

Plastered

"God looks after fools, drunkards, and the United States."
Anonymous

My wife and I laugh about it now, but at the time it wasn't very funny. Of all the embarrassing moments in our life, the episode with the drunken wife takes the prize. Our unit was just a few days away from deploying to the Middle East as the Gulf War was drawing down. The battalion threw a farewell dinner, a "dining out" where all the ladies in their lovely gowns would be taken out to a fine military dinner hosted by the battalion. Every officer wore dress blues, one of the Army's formal dinner uniforms.

The Officer's Club banquet hall was decorated for this occasion and several big-whigs of the Division were in attendance, including the Division Commander. The spacious dining area was set up with a large main table for the VIPs. Numerous other smaller, round, eight-person tables were all spread out to the front of the head table. Each table setting had fine china, fancy tableware, and pre-poured wine.

Before any dinner in the Army there is the usual pre-dinner mixing. People chat, drink and enjoy some hors d'oeurves. Soon, we all made our way into the large hall and settled into our seats. Irene and I sat with three other couples, just to the front left of the VIP table.

A friendly, nice-looking lady sat next to Irene. She was the wife of one of the battalion's staff officers. Over the next hour this dear lady became ever more friendly towards Irene as the pre-dinner booze and several toasts to everyone and his brother began to take effect. As her blood alcohol rose, she became louder and began to sob, the sad drunk with her hundred proof breath now clinging like a barnacle to poor Irene.

Obviously, the main table had noticed the commotion by then and we had to do something. Hardly one to mingle with intoxicated people, the very public place only added to Irene's desire to leave, but the inebriated parasite held on for dear life. The nervous looks from the brass only paralyzed Irene even more. I had to act. With cajoling looks and low whispers I finally got her husband to action and we managed to get the drunken wife to the lobby, who still held on to Irene for dear life.

Outside the lady came to her senses a bit, enough to momentarily let go of Irene. Quickly, Irene escaped and the lady's red-faced husband whisked her out the door, no doubt home to sleep off her sorrow.

I offered to take Irene home. No, she insisted we return to the dinner. She wanted to make sure the crowd knew this Army wife was not the drunk, just merely an unwilling by-sitter looking after a foolish drunk for the good of the U.S. Army.

Unaccompanied Tour

"Solitude is a good place to visit but a bad place to stay."
Josh Billings

An unaccompanied tour can be very hard on someone with a great marriage and wonderful children. The prospect of being ordered to such a tour over a twenty-year military career is pretty good, so one tries to mentally prepare for the six- or twelve-month separation. When the moment finally arrives, however, despite the best preparations the parting is still difficult. When you have a good thing going, it is hard to go.

Though we hated being apart, my wife and I coped with the difficulty of prolonged absences from each other in several ways. First, we kept in constant contact, initially by mail and phone, later by the addition of that blessed invention called e-mail. Second, we immersed ourselves in our different jobs—she with teaching and me with military duties. Third, we resurrected hobbies and reading that we otherwise could not do.

Even with the best of plans though, all these things simply could not fill the empty spots when all our stay busy strategies would flounder. I suppose that is when we should "savor the solitude," as my wife would say. Learning to be content when alone is a good lesson, but personally, it's never going to be a lesson I'll be able to stick with. Like taking awful tasting medicine, I'll take it. But that does not mean I'll like it.

By parting we appreciate. Up to a point. Too much parting, though, does not yield more appreciating. It is hard to keep the fires burning when no one ever uses it. The fire of a family needs the fuel of close friendship.

Personal relationships and family are very important. Yes, military service requires sacrifice from both service members and their families, but long after our time in the service is over, when the uniform is hung up for the last time, we become civilians again. You will stand in your last parade, wear the Kevlar for the final time, and be blessed with that last physical fitness test. Maybe the Army will give you a medal and say good-bye. You'll get a modest pension and a heart full of memories. The fortunate ones will still have their families, unlike others who lost theirs over the years.

Caring for us and those we love will keep life focused and balanced, long after the Army is finished with your services. There are no 75 year-old soldiers, but there are some outstanding veterans who served their country with honor, took care of their families, and made super grandparents. I bet these veterans also know how to visit solitude, but rather not stay there.

Needles and Pain

"A pleasure so exquisite as almost to amount to pain."
Leigh Hunt

My first memory of getting shots was at the Buncombe County Courthouse, just days before I first entered school. To this day, a brief shiver runs up my spine as I enter imposing government buildings like that courthouse, with large columns out front, polished marble floors, and high ceilings that produce an eerie echo when people talk.

Even as a five year-old I had a premonition something was about to happen. Mother held my hand a bit firmer than normal. I could hear the screams of some other small victims down the hallway, growing louder with every step we took. Soon I could smell rubbing alcohol in the air, but at the time I hadn't a clue what it was. Before long I would find out and would forever associate this smell with needles.

Many years later I would join the U.S. Army. Getting vaccinated is a part of the Army experience, and in the Army getting shots is not a single event, but a series of events over the years. They really stick it to you, and woe to those who cannot produce that forever misplaced yellow shot record. Forget this international record, and you might as well roll up your sleeve.

Civilians need to appreciate just how often their sons and daughters in uniform get stuck. Maybe you'll get a tetanus booster once every 10 years outside the Army, but within you receive so many more vaccinations, all gratis of course. There is a polio booster, a typhoid series, and shots for meningitis, yellow fever, tuberculosis, hepatitis, measles, mumps, and rubella. Go overseas to certain areas and you'll get the plague series, the encephalitis shot, and the ever-popular anthrax ordeal. Finally, every year it's a flu shot. Yep, the recruiters will never tell you about all those shots.

As an Army medical officer, it became my duty to keep my troops squared away with their immunizations. The medics and I got very good at this, even with the squeamish and needle-phobic types in our units. We could also handle the occasional warrior who always fainted at the sight of needles. Loaded with vaccine and an allergic reaction emergency kit, we'd hunt each soldier down till we were 100% done, including the occasional soldier wearing stars on his collar. They could run, but they couldn't hide.

Starting with the Old Man and the Sergeant Major, we'd have everybody immunized before too long. It was a pleasure ensuring all our soldiers would not get sick on deployments to exotic lands because of the immunity from disease they received from so many shots. When it comes to needles and pain, take it from me: it is more blessed to give than to receive.

Air Sickness

"Sickness is not of the body but of the place."
Seneca

The U.S. Air Force makes some truly delicious boxed meals for passengers on their longer flights. A couple of hearty sandwiches, some cookies, fruit, crackers, chips, and a drink make up the basic box, with a condiment packet and candy bar thrown in as well. With the Air Force loadmaster's safety brief done, we settled into our cargo seats, earplugs in to drown out the noise of those jet engines, and began to savor the contents of our small, white cardboard boxes.

En route to Egypt via Europe with a contingent from my infantry battalion, it would become obvious over time that there was at least one of my riflemen who failed to come to me for motion sickness medication. Perhaps he wanted to be tough. As things turned out, the trip would be tough on everyone, starting with him.

Our meals eaten, we drifted into a nice nap. A couple of hours later, the air turbulence over the North Atlantic began to make sleep difficult as our C-141 transport plane tossed about and the thin cargo seat padding left something to be desired. With all the bumps and dips, it wasn't long before the familiar smell of partially digested food began to fill the plane's cargo hold, not known for superior ventilation. The first rifleman had lost his cookies. Little did we know that it was merely a warning of more to come.

Thirty-five thousand feet over Greenland things became even more interesting. Despite the general air turbulence, the Air Force has to train. Today it would be a mid-air rendezvous and air turbulence was not going to cancel that training. With an aircraft full of infantrymen, our transport plane lined up behind a KC-135 refueling plane and the real fun began.

Up and down, a bump here, a dip there—for twenty minutes we became greener and greener as the pilots did their best to refuel and make some infantrymen wish they had walked to Europe. Many more succumbed to the general urge to refund the boxed lunches into special bags provided. The drama even challenged veteran flyers who now prayed for antiemetics.

In the end we made it to Europe, many on a now empty stomach. The loadmaster in charge of the cargo on the plane where our ordeal occurred was finally seen again as we deplaned, having mysteriously disappeared when all the fun began. He didn't look well either. They said the Air Force dining facility at the Rhein-Main airbase had made good chow for us after we landed—I don't think there were many takers.

184

History

"Those who cannot remember the past are condemned to repeat it."
George Santayana

The cockpit of the C-141 Air Force transport plane was brightly lit by the early morning sun, rising above the eastern Mediterranean Sea. We had been airborne about three and a half hours, having refueled and recovered from our nausea at Rhein-Main Airbase in Germany during the night. Our destination was Egypt—the land of the Pharaohs.

The pilot and copilot sat comfortably in their seats, with hundreds of interesting buttons, levers, knobs, and gauges all around and above them. The flight engineer sat on my right, monitoring a nearby weather system. From my seat, near the middle of the cockpit, I had a good view of everything. Though I did not understand most of the crew duties and gadgetry, it was all very fascinating.

In the early morning light, the tan coastline of Egypt began to appear. The Nile River delta and Alexandria were just to our right, the Egypt-Israeli border and the Gaza Strip to the left, and the Sinai desert, our destination, dead ahead. We were inbound to one of the oldest places on earth, rich in history, culture, and marvels western eyes seldom behold.

As the Sinai coastline and the Suez Canal passed below us, the desolate yet beautiful sands of the desert began. This small land bridge between Africa and the Middle East appeared nearly barren from the air, but the pages of history are not barren with the importance of the Sinai. Alexander the Great, Moses, Caesar and Lawrence of Arabia all crossed the wastes of the Sinai. Even a Teacher from Galilee would pass through, fleeing as a baby with his parents from the wrath of some crazy, power-jealous king.

Seldom does the U.S. Army post soldiers to an area so rich in history. Egypt and the Middle East offer wonderful opportunities to see history where it actually happened, whether a few years ago with the battles for the Suez Canal, or thousands of years ago with the Pyramids and the ancient Nile River. There is no better place to experience the past up close than where it actually happened.

I remember Egypt well. Of all world destinations, it was and still is "number one GI." The culture, sights, sounds and past came together in a feast of experiences seldom afforded by travel to any other location in the world. For once what Army recruiters promise paid off handsomely.

Those who are blessed with the memory of an Egyptian experience would gladly repeat it.

185

Short-Timer

"Time is the stuff life's made of."
David Belasco

For every soldier, the Army experience is punctuated by times when you have to pack your bags and move. Whether it is a permanent change of station (PCS), an end of your term of service (ETS), or that final retirement date, all soldiers, from private to four-star general, will move on. Moving is the great leveler.

"Short-timers," also affectionately known as "two-digit" or "one-digit midgets," are those soldiers who are within one hundred days of leaving an assignment. For those who anxiously await their transfer or the opportunity to leave the service, "short timer" is a coveted label.

Special short-timer calendars are available, particularly in those assignment locations that are less desirable. Soldiers can mark off each day, counting down to that glorious day when they can leave.

I always found these "short timers" a particularly irritating lot. Here you are, often on a difficult assignment, and there are people around you as happy as larks, marking off their final days and ever ready to remind you that they are about to leave and you are not.

An episode deeply ingrained in my experience was the arrival of our seventy-man group to a six-month assignment in the Egyptian desert. As we debarked from the Air Force transport plane into the scorching August heat, the group of soldiers we were replacing stood by.

These short timers were obviously excited about getting on the same plane for the outbound "freedom flight." As we "new guys" lugged our gear and marched past them, one of the zero-digit midgets called out, "See ya. Wouldn't want to be ya!"

Thanks a lot, welcome committee!

These difficult assignments far from home can seem like an eternity. Whether it is a combat zone, duty along the DMZ in Korea, or a stint of service in the desert watching the Iraqis, you often can't help but count time. There is so much you miss—family, food, stores that are open at three o'clock in the morning, the chance to be freer. Soldiers find the time creeping by when they really look forward to going home.

The clock faithfully ticks on, sometimes fast and sometimes slow, but it waits for no one. Every soldier is eventually a short-timer and then they go on to some new adventure in or out of the Army. Being a short-timer is part of the stuff of what life in the Army is made of.

The Close Call

"Pride goeth before destruction."
Proverbs 16:18

My unit's posting to Egypt was during the Gulf War. The infantry battalion I was assigned to as medical officer was filling in for another unit that had been diverted to Saudi Arabia. We looked sharp in our new desert uniforms as we assumed duties keeping the peace between Egypt and Israel. It was important work and we were proud to be there.

As our unit set up operations, one of my duties was to gather information on the locations and capabilities of local hospitals we could use in an emergency or for referrals, whether Egyptian or Israeli. Part of this effort involved a 150-mile trip to Elat, Israel to inspect the hospital there. So, my driver and I headed north from our base camp in the Sinai desert.

We crossed the Egyptian-Israeli border, completed our visit to the hospital, and began our return trip. As we drove, my driver and I talked about how proud we were of the job and how everyone treated us as VIPs.

As we headed back into Egypt we noticed a "Welcome to Egypt" sign. My driver suggested we stop and get a photo. Seeing no harm in this, I told him to pull off and we'd snap a couple of pictures. We stopped just short of the sign and I got out. I walked to the sign and turned around, facing my driver who was also outside the truck, preparing the camera. To my utter horror, I saw our new truck running backwards across the main road and down a small embankment on the other side. Yelling at my driver, we both scrambled after the truck. To add insult to injury, the truck was heading directly at a group of Egyptian ditch diggers on the other side of the road.

A serious international incident was about to unfold. Imagine my relief when the truck, all on its own, came to a sudden halt. The differential casing on the underside of the truck's rear had caught on a small pile of dirt the Egyptians had made just a meter or so away from where they were working.

Embarrassed, I mumbled a short apology in English to the workers, which I'm sure wasn't understood, and sheepishly got back into the truck. Fortunately, the engine started and we easily pulled away from the small dirt pile. After a short rebuke to my driver to make sure the truck is in park when we stop, we pulled back onto the road and headed home. We forgot the picture and how proud we were. Instead, we both were humbly thankful that Providence had averted disaster. I am sure the Egyptian workers thought they were lucky too.

The Ten-Shekel Woman

"Travelers from afar can lie with impunity."
French Proverb

My patient, an infantry company commander, was suffering from manic depression, an interesting medical condition which manifests itself as a heightened mental state, rapid speech, shifting thoughts, and hallucinations. He was no good to our unit in Egypt, so the commander ordered a captain and I to escort him back to the United States.

We passed through Tel Aviv, Israel, spending the night there at a beachside hotel awaiting a flight out to Paris and then on to the United States. Arising early the next morning, we got prepared to check out of the hotel and get a taxi to the airport. My patient, now on haloperidol, a major tranquilizer, stood obediently by our luggage as I stepped back into the hotel to get other bags, porters not being available because of the early hour. Meanwhile, the other officer checked us out of the hotel.

As I returned to where my patient was supposed to be, I was shocked to find him gone. In a near panic, I could faintly make out in the distance a couple walking arm-in-arm away off to the left in the foggy early morning darkness. Hoping it was my patient, I set off in hot pursuit, leaving our baggage in God's hands.

Tel Aviv at the time had a significant presence of those who ply humankind's oldest profession. These ladies of the evening were still at their trade even in the early hours of the morning. To my relief, my patient was in the company of one of these well-endowed ladies, who had offered her charms to my patient. Already acting like old lovers, these strangers of the night were off on a great international adventure.

Glancing at my watch, I had only a few minutes to untangle this love nest or we would miss our flight. As I caught up with them I discovered to my relief that the lady understood English. Tactfully, I pulled her to the side out of hearing of my patient. Slipping her an Israeli ten-Shekel bill, I said, "I'm sorry, but my friend here has AIDS. I am taking him back to America." She gasped, profusely thanked me, vigorously shook my hand and disappeared into the night. Recovering my now bewildered patient, we made our way back to the baggage and into a taxi.

Later, on the plane, I confessed to my patient what I had done. He laughed and laughed. I laughed too. The Jews have a saying that truth is the safest lie. Perhaps, but for the sake of time, I had to transgress with some creative maneuvering with an Israeli prostitute. She would forever remain for my patient and I, the "ten-shekel woman."

Mountain High

"Hear no evil, see no evil, speak no evil, and smoke no evil."
David Kay

The eight of us made the Saturday afternoon climb up Mount Sinai in typical infantry fashion—fast. Our battalion executive officer, MAJ Dave Shanahan, set the pace as his faithful staff officers followed. The three or so mile hike on that warm Egyptian day was a good workout. The goal was worth it, to stand on the summit of the supposed mount where Moses received the Ten Commandments from God.

The top of Mount Sinai itself is not very impressive—a small chapel, a low wall to keep folks from falling over the edge, and a couple of shanties set up by enterprising Egyptian vendors catering to tourists of all faiths and persuasions. The view on top, though, is spectacular. Spreading out in every direction are the rugged, reddish mountains of the Sinai Peninsula. These were mountains that sheltered the children of Israel fleeing Pharaoh's Egypt.

The climb to the top inspired us. We would learn that there are other inspiring things to be had on Mount Sinai as well.

In addition to the view and the thought that here is where God gave us the Ten Commandments, the clever Egyptians at the summit seemed to be an unusually happy, inspired lot. With their meager supply of sodas, water, and snacks, they possessed and sold yet another source of inspiration. There was an interesting aroma from the rolled cigarettes they smoked. Indeed, they were smoking pot. They were content to enjoy life in general and the view in particular. They were also eager for these American visitors to join them in their experience on high. We declined, of course, and finished our visit to the top with a soda, something far less intoxicating and also less dangerous to our careers.

On the way back down to the valley, the evening shadows began to advance. As the darkness came I reflected on the irony of the whole experience that day. At the very spot where God gave us the law sat those of the human race ready to disregard it again. The tempter was still at work. The darkness still comes.

I was reminded of a text from Psalms that many Christian soldiers have often referred to for strength—"I fear no evil, for Thou art with me." Many evils are out there to potentially lead you in the wrong direction. The senses and desires will always remain under some sort of assault, good or bad. Amid all the blitz of bad temptations, may soldiers always stand ready to hear, see, speak and also smoke no evil.

Checkers

"The chess board is the world;
the pieces are the phenomena of the universe;
and the rules of the game are what we call the Laws of Nature."
Thomas Huxley

It was the most novel checkers game I ever saw. Near a tourist site in Egypt a couple of enterprising Egyptians made a livable wage watching the cars and buses of visitors. To pass the time between customers they indulged themselves in a game of checkers.

Normally, checkers is played with round, plastic, disk-like pieces, twelve red and twelve black. What made this game of checkers so intriguing was how these businessmen made do, playing entirely with pieces and a game board provided by the environment.

Now these unique checkers pieces were what immediately caught my attention. Prepared, no doubt, from an assortment of basic raw materials, one would have never thought they could be employed in a checkers game.

I remember as a boy playing checkers with Pepsi and Coca-Cola bottle caps. These were, however, not nearly as environmentally friendly as those of these Egyptians. In the dry, nearly rainless desert world, these pieces were practical and came in two different colors, dark and light brown. Among the variety to be had, some came in just the right size. They were lightweight, and easily replaced by their overabundance in the general area of the parking lot.

The checkers board was simply marked out on the ground, the standard eight by eight checkered-square pattern drawn with a stick in the sand. The two squatting players were intensely focused on their game, played in the dirt and gravel near an old shack with animals on tethers nearby.

In time, I figured the whole thing out, having little else to do during my R&R but wait for my comrades to return. The animals were the key.

The local tourist business was doing well. Numerous animals nearby provided photo opportunities for visitors or carried burdens up the steep hills. The animals were well fed and therefore produced an abundance of droppings that, given a day or two of intense sunshine, baked some of them into hard, quarter-sized game pieces. From there it was a small step to using them along with small stones as game tokens.

Animal dung and pebble checkers—the most environmentally friendly, economical game I ever saw.

A Lesson from MARS

"Listen or thy tongue will keep thee deaf."
American Indian Proverb

We were given fifteen minutes to talk. Once a week I'd queue up in the line of troops to get a radiophone call through to my wife in Hawaii, halfway around the world from Egypt. The long wait in line would be worth hearing her soft voice and catching up on events with our four children.

The Military Affiliate Radio System, or MARS for short, provided our free link back home. Involving a special connection between radio and telephone systems, it required the help of radio operators on each end of the call who would hear every word of any conversation. Unlike a normal telephone call, though, speakers on both ends of the transmission had to end any portion of their conversation by saying "over." This would alert the radio operators to switch the transmission link to either receive or transmit, depending on the last person to talk.

After a couple of calls, my wife and I got the hang of this peculiar way of communicating, but not without some wasted conversations. You see, on the MARS system, if both people talk at once, then no one hears anything. You can also imagine how confused the two radio operators get when this occurs. Now what do I do? Do I transmit or receive?

It would be difficult to have an argument over the MARS system, unless, of course, both participants always allowed the other person to finish speaking first. This is unlikely of course, because most arguments require the freedom to get the last word in, often at the same time.

I have a rude habit of interrupting people during conversations. Something they would say stimulates some thought and impetuously, I would respond, often stepping on part of what they said. Though this malady plagues me still, a six-month stint in Egypt using the MARS phones reduced this tendency some. I learned more about the important, fine art of listening, giving others the chance to talk, of being patient, and most importantly, keeping my mouth shut.

They say that if the good Lord wanted us to talk more than to listen, He would have created us with two mouths and one ear. Indeed, the mouth does often get us into trouble.

A Roman by the name of Publius once said, "I have often regretted my speech, but seldom my silence." That is good advice.

What do you think, over...?

Simple Pleasures

"Memory is the diary that we all carry about with us."
Oscar Wilde

It had all the makings of a most excellent soft drink commercial. Two very thirsty soldiers, an extremely arid and hot Egyptian desert, an isolated roadside shack with a few tables under shade palms out front, a partially toothless host, and two ice-cold Pepsi Colas on a rusty old table flanked by two equally rusty chairs. Yep, this was right out of an *Indiana Jones* movie.

The drive from Elat, Israel to Sharm El-Sheik on the southern tip of the Sinai Peninsula is a long one. In the heat of an Egyptian September day it is even longer, with the afternoon temperatures soaring to 130° in the shade. With some cooking oil you can fry an egg on the hood of a car. Honest.

The hectic Western pace of life seems so out of place in the mountains and desert of the Sinai. Time almost stands still here. The scattered Bedouin nomads live their extremely simple life as they have for hundreds of years. Their pace of life is as slow as still photography, especially on a hot day. Even the occasional camels or goatherds seem to move in slow motion and the hot yellow sun appears to linger in the sky—prolonging it's relentless scorching of the earth below.

The long drive over the barren, ancient terrain mandates a stop at one of the infrequent "restaurants." My driver and I dared not eat the food, much to the disappointment of our host. Our digestive systems were not yet accustomed to the unseen bug additives that come at no extra charge.

But bottled Pepsi is always a safe bet, especially if you clean the tops before drinking and check to be sure there are no floaters. Though labeled in Arabic, the bottle's shape, color, and trademark red, white and blue emblem is familiar enough. And the ice cold, sweet taste, well… it's the stuff commercials are made of. Maybe those Pepsi people should travel more often for fresh ideas.

I don't think I've ever had a better soda, especially for just ten cents in 1991 American money. Need, circumstances, mood, and product came together in perfect harmony that day. The draining of those bottles filled our spirits and braced us for the remaining heat of the day.

Some things in life should be savored. Simple, inexpensive pleasures are often treasured the most. Their uniqueness and perfect timing leave their mark on our souls. The memory of those experiences should be cherished. And for some of us even the memory recalled can be like the real thing.

192

Burnout Latrines

"Everything is funny as long as it is happening to somebody else."
Will Rogers

In the United States we take bathroom facilities for granted. Combining the total number of public and private bathrooms all over the country, there are probably four or five for every man, woman and child in the nation. Post-World War II Americans have grown up with the relative luxury of not having to go far when they had to go.

Leave America and going to the bathroom is a very different story. Books can be written about the subject of toilet facilities abroad. There are near-coed bathrooms in France and cleaning ladies in Austria who press on with their tidying up even as you sit doing what everyone has to do.

You have the hole in the floor toilet in most parts of the world, with two footpads, one on each side allowing you to position yourself for the universal squat. Spend some time in countries with hole in the floor toilets and you learn to appreciate opportunities to sit on the throne once again.

The Army has to deal with this bathroom need when troops are deployed abroad. It is a big job, especially when large numbers of troops occupy a small area. The logistics of just taking care of waste becomes a fulltime job for some soldiers. But it is an important job, for Armies have been decimated from disease arising from improper disposal or handling of human waste.

Every soldier is familiar with U.S. Army doctrine on how to set up field bathroom facilities. Plop troops down in one place long enough and creative folks will find lumber and nail together some outhouses. Instead of digging a hole, troops will often place the cut-off end of a fifty-gallon fuel drum under each seat hole of the outhouse.

Once each day a detail of soldiers is sent out to cremate the accumulated waste of the last day. A small rear access door allows easy removal of the drum basin and the smelly contents are carried off some distance to a burning point, often an elevated area to carry the smoke away. Four parts diesel fuel and one part gasoline is added in sufficient quantity to the basin and then ignited. The resulting fire burns and burns, smokes and smokes, giving off a memorable scent, the incense of field duty.

Latrine duty is lousy work, but someone has to do it. Looking back over time, those who did this duty can perhaps now laugh about the experience, but it was not funny at the time. In fact, I would bet the term "job burnout" originated with burnout latrine duty. It is a job you only have to do once in order to experience burnout.

The Test

"Nothing is so much to be feared as fear."
Henry David Thoreau

The spouses of service members have a tough row to hoe, especially when the Army takes the soldier away for prolonged periods of time. My wife, Irene, has endured many such separations, and I do not believe I will ever fully understand the sacrifices she made while the Army kept me away.

Whether the spouse is gone for a week or for a year, the one who remains behind must confront a variety of challenges, especially if it is complicated by the responsibilities of raising children. A particular challenge, or really a fear, that my wife always had was what to do if the car broke down while I was gone.

We are primarily a new-car family. I make no apology for my innate disdain of trying to repair things that break. Tis better to have a warranty and peace of mind. It is therefore a tribute to the car industry that our new cars generally stayed in good shape when we had them.

The time did come, however, when even our new car broke down. Unfortunately, the always-dreaded event occurred while I was on yet another long deployment with the Army. Irene had to face the sum of all her fears— being broken down on the side of the road.

My oldest son had broken his arm and my wife was on her way to an appointment at Tripler Army Medical Center in Hawaii. Irene had pulled off the main highway and was heading up the hill towards that "pink palace" on the hillside known as Tripler. Without any warning, the engine to our new van died. Coasting to the side of the road, Irene faced the sum of all her fears.

Staying calm, Irene said a prayer as she, now near tears, reflected on what to do. It wasn't too long before she headed out on foot to get help. A friendly motorist picked her up and brought her on up the hill to the hospital. There, Irene sought out Army Chaplain Ed Bowen, a family friend, who helped her get the van to a garage. Providence intervened with someone on the Lord's (and the taxpayer's) payroll.

Through it all, Irene faced the ordeal with courage, a clear head, and with faith. In the end she emerged much stronger for having successfully confronted one of her worst fears. It is a tribute to Army spouses that time and again they make do on their own. The declaration of independence for my wife and other spouses is written from those bitter and difficult ordeals where they alone stared fear in the face and overcame.

The Corporal

Observation Post Six is perched atop one of the highest mountains in the Eastern Sinai desert. To the west lie the bleak mountains of the Sinai Peninsula. To the east is a vista of the Gulf of Aqaba, with the faint outline of Saudi Arabia in the distance. The mission of the thirteen-man crew of OP Six was to observe air and sea traffic up and down the Gulf of Aqaba.

A narrow, precarious road threaded up the mountainside to OP Six. The danger of moving up and down that road was underscored a few years back, when four men were killed because their vehicle tumbled off the side of that high mountain.

The one survivor of that awful accident, now promoted to corporal, stood with me as we watched the weekly delivery of helicopter slingloads bringing food, fuel, and water. Since that terrible accident, supplies are ferried by air up to the top where the OP lay. The Corporal was a quiet fellow. He and I were both entranced by the movement of the white helicopter, flying up and down the side of that high mountain. Each trip brought precious cargo dangling in the large cargo net below the helicopter.

We'd squint and turn our faces as the helicopter's rotor blades kicked up the sand and dirt with each landing. Quickly, crews would go forward to unhitch the net and wave the aircraft off to fetch another load. Our eyes followed their every move.

Back and forth the operation continued. The Corporal and I marveled at the efficiency of the men as heavy barrels of fuel, boxes of food and canisters of water were moved away from the landing zone. In the background, near the edge of our hilltop perch, the black smoke from a burnout latrine lazily climbed upward. Gaps in the smoke created by the helicopter gave the impression of some Indian smoke signal.

To the Corporal and I, all the scenery and work were fascinating. We could sit and enjoy it all day, but it had to end. The OP's senior sergeant called the Corporal away. We parted cordially, but without words. I patted him on the shoulder as I headed off to the waiting helicopter for a quick ride back down the mountain. The Corporal, tail wagging, trotted off on all fours to his fresh dog food. I envied him. He'd been through a lot, but the U.S. Army took good care of him. It was a good life for that dog, and anyone else who wears dog tags.

> "Therefore to this dog will I,
> Tenderly not scornfully,
> Render praise and favor."
> Elizabeth B. Browning

Herb

"Every man over forty is responsible for his face."
Abraham Lincoln

The man is a legend in his own time. The legend is in the number of people who think highly of him. You will meet many people in the Army who know people you've met or served with. In my experience, no one tops how many people know Herb Brav.

If you've been posted to Egypt with the multinational force peacekeeping mission there, you know about Herb. A retired Army Sergeant Major, Herb was already up in years when I met him there during the Gulf War. Still sharp and energetic despite his age, he was phenomenal. In charge of the recreation services for troops rotating there, year after year Herb became almost synonymous with South Camp, a fortified base in the south Sinai desert on the Red Sea.

I've never met anyone quite like Herb. Slender and fit, he was a physical fitness machine when most folks his age gave up long ago. You could see him out running everyday. The camp weight room was another place often graced by his presence. He kept going when everyone else in his year group was retired and on social security.

Herb was easy to get to know and very friendly. Some of his more unique qualities were enthusiasm, an upbeat attitude, and a genuine concern for soldiers that was second to none. All these things left deep impressions on everyone who met him, regardless of age or rank. These qualities have given Herb many friends around the world. Indeed, I truly have never met anyone else who knew more soldiers and famous people than did Herb.

Over the years, thousands of soldiers, many of whom are now civilians, owe a deep debt of gratitude to Herb. He made their stay in the Sinai so much better than it would have been without him. Year by year he dedicated himself to improving the off-duty services to lonely soldiers posted in the Sinai desert. He made things happen, from scuba diving and weight rooms, to sports programs and the Army's own private beach on the Red Sea, affectionately known as Herb's Beach.

Throughout the years and around the world I've encountered many, many soldiers of all ranks who smile when Herb's name is brought up. They knew him well and with great affection. What a man! What a legacy!

For many soldiers Sergeant Major Herb Brav has been the very best face of the Army they ever saw.

Zealots

"One man with courage makes a majority."
Andrew Jackson

In 72 AD, the Roman Tenth Legion under Flavius Silva laid siege to the Jewish mountaintop fortress of Masada, which lies just west of the Dead Sea in Palestine. About a year later the Romans completed a mammoth ramp, constructed from the valley floor to the top of the mesa-like mountain.

The Romans used Jewish prisoners of war to build the ramp. Many of these people were captured during the recent destruction of Jerusalem. The ramp they constructed was huge, measuring 330 feet high and 645 feet long. Its width would be just enough for troops and siege machinery to reach the top in order to engage the defensive wall.

With the ramp completed, Silva's Legion proceeded to make a breech in the wall of the Jewish defenders under the leadership of Eleazar ben Yair. Realizing the hopelessness of their situation, the Jewish defenders elected a final act of defiance rather than endure humiliation and enslavement by their Roman attackers, now poised for the final dawn assault. As the Legionnaires stormed the hastily built wooden palisade the next morning, they found that the defenders had committed mass suicide, finding only a woman and two children still alive, hidden in a cistern.

The Jewish historian Josephus wrote: "Nor could they (the Romans) do other than wonder at the courage of their resolution, and at the immovable contempt of death which so great a number of them had shown."

I stood at the top of Masada, looking down the massive ramp to the valley below. An R&R trip from our Army jobs in Egypt gave us the opportunity to see firsthand this most famous of last stands. The yellowish-white rock, sand, and ruins of Masada spoke volumes about the events that occurred here nearly two thousand years ago.

The loudest message of Masada for me was that of courage and counter courage. The formidable resolution of the Romans was displayed time and again throughout their rich history. They overcame any obstacle in their path, be it mountains, people, or fearful odds. The tenacity and determination of the Children of Israel are also almost unbelievable. Laid low time and again, the survival of these people through history bespeaks of a Power unique among human societies.

Soldiers should study the lessons offered from the history of these two great peoples, the Romans and the Jews. Though we may not agree with everything they did, we cannot err in studying their incredible example. One man with courage may make a majority, but two with courage will make history.

Sees

"...if ye have faith as a grain of mustard seed, ye shall say unto this mountain, remove from hence to yonder place; and it shall remove."
Matthew 17:20

It had been nearly two thousand years since the Roman General Titus stood on the exact spot where the 25th Infantry Division Commander, my battalion commander, and I now stood on the Mount of Olives. Just a short walk to the west lay the city of Jerusalem. Titus needed two months to conquer the city. We had two hours.

We set off at a brisk pace going through a pre-determined walking tour of the main highlights of Jerusalem. The General was thrilled as we passed through biblical and historical places: the Mount of Olives, the Via Dolorosa, the Garden of Gethsemane, the Wailing Wall, the Temple Mount.

The divided city, part Jewish, Arab and Christian presented a contrast of cultures, politics and history. Every group claimed this piece of ground, barely five or so kilometers square, as very sacred. Like the Romans of old, the three of us were foreigners in a strange land. It was and still is a land whose customs were vaguely familiar, yet still very foreign.

A lot of territory can be covered in two hours. We paused at a Jewish cemetery where, according to Jewish custom, stones laid on top of the tomb are used instead of flowers as a sign of honor and visitation. Then it was on to other sights including the Wailing Wall where prayers, written on small pieces of paper, are stuffed into cracks and crevices of the only remaining section of wall that was once the glorious King Solomon's Temple.

We walked where Christ walked. We paused to pray where He prayed. We stood where many think He was crucified. We also stood where Mohammed purportedly ascended to heaven. It was indeed the most interesting terrain walk I ever had with an American General officer, a feast for the senses against the panoply of cultures and history.

One detail stands out above all that we experienced during those two hours. As we passed the southeastern corner of the exterior wall of the ancient Temple Mount, we came upon a small mustard tree, growing outward from the base of the wall. We stopped and I picked a small seedpod from one of its limbs. Opening it, I removed the tiny seeds and showed them to the General. No larger than the period to a sentence, he was impressed with the idea reflected in the teachings of a Carpenter from Nazareth concerning these seeds and faith. It was an illustration so tiny, yet so powerful. Yes, moving a mountain takes just a little faith and Generals, in particular, are known to move many mountains because of their faith in the men they lead.

Kindness

"Kindness is a golden chain by which society is bound together."
Johann W. Goethe

A knock at the door at four o'clock in the morning does not bode well. In a deep sleep, I slowly came awake to the rapping at my door in the bachelor officer's billets. "Who is it?" I asked. "Dave, this is Major Shanahan." I came wide-awake now. "The XO," I thought, "this cannot be good." I invited him in as I struggled in the darkness to find the light.

I sat on the edge of my bed as he entered my room and there was a look of deep concern on his face. "I have some terrible news for you, Dave," he said. Immediately thoughts raced through my mind. A tragedy. Oh God, please not my wife or my children.

Gathering courage, Major Shanahan said, "Dave, your mother has passed away."

One's memory fails when trying to go over the immediate details of what happens after being informed of a tragedy. It all becomes such a blur. For the messenger and the recipient, there is just no easy way to give or receive bad news. A shock sets in and events become dreamlike. There were tears, a phone call back home in the wee hours of the morning, hurried packing, and getting Army emergency leave orders cut.

From where our unit was in Egypt, the Army had me in Tel Aviv, Israel and on an airplane home within hours. The system that energized to make this happen on very short notice is called emergency leave.

No system on earth is better than the U.S. military's ability to get service members home when there is a serious emergency. Having seen it in action for others many times before, I was very impressed when my turn came to experience it first hand—especially with the complication of being pulled out of the Middle East during a conflict.

The part about my emergency leave I shall always cherish the most was the manner and concern shown by my battalion XO. His task was difficult, but Dave Shanahan's genuine attentions translated into rapidly making things happen to get me home. The chain of events accomplishing this feat all within twenty-four hours left a deep and lasting impression on me.

How the Army takes care of soldiers with an emergency is a golden chain of kindness which bond soldiers even more to the organization and country they serve. The kindness always begins with a sensitive leader who makes things happen. Such kind leaders are worth their weight in gold.

199

Individual Uniformity

"…And our public opinion welcomes and honors talent
in every branch of human achievement."
Thucydides

One thing that distinguishes the military from civilian life is the distinct decrease in the amount of privacy one can enjoy. Living, training and sleeping in close quarters with a large number of people makes it nearly impossible to hide anything. In the old Army, for instance, even the bathrooms had no privacy walls—just eight toilets in a row facing an equal number of sinks.

It is difficult for some people to give up their coveted personal privacy. Though the Army has changed some over the years, there is still a general lack of privacy when compared to civilian life.

Another unique thing about military life is the uniformity. It all starts with your basic uniform, but there are also haircuts, equipment and regulations that are designed to homogenize the military organization, making everyone look alike. Individuality takes a back seat to uniformity. Everything being the same ensures that tens of thousands of people will quickly recognize, understand each other, and work together even though time and distance may separate them.

Like a glass of homogenized milk, the Army is built to look the same everywhere. But every now and again individuality legally exerts itself, especially sub-group individuality. In fact, the Army encourages some of this expression. The system sometimes acknowledges the value of being different, especially when the difference has special meaning. Rank is certainly the most common expression of individual differences, something every new recruit discovers their first day in the Army. There are other things too, like a "Ranger" haircut, a sleeve patch, cavalry spurs, or some special headgear like the Green Beret. All can be found if you look carefully. Each contributes to esprit de corps, or group pride.

In a sea of green soldiers the trained eye can see those who stand out, the individuals there in that large group. There is that especially sharp uniform or the row of sleeve hash marks. There is the guide on bearer, the gold trim on headgear, or a star on someone's collar. Though rare now, there is the soldier or veteran with a multicolored set of ribbons on their chest, one of which is pale blue with five tiny white stars. Truly, far from being a pack of identical military automations, today's military reveals a lot of talent and achievement within the outward uniformity.

Points of Contact

"And on the highest throne in the world, we still sit only on our bottom."
Michel E. de Montaigne

"The most difficult thing about jumping out of airplanes," the Airborne Training Sergeant said, "is the landing." He had our undivided attention, as it was our first day at jump school in Fort Benning, Georgia. "When you hit the ground," he continued, "there is a right way and a wrong way to fall. To fall properly, you need to use your five points of contact."

Over the next couple of hours we were repeatedly taught about these five points of contact. They are:

1) the feet
2) the side of the lower leg
3) the side of the thigh
4) the buttocks
5) the upper back and arm

Before we could even think about putting a parachute on, we had to pass muster on the proper way to fall. You have to fall before you can soar.

"Get up, Alpha 174, and do it again," the black-hatted staff sergeant instructor barked at me. Over and over I'd do the drill in the sawdust pits of airborne school until those wonderful words came, "That was pretty good, Alpha, now move on to the next station."

Over time, I came to understand the meaning of "get off your fourth point of contact," the buttocks. The modern Army has become less vulgar in expressing the messages that were more colorfully said in times past. Army sergeants today cultivate a vocabulary far removed from the cursing of yesteryear, but the delivery and manner are much the same. The fourth point of contact is merely a synonym for other more vulgar ways of identifying anatomy and potential laziness. In fact, you'd be surprised how many words and phrases mean buttocks.

Some say the Army should be tougher and that "soft talk" softens the Army. Others want to "soften" the Army's image further by keeping the military politically correct. You'll find heated debate on this "tough language topic" from soldiers and veterans alike, debates that might involve interesting speech and hot tempers from time to time. The debate is often so intense that even advocates of temperate speech have been known to use intemperate words.

The tincture of time will no doubt settle this linguistic debate. At times it is best not to take sides. The best course might be to wait the issue out by sitting on your fourth point of contact.

Tight and Ready

" We owe almost all our knowledge not to those who have agreed
but to those who have differed."
Charles Caleb Colton

About one hundred nervous soldiers gathered in the rigging shed next to the airfield at Fort Benning, Georgia. It was our third week of parachute training—jump week. The first two weeks were behind us. All the running, calisthenics, and classes on how to parachute were finished. Now, our final week would be the real thing. Most of our group was still intact, having only lost a couple of people to injuries.

On large wooden tables in front of us lay each soldier's parachute, neat bundles of green with yellow safety tags. The main chute looked like a small, flat backpack with a confusing array of harness straps attached. A small reserve parachute lay on the front of the harness below the main chute. That was a portion of the gear each of us hoped would not be needed.

In a loud voice the cadre sergeant began instructing us on the proper way to put a parachute on. In language a fourth grader could follow, he broke everything down into simple steps. Each part had a purpose and a position. Everything was important. He had our attention.

On his signal we began to put the awkward gear on. As each person donned the parachute, we knew that in a critical moment our very lives would depend on how well we followed instructions. This strap here, a snap there and everything seemed to be in position. Each of us checked the man next to us. Yes, everything looked good.

Slowly, the jumpmaster made his way down the line, carefully re-checking every person's work. Everyone, it seemed, needed some correction or adjustment of his or her gear. My turn came and the sergeant carefully looked at and checked every part of my equipment. "It looks good, sir," he said. "Just needs a little tightening." With that he proceeded to pull my groin straps tighter, my family jewels narrowly escaping serious discomfort. "I don't want you slipping out of the chute on the way down, lieutenant," he remarked, as he moved on to check the next man.

"Thank you, sergeant," I said in a now slightly higher voice.

In time our entire group was ready. We filed out onto the tarmac to the waiting Air Force cargo jet. There was not a loose parachute among the bunch of us as we waddled forward in our tight harnesses. We silently prayed that the riggers did a good job packing our parachutes. We also thanked the good Lord for sergeants who knew their stuff and who begged to differ with our best efforts.

Fear

"Courage is doing what you are afraid to do.
There can be no courage unless you are afraid."
Eddie Rickenbacker

Parachuting from an airplane for the first time can be a near terrifying experience. It isn't natural to "jump out of a perfectly good airplane," as some have said. We're all familiar with the fear of flying—that fear is a reality when you stand in the open door of a plane at an altitude of 1200 feet. That's when palpable fear hits you.

My jump school buddies and I were pumped and excited. Finishing two weeks of preparatory training, we headed into jump week ready but nervous. Five parachute jumps—two being at night—and we would get the coveted silver parachute badge to wear on our chests.

No matter how much mental preparation you go through, you can never be fully ready for that very first jump. You just do it. There we were, the hundred of us with full parachute gear on, all crowded into an Air Force C-141 jet transport plane. Everyone is nervous as the aircraft takes off and banks to the right and then left as it maneuvers into position for the drop zone. It's warm inside. There are no windows. Everyone is quiet—just the whine of jet engines and the smell of military gear and jet exhaust. There are nervous glances toward the rear of the plane where the red and green lights are. The red light is on. The doors on each side of the plane slowly come open and the noise level intensifies as the jet engines roar. You can hear the rush of wind. The fear meter inside rises. There is this puckering feeling in your fourth point of contact.

The jumpmaster yells above the noise, "Ten minutes!" After a few more minutes he yells, "Chalk one, stand up. Hook up." We all struggle to our feet encumbered with bulky parachute gear front and back. We hook our static line ripcord to the tight cable above our heads that leads to one of the doors at the rear of the aircraft. The activity keeps our minds focused, but I find I'm whispering to myself, "Be brave, Dave. Be brave." The remaining moments race by. The light turns green. The jump master yells, "Go!" I waddle to the door right behind the man in front of me with six more people clustered in line just as close behind me. The first man is gone, and then…

The whoosh of the wind and the sudden silence are the first things you notice. As the plane moves away, you feel the tug of the parachute canopy opening above your head. There is the smell of jet exhaust in the air. You hang there, slowly descending to the ground. You did it.

Now, where do I land?

203

PLF

"He that is down needs fear no fall.
He that is low, no pride."
John Bunyan

As the Air Force transport plane continued to move away, I was struck by the wonderful feeling of weightlessness, hanging there below the green canopy of my first parachute. Behind me were six other jumpers, slowly drifting downward. The ground was a thousand or so feet below.

About thirty yards in front of me was the first person of our eight-man "stick." A bit heavier than I, he was already well below, approaching the edge of a forest. Anxious, I watched him for a moment, worried that he might land in the trees. Presently, I realized my own need to pay attention and quickly surveyed the ground below for the best landing spot. In no time the first man landed safely, and I soon followed.

You hope for a good landing. Most parachute injuries occur with the landing, hence the reason so much of jump school is spent teaching want-to-be paratroopers how to land. Mentally, I repeated to myself the five points of contact drill over and over during my remaining seconds aloft.

Quickly, the ground was upon me, and I assumed the position of feet and knees together, legs slightly flexed at the knees.

SPLAT! My boots disappeared in about ten inches of muck, hidden under the light covering of mown hay. As water immediately began seeping into my boots, I fell backwards onto my buttocks, thoroughly wetting the seat of my pants.

Thus ended my first PLF. My attempts to go through the five points of contact with a proper PLF ended with the only points in contact with the ground being numbers one and four—my feet and my butt.

The water was cold and the mud stank, but I was not injured. Embarrassed but relieved, I said out loud, "I'll take it!" It took some effort to extract my feet from the mud as I pulled myself up. Before too long I was sloshing my way to the assembly point looking and smelling like I had wet my pants.

I was luckier than others. Some did break an ankle or sprain their back with a bad PLF. My inglorious PLF was without injury, other than my pride perhaps.

If you can walk away from a PLF then it is a keeper. I may not be able to win the lottery, but leave it to beaver to find the only twenty-square foot mud hole on a two-square mile drop zone.

A Leap into the Dark

"I am about to take my last voyage, a great leap into the dark."
Thomas Hobbes

One thing you learn at airborne school is how to parachute at night. Now, let me say up front that every time I have parachuted from an airplane, it has essentially been a night jump, for I had my eyes closed every time.

It was our final jump at parachute training school. Packed into an Air Force C-130 Hercules cargo plane, we anxiously awaited our turn to "exit the aircraft." We were fully loaded with equipment—Kevlar, parachute, rucksack, and a weapons carrying case strapped to our leg, complete with a wooden 2x4 board inside simulating an M-16 rifle.

We all sat squashed together in the troop seats. The dimly lit interior cast an eerie glow to this very personal drama, this jumping out of airplanes into the darkness. The plane's four propeller driven engines were very loud, especially as the rear doors came open. Eventually our turn came to begin our slow shuffle towards the wind and noise at the rear of the aircraft. Our jumpmaster stood like an executioner next to the door. The red glow of a light near the rear door only added to the ominous mood.

There was no time to get too scarred though. Above the noise he commanded the first man in our "stick" of eight men to "stand in the door!" A short moment later the red light turned green and people in front of me began to disappear into the night. I instantly followed.

I felt like a cockroach being flushed down a giant toilet. And this time the lights were off. The turbulence ended as I felt the now familiar pull of the canopy deploying. I could see nothing, even with my eyes wide-open. Somewhere below me was the ground. The question was, when will it arrive and are there any trees? I glanced up at the stars and then towards the horizon. "There!" I said out loud to myself, "The treetops. Get ready." I quickly pulled the rucksack release straps and the rucksack fell away, now only attached to me by a ten-foot cord. "Oomph!" I groaned as I hit the ground, tumbling over my rucksack.

"Great PLF, Alpha!" I sarcastically muttered to myself.

I lay there on the ground, flat on my back, looking up into the night sky. Follow-on C-130's crossed overhead like giant, black condors releasing tiny black dots into the darkness, each dot carrying another soldier on his or her final jump. A cadre sergeant nearby on the drop zone ran over to me. "Are you okay?" He asked. Scrambling to my feet, I answered "You bet!" "Good," he said, "now police up that parachute and move out." Gathering up my parachute, I congratulated myself on my final leap into the dark, a voyage I would never forget.

205

Optimism

"The optimist sees the donut but the pessimist sees the hole."
McLandburgh Wilson

Optimism can be very powerful stuff. A good dose of optimism in a group of people can make things happen, and making good things happen is very rewarding. If only we could buy optimism in the store.

Participating in a change of command ceremony is usually an unnerving affair for officers and non-commissioned officers. Everyone has to brush-up on their drill and ceremonies as the big day approaches. Training schedules are adjusted. Practice parades and equipment layout preparations keep everyone hopping. Stress is a given.

One significant pressure on everyone, though not spoken of a great deal, concerns questions about what the new "Old Man" will be like. Despite the Army's best efforts to train leaders in the same methods and doctrine, the result of special commander schools is an incredible variety of leadership styles. There are good, bad, and indifferent leaders. There is the micromanager, the ruler from a desk type, the worried character, and the penny pincher. Everyone hopes for a great new commander, but mentally prepares for the worst.

My opinion is that the best commanders are the optimistic ones. These people arrive to their new command with an attitude and demeanor that say, "You are the best." Their bearing and method display a sincere charisma that attracts junior leaders and makes them want to do their best. They foster an atmosphere of growth and progress. The motto in their method is "You can do it and I'm going to do all I can to get you there."

The result of such optimism is a momentum that produces outcomes like victories, trophies, awards, time-off, promotions. Positive momentum can win wars too.

Under a positive, optimistic leader everyone can succeed. Optimistic people, for example, can help turn setbacks and defeat into victory. A part of the power seen in enlightened leadership is their sense that all things can work together toward something better. They know that winning can and does happen, and that success involves every member of the team.

Which brings me back to new commanders. There is no perfect commander out there. All are merely fractions of that ideal whole. There is no special course or school that makes them perfect either. But a good common denominator of those outstanding souls who lead groups of people to their greatest height of achievement is optimism. I am confident the Army will continue to produce many commanders who do not focus on donut holes.

Monument

"I found Rome a city of brick and left it a city of marble."
Augustus Caesar

Every now and again, but sadly not often enough, we meet someone who makes an extraordinary difference. In workplaces characterized by more of the same every day, it is refreshing, but also sometimes scary, to have someone come in who improves things.

One of the most uncertain of Army experiences is to be in a command when a new commander comes on board—the so-called change in command. There is a great deal of uncertainty as officers and men wonder what the new commander will be like. Will he or she be lax or strict? Enlightened or a despot? A father or a devil?

LTC Dorian Anderson was an extraordinary man and commander. He found our infantry battalion in brick and left it in marble. He was also the first African-American battalion commander I served under.

To be honest and up front, when LTC Anderson got on board, we were nervous, not unusual with a staff getting to know any new commander. The concern was greater as we were also worried about how he would interact with his staff of thirty or so officers, all but a couple of whom were Caucasian or Hispanic. Most of us had never served under a black battalion commander. It all promised to be a good learning experience for everyone.

There was no need to worry. Our new commander was likeable, very approachable, and showed sincere concern for each officer and soldier in his care. Highly educated and reasonable, what he desired made good sense.

In order to build you need many workers. A master at leadership, LTC Anderson expertly marshaled the strengths of his subordinates and set a course towards excellence. He was not an office-bound commander, but got out among the troops regularly. He also did not micro-manage his people as he did the walk about. His creative leadership allowed for error, but had absolutely no room for ineptitude, laziness, or favoritism.

Over time, our experience and abilities as officers improved under LTC Anderson's expert style. Unbeknownst to us at the time, our crude leadership methods began to change. Following the example of our extraordinary commander, our individual styles of leading soldiers improved. The results were polished and refined junior leaders, better prepared for the next level. Instead of tearing down, LTC Anderson built his men into something stronger and better. Instead of bricks unwillingly baked under arbitrary leadership, we became better at what we were all about—like polished marble. I can think of no better monument to any commander.

Early Birds

"Tis easier to obtain forgiveness than to ask for permission."
NCO Wisdom

When it comes to money, I have no trouble spending it. My relationship with money goes way back, through thick or thin, and, as you might correctly guess, more thin than thick. Though I have become a bit more conservative with age, my wife will testify under oath that money does not homestead within my wallet.

Spending other people's money is even easier. In the often austere world of military budgets, from time to time money suddenly appears, especially with special projects or missions. I can spend this quickly.

An interesting phenomenon in the Army is the so-called "end of year" spending. As far as military budgets are concerned, the financial year does not end on December 31. September 30 is the endpoint for annual DOD spending. This being the case, August and September can be shopping months in the Army, particularly when residual money is yet to be allocated in a "use it or lose it" accounting system.

I developed the habit of making a wish list of Army supplies and equipment that would be nice to have. From this list, purchase requisitions were prepared and submitted, even though I knew full well that no money was available at the time I submitted them. Some years were good and others were fruitless.

One particular year, I was fairly liberal about pre-positioning these requests and lo and behold, when September came, money had to be spent. Lacking any other requests, the supply folks sent mine forward and they were paid for out of unspent funds from the budgets of other folks who were less inclined to spend money. Penny-pinching Peter pays proactive Paul.

Come October, the goodies I ordered began to arrive. Word got out, and naturally, some folks were upset. They made some phone calls, and before too long, the XO pulled me aside. "Doc, what's all this money you've been spending?" "Sorry, sir," I said, "I suppose I was leaning forward in the saddle too much." He grinned and said, "You're forgiven. Now, tell me how you did it so I can educate my less aggressive officers."

In a hundred words or less I explained to the XO how my system worked, something an old supply warrant officer taught me. Essentially the ordering was a gamble, but no more a gamble than birds that get up early to have a better chance at the worms.

In this case, there happened to be a lot of worms that year.

Battle Offering

*"Consider the postage stamp: its usefulness consists in the ability
to stick to one thing until it gets there."*
Josh Billings

The war games against the opposing force (OPFOR) at the Army's
Joint Readiness Training Center were not going well for our infantry
battalion. The bottom line up front was that we were getting our tails
spanked. As medical officer, there was little I could do to help my infantry
comrades in rectify the deteriorating situation. They were not doing well
especially when the "bad guys" overran the battalion command post.

Each day a new battle scenario would be played. Screening,
movement to contact, defense, attack, you get the picture. After a few days
we would be in the defense. The old man had had enough of being beaten—
the new plan implemented the evening before the defense began would be
unorthodox—a full infantry company would be positioned as bait to draw
the bad guys out into a "kill position." Our brigade's defense would be a
counterattack of the bad guy's attack. The anvil receiving the attack and
counterattack would be an augmented infantry company of 130 men.

Reinforced with a mortar section, some combat engineers, and a
forward surgical team that included me, Charlie Company dug in for the
coming onslaught. I too made my foxhole deep and covered it with a piece
of ¾" plywood, piled eighteen inches of dirt on top, and added a final touch
with a camouflage layer of leaves. The umpires were impressed with this
"doc" who dug his own ditch.

At dawn the attack came, first with simulated artillery fire, then a gas
attack followed by the main mechanized infantry assault. I hunkered down
into my foxhole, gas mask on, laying low as the guns blazed away. The
MILES, or laser tag, systems on each "hit" soldier began to beep. Within
moments the OPFOR had overrun the company and moved on into the
brigade "trap" behind us.

As Charlie Company regrouped, only thirteen men were "left
standing." In the storm that was our teacup, we had managed to hang on
long enough to maul the OPFOR.

Meanwhile, my medics and I were pretty busy with the bulk of
Charlie Company's "wounded." The umpires took note that the medics laid
low while the world fell apart. We were still there when the storm moved on.
Now they watched us do our stuff. Though the company had gone down the
drain in the simulated fight, the medics were there to save what was left. All
in all, it was good fun, but one wonders how different it would be had it
been the real thing.

A Dirty Story

"And so, from hour to hour we ripe and ripe,
And then from hour to hour we rot and rot, And thereby hangs the tale."
William Shakespeare

We Americans take for granted the relative luxury of being able to shower or bathe each and every day. We grow so accustomed to this that our keen sense of smell can immediately detect that person near us who emits the unspoken message that they have not bathed in a few days. They hit us with a familiar blast of ripe, human body odor.

I remember during basic training some of our number needed remedial lessons in the important art of personal hygiene. Too lazy to take a shower like the rest of us smell goods, they stood in our close ranks broadcasting their stink to everyone with a normal sense of smell. It didn't take long to figure out who used *Dial* and who didn't. The bad cases received a midnight shower party. Select members of the platoon with a particularly strong desire to enforce the Clean Air Act, formed an ad-hoc committee for public safety and took it upon themselves to rather rudely interrupt the stink bug's sweet slumber and haul him off to a cold shower. One such lynching was enough to inoculate soldiers on the benefits of baths.

Thankfully it isn't often, but there are times when the United States Army gives you the opportunity to go for extended periods of time without a bath. A tour of duty with a combat arms unit, especially light infantry, will at some point provide the chance to get dirty and stay that way for awhile. My personal record is eight days without a bath, but I have on good authority that many others have far exceeded my record and lived to smell the tale.

Ironically, when everybody stinks then you don't stink so badly. Maybe our sense of smell adapts to unpleasant odors. Stinkers enjoy the company of other stinkers. Hey, what's a little BO among friends?

But the family sure does notice when you get back home. Your reputation precedes you. Days and days of good, dirty training have produced a good case of grand funk that is in desperate need of a long shower, lots of soap, and a hard scrubbing. You are so dirty your discarded uniform stands up by itself and the wife wonders whether to wash or burn it.

The miracles wrought by soap and water cause you to become a new creature. Add a touch of deodorant and cologne and you are a civilized human being again, ready to join the ranks of sweet smelling soldiers. I highly recommend everyone get real dirty at least once in his or her life. It builds character. If America ever goes to war again you can bet dirt will be a basic issue item, but a regular bath will be optional.

A Little Rest

"Sleep is a divine oblivion of my suffering."
Euripides

We had been at the Joint Readiness Training Center (JRTC) for four days. The OPFOR was eating us alive. Day and night our light infantry battalion took heavy "casualties" as the smaller, smarter, faster OPFOR units harassed our conventional efforts.

Within the first twenty-four hours all our helicopter support had been "shot down." Every re-supply convoy was ambushed, with many vehicles "destroyed" with the resultant loss of supplies. Communications, medical, and logistical support struggled to keep functioning despite personnel and equipment "losses." The brigade commander's grand strategy was failing.

By day four our colonel was tired, very tired. I came up to his vehicle to check in and he couldn't even remember my name. Bags were under his bloodshot eyes. All this was no war game for him—it was real. He was at the point of total exhaustion.

I pulled the XO aside and asked when the Old Man had last slept. Learning that he hadn't slept more than a couple of ten-minute catnaps in four days, I made my way back to the commander's HUMMV with the XO. Slightly nervous but determined, my words shocked even me as I proceeded to order the Commander to bedrest. I felt like *Doctor McCoy* on *Star Trek*. "Sir, you're no good to anybody, please sleep."

Reluctantly he agreed, and the XO, who had been saying the same thing in vain for two days, took over. The commander had a good sleep. We saw to it. Guards posted, no interruptions, no noise, and a dark tent with a soft bed. For four hours he slept the sleep of the dead.

When he awoke it was dusk. Refreshed, the Old Man called all his officers in and laid out a new plan to fight the OPFOR. Tactfully abandoning the brigade commander's failed strategy, we witnessed a new commander turning his troops loose to fight fire with fire that night.

By dawn the OPFOR were on the run. Instead of making us sitting ducks, units were busted up into small maneuver elements that searched for the enemy patrols and ambushes. Convoys were enlarged and fortified overnight. We were transformed into a battalion of guerilla fighters giving the bad guys a dose of their own medicine.

Still superior in numbers, our tactics paid big dividends. One of the best payoffs was that our suffering lessened. Supplies were regular. Aircraft could fly again. We all could get some sleep, too, including the Old Man. A little sleep changed us from losers into winners. Sleep sent our suffering into oblivion.

Dr. Jeckyll and Mr. Gunner

"God himself helps the brave."
Ovid

The Army has a system in place whereby if a war breaks out many professional medical people come from all over the place to join units heading into the fight. Some people will come from the Army Reserves and National Guard. Others come to us from permanent U.S. Army hospitals.

My three-year stint as a medical officer to an Infantry battalion included some interesting trips and training. The U.S. Congress authorizes a second medical officer as part of our combat training. When the time came for my battalion to deploy for a month to the U.S. Army's Joint Readiness Training Center for realistic combat training, the Chief of Internal Medicine Clinic at Tripler Army Medical Center joined us for the trip.

It was his first real exposure to the Army, having spent most of his short career in hospitals. You might think getting pulled out to play war games would be a real pain for these specialty-trained physicians, and for many, it is. But for this doctor, it was a great adventure. Though he knew little about the real Army, he learned fast, like cramming for some test.

As the war games commenced our doctor played for real. He pitched in with all the details of providing front-line medical support, such as finding places on a map, making do with what medical supplies the Army gave us, or digging in to hide from the bad guys. Though we'd probably never do this in a real war, he and I shared the same foxhole for company. In a real war you would not want both doc's in the same box, so to speak.

Day by day I was struck by how this mild-mannered, board-certified internist was transforming into GI Joe. One day we were getting harassed by a genuine Soviet-made HIND attack helicopter the bad guys had. This flying tank was making a mess of our light infantry battalion. As the beast strafed us, our chances of "surviving" around the umpires worsened.

The Doctor became exasperated with this winged tank. Grabbing an M-60 machine gun and a belt of training ammunition from one of our 'casualties,' he loaded the weapon up and jumped out of our trench, General Patton style. "Enough is enough," I heard him yell as he aimed the machine gun at the HIND helicopter heading straight at us. Tossing away his Geneva Convention status as a noncombatant, he opened fire.

"Boy!" He exclaimed as the last of his ammunition blanks were expended and the helicopter had flown on, "That felt good!" A spontaneous applause erupted from grunts and medics hiding in ditches, holes, and culverts all around. "Good job," I said, "but try not to look so conspicuous around me. It draws fire."

Sailing

"When a man does not know what harbor he is making for,
no wind is the right wind."
Seneca

My wife has always had this strong desire to learn how to sail. To her, sailing carries with it an intense sense of freedom and romance. To travel on the open water under your own power is a neat thought. The quiet solitude is attractive, taking one away from our often-hectic life.

I was never as enthusiastic about the adventure of sailing as Irene was. Nevertheless, I consented to take lessons with her at the Naval Marina in Pearl Harbor, Hawaii, right next to where the big United States Navy ships dock.

The day came for our joint experience and we found ourselves being taught the ways of the sea by a seasoned sailor working with the armed forces recreation services center. After some brief shore lectures, our lean, well-tanned instructor took us out in a small sailboat, not too far from where many ships were sunk during the Japanese attack on Pearl Harbor in 1941. Our instructor seemed to effortlessly steer the small craft over the gentle waters as the warm tropical breezes took us from point to point. Enormous Navy ships moored nearby dwarfed our small boat, but we paid close attention as the expert seaman ably showed us the various techniques.

In time, it was my turn to take a boat out. The task was quite simple: take out the small sailboat and pass three specially placed orange buoys in the harbor. Then, simply return to the starting point. Right. Piece of cake.

Well, not exactly. In full view of Navy crews manning an aircraft carrier and a couple of other ships nearby, I proceeded to entertain them with my efforts to control both ship and sails. I couldn't seem to get the thing to go where it was supposed to and the wind wouldn't cooperate either. After upsetting the boat a few times and failing to clear the last buoy, I struggled to steer back to shore, now also soaked to the bone, landing as close to the starting point as possible. Clearly, the problem lay not with the boat or the wind. It was a user problem. Irene, on the other hand, expertly sailed and landed without mishap. I envied her obviously inborn nautical skill.

Sad to say thus ended my naval career for a time. Work and a deployment abroad for the Army interrupted my further studies, but at heart I just didn't want to go back. Becoming a sailor may be in the cards someday, but for now I'll stay on shore. I'll need more motivation and a more opportune time to correct my operator difficulty with both sailboat and wind. For now it is a boat too far.

Kay's Law

"Do more with less."
Unofficial Army doctrine

For years I wondered what held the Army together. Fat and lean years, happy and mean years, you have to have something that keeps things going through it all. With all the fluctuations in the Defense budget year after year, there are times when the Army does well, and others when you just have to make do. The real strength of the Army's ability to function comes in the 'make-do' years.

There are many that wish the Department of Defense was on a more fixed income. But the vicissitudes of the American way of life and fluctuations in the political landscape will forever have an effect on the Pentagon's budget. You might say the Pentagon holds everything together. Maybe so, but I for one, believe in *Kay's Law*.

Kay's Law states that there is an inverse relationship between the amount of money the military has to spend and how much duct tape soldiers use. The more money the Army has, the less duct tape is used, and vice versa. I just know the manufacturers of duct tape cringe when they see a rise in defense spending.

They should issue every soldier a roll of duct tape. It is wonderful stuff. I can think of no other substance that has so many applications. You can patch things, hide blemishes, plug holes, cover over glare, and hold about anything together imaginable. In the Army, this special tape has 1001 uses, especially in the leaner times, when it is necessary to save money and cover a lot of sins.

But you know, too much of a good thing has the opposite effect. You might call this a corollary to Kay's Law. Too much DOD money causes the Army to use less duct tape to make things last. I mean, why use duct tape when there is plenty of money to get new stuff? So soldiers throw away repairable things and buy new items. Duct tape sales go down.

All this buying and living without duct tape drains the budget, gets up the ire of conservative penny-pinching types in Congress, especially those with heavy interests in tape manufacturing, and before too long the DOD budget gets cut. Duct tape sales go up.

It is all very clear now. Decreased military spending is not a peace dividend. It is a duct tape dividend. We can always do more with less, if we have duct tape. Furthermore, it isn't red tape that holds everything in the Army together. It is duct tape.

Paradise

"What! Wouldst thou have a serpent sting me twice?"
Shakespeare

Hawaii is a gorgeous place. Of the fourteen or so assignments I've had in the Army, my wife and I especially appreciated these tropical islands. The warm temperatures, lovely trade winds, and lush greenery combined with the warm spirit of Aloha in the people who live there, created for us a place as close to the heavenly kingdom as you will find on this earth.

But there is a devil in Paradise. You will not see him on the beaches of Waikiki or in the fine restaurants of Honolulu or Maui. No, this prince of darkness crawls in the hills and boonies of paradise.

Hawaii has done an excellent job in keeping snakes and rabies out of the islands. Strict inspections and mandatory quarantine periods provide a strong barrier to the entry of unwanted pests and disease. But when the devil came to Hawaii, he managed to sneak in as a centipede.

Troops, especially light infantrymen, stationed in Hawaii are very familiar with this orange/brown critter. Spend any amount of time training in the Kahuku Mountains training area and you'll meet this fellow, always on the move, getting into interesting places like empty boots or sleeping bags.

It is fascinating to watch this creature from a safe distance. Dozens and dozens of legs busily work in unison to bring the whole to some unknown destination. The dramatic head armed with two pincers looks menacing, but the danger lies in the V-shaped tail.

I was taking care of a sick infantryman one morning, high up in the hills on the island of Oahu. Off in the distance you could see a hotel resort on the beach and imagine the amenities there. Good food, swaying palms, refreshing pool, and beautiful women. But today the task at hand was dramatically different. As I worked on this soldier, I had laid my Kevlar helmet down in order to use my stethoscope. Finishing my examination, I placed the Kevlar back on my head.

Everything went okay for a couple of minutes, but then I began to experience a sudden stinging headache, the likes of which I'd never had before. I thought I was having a stroke. Then there came another headache, now on the other side. I immediately pulled the Kevlar off, and as I laid it down I caught a glimpse of a centipede tail in the webbing. One of these ten-inch monsters had nailed me twice. Thankfully, I didn't have a serious allergic reaction as other victims have had.

In every paradise there is something that brings knowledge of good and evil. In Hawaii it is not a tree, it is a serpent of a different sort, a devil with a stinger.

Eagles

"They shall mount up with wings as eagles."
Isaiah 40:31

No matter where the Army managed to send our family, Irene and I always appreciated the support commanders gave to Boy Scouting programs at each post. Commanders understood how important it was to keep young boys busy and out of mischief. Like the youth sports program, Boy Scouting is alive and well in United States Army communities.

One of the things I am most proud of is being the father of a couple of Eagle Scouts. It was a long but fun road to assist each son in getting to this coveted achievement, the highest rank in Boy Scouts. Spanning many years and three different continents, we managed to help several great troops and scoutmasters get the boys through hikes, camping trips, merit badges and service projects. In a sense Scouting helped give meaning to the boys amid all the disruption of moving and the turbulence of adolescence.

One of the very best Scouting programs we experienced was at Schofield Barracks, Hawaii. Each year the 25th Infantry Division command would sponsor a survival program for Scouts. It was a big deal that included obstacles to cross, survival food to sample, rappelling towers, and special equipment to try out, all supported by dozens of soldiers, volunteer leaders, and involving hundreds of Cub and Boy Scouts.

My youngest son, Brian, was a Cub Scout at the time we were there. He was all fired up about participating. With all his hyperactive buddies in the pack, they were off to do what their daddies did.

I was unable to be there for most of the day, but by mid-afternoon I arrived just in time to see the boys negotiate a rope bridge. My son lined up with the other boys across a large ditch filled with mud. He managed a wave to me as I stood on the other side with other watching parents.

One by one scouts slowly shimmied their way across as we gazed on. Some of the boys would loose their grip or grow tired and fall into the mud pit four or six feet below the rope. Splat! Laughter would erupt as each boy received his chocolate coating. Soon, every boy, including my son, could not possibly hope to cross the pit unsoiled due to the enthusiastic assistance of scouts bouncing on both ends of the rope.

The fun-filled day ended with muddy boys receiving their patches and awards. They had a great day learning about what their dads did in the Army. Some of those muddy boys would one day rise up and become eagles in Scouting. Some of their dads would rise up to become eagles in the Army.

Where do eagles dare? Scouting is a good start.

Lessons

"Be ignorance thy choice, where knowledge leads to woe."
James Beattie

We were working hard in the tropical heat of Thailand. In country for over two weeks, we were finally going to have a full day of rest and relaxation. For most soldiers it was a chance to go to town.

Lesson #1—Try to relax when you can.

The city of Phitsonoluk lies in the center of Thailand. A thriving market town, it offered plenty of sights, sounds, and smells for soldiers weary of the daily military routine. It also offered opportunity for mischief.

Lesson #2—Never pass up opportunities to learn.

Our battalion commander ordered that all soldiers stay in at least groups of four when on pass. So, three warrant officer aviators dropped by the aid station the day prior to R&R and asked, "Hey doc, we need a fourth person. You want to go to town with us?" "Sure," I said, little realizing the education I was about to get.

Lesson #3—Don't do R&R with Army pilots.

The next day on the way to town, my companions had things in mind to do far different from my idea of a good time. Surmising their plan to visit a house of ill repute, I expressed a desire not to partake, but that I'd drop them off and pick them up. Soon we arrived at the prostitute palace.

Lesson #4—There will always be things you have never seen.

Entering the lobby, we found a typical looking barroom with tables, signs, bottles, and so forth. Of distinct difference were the large two-way mirrors along the far wall behind which approximately fifty Thai beauties were seated in orange bathing suits. Prominently displayed on the covering for their ample upper anatomy were numbered signs for selection purposes.

Lesson #5—Never judge a book by its cover.

My aviator friends disappeared for three or four hours to have a good time, and I, the self-righteous one, found a restaurant and did some shopping, ignoring the old man's order to stay together. The pilots had a good time and so did I.

Lesson #6—Sometimes you cannot follow orders.

The restaurant meal sat well with me, with no gastrointestinal haunting. I'm not sure the excitement sat well for my pilots. A couple of the them left with something extra for their good time, as they would discover a few days later. Despite doc's prior advice, their hormones overruled and the body later paid a health tax.

Lesson #7—Sometimes you get more than you bargain for.

Saint Not Sober

"A visit from St. Soldier."
David Kay
(Adapted from *A Visit from St. Nicholas* by C.C. Moore)

'Twas the night before Christmas, when all through our stake,
Not a creature was stirring; no one was awake.
The presents were placed by the tree with care,
And all hoped that morning soon would be there.

Our children were nestled, all snug in their beds,
While visions of video games danced in their heads.
And my wife in her nightgown and I in my briefs,
Had just settled our brains for a tropical night's sleep.

When out on the sidewalk there arose such a chatter,
I rose from my bed to see what was the matter.
Immediately to our windows, I jumped like a jack,
Lifting up the blinds and pulling the curtains back.

The moon shown bright in that Hawaiian sky so wide,
And gave the luster of midday to everything outside;
When what to my wondering eyes should appear?
But an intoxicated soldier that everyone could hear.

With his slurred voice, so garbled and brash,
I knew in a moment it was a drunk about to crash.
I could see his flushed face and a little round glass,
That spilled when he laughed, fertilizing the grass.

He staggered and swayed, a right intoxicated old elf,
And I laughed when I saw him, in spite of myself;
But the direction of his gait and the tottering of his head,
Soon gave me to know I had nothing to dread.

He spoke loud words as he continued his great work,
Of filling the night with sounds and acting like a jerk.
And waving his hands at the sky and our abode,
He gave a nod and on down the sidewalk he strode.

Sometimes he'd spring to his senses and into the night he'd yell,
But always on down the path it grew quieter. You could tell.
I finally heard him exclaim as he staggered out of sight,
"Merry Christmas to all! Do you want to fight?"

Bragging Rites

"Experience inspires this work."
Ovid

With four children in our family, every opportunity to travel while in the Army inevitably includes a stop at any theme park along our path, especially those with roller coasters. These man-made terror machines with their dose of thrill and excitement attract my children like moths to a front porch light. They get this tendency from their father, who is, of course, the worst of the bunch.

Meanwhile, mother is content to merely sit and watch.

Over time we have ridden many coasters. We rate the thrill from each ride. The terror meter was higher on the one with the two loops for example. I rate roller coasters according to nausea or pain. With each new park my children have taken me to new levels of both.

The best of all rides is an experience my children will never know, unless of course they enter military aviation. The best experience is in the front seat of a Cobra attack helicopter—especially with a veteran warrant officer pilot at the controls.

My opportunity came while serving as a flight medical officer for a helicopter squadron deployed to Thailand. Our four-week sojourn was full of new sights and experiences. After helping this particular warrant officer with some medical problems, I was able to cash in on an offer he made for a ride I had long looked forward to. The ride became my best experience in Thailand and one of the best of my Army career.

Strapped into the narrow front seat, the clear canopy overhead offered a full field of view ahead and to each side. Effortlessly, the aircraft lifted off and a feeling of weightlessness overwhelmed me. The pilot flew low—very low. Narrow valleys, pathways, roads—all were areas explored three dimensionally. Sharp turns and sudden surges in altitude added to the thrill and wonder of the ride. Instead of going around in circles like a roller coaster, the scenery constantly changed.

It was a ride that went on and on. Unlike a sixty-second roller coaster ride, the Cobra ride lasted over an hour. What an experience! What a memory! For the time being, dad is one up on all the roller coaster tales each of my children can tell. We've ridden *The Rattler, The Scream Machine, The Big Bad Wolf, The Mind Bender* and a dozen others, but only dad has ridden the Army Cobra. Those bragging rights have been one of the top fringe benefits of my military experience.

Temporary Housing

"This too shall pass away."
Abraham Lincoln

We seldom got it right. Probably only once or twice could Irene and I honestly say we lived in a great house. Living in not-so-perfect temporary circumstances is one of the curses of the Army experience.

Allow me to elaborate. One of the most significant pressures on a soldier with a family is to make sure they are all settled in once you arrive at a new duty station. The need is often at the mercy of what lodging is available at the time. Even when you choose from the best houses that might be up for lease, you learn to never judge a house by its exterior.

Deerpath Drive had a nice ring to it. The brick house was in a beautiful neighborhood with friendly people. Yes, this would be a great home during our one-year sojourn at Fort Bragg, North Carolina. But after we had gotten all settled into our new home, the wind shifted. Literally. The realtor failed to inform us of a large pig farm to the north. Never, my friends will you smell anything more repugnant than a pig farm. The deer path led to a farm full of pretty pink pigs in a piggy pooh pit.

Another home we lived in was full of cockroaches. We owned the day, and they ruled the night. We attacked these creatures mercilessly and took no prisoners. Even my peaceful Irene joined the fight. In the end, we had to violate international laws on the use of weapons of mass destruction to finally subdue their prolific and tenacious civilization.

A couple of times the Army blessed us with rather tempestuous neighbors. How these people ever fell in love and married escapes me. The things they said and did would make Jackie Gleason's *The Honeymooners* look like *Sesame Street*. A civil war would rage next door, always teetering on the brink of outright violence. How skillful human beings are in the artful manipulation of the English language in order to cause harm!

Once we found the perfect house, just the right size, near to work and church, in a quiet clean neighborhood, or so we thought. But down by a nearby creek a hunter kept his hound dogs. These adorable animals became abominable pests as they began their serious howling in the predawn hours, especially if there was a full moon.

From sights and sounds, smells and some interesting neighbors, I suppose one is never going to find paradise on earth. Every rose has a thorn. Whatever housing inconveniences we have had to deal with in the Army, we took comfort in one fact: sooner or later, the military would send us somewhere else. This too did pass.

Nerf Wars

"Old men are children for a second time."
Aristophanes

I asked my three sons, now practically grown men, what one of their fondest memories about being an Army kid was. Their answers surprised me. They had many memories of life in the Army, from taking rides in Air Force planes to seeing places few kids their age ever dreamed of doing. But without a doubt, all three of my boys rate the Bachelor Officer's Quarters (BOQ) Nerf wars right at the top of their "Best Army Experience" lists.

Our family had just moved to Fort Sam Houston, Texas, from our previous assignment in Hawaii. While waiting to buy a house near post, we stayed in a small two-room suite on the fifth floor of the BOQ. It was summertime, and three grade school age boys were a handful to keep entertained, especially when cooped up all day.

Visiting the PX one day, my boys discovered the merits of the soft, foam Nerf toys. For a young man looking for action and excitement, the array of Nerf weapons was just the thing. We bought some, of course, and my young warriors would anxiously await the return of dad from work each day, knowing that with my arrival, the Nerf wars would begin. The entire fifth-floor hallway became our private battleground as we fired our Nerf weapons at each other. Day after day, it was high adventure as the fledgling warriors practiced assault tactics in an urban environment against dad.

We had small Nerf guns and a large Nerf cannon, all with soft ammunition that made little noise and didn't hurt when you got hit. For hours we would battle back and forth, maneuvering and attacking, taking prisoners and being taken prisoner. It was great exercise and great fun, especially for Dad, playing different scenarios as only boys know how.

Mother appreciated the relief of being without the boys for a while each day. Over supper they would entertain her with the tales of our imaginary battles and victories, and I too entertained her with stories from the Nerf wars.

Time marched on, and soon we moved into our new home. The Nerf guns were played with less and less. I was rummaging through some old toys for my boys the other day, and there was one of those Nerf guns. After ambushing my wife I discovered it was still serviceable after all these years.

My grade-school sons are men now, but I know that they would readily join me in a second Nerf war if only given the chance. Perhaps we'll do it again when we're old men and the legend of the Nerf wars needs passing on to the grandchildren.

Poetry in Motion

"Forewarned, forearmed; to be prepared is half the victory."
Cervantes

It's early morning and dark outside. The cold air is crisp and sounds are amplified by the stillness. Out of the distance you hear them coming. There are calls and chants. The rhythmic stamping of a mass of people approaches, hundreds, thousands of them in unified motion. Synchronous impacts of running shoes against the pavement. The guidon flags are out front. A single voice of a side runner calling out a verse and the group responds in a unison chorus. It's physical fitness training time again.

First comes the Division Commander and his immediate staff, with the U.S. flag and Divisional colors with battle streamers out front. No one wears rank, only their gray PT clothes. The only variety seen is in the different types of running shoes everyone wears. You can identify the leaders by where they run in formation. Center front is the commander. On either side of the commander are often the XO and the Sergeant Major. Behind come massed phalanxes of soldiers, four abreast. Each unit has a talented cadence caller, some undiscovered Billy Joel. He runs on the left side, calling the chant that keeps everyone in step. In addition to puffing and sweating, you have to sound off too. "C-130 going down the strip…"

Military group PT is poetry in motion. Strange poetry to a civilian, but poetry nonetheless. Across the different military services, the ritual of group physical fitness training in the early hours of the morning is repeated each duty day around the world. Painful to all, inspiring to many, this mandatory event builds unit cohesion, wears out its participants, and bugs the non-participants in their cars trying to cross a post with key roads blocked for the runners.

The group is stronger through this very public ordeal. Individuals will recover from their aches and pains and be strengthened. The end result is unit and individual pride in their joint experience. For the Army, physical fitness training builds fit soldiers and weeds out those who are not. More importantly, there is an intangible payoff for unit leaders molding a team. For the casual observer, this uniquely military devotion to physical fitness brings an appreciation of the worth of our Armed Forces.

Though some may not be able, there are others who can and will be ready—even in the wee, dark, early hours of a morning. They train to fight. They train to be winners. The price is sweat. The payoff will come in the crisis later today or tomorrow. "So here we go. We're at it again…" We can all take comfort in the fact they are at it again and again.

Big Brother

"You don't live in a world all alone. Your brothers are here too."
Albert Schweitzer

There are times in a person's life when you wish you could go back and do a retake of some episode, some bad experience for which you were the cause. I wish for a redo of a particular staff meeting at the Army Medical Department Center and School at Fort Sam Houston, Texas.

Jan "Casey" Bond and I were instructors at the school there. We shared the same office. We hit it off well, and our shared background as medical officers in combat arms units helped solidify the relationship in a school-house world surrounded by nerdy medical types who just did not know what the real Army was all about.

Though I arrived at the school before he did, I looked up to Casey, who was senior in date of rank and age to me. Just back from Somalia, he would entertain me for hours with tales of the adventures and escapades he had had there. It time I could honestly say he became almost an older brother to me.

Casey was chairing a departmental staff meeting one day with twelve or so instructors and support personnel in attendance. In hindsight, I should have missed that meeting, but a seat was duly occupied by yours truly. The meeting agenda went well until the subject of communication equipment came up. To this day I don't know how it happened, but within minutes Casey and I were having a war of words in front of the staff—me, the temporary liberal, wanting to buy the stuff and he, the conservative, telling me there was no money and never would be.

I cannot speak for Casey, but I had definite opinions on the matter and my contrary streak dug in. "No" was not an option. Well, no was the option. In my bullheadedness, I made a mountain out of a molehill and tarnished the friendship, too.

Now here is where the true gentlemanly side of Mr. Bond came out. I was primarily at fault, making a debate public before any preliminary staff work or discussion behind closed doors was completed. But it would be Casey who made the first genuine gestures toward reconciliation. My pride melted. Friendship mattered more than differing opinions or embarrassment.

Casey retired out of the Army long before I did. Our chance meetings over the years stand out clearly in my mind. His enthusiasm and constant smile always revealed what a great man he will always be. He was truly the big brother the Army never issued me. May he live long and prosper.

The Big Fish

"I have laid aside business, and gone a-fishing."
Izaak Walton

There is nothing quite like a fishing trip to forget about life in the Army for a bit. That old uniform gets hung up and you don those old blue jeans, a flannel shirt, that lucky fishing vest, and a raggedy old hat that, though it looks pretty sorry, will still keep your head dry. There is nothing like being in the proper uniform for fishing.

My oldest son, Nathan, and I went on one fishing trip I will never forget. The lakes of Manitoba, Canada beckoned and we headed out in our canoe for a great adventure. Tulabi Lake lay undisturbed as the morning sun rose in the east. A hint of fog lingered over the dark waters. Our canoe glided gently over the glass-like surface as we headed across the lake to an area we had not as yet fished. On our way across we trolled and managed to get a couple of hits: two small walleye and a medium-sized pike. The fish were biting and we knew we were using the right lures.

Arriving at the other side, Nathan made the first cast into shallow water near shore, maybe two or three feet deep. "Aw Dad," he complained, "It looks like I've snagged a limb." I glanced over to where he had cast. As he reeled his line in, a small wave of water followed, but unlike a wave created by some inanimate object being pulled under the water, this wave quivered. "Nathan," I said, "I'm not sure that is a limb."

As soon as the last word was out of my mouth, Nathan gasped. An enormous tail had flipped up out of the water. "Oh boy!" I screamed, "I'll get the net ready." Nathan had caught a giant in the shallow water—a fifteen-pound, thirty-seven inch Great Northern Pike. The toothy giant made us a bit nervous as he lay in our tippy canoe.

That big fish was definitely a keeper and found a permanent place mounted on our family room wall. It is a most excellent momento of a great time with my son while away from the Army. Indeed, when I see that fish I am reminded that a soldier's children, and not the Army, are among the most important things in his or her life.

You can have a very successful career. Promotions, prestige, medals and honors are all well and good. But as far as life is concerned, doing the Army thing at the expense of your kids cancels out the other successful parts. In the big scheme of things the big fish gets away.

For soldiers with children it is important to sometimes lay aside the Army and build some memories. It is the only way to land the big one.

Trouble and Rocks

"I have had many troubles in my life
but the worst of them never came."
James A. Garfield

All of God's children have troubles. Sometimes we might be tempted to think that we have received a disproportionate serving of trouble, but over time some of us learn that there are others who have far greater troubles.

While I was an instructor in the Army's physician assistant school it was my periodic duty to serve as an advisor to a class of PA students. As a class advisor, one quickly learns that everyone has his or her individual struggles.

With regards to trouble, one particular student comes to mind above all others. He was a great soldier and was very intelligent. He made good grades and was always at his appointed place of duty. The only trouble in his life was his spouse—and she became trouble in my life as well.

My first meeting with her went off well enough. Cordial, but in hindsight I now know she was merely sizing this captain up preparing for the coming assault. You can imagine my shock when on the very next day after our meeting she entered my office unannounced and in an emotional outburst dumped all her anger and frustration at the Army in my lap.

Great Scott, by the time she finally slowed down was that a pile of trouble! Money problems, unable to get into post housing, medical needs with their three children, pregnant with a fourth, husband should be home more, and generally a hatred for all things military, were just a few of her complaints. Naturally, most spouses are super people and don't have nearly as much trouble, but as we began to tackle each problem, I came to realize that this lady expected the Army to do everything to make her happy.

Gently, I attempted to give her a more realistic expectation of Uncle Sam. She would have none of that. She was a "got to be in the front of the line" kind of person. No matter what I did for her, since I was "part of the system" it wouldn't be good enough. Like the child who dreads going to an immunization clinic, I began to dread her periodic visits to my office.

Rather than allow hateful people to get under your skin, one must remember it's their problem, not yours. Do what you can, but some people will be never satisfied. Refuse to be drawn into their self-imposed purgatory.

God bless those rare soldiers with really troublesome partners. They are stronger than I am. Generally, one can do only so much for their problems. Beyond that, you have to move on, like water in a creek that flows on by the pesky little rocks in the way.

Survey

"The more laws and order are made prominent,
the more thieves and robbers there will be."
Lao-tzu

Some equipment was missing, about $5,000 worth. Repeated searches were fruitless. The Commander ordered an investigation, so a report of survey began. The Sherlock Holmes of missing property is the report of survey officer.

A report of survey is not unlike that of a private investigator or special counsel. Evidence and statements are gathered. Piece by piece, you trace where the missing item was and where it disappeared. Slowly, you narrow down the person or persons most likely responsible for the loss. Often, the answer isn't very clear. Other times you uncover some serious stuff.

Report of survey duty is something any officer in their right mind does not look forward to doing. The job usually comes without any advance warning as an order from the Commander. It is not a "we'll get to this when we can" priority either. It has high visibility and importance to the command, the progress of which is often tracked on a daily basis. So, over the next two to four weeks your schedule is trashed, for the survey process is often long, tedious and time-consuming. In addition, the task is often thankless. And the paperwork bears witness to the fact that many trees have given their lives for this process.

Throughout my career, I've known and heard of cases where soldiers destroy their careers with acts of dishonesty or larceny. Some interesting cases were: a dentist taking Army dental equipment home; a sergeant selling Army equipment to feed a drug habit; a colonel caught shoplifting in the post exchange; and a soldier selling rationed items on the black market. Often they are caught by the report of survey officers.

It is ugly work ferreting out the wicked, but someone has to do it. You see the dark, often stupid side of human nature. As the process nears completion, you see the system at work bringing justice to the abusers of taxpayer dollars—the fines, article 15s, letters of reprimand, or actual jail time. Any negative outcome will potentially ruin careers.

There is a dark side in each of us, some bit of barbarism or selfishness we struggle to keep under control. Every now and again, some of us have a serious idiot attack and the dark side shows itself. Sometimes we are caught. If not caught, then the stupidity is likely to repeat itself ever more easily. Being all you can be should not include being a criminal. You don't even want a little bit of that in your life.

Faith and Allegiance

"...That I will bear true faith and allegiance to the same..."
From the U.S. Army Enlistment/Commissioning Oath

The battle dress uniform of every soldier has two cloth tapes sewn to the front of their tunic or blouse. Over the right upper side lies the soldier's last name and on the upper left is a tape displaying "U.S. Army." If soldiers are ever in doubt regarding to whom he or she needs to remain loyal to, they need only look at their chest. Prominently displayed on the front of Army uniforms are the three things in life that soldiers should bear true faith and allegiance to: their family name, the United States, and the Army.

The first loyalty of a soldier should be to his name, symbolized by the right nametag. Shakespeare wrote, "To thine own self be true." By taking care of yourself and those you love who bear the same name, you perform your first and most important duty. It is always the right thing to do. This is where all honor begins.

The second loyalty of a soldier is to the United States of America, the U.S. part of the left tag. The ideas embodied in the Constitution, the Bill of Rights, and the subsequent amendments to the Constitution form the basis of our unique experiment in democracy. Such an experiment could not continue without people who are willingly prepared to defend it against all enemies, both foreign and domestic.

The third loyalty of a soldier is to the Army. Take care of the Army and the Army will take care of you. The Army forms the largest and historically most important branch of the Department of Defense. You can never truly defend this great nation without the capability to seize and hold ground with American flesh and blood. Smart bombs, planes, or ships cannot do this. The Army is nothing without people.

For those Americans who never enter military service, there is only so far they can go with patriotic loyalty. Not to question the sincerity of their motivation, it still takes a higher level of commitment and love of country to willingly give up certain freedoms for a time in order to serve in uniform. The civilian leadership of this wonderful nation would benefit from leaders with military service credentials, something the voters should always remember.

In a world of faithlessness and disloyalty, it is important, critically important, to maintain a group of citizens sworn to be loyal to the timeless ideas of Family, Nation, and Army. And to duty, honor, country. May America, in turn, always bear true faith and allegiance to her soldiers as well.

A Lesson For All

"The secret of teaching is to appear to have known all your life
what you learned this afternoon."
Anonymous

When cast in the role of teacher, every now and then you have to give a lesson that is not found in a textbook or manual. Some lessons, particularly the difficult ones, are given experientially and must be learned quickly. It fell my duty to give a group of soon to be officers an important lesson, which in turn became an important lesson for me as well.

The forty PA students in the class were among the best enlisted soldiers in the United States Army. Selection to the school is highly competitive, so those who come are sharp, motivated, and very intelligent. It was a pleasure to teach them and the class would honor me with a small plaque near the end of their training, one that still hangs in my office.

Unfortunately, coinciding with their class gift to me was an incident that threatened to mar everything. One of their number, also soon to be an officer, was frustrated with the results of a test posted on a classroom bulletin board. In his anger over a poor score, he wrote in large letters B.S. over the score sheet. It was a behavior unbecoming of an officer.

Upon my discovery of the act of written vandalism, I struggled with what to do. Such a deed could not go unaddressed, especially for officers who must be leaders and also example setters. A student conducting himself in this publicly obnoxious manner would bring into question his fitness to lead. The last thing we need are officers with a graffiti problem.

I nervously stood before the class. On the table in front of me was the plaque they had recently given me. My opening remarks were on the proper behavior of officers. This led to a review of the deed and my desire to find out who the perpetrator was. It was my hope that this person would quickly come forward, acknowledge his error, and publicly apologize. If not, then I was prepared to temporarily return the plaque to the class, unable to honorably display their gift to me when an unknown class member had acted with such dishonor. It was a difficult lesson for me and for them.

Much to my surprise and relief, the guilty one came forward quickly. Contrite and embarrassed, he publicly made amends for the trouble he had caused. His courage to accept responsibility for his actions restored the honor of his class and my confidence that he would learn from the error and become an even better officer.

I shall never forget that experience. It is something you cannot learn from a book, these lessons about duty, honor and country.

Teamwork

"If it is broken, fix it. If it works, don't break it.
If it refuses to work, then DX it.
That about covers it. Any questions?"
NCO Wisdom

The basic functional unit of the Army is a squad or section that numbers anywhere from five to eleven personnel. Soldiers in a squad or section normally work in close proximity to each other. It is therefore nearly impossible for any member of such a unit to goof off or "sham," since each soldier usually keeps a sharp eye on the other. This is a part of teamwork. You drop the ball and fellow team members know right away.

In the Army there is always a job or some collective task to do. To get the work done each member needs to pull his or her own weight. Each member also needs to understand the jobs of other members of the unit, for unexpectedly the job may be thrust upon you, especially in combat.

Within small units, cheating on the job or cutting corners has a short life. Each member quickly feels the omissions or mistakes of others. Individual failure can lead to collective failure.

For example, a squad in Ranger school does not find its rendezvous point because one man failed to read a map properly. They therefore miss their daily food ration. A tank crew down range fails to qualify because one crewmember omitted a key step in their battle drills. A litter obstacle course team drops the patient because one member failed to pay attention, thus causing the whole team to disqualify for the Expert Field Medical Badge. Or a Chinook helicopter crashes and causes four deaths because a maintenance team failed to correctly place a bushing part.

We all lose when some do not pull their own weight, but we win big time when people come together and, like a finely tuned engine, accomplish great things. That is what a team is all about, each member pulling with and for the other towards a common goal. Many people can do far more together than what one could do alone.

Teamwork is the essence of the military. If one team member has trouble, the others pitch in to help. They take care of one another. If a group member is broken, they try to fix him. If a member works like he is supposed to, then the team tries not to break him. If the soldier is broken, then they DX him.

That just about covers every kind of soldier out there. No more questions, sergeant!

Self-Study

"Whoso neglects learning in his youth,
loses the past and is dead for the future."
Euripides

Education is a lifelong process. A commencement ceremony is the time when someone gives you a diploma and launches you out into the working world. You normally receive a piece of paper to hang on the wall which ends the long hours of study and boredom punctuated by bouts of prayer during examination times.

But life's school really just begins at graduation. Wisdom is often referred to as pearls, the so-called "pearls of wisdom." In all the bits of wisdom that come from people who have made a career in the military one pearl seems to stand out: always look out for yourself. At first this taking care of numero uno may seem a bit selfish. But the fact is that in the lesson book of life few people will watch out for you. Ultimately you have to take care of yourself in order to help others.

One of the very best ways to take care of yourself is to read. Most of us have to develop a taste for reading. We may have time for a quick glance at the newspaper or a magazine, but few of us dive into complicated reading. A *Tom Clancy* novel may be the most difficult reading some of us immerse ourselves in. In a world fast becoming internet-dominant, soldiers have got to read and become computer literate in order to stay ahead.

One of the most favorite moments in my military career was to take a break and visit the post library. Generally, the Army does a good job of outfitting each post with a good supply of books, newspapers, and magazines in the local library. And it is all free to card-carrying service members.

Albert Einstein once said that the mark of a genius is not knowing everything, but knowing where to find it. A good start is at the library or on the Internet. There is nothing quite like settling into a comfortable chair and reading up on the latest, whether it is a copy of the *Army Times* or visiting the PERSCOM web page. Every now and again you run across some bit of information that helps you stay ahead of the game.

When I was an NCO the Army taught me a key leadership principle: keep your soldiers informed. Excellent leaders will do this. They will listen and study and pass the information on. Unfortunately, the Army does not always issue you good leaders. That's when you have to make up for the shortfall. The best insurance is to keep yourself informed. There are three ways to do this: read, read, and then read some more.

TDY

"He seen his duty and he done it."
American Saying

It was tough duty, but someone had to do it: Temporary duty in Washington, D.C. at Uncle Sam's expense. Your hotel room cost $212 per night. Rations and incidentals allowance brought in another $92 per day. Life was good.

Temporary duty, or TDY for short, is good news to most soldiers. Yes, you have to be away from home, but at least there is some extra money involved. Instead of sleeping on the ground or in the back of some vehicle, you get a queen-sized bed with fresh sheets, room service, cable TV, fresh coffee, and donuts. No doubt about it—TDY is great duty.

An Army career can offer temporary duty in just about any place you can think of—anywhere where the U.S. government needs you to attend school or needs your special skills. From Jerusalem to Hawaii, from Florida to Heidelberg, Germany, I have had the opportunity to live like a wealthy traveler, with not the slightest worry about how much the room tab would be or what the airfare costs.

Certainly the special duty performed or school one attends while on TDY is important. That is why you are there. But despite the school, work or special project to be done, TDY has got to be one of the best fringe benefits a career soldier can stumble upon. It is like winning an all-expenses paid trip—like a miniature rebate for the Federal taxes we all pay. Take your family along, at your own expense of course, and you can make a full-blown vacation out of the deal.

A military career will not make you rich, at least not through legitimate means. But there are some rich experiences and the occasional perks, perks that everyone from private to general get a shot at. Temporary duty, especially in a plum location, tops the list of special experiences. Thank goodness a career that affords ample opportunity to work, eat, and sleep out in the rain, the dust, or freezing cold also offers the oasis of TDY.

When that TDY opportunity offers itself, it is the rare soldier who passes it up. At least for a few days you can forget the grunge of field training exercises and live out the good life around the edges of your daily special course or duty. It is an excellent change of pace, a chance to renew yourself. In fact, one way to spell recreation in the Army is "TDY."

There are times, especially when you are lying outside by the hotel's swimming pool that you can even forget you're in the Army, all at government expense. When the Army offers you temporary duty, do it.

231

The White House

"The Presidency is a splendid misery."
Thomas Jefferson

A high point of my military career was a call from the White House to interview for a position on their staff. Active duty military personnel are called to fill positions from protocol and communications to medical support and logistics. Only the best the Department of Defense (DOD) has to offer, I am told, are even asked to interview. So, it was quite an honor to be even summoned to a screening.

The interview process was very detailed. White House Security personnel had me complete a small stack of background check questionnaires. They wanted to know everything—any divorces, family problems, debts, foreign friends or travel, family in prison, or listing of being a conscientious objector. No detail was forgotten.

After the security folks were done with me, I was ushered into another area for an interview with the medical staff of the White House. The staff was comprised of service members from all branches of the DOD. For three quarters of an hour we had a cordial time as two doctors, two physician assistants, two nurses and one medic asked me questions. I was nervous and, as usual, probably talked too much.

After the interview, I received a personal tour of the White House by one of the staff PAs. The President and Vice President were out of town when I was there. They had important things to take care of. Too bad, otherwise I would perhaps have been able to meet them too. But there was a behind the doors tour of The Rose Garden, the press room, the halls and offices of our nation's highest leader.

The highlight came with the opportunity to stand in the Oval Office. To see that famous American room up close was a good consolation prize. The paintings, the Remington statue, the large desk and immaculate carpet, along with office furniture pieces, each with a unique history dating back to previous presidents, were all in good taste.

Later that day I learned that I was not selected for the job. It was unfortunate news, for I think I would have enjoyed the job very much. A good friend of mine was chosen. He was the best man for the job.

Sometimes the things we desire can be a bridge too far.

I am sure that even a job in the White House offers times that are difficult or tough. But even a miserable job in our nation's most famous house would at its worst be a splendid misery.

Of Pens and Swords

"The pen is mightier than the sword."
Edward Bulwer-Lytton

The Skilcraft company puts out a pretty good ink pen, so good that the U.S. Government continues to buy them each year by the tens of thousands. These small, black ballpoint pens have "U.S. Government" imprinted on the side. It is said that a job isn't finished until the paperwork is done. I say the paperwork will not be finished until someone finds a pen, and in the Army, it is often a Skilcraft pen.

You know you are near a military post or major government installation when you see these small, black pens. They can be anywhere— with the cashier at the Walmart checkout register, at the grocery store check writing counter, or at the local bank where you fill out deposit slips. You can rest assured that no matter where troops have been sent, a fair supply of these pens will follow and are left behind. The tales these pens could tell!

Unofficially, they say a soldier is "out of uniform" if he or she does not have a pen in their possession. Many times I've seen soldiers squirm as they ask to borrow a pen from another soldier in order to sign some document. My own experience has been no exception either. I was often found without a writing instrument. So, everybody works hard at making sure one of Uncle Sam's little pens is in their possession at all times.

Over the years the government has bought other pens, many varieties from different manufacturers, always in black or white colors. This whole pen-business is probably some congressional deal to create jobs in a job-scarce district somewhere. There are brief flirtations with different pen manufacturers, some quick deal with a different distributor or company. Despite these brief flirtations, however, the short, black, and obviously economical Skilcraft pens remain the mainstay of U.S. Army penmanship tools.

Weapons systems have come and gone. It seems the Army gets new "swords" every few years. New toys keep us ahead of the game of preventing war. The Abrams replaced the M-60 tank. The .45 cal pistol is gone. Hawk missiles gave way to Stingers.

Many things change over the years. Uniforms have changed. Even the names and designations of units change. Few things survive the test of military time. The Skilcraft U.S. Government pen, on the other hand, is still around in full force.

The pen has indeed been mightier than the sword.

Honesty

"A few honest men are better than numbers."
Oliver Cromwell

Of all the U.S. presidents, I admire Abraham Lincoln the most, even more than George Washington, who was for me a close second. Washington was an aristocrat, but Lincoln was a self-made man from the backwoods of Kentucky and Illinois.

In the backcountry of the American Midwest, Abraham Lincoln had plenty of experience with swindlers and liars, those nameless characters drifting from one heist to another. He reveled in spinning tall tales based on his encounters with these nameless drifters evoking a good laugh, but he personally was renowned for being a man of his word.

Lincoln is gone but times have not changed regarding liars and swindlers. What the world always needs is honesty. We need people who are not afraid to tell the truth. The last thing we need are people who "pop smoke," who try to cover up what they are doing.

I think all of us have fibbed at some time in our life, but some do it more often than others do. We can weave some tall tales indeed. Someone once said, "you can tell when some people are lying because their lips begin to move." We have examples of this from presidents on down the chain of command. There's the soldier who covers up some theft. The senior officer knowingly provides false data to Congress. Or a sitting President lies about an affair.

Lying, or partial truth, has its advantages. There has to be or we wouldn't see so much of it. We often get away with our white lies. Some temporary gain is ours. But every so often we're exposed. We get caught as one of our whoppers come out as a true misstatement of the truth. The big lie is revealed. Our honor is trashed.

Many people didn't like Abraham Lincoln back during his day. His enemies, southerners and northerners alike, often called him a liar. It is interesting that when the facts came out many of these same people turned out to be liars themselves. Lincoln was right and truthful so consistently that people called him Honest Abe. Perhaps that's why we Americans revere him so much.

If you are ever in Washington, D.C. take the time to visit the Lincoln Memorial. There sits old Abe, watching over the legislative branch at the other end of the Mall. Symbolically, he still keeps an eye on things. It would be his hope that all who serve in our government will always speak the truth and nothing but the truth, so help them God.

Friends and Flocks

"The gods help them that help themselves."
Aesop

The Combined Armed Services Staff School at Fort Leavenworth, Kansas, offers training to Army captains in the fine art of being a staff officer. Many lessons are imparted at this important school. Some of these include how to stand up and do a military-style briefing, how to do research, and how to prepare military correspondence.

The most important lesson for me came from the Canadian geese that lingered on a small lake next to the military library there. The geese numbered perhaps twelve or so and reminded me of two things. First, that my wife was also from Canada and she was missed a great deal while I was a geographic bachelor. Second, the geese served as an object lesson on teamwork.

With every class going through school at Leavenworth there is an overriding theme, some great idea the generals want to make sure their young captains absorb. These geese represented that carefully chosen theme for my sojourn there: teamwork.

Many of us have seen geese migrations each spring and fall. The Canada goose is one of the most familiar fowl of North America. Beginning its journey from the northern reaches of Canada or Alaska each autumn, it flies south to winter in Mexico or Florida. The trip, hundreds of miles long, cannot be made alone. Each goose joins a flock that stay together for protection.

The flock also provides a unique way of conserving each goose's strength. By flying in their trademark "V" shaped formations, geese always rotate the lead position at the tip of the formation. Scientists say that by rotating and staying in the airstream created by the V-formation, each goose will save a great deal of the energy that would otherwise be needed if it flew alone.

The geese offer a good lesson from an idea in nature that works. That idea in the military experience is very much the same. Working together is the name of the game. A military career is a long journey, one best not made alone. Stick with the group, obey the rules, take charge every now and again, and learn how to follow. Do this and you can't lose.

Those geese can teach us a few things, even when the generals move on to some other theme. Chief among those lessons from these birds of Canada is that the team helps those who help the team.

235

Leavenworth

"'Cause I's wicked—I is. I's mighty wicked, anyhow. I can't help it."
Harriet Beecher Stowe (*Uncle Tom's Cabin*)

The U.S. military attracts all kinds of people. You will see the good, the bad, and the ugly. Some pretty wicked people join the service and are good just long enough to get a chance to be bad. Given the chance some of them can be very bad. Many of these fallen angels wind up involuntarily assigned to the ugly side of Fort Leavenworth, the so-called "long course."

The prison at Fort Leavenworth holds former soldiers, sailors, airmen, and marines. In 1994 I was attending an officer advanced training school in what I will term the "short course" of Fort Leavenworth. One day during a break in classes, my class took the opportunity to tour the prison up close. Behind the bars and dank walls we received an impression of justice far different than standing on the outside looking in. I don't know who had the idea prison was a soft place. They haven't seen Leavenworth.

Seven hundred and forty-three inmates were all there for some very significant crimes—drug dealing, child abuse, armed robbery, assault, rape, murder. Some residents of this institution had been leaders in the military. There were former chaplains, commanders, and first sergeants. Others were merely the low life of American society who never made much rank before they met their match in the military's justice system.

The cells were dark and small, the food austere, and the guards were tough on the prisoners. These guards meant business. Not a smile in the place. I bet they took a dose of serious sour pills every day. These prisoners had been wicked and they were paying for it. The military police guards made sure of that. It was a prep school for Hades.

In time, and in most cases lots of time, those with fewer sins earn the opportunity to leave this military-made purgatory. Easily recognized in their brown prison uniforms, the prisoners are put to work around post doing odd jobs like bagging groceries, mowing grass, or landscaping. As a result of their penance, Fort Leavenworth becomes a very pretty post. In time, if they behaved, they would be freed. They pay their debt and finally return to society, hopefully ready to play by the rules that govern us all.

And so there are two types of officers that go to Fort Leavenworth—those there for the short course and others for the long course. The most promising officers of the Army go there for the short courses. The wicked ones go there for the longer one. One school teaches those to lead who know how to obey. The other teaches failures how to obey who will never lead soldiers again.

Purple Suits

"Vision is the art of seeing things invisible."
Jonathan Swift

The founding fathers and their successors over the years probably intended for the United States military to remain divided into different branches: First, the Navy, the Marines, and the Army, and then later the Air Force and Coast Guard. In earlier times the missions of each service were crystal clear with very different and distinct jobs and responsibilities.

But times have changed. Within the different branches of the DOD, there has evolved over time a dramatic blurring of lines. Necessity has led each service to create within their own areas certain elements of the other branches. Today it seems as if each service literally has their very own infantry, aviation, water support capability, and special operations.

I have a vision that the time will come when we can combine the services. The bureaucracies and redundancies currently in place would yield significant savings, and their reduction would enhance overall mission capability and efficiency. I only hope my vision is not a hallucination.

The opposing view would argue that to combine the services is fundamentally dangerous, concentrating power into the hands of a few. Poppycock. The checks and balances between the civilian and military organizations are in place to forestall a coup. Besides, a coup is just as possible even under our current, more expensive system.

Refer to combined service operations and military folks often disdainfully use the term "purple suit," meaning a blending of different uniforms symbolically creates an off-color. The higher up the chain of command you go, the more skeptical they tend to be about combination and sharing turf. This is not surprising. Military authorities argue against blending because they have a vested interest in stars and fiefdoms. Which general officer billet do we give up?

My vision remains fixed on the idea that the services can combine. We should start small, perhaps with a joint task force comprising a two- or three thousand-man organization representing every service. At first their mission could be primarily disaster relief. This would provide a classroom for the services to learn that yes, we can work and live closely together.

What color this organization should be is immaterial. I don't think that it would be purple. I would prefer something more like red, white, and blue: *All-American*. Perhaps this is only a mirage, but in time hopefully more influential people will see it also.

Self-Forgiveness

"Only the brave know how to forgive...
A coward never forgave; it is not in his nature."
Laurence Sterne

Every human organization has leaders. The family, the church, the community, the school—all have specially chosen individuals who stand out and take the reins of guiding others. The military epitomizes leadership, for its very existence is built upon people who are willing to lead and those who are willing to follow, even to the death.

I have seen many leaders come and go in my Army career. Spending time in artillery, infantry, armor, aviation, cavalry and hospital units brought me into contact with leadership from all around the Army. In time I too became one of those leaders, albeit on a modest level at an even more modest rank.

All leaders make mistakes. I've seen some whoppers and, sad to say, some of the big ones could be traced back to me. Most often, however, we tend to see the mistakes of others rather than our own. For a long time I dwelt upon the mistakes of my leaders. I enjoyed sitting in judgement, Monday morning quarterbacking their performance. When finally walking in their shoes, however, I found that my methods were as humanly fallible as theirs were.

Dwelling on mistakes drags a leader down. Focus too long on the negative and you will also become negative. Over time, good leaders learn that it is the lot of leadership to take risks. With risk comes a margin of error into which they sometimes fall. The Army terms this acceptable risk. Acceptable losses.

Some do not get back up once they fall. They quit. Others rise like phoenixes from the ashes of what seemed like a fatal error. Why?

One answer is to look for common threads in successful people. Like others, successful people leave a past history strewn with some mistakes. Bad words said. A loss of patience. Inconsiderate. Half-truths told. Despite their failings though, they move on. A major reason they continue is because they learn to forgive themselves. They know how to say they're sorry and they know that leadership is not an exact science. It is an art.

I heard an idea once from a Great Man who spent a good deal of time studying from a Great Book. His advice was simple: people need to forgive themselves before they can forgive others. Good advice. Don't be too hard on yourself. Like learning to walk, you have to fall every now and then. Forgiving yourself is getting up and trying again.

Volleyball

"Win this one for the Gipper."
Knute Rockne

When God was issuing athletic genes, I was passed over. Don't get me wrong, I can pass the physical fitness test and even maxed it twice, but only because I got older and tested under the standards for older soldiers. With sports, though, I am not your first round draft choice. In fact, I'm not even draftable at all.

With such athletic credentials as these, I reported to Fort Leavenworth for the officer Combined Armed Services Staff School. In addition to classes, I had to participate in organized volleyball games with eleven fellow classmates.

The bottom line up front is I am a klutz at volleyball. I didn't even know the rules much less know how to play properly. I'm hard pressed to recall the rules or play well at any sport. In any event, onto the court I went, and true to form, my performance was under whelming. I was poor and consistently so. I was a serious "REDO." No spikes from this 5'6" wonder, and a less than a 50% effective rate of fire over the net into the bad guy's area of operations wasn't going to take us to the super bowl of volleyball. Essentially, I was merely a nuisance on the court.

Our staff group leader, an aviation lieutenant colonel, was patient with his twelve captains, especially the vertically challenged ones. He had three championship teams in a row and we could be fourth, he said, but "no pressure." Yeah, right.

Winning for the Colonel was indeed not everything. But in his quiet, professional way, he set us up for success. He improved our odds. He placed us so that our weaknesses were offset by the strengths of others in our group. He emphasized those strengths in each of us, even if they seemed almost nonexistent.

The Colonel focused on the positive. He essentially made us into a team and we did well. Very well in fact. Of the fourteen teams in our league ours came out on top. *Numero Uno.* We were fourth in a row of championship teams.

I learned a great deal at Fort Leavenworth. Second only to the geese lesson, I learned that even though I did not play volleyball very well, I learned to enjoy doing it poorly, especially with great players on the team redeeming my sins. Thank goodness for a little help from my teammates, which is probably what the Creator and our staff group leader had in mind for me from the beginning.

The PT Pain

"When the head aches, all the members partake of the pains."
Cervantes

To stay in the Army, soldiers have to endure a unique form of torture twice each year: the physical fitness test. Administered throughout the year, most career soldiers opt to take the mandatory test in April and October. Spring and fall are good target seasons. No need to complicate the ordeal with the heat and extra sweat of summer or the cold and ice of winter.

Periodically, physical fitness experts tinker with the test to make it "better" than before. When I first joined the Army, the test consisted of five events: the sit-up, the push-up, the run-dodge-and-jump, the crab walk and the two-mile run. Now we just do sit-ups, push-ups and the two-mile run. Despite the adjustments the test still creates pain for most, but probably fewer serious injuries than the five-event version.

A sure way to end your military career, or at least to stall any further gains, is to fail to take the PT test or fail it altogether. Therefore, on the day of a PT test most folks are nervous. The general mood is "let's get this over with." The graders, normally specially selected sergeants who always look like they are on steroids, line you up and demonstrate the proper exercise technique. They demonstrate improper technique for each event and perform picture perfect sit-ups and push-ups. I found it interesting that they never demonstrated the two-mile run for us.

Generally the sit-ups and push-ups go quickly and most soldiers perform at least the minimum number of repetitions required. But then comes the run. For the next fifteen minutes or so, the pain really begins. Like a miniature marathon, a herd of soldiers, each tagged with a number, start the run. Woe to the soldier who fails to yell out his number to the grader as each lap around the track or route is complete during this timed event. They will run even further.

By the second mile, runners begin to really hurt. Older soldiers hurt even more, desperately working to finish the run within the allowable time. Heavier soldiers begin to feel just how much extra effort it takes to move their stuff around the track. The body wonders if the torture will ever end.

Soon the run does end and you've passed the test. Relieved, you feel like you are about to die. The muscular graders grunt a "good job" at you as cross that finish line practically coughing up blood from heavy breathing.

Now you get to go and take a long shower and also have a valid reason for being late for work. Who said pain never gives you gain?

240

Time Management

"Make haste, slowly."
Augustus Caesar

Hurry up and wait. It ought to be the Army's motto. Being all you can be means that the Army will develop your abilities both with speed and patience, and usually at the same time. Every soldier is familiar with concept that in the Army there are times when leaders hurry us along to a specific end, only to discover that we end up waiting for something else to occur anyway, which eats up any time gained. Things finally do get done, but often with a good dose of frustration at poor time management.

You hurry like crazy to get a railhead set up for a train delivery, only to learn that the train will be late. You rapidly get troops into position only to find out that events now have changed to the point that haste was unnecessary. You rush to that appointment and learn upon arrival that you are an hour early.

Time management. In the business world, proper use of time is treated like religion. Time equates to money and apparently, faster is better. Maybe. Certainly for a profit driven system that may hold true, but in order to get quality that lasts, sometimes you need to take your time.

Paradoxically, to get some jobs done quicker you need to take your time. The quick way may be the wrong way when tested by time. If a job is worth doing, they say, it is worth doing right. Doing it right means taking whatever time is necessary.

I remember being in a troop convoy that was behind schedule. In our stress over being late we made wrong turns that caused even further delay. Our haste was making waste.

Everyone has slack time—that left over time that may have no immediate use. In the Army soldiers call it "down time." Slack time is a window of opportunity to use a certain amount of hours or days that outwardly have no use.

Sometimes it is good to have time where it looks like you're doing nothing. This "do nothing" period may best be used for planning and reflection. Thoughtful planners can save a lot of wasted time. A planner's job is to get the job done with less time and energy. You have to slow down and figure out the best way to do something.

But when the metal is hot, you should strike quick. Seize the initiative. Take advantage of opportunities when they are offered. Like a chess game, make your move, and then slow down to reflect and think clearly. Consolidate your gains. Plan that next move.

Make haste, slowly.

Rain Man

"Into each life some rain must fall."
Henry Wadsworth Longfellow

They have a saying in the Army that goes like this, "If it ain't raining, we ain't training." Spend any amount of time in Europe, Hawaii, Korea, or Fort Lewis, Washington, and you'll see a fair amount of rain. And for some unknown reason, it seems as if most of the rain comes only when you're out in the field on training exercises.

Maybe that's why the Army does not authorize male soldiers to use umbrellas. Honest. I guess Generals figure that rain only falls on civilians and women, and how embarrassing it would be to have hundreds of male soldiers walking around with umbrellas. Female soldiers are allowed to carry a black umbrella, while their male counterparts get soaked.

Now, I'm all for equal rights. Everyone should be equal before the law. And Army uniform regulations. The military, however, does have some curious exceptions to this equal-rights business. In addition to the umbrella issue, males have to maintain short haircuts, while their female counterparts have some truly lovely, often long, finely maintained hairstyles.

But the umbrella thing takes the cake.

Forgive me for seeming a bit chauvinistic here, but clearly a soldier is a soldier. Male or female, black or white, private or general, all are soldiers, and should be subject to the same rules, eat the same food, wear the same gear, and have equal opportunity to get wet. Cultural baggage is one thing, but combat is no respecter of persons. I have it from good sources that in combat everyone will get wet when it rains.

There is an interesting metamorphosis that occurs when people advance in rank. There is an inverse relationship between how much rank they hold and how often they get wet from the rain. The higher up you go, the less wet you get. Maybe the authorities that make the decisions have forgotten from whence they came, how wet they used to get.

Sitting in their finely furnished offices with plenty of "I love me" accessories hanging on their walls, it is easy for a general or the high-ranking civilian to forget that maybe, just maybe, there are still some inequities out there in the ranks. As they peer out the window on that rainy day, perhaps they should reflect on the fact that those with testosterone are getting wet, while those of the fairer sex can remain dry under their umbrellas.

It might be well, then, when into the life of our nation's big decision-makers, a little rain could fall. A visit from the rain man might be, for them, some good training.

Sleepers

"I think, therefore I am."
René Descartes

Daydreaming is endemic to humans, part of being a mammal. Our proneness to short attention spans becomes really apparent when people are confronted with a boring class or lecture. They say that if you have a message to give people, it is best to get it across within the first ten minutes. Otherwise you lose most people if you take any longer.

The whole "bottom line up front" doctrine probably stems from commanders who have short attention spans and who don't want to go through all the tedious details. Therefore, getting to the point quickly has become a religion in the art of military presentations or briefings.

From time to time, though, audiences face a speaker who rebels against the brief briefing doctrine. As the audience's attention level drifts lower, their thinking wanders to other things: What's for lunch? What will I do this evening? How will I come up with the money for that special item? They think, but they are no longer there.

Daydreaming in an Army briefing can be dangerous. Nothing can be more embarrassing than to have a General officer publicly humiliate someone, say a lieutenant colonel for example, for not paying attention during a staff meeting. Far worse is the narcoleptic officer who is awakened during a meeting by the hand of the Chief of Staff or the Sergeant Major.

Soldiers new to the Army learn very quickly to stay awake. A common challenge comes during those long, trying lectures in halls where the room temperature mimics the tropics. One quickly develops a Pavlovian response as he witnesses the reaction and results of sergeants singling out soldiers who do not pay attention. A renewed vigilance to stay awake sets in as the sleepy perpetrators endure the consequences of their lapse of attention—usually having to stand for the remaining time, not infrequently for hours. One pities those poor souls who fail to stay awake.

The reason for staying awake in combat is a no brainer. Your own safety is at stake and often that of others is too. To endure the boring times you must develop certain skills with an end goal of staying awake and alert. Maybe you chew on sunflower seeds. Or indulge in short bursts of thought and daydreaming punctuated with alertness. The mind reflects, but you are also in touch. You think, therefore you are. You dream, but you do not doze. For if you dream too deeply or fall asleep, you run the risk of a more permanent sleep.

If you think not, you will not be.

Talented Fools

"A fool is every man in some man's opinion."
Spanish Proverb

In the Army one learns to make things idiot proof. It's doctrine. Keep it simple. The simpler method is the best way. Up and down the chain of command brevity is worshipped like a religion. Nothing captures this idea more than the KIS Principle: Keep It Simple.

Born no doubt in the crucible of combat, keeping things as simple as possible makes good sense. When the world around you is falling apart—leaders gone, enemy or friendly fire coming at you, advantages lost—you have no time to follow complicated procedures or debate. You have to act quickly or die.

Just ask helicopter pilots what he or she would do with a fully loaded aircraft and total engine failure at five thousand feet. By heart and in simple language the pilots can coolly recite step by step what actions to take to save crew and passengers. Like well-drilled children reciting memory verses from the Bible, they can state verbatim and in proper sequence what they would do and when. Talk to tank commanders or artilleryman and they can do the same type of recitation of what actions to take if a round misfires in the gun barrel. Their recitations come in a language that a sixth grader could easily learn and understand.

One can never remove all risk however, no matter how simple you make something. Try as we might things still happen. Often fools, and that sometimes may include us, are attracted to risk like moths to the purple light of an outdoor bug-zapping machine.

The fool is the one who failed to learn the emergency procedure or the leader who fails to keep people on their toes. The fool is the one who dies needlessly or the soldier who drinks too much.

Battle drills minimize losses. Emergency procedures save lives. You can try hard through drills and procedures to make something foolproof, but human nature is such that given the chance we always manage to invent a more talented fool.

There are times when each of us displays a moronic tendency in one form or another. Given a mirror we might all see the fool in ourselves from time to time. With the same mirror of self-evaluation and experience, we can purge ourselves of our daft tendencies. The self-evaluation part is the first lesson every talented fool should learn if they sincerely desire to be more foolproof.

The Army Way

"There's the right way, the wrong way, and the Army way."
Anonymous

My fifth grade teacher will always remind me of the ordeal of learning to write correctly. Mrs. Davis was a cultured, well bred, and educated older woman in our small town in the mountains of North Carolina. She was determined that the barbaric children in her care would one day become like other famous writers of America, perhaps a Robert Frost, a Carl Sandburg, or a Thomas Wolf. We would be her literate legacy or else.

Tattooed in my memory is the writing a formal letter lesson she gave us. It was the first real, academic hurdle of the year. "In order to succeed," she would say, "you have to write excellent letters." Day after day she drilled and corrected us. Re-do this. Change that. In a world before computers, it truly was an awesome task for an eleven year-old upstart. And it did not help matters that we had to write with a fountain pen, that messy dinosaur of the past. That pen added insult to injury.

Finally, after much academic tribulation, our letters met her approval. We were able to move on to other things, much to the relief of her weary pupils. I mistakenly thought my letter writing challenges were over.

Years later, while at staff officer training at Fort Leavenworth, Kansas, I faced another ordeal of a similar letter-writing nature. Our group leader in the staff officer training school was determined that his officers would become experts in preparing professional military letters, the famous Army memorandum. "Pay attention to detail," he said, "and don't use the passive voice. Follow the regulations."

We worked hard at preparing those memorandums. Each day the memorandums would return to us with the now familiar blue corrections of our group leader all over them. Nit picky stuff—indent here, extra space there, or use of passive voice. His "Redo" written in blue across the top page of our daily offerings became our class motto. I had uncanny flashbacks of Mrs. Davis, only now she was a lieutenant colonel.

We eventually got the hang of how the Army wanted us to write. Brief. To the point. And we *never used* the passive voice.

My fifth grade teacher did her best, but to the Army her details were passé. I've learned that when it comes to letters, you learn that there is a civilian way and an Army way. In order to succeed in either world, play by the rules, sing the right music, and follow the rules of whatever side of the fence you might find yourself. Above all else you do not want to be a "redo."

A Picture is Worth...

"Appearances often are deceiving."
Aesop's Fables

As far as the Department of the Army (DA) is concerned, three things make up the official soldier: the basic personnel briefing form, his or her evaluation reports, and an official photo. The first provides information on who and what you are, the second offers details of what bosses think you are, and the last, an image of what you look like. It will be these three items any DA board will have in hand to determine a soldier's future career.

Every fair-sized Army post has a small studio that takes DA photos, these official portraits of soldiers in their Class A uniform suits, better known as "greens." After expending a small fortune for tailoring, dry cleaning, and outfitting the dress uniform with various accouterments, a soldier arrives at the appointed time at the photo lab with the uniform encased in a suit carrier or the plastic dry cleaner's cover.

Now the real work begins. In a nearby changing room, the precious garment is put on. Assisted by large mirrors, a careful search is made to remove all lint and loose strings. And if they are smart, a fellow soldier helps. All awards, badges, buttons and tags are perfectly positioned according to Army regulations. This measurement business is very important, for every soldier is told about promotion boards that use rulers and magnifying glasses to look for mistakes. There is no independent UN confirmation of this rumor.

If the photographers are worth their stuff, the real deceptive work now begins. Clever and hidden placement of double-sided tape smoothes out wrinkles in the uniform and flattens those protruding pocket flap edges. Those crooked trouser leg creases magically straighten into even ridges with more tape strategically positioned in the buttock area, away from the camera lens. The addition of pads or paper under the jacket fleshes out gaps, giving the wearer a more muscular, professional appearance.

Finally, the body is positioned so that all is at attention, facing toward the camera, arms just so at the sides, chin and head at the proper angle, and a deep breath of air inhaled to enlarge the chest. Hold it. 1, 2, 3…. Flash!

In the old days, one had to wait a week or so to check the finished photo for errors. Today, digital photos offer immediate feedback and on the spot retakes if necessary, complete with any further deceptive work. In the end, the Army gets a photo of a sharp looking soldier in a "perfect" uniform.

Right. Anything you say. But only the photographer knows for sure.

Wrong Turns

"If you board the wrong train, it is no use running
along the corridor in the other direction."
Dietrich Bonhoeffer

Every once in a while we make a wrong turn in life. We make a mistake. We think at first it looks like the right way to go. We start down the chosen path, but we begin to realize that it is the wrong way. It is then that the often-painful process of turning around faces us.

The U.S. Army has a scholarship program for advanced training for officers in civilian universities. It is called the Long Term Civilian Education Program. Participants get full pay and allowances during the training, plus their books and tuition are fully paid. It is a great deal. In return, the officer incurs a service obligation for each year in school.

The doctoral program in education met the needs of the Army and I qualified. After applying for the scholarship, it was not too long before the Army picked me up for this program. Orders came down and soon thereafter I was off to the University of Texas in Austin. It all went so quickly.

I was not accustomed to school after fifteen years in the Army. "No problem," I thought, "I can adjust." Right. In my heart I began to feel that becoming a research expert while doing a Ph.D. in this particular field was not for me. It also dawned on me that follow-on assignments after school would take me away from troops and patients, keeping me in a research lab or pushing paper.

Though the scholarship was sweet, the area of study was not. For me it became a wrong turn. I knew in my heart that it was more important to go back to those things that I enjoyed rather than continue down a path that would make me miserable for many years to come. A lot of people were upset when I resigned from the program and, as expected, I was reassigned according to the needs of the Army: Fort Hood, Texas.

I settled into a new job at the new post doing what pleased me the most—seeing patients and taking care of soldiers. Over the years many of my colleagues have asked why I would turn down such an opportunity as was made available to me. My answer is simply that one man's opportunity can be another man's nightmare. Never willfully follow a direction you do not wish to go. You need to follow your heart, as my wife often says.

The wind can blow pretty hard at times. Someone once said we cannot control the wind, but we can adjust our sails. It can take a while to adjust the sails. But adjust you must and without any regrets. Learn from a mistake and it ends up not being a mistake at all, but another one of life's training opportunities.

Swords

"If you go in close enough your sword will be long enough."
Viking Saying

Most people would think the quote above deals with ancient battles where the skillful use of the sword ruled the day. Probably so, but for me it means something entirely different. Like most bits of wisdom it has several potential meanings. Confronting our fear of the unknown is a good start.

The unknown scares most people. If we are truly honest, we all tremble just a bit. Our imagination takes what might happen in the future and causes us to get nervous, to loose sleep, to be unsteady in the ranks. Incomplete information about what lays ahead traps us into forming opinions about the future, opinions that are often incorrect. It might be our concern about a move to a new place, a new job, a new baby, or a new boss. These are examples of future events that may cause anxiety in most, if not all of us at times.

Though fear of the unknown can be quite a normal reaction, some of us, especially in the Army, pre-play upcoming events in ways that often cause us to make mountains out of molehills, to overestimate the size of our foe. We hedge our bet. We're unsure of success. We do not want to fail. We fear we will turn and run like a spooked coward. Maybe we have even seen some folks who have run from similar challenges before.

Events we anticipate in our minds often finally do arrive. The clock will always tick on. We have to face the music. The dose of anxiety has to be taken. Though understandably nervous, in our more honest moments we'll admit that the fearsome event was little if no trouble at all. The move wasn't so bad. The neighborhood is better than the last. The new job is exciting. You love that new baby more than anything and even the new boss is a likable person. Where have all the monsters gone?

Our sword, or coping mechanism, turns out to be long enough, more than adequate to meet the new challenge. The mountainous fears seen from a distance got smaller as we drew closer. The dreaded monster of tomorrow is nothing more than a shadow of something not very scary at all. We found ourselves expert in building up the unknown, masters of fiction.

Those who turn and run from the challenges of life never get close enough to conquer and subdue their fears. They never draw their sword. The bold and the brave face the challenges and prevail. They really do go in close enough with tomorrow's giants and find their sword long enough for the task, even in an Army that no longer issues literal swords.

Best Kisses

"What is a kiss? Why this, as some approve:
The sure, sweet cement, glue, and lime of love."
Robert Herrick

There are kisses and then there are kisses. You have the basic peck on the cheek, the smooch, a little bit of sugar, or that very brief touch of the lips. And then you have those soft, smooth, warm, moist, drawn-out encounter lips to lips that warm a soldier's heart for months. From sugar to sucking face, somewhere is the kiss we remember above all others.

The lips are some of the most enervated parts of the human body. A large section of our brain is dedicated to oral sensation. I remember in my medical training seeing a chart that illustrated a head drawn proportional to the amount of nerves each part of it received. The skull was quite small, but the lips, man, those were some big lips!

Soldiers generally develop a high esteem for kissing when it comes to departing or greeting their spouses or lovers, especially when long periods of being apart are involved. Some of the best kisses are in airports and embarkation points where troops are once again either coming or going. I've sat in terminals and observed these magnetic encounters between male and female mouths. The intensity, attention, and tenderness of the display are an art form. The lovers are frequently oblivious to stares these passionate public performances generate. Some, particularly the male of the pair, can forget where they are and sometimes get carried away a bit, allowing their hands to wander to some generally interesting anatomy. The female often gently removes the errant hand back to a more acceptable location, all the while maintaining an uninterrupted dedication to the kiss in progress.

Of farewell and hello kisses I prefer the hello type. Nothing beats these kisses which are full of excitement, anticipation and joy, all wrapped together in a surge of feelings and hormones. They erase so much loneliness in one warm embrace of arms, bodies, lips, and, for those familiar with French lessons, even tongues.

An Army career will be punctuated by absences from those we love. Whether for a few days, months, a year, or the "duration." Each departure calls for strength to endure and hope for kisses to come. Kisses strengthen bonds that time and distance cannot destroy. Few things match the power of a relationship between two very special people than by sealing it with a kiss. A kiss is still a kiss, but there is something special about those warm, soft encounters of the lips in public places, especially between soldiers and those they love with a passion.

Success

"In all things, success depends upon previous preparation,
and without such preparation there is sure to be failure."
Confucius

What is the definition of a successful military career? Who makes the determination of success or not? Do we even need to focus on "success?" These are important questions for which there are many different answers.

Each soldier holds within his or her heart a differing definition of what success is. For some, success in the military can be defined as higher rank, meaning more prestige and more pay. He who goes home with the highest rank, wins. For some, awards and recognition for display on the "I love me" wall brings meaning. Still for others, completing military service without getting into trouble is success. The mold that fits most, though, is to simply try and be all you can possibly be. For many people, a successful military career is the experience, the journey, rather than the rewards or destination. Emerson captured the meaning of a successful life in the poignant prose below. It is a message directly transferable to the military experience, whether it is for a three-year enlistment or for the thirty year "lifer."

What is success?
To laugh often and much;
To win the respect of intelligent people
And the affection of children;
To earn the appreciation of honest critics
And endure the betrayal of false friends;
To appreciate beauty;
To find the best in others;
To leave the world a bit better'
Whether by a healthy child,
A garden patch,
Or a redeemed social condition;
To know that even one life has breathed easier
Because you have lived;
That is to have succeeded.

Ralph Waldo Emerson

The Starched Friendship

"Dress is the soul of a man."
William Shakespeare

The freshly cleaned uniform hangs in your closet like a thin, speckled green piece of cardboard, covered with a transparent plastic protective cover. For three dollars, you bought a good wash for the old duty uniform and a starched press you could never get from household spray starch, a conventional iron and an ironing board. Despite the uniform's age, it still looks sharp with the flattened pockets and patches on the clean, though now slightly faded, cloth.

It is time to begin a new day. Part of the routine is the ritual of donning the starched uniform. Removing the trousers from the hanger, you almost have to force each leg into each pant leg. The crackle of the stiff cloth resists your efforts, reluctantly giving way, but also staying firm against your legs. As you stand up in the rigid trousers, it feels almost like a suit of light armor, with straight creases going down the front of each leg into the boots now on your feet. It is almost as if the pants could hold you up by themselves.

The shirt comes next. You roll up each sleeve in typical Army fashion, inside out until a few inches above the elbow, a couple of two-inch rolls and then the final outside end covering the whole roll. The squared stiff cloth makes a perfect cuff, just below the unit patch on your sleeve.

Putting the tunic on, the clean aroma of starch and thread wafts around you. Sliding each arm into place, the rolled sleeves press firmly against your upper arms, as if stapling you to the shirt.

After removing the small paper number tag stapled to the tunic front, it is a small struggle to fasten the four buttons, but you're used to the routine of sliding them into the uniform's front underflap buttonholes. The compressed tunic feels firm against your chest. The pressed nametag and U.S. Army label above the front pockets remind you once again of who you are and to whom you belong.

You look sharp in the full-length mirror. The old uniform and you have been through a lot together. You complement one another. It has been a synergistic relationship. It makes you look good and you see to it that it looks good too.

In a sense, you and that uniform hold each other up. Together you look like a soldier. With the friendship of that old, now starched uniform, you become, as Aristotle once said, "a single soul dwelling in two bodies."

The High and Low Roads

"When we build, let us think that we build forever."
John Ruskin

If you look at my high school graduation picture, you'll see a fairly longhaired kid in a tuxedo. I looked good then. No wrinkles, a good head of hair, and so innocent you could smell it. Some things happened along the way to wear me out, but for a time I was brand spanking new. Below that fresh high school picture is a caption with my life's ambition. My goal at that time was to go to West Point and become an Army engineer.

Neither happened. I missed out on West Point to some high school football star in Charlotte, who got the available academy seat from North Carolina Senator Sam Ervin. After this setback, I eventually shifted my focus and my career choice from engineering to the medical field, probably because I am a people person deep inside.

In some ways it was too bad West Point didn't work out. That would have been a high road. I probably would have retired as a colonel instead of a major. Let's not go there, Dave. But wait a minute. The so-called low road in the Army was not so bad either. Yeah, the pay as a private isn't as good, but look at the experience. And over time, it does get better, if you stick it out and continue to build on what you already have. Six years enlisted time, seven years as a warrant officer, and seven as a commissioned officer. It was definitely a road less traveled.

Most Army officers are fast track types. They go to a college or a service academy right out of high school, and in four years you produce an empathetic team leader that understands the real Army and the soldiers they lead, right? Not necessarily.

It is the biased opinion of this man, who was there and got the tee shirt, that the best officers were former enlisted soldiers. That's the bottom line. Opinions to the contrary are probably from officers who bypassed being a private or a sergeant. Talk to any Army enlisted person and they will more than likely endorse the same opinion.

If you build something, you need to ask how long it needs to last. You can cut corners on material for short-term jobs, but you pay a price later. Officers built from scratch, those who come up through the ranks, people the Air Force calls "Mustangs," are leaders that are built to last forever. We will not be able to make all officers like this, but the "head shed" would do well to build a few more this way, even if it might seem like a low road to some.

Vacation

"You will soon break the bow if you
keep it always stretched."
Phaedrus

Not many jobs out there in the civilian work world give you thirty days of paid vacation each year. Most regular jobs give you two weeks, maybe three after you've been with the company for ten or twenty years. Not in the Army. From private up to a four-star general, everyone gets thirty days.

The English call it "going on holiday." Americans call it vacation. In the Army it is called leave. Leave is official permission to be away from the Army for a given period of time, something they once called furlough years ago. Any name you give it, this is a soldier's chance to hang up the uniform, grow a beard, and be a temporary civilian again.

Strangely enough, some soldiers have to learn how to go on vacation. They find it difficult to be away from being all you can be. They are hesitant to go away and take a break. When they finally do take leave, they hang out in their room or at home watching TV. Some even show up at work to see how things are going. They just can't seem to get away.

A good number of us have no problem getting away. Seldom do we accumulate leave days to the point where we have to "use it or lose it," that is, having more than sixty days of accumulated leave days by 30 September each year. Those unused days over sixty are taken back by the Army. No, work up seven or ten days of leave and we're off again on some excursion, fishing trip or anything away from the Army.

Once I was gone from the Army for forty-five days. I had a great time and before long, I almost forgot I was even in the military as my hair grew longer. Each morning without a wake-up call was nice too. A person can get accustomed to that. When I finally returned to work again, it took some readjusting to the routine, this being all you can be.

Whether you are on leave for ten or thirty days, for career soldiers it is good to go back to work. You actually look forward to getting back to the routine. The mission, the uniform, the camaraderie all return with that satisfying sense of belonging to something bigger than yourself.

Though the Army often rides soldiers hard the other 335 days a year, every soldier knows they get thirty days on their own. Those sweet days of annual freedom are a Godsend to most soldiers. A short break every now and again helps everyone be even better at being all they can be.

Citizens

"The first requisite of a good citizen in this Republic of ours
is that he shall be able and willing to pull his weight."
Theodore Roosevelt

A Federal judge in a long, black robe entered the large auditorium in downtown San Antonio, Texas. Just over two hundred registered aliens rose in honor of his arrival, one of the aliens being my Canadian wife, Irene. But she would be a Canadian for only a few more moments, for this was a citizenship ceremony. The judge would make the naturalization to U.S. citizenship official for these people literally from all ends of the earth.

Amidst all the various cultures represented in that large group, it was intriguing to see three soldiers standing, two sergeants and a staff sergeant. They stood there looking sharp in their Army dress green uniforms. They were becoming citizens to a nation they were already sworn to defend.

Few Americans realize that a large number of foreigners serve in the enlisted ranks of our armed forces, officers being the only group required to have U.S. citizenship. Many native-born American soldiers have seen first hand the drive and determination of these green-card-holder soldiers. Immigrants see serving in the military as an opportunity to excel, to get ahead, and to take advantage of this land of opportunity.

In another time and another place, Rome stood for a thousand years partly because Roman citizenship meant so much to those non-Romans who desired it. Service in Rome's armies often brought citizenship.

American citizenship also means a great deal to the world today. Many, both Americans and foreigners, sometimes put down being an American. They point to our continuing struggle with murder, crime rates, and decaying morals. Yet despite the blemishes, this great nation remains a magnet for those who see beyond the tarnish to the shining metal of security.

They come from all lands, these aliens amongst us. They cherish the hope and opportunity that being an American affords them. They do not see an exodus of Americans to the citizenship of other nations, despite the naysayers of our country. No, they, like the non-Romans of old, see American citizenship as a coveted possession, as golden as it ever was.

These three sergeants had already demonstrated by their service what they were willing to do for our country, and now our grateful nation would do something for them. They raised their right hands once again, and my wife for the first time. They all took the oath freely, without any reservation or purpose of evasion.

254

Fireworks

"Cut an American into a hundred pieces and boil him down,
you will find him all Fourth of July."
Wendall Phillips

Here is a good tip: The best position to see the fantastic Fort Hood,
Texas, Fourth of July fireworks display is by the main gate in the large fields
by U.S. Highway 190. Tens of thousands of people flock to this annual
event. Local Army officials spare no money in making this extravaganza
into a serious high for the pyromaniac in all of us.

As the sun slowly sets to the west over Copperas Cove, thousands of
pick-ups, four-wheel drive vehicles, and cars pull off the highway into the
grass. Lawn chairs and blankets, like prayer rugs, come out all oriented at
the main gate, the launching point for the patriotic pyrotechnics program.

As it gets darker, everybody and his brother sets off their own rockets,
firecrackers, and assorted bombs as personal offerings to this annual ritual.
You can gauge the state of the economy by how much civilian acquired
ordinance is exploded. 1999, for instance, was a great year, as thousands of
rockets and explosions lit up the sky around us before the main show.

With the arrival of darkness, the big event commences with the sound
of multiple thumps in the distance—mortars launching the opening salvo of
fireworks. For the next thirty minutes, spectators are offered a visual and
audio display of fantastic proportions. The show dwarfs any other you've
ever seen and rivals the Washington D.C. and New York harbor shows.
Averaging at least one or two explosions per second, the viewer feasts on the
complete array of modern pyrotechnic possibilities. "Wow," my daughter
screams. "Oooh," my wife exclaims. With every blast of sound and light,
the folks around us respond with "aaahhs" from their lawn chair or tailgate.

The marvelous show is free, brought to us by Fort Hood. The
experience is, for young and old alike, a uniquely American phenomenon.
Though ideas and opinions may divide us, the fireworks display of the
Fourth of July each year brings us all together, Republican and Democrat,
Catholic and Protestant, soldier and civilian. Everyone enjoys it.

The show finally ends and the hour-long traffic jam on highway 190
begins. The lines of vehicles make their way home with their individual
loads of Americans. A few remaining pyromaniacs fire off their last rockets,
streaking into the night sky overhead, accenting the thousands of head- and
taillights on the highway below. The cars on the road and bombs bursting in
the air gave proof that night that our booming economy was still there.

Government Quarters

"Misfortunes never come singly."
Ausonius

Over the years, we have had the opportunity to live in government quarters on various Army posts in the United States and abroad. Military housing was generally a good experience for our family. The glaring exception was Fort Hood, Texas, where the Army unknowingly issued us a home haunted by mechanical poltergeists.

The location of the townhouse-like quarters was excellent. A quiet cul-de-sac nestled in next to the post golf course. We just knew it would be wonderful living there and in no time settled into our new home with plenty of space for my large clan.

Little did we know that over the next sixty days we would endure twenty-two mechanical failures, constantly reminding us that the three most important things about real estate were not location, location, location. No, the most important things are location, no breakdowns and peace of mind.

We moved in during the month of July, well known for being very hot in central Texas. Naturally, the air conditioner failed. Maintenance crews messed around with the old unit for a few days. They finally gave up and installed a new one after affording us ample time to bake.

Perhaps the heat inside the house triggered the plumbing leaks that began within our first week there. The upstairs bathroom, followed by the bathtub and shower, all decided it was time to hemorrhage. Repair crews created gaping holes in walls and the ceiling in their attempts to repair the pesky leaks. In quick succession the water heater, dishwasher, and kitchen lights failed too, causing further opportunity for us to visit with maintenance crews with whom by now we were on a first-name basis.

The coup de grâce came with the flooding of our kitchen from an improperly installed garbage disposal that also had failed. I'd had enough by then and begged the family housing office to allow us to move into another house. Nothing doing. There were no others available.

In time, it seemed like the repair people replaced the entire house around us. Even the musty, rotting odor in the laundry room was gone. Perhaps that was the end of that poltergeist. I am sure the repair help-line operator was relieved when my calls became fewer and fewer. You know you have a problem when you call the help-line and you overhear her say, "It's him again."

Yes, like some *Poltergeist*, I'm back.

Little Things, Big Consequences

"The Devil is in the details."
Anonymous

The day at the aviation troop medical clinic had been a slow one. By lunch, each of the flight surgeons was off on different errands or duties, and I was left as medical officer on duty. I had just settled down to read a medical journal when the phone rang.

"Captain Kay, this is range control. We've got a helicopter that has crashed." Holding the receiver next to my ear, my mind began to whirl as accident procedure lists came forward from my memory. "Roger," I said as I fumbled for a pen and paper, "Do you have the location?" Over the next couple of minutes, I scribbled down grid coordinates, several phone numbers and names, and then hung up. Over the next several hours, dozens of procedures would be set in motion to investigate the crash and recover the remains of the five deceased aviators.

It was a beautiful day and many helicopters had been launched on various training missions. Several were Chinook helicopters, those large Army transport helicopters with two large rotor blade systems, one on each end of the airplane.

The flight had been for orientation of a new pilot and crew chief, done by two other experienced pilots and a crew chief. They had taken off and were about twenty miles from the airfield when they went down due to a sudden failure of the tail rotor blade system. Apparently, the dropping blades cut the aircraft in half at two thousand feet, scattering debris and crew over an area a mile and a half wide. There were no survivors.

After days of crash investigation work, it was determined that the cause of the accident was a ninety-nine cent part installed backwards. Despite the initial error of the primary mechanic, three senior inspectors had also failed to notice the mistake. The result was a drive shaft failure due to too much vibration from the poorly placed part. A small detail caused a fatal accident.

The inventions of man often take us to great heights. We marvel at how much knowledge and ingenuity can provide for our world. But we would do well to remember that technology could also cause us to fall because of our failure to pay attention to the little things.

Whether it is a small part, an apparently insignificant worker, or a minor detail, sometimes we learn the hard way that parts, people, and details are all as important as the whole. Failure to pay attention to those details can potentially unleash a devilish result.

Vowels

"Good kings are slaves and their subjects are free."
Marie of France

What is the essence of leadership? If you strip away all the titles, pomp and trappings of great people, what is left? The answer is probably as varied as the people who answer the question. Allow me to submit my version.

Have you ever thought about how English would be written without vowels? Consider the quote above written without the vowels:

"Gd kngs r slvs nd thr sbjcts r fr."

Pretty confusing isn't it? Without vowels our language is gibberish. The same is true of a people without good leadership. Just as vowels hold the language together and allow sense to be made of what is written, so also does good leadership hold people together and make sense of what they do.

A, E, I, O, U and sometimes Y. To help understand what good leadership is we might consider using each vowel to characterize some key aspect of what a leader should be:

A - Aggressive: They are self-starters who get things done.

E - Example: They talk the talk and walk the walk.

I - Integrity: They keep their word or have a good reason for lying.

O - Others: They are selfless in taking care of others.

U - Uniformity: They are consistent, predictable, without favorites.

and sometimes...

Y - Yourself: They care for themselves but not at anyone's expense.

What exceptional leaders are can best be summarized by a quote from John Updike. He wrote that a leader is someone "who out of madness or goodness, volunteers to take upon himself the woe of a people."

I, for one, wish we could find more of these people.

Trouble

"When we see men of a contrary character,
we should turn inward and examine ourselves."
Confucius

The Germans have a saying that is difficult to translate exactly into English. *Er ist mir nicht sympatisch.* The general interpretation is we don't have the right chemistry between each other. The phrase could apply to many of us concerning some of our interpersonal relationships.

We all encounter people in our lives with whom we do not hit it off. Unfortunately, some of us experience this more often than others. Maybe it was a poor start, a bad first impression, some preconceived opinion, or a smoldering piece of bigotry we cannot purge from our soul. Sometimes these interpersonal wrinkles explode into open conflict.

Two physician assistant lieutenants sat in my office. They were angry, fortunately not with me. As intermediary, my job was to sort out and possibly settle the conflict between these two fine medical officers.

To state the case simply, these two couldn't stand each other. We began with a venting session. One at a time, and without any interruptions, each presented their side of the problem with a liberal sprinkling of accusations and judgments about the other. Like prosecuting attorneys at a war crimes trial, it was ugly, but everything was on the table.

Though no expert at negotiations and conflict resolution, I began to sort through the differences. There was guilt on both sides. The overall lack of communication had only made matters worse between the two. Perceived misdemeanors became major crimes in their eyes over time. Both parties were equally mired in hurt feelings and sadly, unwilling to acknowledge that perhaps they each might be a major part of the problem.

Eventually, they reached an uneasy truce. They agreed to disagree. They never became friends or even close working colleagues. Circumstances forced them to work together, however grudgingly, but successfully. Things healed somewhat, but there was a scar. And scars nearly always have an influence on performance.

Each of us can probably recall a similar situation in our own experience. There are folks with whom we choose not to interact. In our more honest moments, our conscience might prod us to reflect on our side of the situation. Indeed, when we point the finger at someone, three of our remaining fingers point back at us. If we fix our part of the problem, then the rest is on them. It is one way to get unstuck from this tar baby of ill feelings even when the other side refuses to cooperate. Sometimes that's the best we can do.

Patience

"Labor disgraces no man;
unfortunately you occasionally find men disgrace labor."
U.S. Grant

In the Army, being a cook has got to be the most difficult job of all. Their work is constant, poorly appreciated, and they put in long hours at weird times. Whether in garrison or in the field these folks earn their pay.

At the opposite pole of the difficult job scale has got to be the personnel clerk. This must be the easiest job in the Army. These people work in a clean and dry environment. They stay cool inside at their desks when it is hot outside. On cold days they stay warm in their well-heated work area. It is rare to see these soldiers break a sweat or in dirty uniforms.

I normally would not say anything about Army personnel offices if only my perception was not reinforced by repeated personal experiences. From Germany to Fort Hood, from Fort Bragg to Schofield Barracks, I've been hard pressed to find an Army personnel customer service desk that really does just that—provide great customer service.

Most personnel offices do not work off an appointment system. You walk in. The customer service desk often is a closed counter, probably to keep the less patient customers from climbing over. More often then not, you stand there waiting for some guidance as to what your next step should be. A quick scan of the office area reveals several clerks looking busy. On closer examination, though, you hear intense discussions on non-personnel issues. There's last night's basketball game, favorite foods, what's playing at the theater, or some childcare problem. These soldiers frequently seem to skillfully avoid making eye contact with you as they restack and reposition those piles of papers on their desk.

One does not dare complain or make a scene. First, it raises the blood pressure and second, these people have access to keyboards that can mess up records or lose paperwork. No, it's best to wait and develop character.

Eventually, someone, usually the lowest ranking clerk, gives in and offers to help. Sadly, they often don't know how to handle your situation, so off they go to some back room office to the NCOIC or a civilian who really knows the answer. After you've paid additional patience dues, the solution comes forward, usually in the person of an experienced civilian or crusty warrant officer. In ten seconds we have it taken care of.

They say a job isn't finished until the paperwork is done. Maybe, but on the personnel side of the house, it is a good bet that a job will not be finished until the patience is done.

260

Tough Times

"When the goin' gets tough, the tough get going."
Anonymous

In truth, he was the most difficult physician I ever worked for. The United States Army was just about the only thing in the life of this West Point graduate who had gone to medical school right after his academy years. He had never married, too dedicated to the various jobs and missions the Army provided. He was a stickler for detail, and those who worked for him learned how he could micromanage anyone who did not live up to his high expectations. He wouldn't blink an eye at staying after duty hours on a regular basis, and if your work was not up to par, then he'd keep you there too, until it was done. His abrupt, no-nonsense manner only reinforced the overall mood that this man expected 100% plus out of his subordinates.

Working as his staff officer I found myself facing a steep learning curve. In addition to running one of his troop medical clinics, I was also his deputy in handling dozens of projects and problems unique to a U.S. Army armored division. It didn't help that the Division Chief of Staff, his rater and my senior rater, was just as obsessed with the Army and missions.

I spent a year and a half working for this man. It was painful at times, and always challenging. The day finally came when he was moving on. There were three of us 'staff weenies' who worked for him: a very capable First Lieutenant, and one of the best Master Sergeants I ever worked with, and me. A few days before his departure he called us into his office. We reported with a sense of foreboding, for we just knew something was up.

We stood before his desk as he began to speak to us, "I know I've been tough on you men," he began. "In truth, I wouldn't have blamed any of you if you had quit on me. Many have before." He paused, then continued, this time choosing his words and with an obvious tremble in his voice. "You have been the best officers the Army ever provided to work for me. I have been a taskmaster, and you each have mastered the tasks. I cannot thank you enough for sticking with me when I gave you any number of reasons for leaving. Please accept this small token of my thanks."

He then gave each of us mint U.S. silver-dollar coins, dated with the years we had worked for him. It was then that I began to realize how much I had personally grown working for this man. Instead of complaining or quitting, we hung on and got to work. Instead of living in the shadows of ignorance, this man expanded our horizons. It was a rough time, but rough and tough times polished our character. This is a point always remembered when I look at those shiny mint coins this great man gave me.

261

Stingy

"If I were a medical man, I should prescribe a holiday
to any patient who considered his work important."
Bertrand Russell

Perhaps I was being cruel. In hindsight, maybe I should have been more liberal in giving "quarters" to soldiers on sick call, allowing them to go home to rest for the day. Compared to how civilian medicine is practiced, I was pretty stingy with sending my patients home in the Army.

It is Monday and soldiers come to see me on sick call. Some have had a rough weekend, albeit often self-imposed through increased food, drink and extraordinary activities. A full day's work looms ahead for them like a dreaded menace. Maybe sick call can be their salvation. They conjure up a cold or chronic back pain and see me for a chance at getting the day off. I prepare their treatment plan at the end of their medical visit. Most will get some medication and treatment instructions, but all will receive a duty disposition. With regards to the final duty disposition section on an Army sick call slip, how many times I've heard the question, "Doc, do you think I could take a day off and get some rest?"

Now here is my chance to make friends and influence people. Cut them some slack. But as I have already stated, more often than not, I give them my "pep talk" about getting back out there and doing what you can for the Army. Come back and see me if you feel worse. Fever, vomiting, increased pain, are good reasons to return. Of course, the overwhelming majority of my patients manage to make it through the day without coming back to see me, either because they improved as the day went on or they felt a return visit would be futile.

Civilian life is a whole different ball game for doctors. Paying customers must be kept happy. "A couple of days off from work? No problem." A sniffle and a sprain will get at least a two-day holiday. The magical doctor's note is filled out and everyone seems happy. Even the employer or teacher reveres the doctor's note as certification that yes, their employee or student was so ill that a small holiday to heal was necessary.

Forgive my slightly cynical mood here. Chalk it up to an "old Army Doc" struggling with how the rest of the world practices medicine. I guess we all should take a medical holiday from time to time. The spirit may need a rest even when the body may not provide enough objective proof. Until an objective measurement of the human spirit is invented, I suppose we should err on the side of rest for the weary in spirit as well.

Giants

"If I have seen further it is by standing on the shoulders of giants."
Sir Isaac Newton

The states of Virginia and West Virginia have offered two very unusual soldiers in the service of the United States. Both men were very devout in their protestant religious faiths. They would become soldiers and serve as medics, one in the Pacific campaign of World War II and the other in the rice paddies of Vietnam. CPL Desmond T. Doss and CPL Thomas Bennett were conscientious objectors who did not dodge the call to serve the United States of America. In time, both men would so impress their leaders by their self-sacrifice under fire, that they would be awarded the highest honor a grateful nation can bestow, the Congressional Medal of Honor.

In honor of their exploits and memory, the U.S. Army Medical Department at Fort Sam Houston, Texas, has a lobby photo display of every medical soldier who has received the Medal of Honor. Their faces, names, and a brief description of their achievements have inspired thousands of medics who pass by the wall display area. Of the fifteen or so great men shown, Corporals Doss and Bennett are unique among the unique.

As mentioned earlier, I have had the privilege to personally meet Corporal Doss. An elderly, quiet gentleman, he looked sharp in his uniform with that distinctive blue-ribboned medal about his neck. I never met Corporal Bennett. He was killed in action while serving in Vietnam. But I had the honor of meeting his family while serving as action officer for the construction of a state-of-the-art medical clinic named in his honor. Both men were an inspiration for me and for others who continue to serve within the dictates of their conscience.

The power of the United States is awesome. What amplifies that power even more is how this experiment in democracy can accommodate the wishes and needs of all people, regardless of their race, religion, gender, ethnic background, or social standing. It is also powerful that this nation will recognize the extraordinary achievements of the minority opinion or belief.

Though soldiers may not always agree with the beliefs of others, they are sworn to defend, as Voltaire said, even to the death, their right to believe it. These same soldiers, and even soldiers who serve without bearing arms, have shown devotion to the ideals of this great nation time and again. When the world is falling apart all around them, there are ethical giants who stand out, who do the right thing.

Doss and Bennett are two combat medics who stand among the giants in more ways than one.

263

The Numbers Game

"When you can measure what you are speaking about
and express it in numbers, you know something about it."
William Thomson, Lord Kelvin

Somewhere, there is a real good reason why the Army adopted their numbering system for buildings on post. There has to be, but the answer eludes me. Unlike civilians who have a somewhat logical progression of house numbers along your average street, the Army seems to be all it can be with confusing building numbers.

Instead of a normal address, say 759 Central Avenue, the powers that be christen a military structure building #23001, Fort so and so, along with the state and zip code. Any permanent man-made structure, even small storage buildings, gets a number. But for some unknown reason street names do not figure prominently in an Army address.

Building numbers assume an identity all their own with the troops. Say the number and troops immediately recognize what activity goes on there. For instance, at Fort Hood the In-Processing Center is simply known as Building 121. Soldiers will know where it is and what goes on there, but they would be hard pressed to give you the name of the street it lies on.

The numbers game with structures would make some sense if the person numbering the buildings would follow some logic. Somewhere there ought to be a building number one, say at the farthest corner of post. Then, on the other end of post would be the highest numbered building. All others would be in an understandable number sequence in between. But no, you're in building 118, the barracks to your left is 9007, and that structure across the street is 270.

I feel for the express delivery trucks or the civilians who visit Army posts. With hopeful looks they stop the first intelligent-looking soldier they can find. "Can you help me find where my son is?" "Sure," comes the confident response. "Do you know the building number?" Now comes that puzzled look. "Building number? Do you mean the address? Well, all he gave us was his unit."

Eventually, through the time-tested "go this far then turn left at the stop sign..." the soldier gives them his best guess and sends mom and dad off with a confused, skeptical countenance. Eventually they get there, most likely after driving in circles and asking a few others for their best guess.

Maybe all this is part of a grand scheme to confuse the enemy. Figure it out and you're in deep trouble. Indeed, those who do eventually figure it out are probably up to their elbows in the Army and not just visiting.

Missing No More

"Let us endeavor so to live that when we come to die
even the undertaker will be sorry."
Mark Twain

It is a fact of history that when America has gone to a major war, many soldiers did not come home. Travel abroad and you will find the cemeteries of America's honored fallen from the Philippines to Italy, from Korea to France. Row upon row of white markers identifies soldiers, sailors, airmen, and marines who gave their lives for the cause of the United States and her Allies. Thousands more whose remains are forever lost are listed officially as missing in action.

The difficulty of creating an accurate method to properly identify fallen service members has plagued military authorities for years. Fingerprints, dog tags, or dental x-rays do not suffice. The lethality of weaponry and the frequent incineration of bodies in the blast and fire of battle leave little to identify. The remains that are found are often unrecognizable.

In the 1990s, the U.S. military implemented a program to identify remains through the use of a person's DNA (deoxyribonucleic acid). DNA is the genetic marker of who we are as individuals physically. By taking a blood sample or a swab from a soldier's mouth, authorities now have on file an important way to confirm the identification of any biological remains that may be found.

One prays that deaths caused by training or combat do not occur. But they do, despite our best efforts to prevent them. Make no mistake: military service is dangerous business. There are times when harm gets in the way.

When America's finest fall, a special group of people steps forward to prepare and transport their honored remains home. Grave's registration personnel perform the important mission of identifying the remains of service personnel killed in action. The advent of the DNA data bank makes the identification job a lot easier and more accurate.

No one knows when his or her life will end. Soldiers know that when sent into the danger zone, they can be assured that America will do its very best to care for them through supporting their service while they yet live, caring for them if injured or sick, and, if necessary, honoring them in death. The American people will always endeavor to do this and more. The people's sorrow over the loss of even one soldier is cushioned by a life lived nobly and that the soldier's actual remains make it home to the ones who will never forget.

An Ounce of Attention

"An ounce of attention can buy a pound of praise."
David Kay

A Command Sergeant Major dropped by the medical clinic one afternoon somewhat in a hurry. He had meetings to attend and things to do. He needed a refill of ibuprofen, which he took for knee pain from all the running he did. We were usually quite busy at the clinic, but for a Command Sergeant Major or a Commander we always tried to make time to get what they need and see them on their way.

So, in between patients, I took care of his medication refill and then asked him in passing if he needed help with anything else. At first he said no thanks, but then he paused and said, "Well, I had my 45th birthday a week ago and lately I find myself getting a bit short of breath when I go running."

It was a hectic day in the clinic and the Sergeant Major was certainly in a hurry, too. It would have been easy to tell him to set up an appointment. But a small voice inside me said, "You need to look at this guy." So, we shuffled some patients around and made room to see him then and there. He protested, but I said to him, "Look, I need to see you now. Make some phone calls and give me a half-hour of your time."

It took more than a half-hour. Some vital signs, a history and physical, blood tests and an electrocardiogram confirmed my suspicion that the Sergeant Major could have some coronary artery disease. We sent him for a treadmill test that same day and it proved positive. He was immediately shipped off to Brooke Army Medical Center in San Antonio, Texas. After a day or so of further observation and testing he underwent by-pass surgery for three clogged coronary arteries.

A busy clinic and military referral systems sometimes cause us to lose track of our patients. With so many patients to look after it does take some work to follow-up on the patients you have seen, especially those seen on the spur of the moment. The next day I checked with the Sergeant Major's unit and learned that he had surgery and was doing well.

A few weeks later, while he was on convalescent leave, the Sergeant Major came in to see me with a big smile on his face and a big scar on his chest under his shirt. Right in front of patients and staff, he said to me, "Now here is the man who saved my life." For a moment there, I thought it was my turn to have a heart attack, but my heart was only skipping a beat or two. An ounce of attention bought a pound of praise.

266

Respect

"The flag is the emblem of our unity, our power,
our thought and purpose as a nation."
Woodrow Wilson

It is a Friday afternoon just before 1700 hr, (or five o'clock p.m. civilian time). Time to get off work and head home for the weekend. Thank goodness it's Friday. You close up shop and get things ready for the Monday morning you know will come.

Outside, that nice car waits to take you home. It is a new set of wheels you really enjoy driving. The engine starts effortlessly and the insulated car shields the engine noise so much that you have to listen carefully to even hear it running. Pulling out of the parking lot and onto the main post road, you're on the way toward home. The air conditioner is on. Your favorite tunes are playing. You begin to relax and enjoy that new car smell.

Before you leave post, though, there is one final duty Army custom requires of you. It is time to render respect to the flag, one of the most important duties and rituals of a United States Army post. Above the sound of the music from the radio inside your car, there is the sudden boom of the post cannon and cars ahead begin to spontaneously stop right where they are. Like some programmed call to worship, soldiers step out of their cars, come to the position of attention, and render a sharp salute in the direction of the post flag. You do the same and faintly hear in the distance a lone bugle sounding retreat.

The flag is lowered, the music ends, and everyone seems to suddenly come to their senses as they step back into their cars to continue their journey home. For a moment, though, the soldiers became one in their peculiar public expression of devotion to something embodied in that grand old flag with fifty stars and thirteen stripes. There is a oneness in these people, standing there in the road. From their scattered positions they salute a distant flag they might or might not see. The spectacle is rich in thought and purpose.

Soldiers feel pride in what may seem to others an inconvenience. Civilians marvel at this phenomenon. That's okay. Soldiers know that the flag will go on being the symbol of this great nation long after they are gone. Soldiers are sworn to defend it and are honored with the same flag in their funerals, that last blanket of red, white and blue covering their remains and tucking them into their long sleep. A small stop at the end of the day for the Stars and Stripes is the least American warriors can do for such a powerful symbol and friend.

Hardheaded

"I have experienced many instances of being obliged by
better information or full consideration to change opinions."
Benjamin Franklin

There are some pretty hardheaded people out there. They have an opinion. You can argue until you are blue in your face, but they will not change. It doesn't matter if they are politically conservative, moderate, or liberal, in all groups you'll find folks who are just plain stubborn.

Now, being hardheaded can have its advantages. They may be sticking to their guns because they have information you don't. Though I've never been in combat, I've read and have been told that the fewer stubborn opponents you have, the lighter the resistance will be. Indeed, contrary people tend to dig in and they dig in even deeper when threatened, so it becomes more difficult to root them out of their position.

Sometimes being as stubborn as a mule is stupid. Maybe they think it is a matter of honor, but often it is simply foolish. For example, take Hitler's handling of the German Army towards the end of WWII. He ordered his generals to hold every position to the very last man, eventually decimating his armies to the point that they ceased to exist except as paper tokens on a wall-battle map.

Sometimes we must change to cut our losses. Even with all available information, some people will not change. Carl Sagan, the late astrophysicist and host of the TV program *NOVA*, developed what he termed the *Baloney Detection Kit*. He believed it was important to change your opinion if certain conditions applied.

Unfortunately, the Army does not issue kits that help identify bogus or false information. You have to learn to detect it pretty much on a trial and error basis. When confronted with the facts, we should be prepared to change our opinion, even if we have to do it in front of the troops. How many soldiers have died because their leaders failed to act in a timely fashion when confronted with outright baloney.

There's a lot of baloney out there. Stubborn people run the risk of feasting on it. Frequently, even leaders can be guilty of at least sampling baloney. Smart people look for better data, encourage debate, get independent confirmation, and see things from multiple perspectives. If the data points to changing their current course or opinion, then they are not afraid to do so. If they see baloney, they stop eating it ASAP.

Do No Harm

"Wherever a doctor cannot do good,
he must be kept from doing harm."
Hippocrates

When you are the flight medical officer on duty, a pager going off is usually not a good thing. A quick call to the emergency room confirmed my worst fears—a fifty-two year-old lady had sustained burns to forty percent of her total body surface and was in need of aeromedical transfer to the Brooke Army Medical Center burn unit.

On the way to Darnall Army Community Hospital, I alerted the duty flight crew to prepare the UH-60 Blackhawk medical evacuation helicopter. Arriving at the emergency room, a flurry of activity surrounded my new patient as trauma surgeons performed an escharotomy, or tissue release procedure, to the patient's left arm to ensure the blood supply would not be cut off due to the swelling of burned skin. The attending doctor gave me the details of her case as I watched.

Cooking breakfast in her kitchen, the patient had to deal with a sudden grease fire from frying meat. In her attempt to put the fire out, she upset the pan and spilled hot grease onto her arms, upper chest and lower legs. A flash burn also singed her face and hair. Fortunately, she did not inhale any flames, but she was still in bad shape.

For the next hour, the patient was in my care as we made the flight to San Antonio. She had a tube inserted into her lungs to keep her airway in control, so continuous chemical sedation was necessary. Two intravenous infusions, oxygen, a bladder catheter, burn dressings, monitors, vital signs, and checks of pulses in her hands and feet kept the flight medic and me constantly busy. A respiratory technician managed her precious airway.

It was my constant prayer that she would do well. At any moment things could change for the worse. In the cramped conditions of a helicopter it would be next to impossible to resuscitate a dying patient. She teetered on the edge of death.

I know of a no greater relief than to successfully complete the transfer of a critically ill or injured patient to the appropriate hospital. The risk involved is worth the trip to a place of better care, in this case a state-of-the-art burn center. But risk does cause a good deal of stress while on the way.

Completing the final entry in the patient's chart after a successful transfer is how I would spell relief. Once again the patient transfer process did no harm.

The Porta-Potty

"The worst is yet to come."
Alfred, Lord Tennyson

The soldier will remain forever nameless to some aviators and I. We wronged him severely one day and I fear he remembers it to this day. Surely he must. I would remember and I have.

Civilized people have cultivated a certain basic expectation when occupied in going to the bathroom. For sophisticated Westerners this requirement can only be met with privacy and preferably a seat, unlike the holes in the floor most of the remaining world uses. Imprinted in practically every American psyche since childhood, is the unwritten rule that we are to abhor smelly, no seat, toilet facilities that circumstances may require of us. The bush will simply not do.

In view of this fundamental requirement and the environmental hazard posed by loose human waste, the U.S. Army provides a thriving business to porta-potty operators during field training exercises. Gone are the days when we simply dug a hole and did our business in the great out-of-doors.

The nameless soldier was no doubt enjoying that daily, private moment in a porta-potty during an FTX. He had no idea that the most embarrassing moment of his life was about to unfold. His experience was one any of us could have faced, for surely all soldiers have done their business in these field johns at some point in time. Only this particular man was unfortunate enough to be in the right place at the wrong time.

Our Blackhawk helicopter came in for a landing fast and low. It was a flawless approach and touchdown, almost poetry in motion. The pilot's work was perfect enough for even the best of recruiting film clips. There was only one defect, one small detail. The winds generated by turning rotor blades upset two or three port-a-potties near the landing zone, one of which held this indisposed soldier.

He emerged from the upset potty quite red-faced, bewildered, and speechless. Buttoning his pants on the run, one could see that though unharmed physically, his clothes and no doubt his soul were soiled from the tumble and shock. He rapidly disappeared into nearby tents as onlookers laughed a laugh they would not soon forget.

It is interesting how our world can be turned upside down so quickly, for some quite literally. I pray that when my time comes, it finds me in a less vulnerable moment. It is a wish I fear is canceled-out by the fervent prayers of this one soldier. No doubt he wants something far different for those aviators who delivered him such a scar to his dignity.

The Crash

"A Hero is no braver than an ordinary man,
but he is brave five minutes longer."
Ralph Waldo Emerson

It was a foggy and cloudy morning. The Blackhawk helicopter circled the airport as the pilot prepared the aircraft for landing. Totally dependent on guidance from the airport tower because of poor visibility, the pilot carefully followed the instructions from the air traffic controller.

Just over the end of the runway at two hundred feet and still in the fog, the pilot suddenly was unable to control the aircraft. The helicopter began lurching to the left, out of control. Still in the fog and on final approach, the pilot struggled to gain control of the aircraft. Already low and without visual references, the pilot's best efforts failed to prevent a crash.

About an hour after the accident I arrived at the scene. The fog had cleared and the helicopter lay on its side in the middle of the airport runway. All four-rotor blades were torn off by the impact. Large gashes in the runway asphalt marked where each blade impacted. Miraculously, there were no injuries or deaths, for all three crewmembers managed to quickly crawl out of the badly damaged aircraft.

At first everyone said it was pilot error. The command, self-appointed investigators, and idle talkers just knew that the pilot was at fault for being unable to handle the helicopter in bad weather. He was new, inexperienced, or just plain panic-stricken. "His career is finished," some had said.

I served on the crash investigation team. For two weeks our team of five sorted through every detail of the accident. Equipment, tape recordings of radio transmissions, scene evidence, and medical records were searched for any clues. No detail was left untouched as we went over the Army's accident investigation checklists, line-by-line, item-by-item. Meanwhile, the crew, and especially the pilot, waited, wondered, and worried.

Finally, the cause of the crash emerged. It was not pilot error after all. An aircraft part failure due to normal stress caused the tail rotor control mechanism to stop functioning. Given the circumstances of the accident, the efforts of the pilot did not contribute to the crash, but rather prevented the loss of life. Instead of a rogue, our findings made him a hero.

Often we judge too quickly. Certainly to judge is human, but to err is also human. We commonly err when conclusions are formed without the facts. It is often a mistake to prejudge. As Jessamyn West once said, "It is very easy to forgive others their mistakes. It takes more gut and gumption to forgive them for having witnessed your own."

271

Headaches

"Bad is never good until worse happens."
Danish Proverb

Things can always be worse. You think things are turning really sour and then all of a sudden, an extra dose of sour is added. Murphy's Law kicks in. If things can go wrong they will. Bad stuff happens, and when you think you see light at the end of a tunnel, it turns out to be the headlights of an oncoming train. In my case, the train is often inside my head in the form of a whopper headache.

On days when everything seems to be going to the devil, I can get some serious headaches. There is stress coming from every angle—people not showing up for work, the boss wanting something done right away, misplaced keys, or a subordinate filing a complaint over some silly issue. And then on top of this bad sandwich of a day comes this headache like a thick slice of smelly European cheese.

The whole world could be falling apart, but when the headache arrives, nothing else matters. The self-survival instinct kicks in. My priorities shift to a quiet, dark room where the freight train inside my head can run its course, usually in one or two hours. A short rest and then it is gone, often just as quickly as it arrived. I can re-enter the world of the living with a renewed vigor and a mind relieved of pain.

Now, with that awful headache gone, I can tackle anything the Army hits me with, be it a lobby full of impatient patients, fellow medical officers not pulling their fair share, or that pesky IG complaint. I can even handle the boss's deadline. Things, though still bad, do not seem as awful anymore when that headache is gone. Eventually, you can even live without those missing keys as long as the headache stays missing too.

An Army assignment may often be difficult, but trust me on this one, it can always be worse. Name a lousy job and someone can get you one that is worse. Someone taking disciplinary action against you can take more. Murphy's law is alive and well in the United States Army. You can get backed into a corner with no way out and then they back you in some more. The experience of civilian life reveals much the same thing.

A few of these lessons and you begin to see that, taken in proper perspective, things may not be so bad after all. Bad is indeed bad, but worse is no better. Given the potential of things, perhaps what we have facing us isn't so horrible after all.

Yeah, right. Headaches excluded.

Chapters

"Freedom exists only where people take care of the government."
Woodrow Wilson

There are many people who cannot endure the military experience. Many tremble at the reality of military life, for literally every moment of each day is managed by someone appointed over you. Managing every minute of a soldier's day is something the Army does well. It's religion. But this constant accountability causes some to want out of the Army.

I read once that approximately one out of four people who join the service do not complete their initial commitment. Their reasons vary for being "chaptered," or released early from active duty. From family hardship and pregnancy, to misconduct or homosexuality, many soldiers prematurely bail out either voluntarily or involuntarily.

Loss of freedoms they have grown accustomed to in civilian life is likely a major reason why some soldiers quit. As a military medical officer, I've seen so many of them come on sickcall with some minor complaint, but with faces burdened with struggle and sorrow. The slightest probing and it isn't long before the tears begin to flow. In an outburst of emotion, they pour out their hearts about not being able to cope.

Most of these soldiers who want out of the service are new to the Army. But sometimes it's a veteran of many years in the service. I haven't seen any generals chaptered out, but from major on down, there have been more than a few. For every one that quits though, three others stay on.

For those who complete their obligations, one wonders what makes them tick. Why did they stay on? Were they ever homesick? What sets them apart from the quitters? Job security, travel, education, pay, and benefits are part of it, but there must be more.

Some soldiers are motivated by patriotism, by a deep sense of an obligation to defend the country that gives freedom to all. Many simply love the job they do. I remember meeting a warrant officer pilot who, coming out of a break in service, came to see me for medical processing. I asked him, "What made you return to the service?" He said, "I had a good job in civilian life, but I have missed the camaraderie and flying the Apache."

For each soldier who stays on, he or she learns to cope with the undemocratic way of the military. They become assimilated. They adapt and overcome. The rules they are subject to are not always arbitrary. Instead of being chaptered, they form another chapter in a long line of green that continue to keep all Americans emancipated from the rule of other men.

Tap Dancing

"I know what I know and I don't know what I don't know."
Colonel Wayne A. Schirner

My wife will readily tell anyone I cannot dance. Though as her husband I can pretty much appreciate almost all forms of music, I remain unable to transfer the beat to my feet. My spirit is willing, but my legs know that I don't know how to dance.

I have always admired those guys would could get out on the dance floor and really dance. Instead of your regular bob and jiggle type-dancer, these guys know their stuff. They can lead a woman through some cool and sophisticated yet smooth routines that ooh and aah the rest of us. Every move they make is the masterful execution of a predictable pattern that becomes a work of moving art. Oh, how I wish I could master the Tango or the Rumba and dance as good as Fred Astarie!

Falling far short of what these agile men can do, I have sought to understand why I am a klutz with dancing routines. To date I have suffered no stroke or other physical impediment to explain why I can't dance. Though not ambidextrous, I seem to be fairly coordinated. Anyone who can fly a helicopter very well ought to be.

I've concluded that when dancing I am too distracted to pay attention to the steps. There I am, up close to a lovely lady. Her perfume and attractive dress, combined with that universal softness and very palpable anatomy are simply too much for my senses. When so close to such beauty as is natural to all women I simply cannot walk and chew gum at the same time, so to speak.

There are times when we act like we know something when we really do not. We bluff. We fake it. We put on a show. In the Army I believe this is called "tap dancing." Out on the dance floor you can bet I'm "tap dancing."

It hurts our ego to acknowledge our limitations. There are things we know and things we don't know, but are unwilling to admit. But here I will admit I can't dance. I wish I could. I honestly try my best when my darling wife hones in on a familiar "oldies" tune on the radio while preparing dinner. Soon we are spinning around the kitchen. I put on a show and go through the motions. Eventually though, it becomes hard for me to focus, to stay in step, and we invariably end up arm in arm and foot on foot.

I know what I know and I don't know what I don't know. Even with dancing lessons I will probably still not be able to dance worth a hoot. But far be it from me to turn down the chance to spin my wife around on the kitchen floor, despite the clear and present danger of yours truly tap dancing on her lovely toes.

Accuracy

"What I advise is that each contently practice the trade he understands."
Horace

For those who are married and make a career out of the military, there comes a time when the ambition and career of their spouse can figure as prominently as their own. When this occurs, a good formula to keep the marriage successful and growing is for each spouse to work at accepting and accommodating the needs and desires of the other. That's my motto, to always be ready to help out with whatever needs done.

My wife spent the first thirteen years of our time in the Army as a homemaker. As our four children grew up, she returned to school and eventually became an elementary school teacher. Boy, did life for us all speed up when she went to work!

Now, for those who don't know any better, let me be the first to tell you these teachers earn their pay, and then some. This is especially true if they teach in a school composed primarily of Army brats. The normal turbulence of Army kids moving in and out, combined with the usual treadmill of lesson plans, classroom discipline, papers to grade, and the pointless drills of education bureaucrats, leave the teachers with little breathing space down in the trenches with twenty or more pupils.

At one point my wife was having a difficult time keeping up. Being the knight in shining armor, I volunteered to help her in any way I could. Desperate, she gave me her grade book and a calculator and asked me to average the grades. Being a medical kind of guy, she figured I could do a good job there.

Wrong. Oh, I did well with the grades of 22 of her 23 students. But with this 23rd student, I was off by five points in one particular grade. Short on time, Irene trusted my work without double-checking. Report cards duly went home with the students and as fate would have it, that one erroneous grade was given to the one student whose father was a hawk on the lookout for teacher imperfections. In no time my wife received a ration of grief from the irate father. My poor wife had assumed risk with her helpful husband who had indeed failed in his attention to detail.

Despite my sin of omission, she loves me still. But no longer am I allowed to assist her in the realm of student grades. Zero tolerance for error there. Hey, nobody is perfect, especially when we fail to check our work twice. It was an important lesson for me, though. It's great to be helpful, but be very careful. If a job is worth doing, then it is worth doing right.

Drive-Thru Training

"Change is to shift one's position and be bruised in a new place."
Washington Irving

A permanent change of station (PCS), or movement from one Army assignment to another, is an event my family always made the best of. The chapters of my four children's lives are divided between places where we have lived. They relish the memory of the journey and each location.

When undergoing a PCS our family always took memorable vacations. Whether it was a coast-to-coast trip across America or halfway around the world, the highlights of each move were visits to just about everything worth seeing along the way. Our family photo albums received a healthy influx of new pictures of places like the Tower of Pisa in Italy, Hawaiian beaches and the Grand Canyon in Arizona.

For mom and dad each move would bring mixed feelings. Joy, excitement, stress, and anxiety all came together to form something akin to sweet and sour. For me, the long drives were a favorite part. Being the son of a truck driver means that enjoying long drives is in my blood. My wife always looked forward to the traveling too, especially since she would not have to cook. The periodic stops for drive-thru fast food were, without question, among the highlights of those long drives between assignments for my wife and the kids.

Now, for dad the experience of a drive-thru was stressful, right up there with having to deal with a multiple source information input situation under a serious time constraint. There are six people in our car as we pull up to the outdoor ordering box. No one ever knows exactly what he or she wants, as I notice through the rearview mirror four or five other cars lining up behind us. The initially pleasant electronic voice of the burger joint employee asks for our order. With some delay in deciding, the voice from the box becomes politely impatient, saying for the umpteenth time, "Will there be anything else, sir?"

Eventually we place our orders, each with some exception or modification—super-size this and hold the pickle that. You get the picture. Seldom did we order a preset meal number, certainly not when you have three growing boys and a couple of vegetarians in our bunch.

Usually, the driver, dad, is fairly stressed and needing an antacid by the time the food is ordered, paid for, received, inventoried and handed out. It's good training, though. Leaders need to cope with change and dealing with pressure in cramped spaces. My advice to the Army is to integrate the drive-thru ordering process with a carload of kids as part of its leaders' training program.

Keeping It Simple

"An expert is someone who can take something
you already know and make it sound confusing."
Anonymous

Keep it simple. It is a great yet frequently neglected philosophy. Too many cooks in the kitchen at one time claiming to know the recipe will spoil the food. My experience with implementing the TRICARE program at a major Army base was an example of a simple concept made complicated by too many voices from experts and the media on this military version of a Health Maintenance Organization (HMO).

My job as action officer for TRICARE briefings in my division was straightforward: make things as simple as possible to understand, and then get the word out to all sixteen thousand soldiers and their families in the division. Use experts on TRICARE if you can. Not too hard a mission, except when having to fight misinformation that comes from rumor and those who know just enough to make themselves dangerous.

The TRICARE concept was in essence quite clear: transfer over to TRICARE or risk potential delays for medical care. The DOD was changing and was asking soldiers to consider choosing the newer system. Bottom line up front was the new system offered more choice at a modest expense, or you could stay with the old way and pay nothing, but risk delays.

Most people understood this brief description on TRICARE. The problems arose with specific questions posed publicly, whose answers only applied to a few. Trying to sound like someone who knew everything about TRICARE, "expert" briefers wound up confusing many with answers they provided to specific questions that had no bearing on the majority. People became lost in a forest of exception and details that really didn't even concern them. The confusion led to doubt and doubt to indecision as reflected in slow enrollment rates within our division.

For damage control, we had to get the briefing process right. We kept it simple and we directed group-setting questions likely to cause confusion to one-on-one encounters or to the TRICARE 1-800 help line. Most folks do not need a lot of detail, just the facts that applied to everyone. People, in general, seemed to like and understand our new tactic. Enrollments went up. The Old Man in division headquarters was happy.

In an age of information we need know many things. Keeping things simple helps. The experts have their place, but their best place is with individuals and not in front of the masses. More information than they need does not necessarily make people smarter.

Of Money and a Fool

"A fool and his money are soon parted."
Anonymous

The Army's suggestion award program for ideas that save money is a good deal, provided you offer some idea or change that really does save money. Depending on how much savings is realized; one could stand to get a sizable sum of money as an award.

I once received four thousand dollars in cold cash for an improvement suggestion. By my calculations it worked out to about a thousand dollars per hour of work. Not bad. Naturally such a windfall makes one very happy.

My medical officers had been complaining about how many unnecessary physicals we were doing on soldiers. It was difficult and tedious work. We suspected that with chapter physical examinations in particular, commanders were ordering them as a scare tactic to get marginal soldiers to straighten up and get back into line.

A couple of phone calls and some numbers crunching confirmed my suspicions. Over half of the physical examinations were indeed not needed. This translated into a lot of time and work done in vain. While preparing the report for the Division Commander, I wondered how much money this excess work translated into. Two more phone calls gave me the answer: $392.00 per physical. After comparing numbers with Personnel, the conservative estimate was that for our Division alone the Army was losing a quarter of a million dollars each year.

In addition to the commander's report, I submitted another to the Army Ideas Program. Maybe the Army would consider this idea worth a cash award. The evaluators agreed and a few months later the check arrived and you would think the rest is history. Not quite, for now comes the rest of the story.

I should have gone out and spent the money. Instead, a stock tip from a friend led to my investing the extra cash into a company whose stock was supposedly about to take off. Well, it crashed while still on the ground trying to take off. The get-rich-quick scheme turned into a lose-it-all fast reality.

Easy come. Easy go. Philosophically speaking, there were at least a couple of lessons here, maybe some ideas or suggestions really worth adopting. Learn from your mistakes, right? Well, first, doing your homework ahead of time is better than blind trust in someone else's opinion. Second, we will all do something foolish from time to time.

Foolishness is a shoe many of us will try on. Hopefully, we will not make a habit of wearing it.

Story Tellers

"Newspapers are to be feared more than a thousand bayonets."
Napoleon Bonaparte

It is hard for me not to be at least a little bit cynical when I read a newspaper. There was a time when I naively trusted the stories and reports, unaware that perhaps the story might not be true. As someone once said, "They might be inclined not to lie, but they're not telling the truth either." After a close encounter with the sometimes-inaccurate press, I quickly learned that they certainly know how to tell stories that suit their purposes.

Allow me to elaborate. A major city newspaper called up our Army Division's public affairs office. They wanted to get the story on a new armored ambulance we were putting through tests and trials. The Division Surgeon tapped me to do the honors of showing the press around, answering their questions, and allowing photo opportunities.

The press corps duly arrived, led by an attractive but talkative woman, perhaps in her late twenties. I could tell it was their first visit deep into Army-land as their questions and interest betrayed their general lack of knowledge concerning things military.

But they seemed to catch on quickly, and in no time they had asked all their questions, taken dozens of pictures, and gathered enough notes and tape recordings to write a small book on the Army's experimental armored medical treatment vehicle.

I received congratulatory phone calls from friends a few weeks later, after the story came out in the Sunday edition of this major regional paper. The story and pictures were syndicated in other papers, too...*The Washington Post* and *London Times* for instance. Smack dab on the cover was a picture of Yours Truly giving the world the scoop.

There was just one small problem. Oh, I was tickled with the publicity, but I was also troubled by several misquotes. "I didn't say that," I thought, or "That's not what I meant." One phrase was definitely conjecture, but attributed to me as a bona fide quote.

I guess what bothered me most was the lack of any opportunity to proofread the story before it went around the world. It is a scary thought how much misinformation might go into print.

Live and learn. You learn not to believe everything that is said or seen. The press is not unlike show business in that truth might not be as exciting as fiction, but for now I suppose it's the best we've got.

A Hero with a Headache

"But the very hairs of your head are all numbered…"
Matthew 10:30

One of the most positive, humorous, and enthusiastic physician assistants I ever had work for me was Lieutenant Mark Dedmon. This "can do" individual never ceased to impress me with his abilities both as an officer and as a clinician. And this was before I learned that he was also a recipient of the Army's highest peacetime award for heroism—The Soldier's Medal. He earned this award when as a medic assigned to the 82nd Airborne Division he rendered emergency first aid and treatment to fallen comrades during a fiery ground collision disaster between two transport planes loaded with troops at Pope Air Force Base, North Carolina.

Mark arrived to work one morning with a headache. The 4th Infantry Division clinic we worked at had an especially large crop of sick call patients that day and Mark plowed right into the work as usual. Passing him in the hallway, I noticed that he did not seem his normal self. "Is something wrong?" I asked. "No sir," he said, " just a headache that will not go away." After telling me he was seeing one of our other doctors in the clinic for it, I told him to let me know if it didn't get any better.

It was not until the next day that I caught Lieutenant Dedmon again. He was back at work but the headache was no better, maybe even slightly worse than before. A bit worried now, I stuck my head into the Doc's office who was seeing him and said, "Hey, I think we ought to get a CT on Mark. His headache is no better."

Later that same day Mark received his CT Scan. A mid-brain mass was found and he was whisked off to Brooke Army Medical Center in San Antonio. In no time they had Mark in surgery and opened up his head. In addition to a brilliant mind, the neurosurgeons found a non-cancerous tumor, a rare glioma.

After a few weeks of recovery and some convalescent leave, Mark was back to work. He looked a bit different now though. A Frankenstein-like scalp scar and some scattered hair loss now complimented his deep-set eyes, square jaw, dark hair and large muscular build. Always one with a great sense of humor, he made the most of the change by going around walking like Frankenstein and stating in a thick, imitation German accent, "Und now I have an excuse not to remember zings."

It was great to have Mark back safe and sound. He had us worried. And though he was left with some scars, we all knew that Someone upstairs was looking after our hero, even if his head hair count went down a bit.

Of Apes and Leaders

"Is man an ape or an angel?
I, my lord, I am on the side of the angels."
Benjamin Disraeli

You can't please all the people all the time. Despite our best efforts, you interact with some folks with whom it is impossible to get along. There are different opinions, different priorities, and different personalities.

She came to work in my clinic as a junior supervisor. Our first meeting didn't go well for I was in the middle of seeing patients and she had another scheduled appointment. Pleasantries were exchanged, but it was not an auspicious beginning.

Being part of the poor start, I probably contributed to a self-fulfilling prophecy. I half expected trouble from her based on my erroneous first impression. I was therefore not surprised when some complaints about her came in. She was gruff with the patients, and wasn't very friendly with the clinic staff. In short, it looked like she had an attitude problem.

It took me a while to figure out what was wrong. Only after a sharp verbal encounter together did I begin to earnestly seek for a solution to my new problem. It dawned on me that I was the problem and not she.

It is easy to point the finger, to demonize people. It is one of our human tendencies. With reflection, I realized I had not made her a team member. I had been too busy. The blame finger pointed at me. The demon was much closer to home.

She was very nervous as we met, probably wondering if I was about to address her performance. Her anger and frustration simmered just below the surface of civility. First, I apologized. The problem was with me, not her. I promised to do a better job of communicating and helping her. With that said, her anger and bitterness inside melted away. A noticeable relief overcame her.

Over time a new person emerged. All along she had been a warm, concerned person who, as I learned, faced personal and family struggles only made worse by an indifferent work environment. Genuine communication and concern helped set things right. The complaints ended. The stress levels dropped dramatically. Productivity increased.

I discovered two things from the experience. First, the entire clinic staff came to know that, instead of a demon, the new medic became an angel on our TMC staff, someone who blossomed into a likable, caring, faithful team player and leader. Second, my performance was ape-like and a simple apology made all the difference. It was a very important lesson and one even an ape like me could learn.

281

Fairness

"Silence gives consent."
Oliver Goldsmith

"It isn't fair!" How often this was my experience! A case in point was my tangle with U.S. Army finance. Here I was getting paid less each month for housing than the guy across the street that had the same rank and time in service as I. The $70 difference each month added up to a nice chunk of change. But Army finance ruled against my claim. No exception would be made and my appeal to higher authority ended with still no extra money for me. Though I was unsuccessful and frustrated, I did take some comfort in the fact that the system did pay attention when I spoke up.

A key component of good leadership is the ability to listen, to disperse justice when appropriate, to make things right. Nothing can poison morale quicker than an uncorrected real or perceived injustice. Leaders should recognize this and be alert to a quick and just solution, be that giving a soldier correct information or making a wrong right.

Most of the time, indifference toward wrong has a very short life in the Army. Part of why an Army of a republic built upon democratic ideals succeeds so well comes in no small part to a soldier's right to appeal, to speak up, and to see the Old Man.

If it isn't right, then say something. And many do. Anyone who has occupied leadership positions in the Army knows well that soldiers do speak up. This is good. They may speak up too much sometimes and some may even say this reflects a lack of good order and discipline. Maybe, but in the face of wrong, it is better to overstate the case than to be silent.

Silent people are not stupid, but sometimes they allow the hurt or ill feelings to run deep, to fester. Far too often it later explodes into something out of control, something bigger than it ought to be. Witness the profiles of people who blow up Federal buildings or mow down innocent people in restaurants or playgrounds with automatic weapons. It is true we should listen more often than we speak. That is one reason why we have two ears and only one mouth. But we still have one mouth. Picking our words and methods carefully, we can find the right time to speak out.

Let the soldiers of a democracy speak up. From a suggestion form to a congressional inquiry, leaders may think the time given to these matters is a pain, but there is a good reason. Every now and again a comment or complaint turns up a whopper of a problem or a brilliant solution to a vexing problem. Listen to them. You might find the seed of a big problem you can fix quickly. A few ounces of words now may prevent pounds of testimony later.

The Raid

"The vitality of thought is in adventure. Ideas won't keep.
Something must be done about them."
Alfred North Whitehead

One warm Saturday afternoon my sons and I sat on the back patio of our government quarters. As mother's wonderful noon meal settled in our bellies, we indulged in typical guy-talk, solving the world's problems and discussing anything to do with ideas and adventure.

Just off our backyard was the fourteenth hole of the post golf course. Each day hundreds of people would negotiate this particularly short but difficult hole. We watched a group of four men tee off, each one unable to land their golf ball on the green, about one hundred yards from the tee off point. Instead, each ball dropped into the pond lying just before the green.

My youngest son, Brian, watched these proceedings intensely. Suddenly he announced, "Dad, I bet there are a zillion balls in that pond. If we could only get them out we could make a fortune selling them to passing golfers." Mulling over his suggestion a bit, I replied, "Yes, but how?"

That evening, well after sunset, two of my sons and I set out in our bathing trunks and old tennis shoes. We scaled the small golf course fence and darted across the green. The full moon was our flashlight as we eased slowly into the warm, black water of the shallow pond. To our surprise there was ten to twelve inches of muck on the bottom. Partly to ease my own fears, I said in a loud whisper, "Don't worry. You'll get used to it."

We worked quickly, using a seine to screen for the golf balls. The adrenaline flowed as we dipped and scooped. There were hundreds of balls rolling around in the warm goo, like hard meatballs in spaghetti sauce. A primordial odor followed in our wake, the result of all our churning and movement through the mud. Boy, did we raise a stink! We came across a discarded golf club and a chill went up my spine. What if there is a dead body in here, or worse, a monster in the mud, some large snapping turtle that bites and never lets go? I quickly banished the thought from my mind.

In the dark we heard the sound of a golf cart. We hunkered down in the water as the night watchman passed by on patrol. My entire Army career flashed before my eyes. Technically we were not supposed to be there, but that was part of the adventure. We were on a mission.

Soon we had a ton of golf balls. We beat a hasty retreat to our backyard, flushed with victory. Brian and Marlan beamed and looked like kids who had won the lottery. We would smell like a swamp for several days, but the memory of our clandestine raid would linger much longer.

Badges

*"At times he regarded the wounded soldiers in an envious way.
He conceived persons with torn bodies to be peculiarly happy.
He wished that he, too, had a wound, a red badge of courage."*
Stephen Crane

The General and I had just completed the weekly visit to troops
admitted to Darnall Army Hospital. Of the eight or so patients, one had his
gallbladder removed and another had pneumonia. There was a female soldier
who had her first baby and an older soldier who had his first heart attack.
The General had a genuine interest in each one of them, taking time out of
his busy schedule each week to do the walk-about and see them personally,
without some entourage in tow.

Driving back to the 4th Infantry Division headquarters in his staff car
the General struck up a conversation with me, his deputy division surgeon.
We had served in the same units twice before, only at different times. I had
just missed serving under his command with the 5th Battalion, 32nd Armor at
Fort Stewart, Gerogia. We both also had served with the 11th Armored
Cavalry Regiment, only he had served as a cavalry troop commander in the
Vietnam War.

We both recalled times with the 11th Cavalry. I told him of a recent
visit I had to Fort Knox where the Regiment had erected a memorial to her
fallen dead from the Vietnam War. I marveled at how many names were
etched in that sacred stone, an eternal testimony to the heavy cost in fallen
cavalry troopers from those bloody fights.

The General grew quiet, gathering his thoughts. After a short pause,
he said, "You know, there was a time in my command of one hundred and
twenty men when there were only a handful of them who had not yet
received the Purple Heart."

Wow! Few remember the accomplishments of armored cavalry forces
in Vietnam. It was difficult and costly work keeping the roads clear of the
Viet Cong. Helicopters could not always fly or haul the tons and tons of
supplies needed by troops out in the bush and rice paddies.

There were many casualties from this important work, fraught with
mines and road ambushes. Helicopters did a vital and important work in
Vietnam, but few appreciate the deeds of armored cavalry in that conflict.
Aircraft cannot always help in a war that does not pause for bad weather.

I envied the General. He spoke with a sense of pride from a job well
done, even if we "lost" that war. He and his men had made a difference in
combat, many earning badges of courage in the process, some of them red.

R&R

"The end of labor is to gain leisure."
Aristotle

After working hard on a hot day there is nothing closer to heaven than to rest in the cool shade with an ice-cold drink. People in the service work hard. The long hours they put in are often combined with sweat and stress. Rest and relaxation, or R&R for short, is something we all need, military or civilian.

The Department of Defense understands this need and has made provision for service members to get away and have fun without losing an arm and a leg in the process. Military personnel can take advantage of several recreation and service centers around the world. From the Hale Koa hotel on Waikii to Camp Darby near Pisa, Italy, the DOD provides getaways most people just dream about.

For my family, tops on the list of these DOD fun places is the "Shades of Green" hotel, located on the Walt Disney World Resort in Orlando, Florida. This hotel lies near the magic of the Magic Kingdom and is indeed a magical experience.

Shades of Green was a paradise for my family. We stayed a week there and should have stayed longer. Large, comfortable and quiet poolside rooms, good food, and so many things to do it was almost overwhelming. You have golf, tennis, swimming, and the wonders of the Magic Kingdom, all within walking distance.

Vacation should be a time you can even forget you are in the Army. This is important. It rebuilds the soul. In fact, recreation means to re-create, to make new again. No matter what form of leisure you enjoy, it should recreate and not destroy. You should not have to go back to work to get over your holiday.

The military has a fair crop of Type A personalities: people who are driven and some who are workaholics. Like the preventive maintenance checks and services (PMCS) we do on every piece of equipment in the Army, we also need to do the same for ourselves, especially if we are a Type A personality. I spell PMCS for soldiers as "Shades of Green."

Leisure time well spent is an excellent opportunity to lubricate the spirit, rest the bones, and reconnect with the real meaning of why we do what we do. Shades of Green is simply one of the many human maintenance depots soldiers can take their tired spirits to. You work hard. Sometimes you need to rest in the shade.

Photographic Memories

"The history of the world
is but the biography of great men."
Thomas Carlyle

Some fragments of who and what we are will one day be stored in boxes and climate-controlled rooms for posterity. Sprinkled throughout the U.S. Government are a small cadre of historians who are the keepers of the past. Their task is to preserve those bits and pieces of the lives of people like you and me.

The last time I had worked with this senior sergeant was at the Joint Readiness Training Center. He was our Observer Controller (OC), or umpire, in the war games there. My infantry battalion was taking part in war games his advisory team was grading. Now I had the opportunity to work with him again, only this time going through the photographic archives of the 4th Infantry Division, where he now served as their custodian.

The Bennett Health Clinic was a brand new garrison troop and family medical clinic at Fort Hood, Texas. To decorate it, we hit upon the idea of photographic displays on the division's history, particularly the medical support. The idea was to piece together six or so mosaics from each major period in the infantry division's history, all with a medical theme.

Nearly one hundred years of photographs lay in carefully stored packages before us. We immersed ourselves into the work, our specially gloved hands carefully sifting through almost untouched old photos of soldiers and events long past, but not entirely forgotten. Famous people and common folk, all were frozen in time on paper. For several days, we went through literally thousands of photos, finally assembling one hundred and fifty or so on medically related subjects. From World War I to Vietnam, the faces, scenes and places came to life as photo mosaics and individual narratives were prepared for permanent display in the new clinic.

At the grand opening of Bennett Health Clinic, hundreds of people participated. As the generals finished their formalities and the ribbons were cut, the crowd dispersed throughout the building to check it out.

Up and down each hall the visitors would linger before any one of the twenty-four photo displays. They saw more than a new building. They saw a bit of the spirit of those who had come before—the medics across the 20th century whose likeness and story was no longer hidden in a box. From the trenches of World War One, the bitter cold of Nazi Germany or Korea, to the steamy swamps of Vietnam, they were not forgotten.

286

The Caveat

"Every man has three characters – that which he exhibits,
that which he has, and that which he thinks he has."
Alphonse Karr

Dr. Jonathan Jaffin is an outstanding trauma surgeon and one of the very best doctors I ever worked for. Unlike some supervisors I've had, he was also a very personable man with a broad range of interests. In fact, he enjoyed tackling difficult tasks and developing skills far removed from the complexities of an operating room. A rising star in the U.S. Army Medical Department, Dr. Jaffin was posted as Division Surgeon to the 4th Infantry Division, the Army's first experimental division of the computer/digital age. I would have the distinct privilege of serving as his deputy.

One could not spend a day working for Colonel Jaffin without learning something, often unrelated to things medical. Once the business at hand was taken care of, I would enjoy just sitting and listening to this brilliant man as we touched on topics ranging from the American Civil War, ethics, anthropology, Wall Street, and, as I would learn, language. You can imagine the conversation as a Johns Hopkins trained Yankee surgeon and an ADHD kid from the mountains of North Carolina interacted together. The discourse was always stimulating, but easily shifted to new topics. I found the richness and variety of our discussions very rewarding.

One of my weakest areas in life is the English language, especially vocabulary. I always marvel at the sophisticated language of highly educated people and fancy myself assimilating some of it from time to time. There is power in words. Sometimes, though, the power backfires when you use newfound words improperly.

Take, for example, the word caveat. For years I had improperly employed this neat sounding word in my efforts to sound intelligent. For some reason I thought the word meant "an exception." My error was probably a half-baked remnant of my high school vocabulary drills. You can then imagine the delicate nature of an on-the-spot correction to my misfired word from my tactful mentor at the height of one of our discussions. I quickly learned from my boss that caveat meant a warning or caution.

Jon Jaffin will forever remain for me an exceptional man, a man who wears the uniform of the United States Army. My brain and character underwent some serious expansion under his tutelage and I enjoyed it. My only caveat to those who work with brilliant people is this:

You may be able to walk the walk, but you also need to talk the talk.

287

Final Clearance

"It ain't over 'till the fat lady stamps your papers."
David Kay

Soldiers about to depart an Army post are very familiar with "outprocessing." Several working days are given to soldiers to ensure they check out of, or "clear" key activities on post, like dental, medical, housing, supply or transportation.

The last place soldiers check out of is the final outprocessing point, but this is a mere formality. Some clerk picks up your "clearing papers," logs you into a book, and you're on your way. The real final outprocessing point is the person stamping your papers at the Central Issue Facility (CIF).

To function in the Army, soldiers need gear, and lots of it. What most civilians would call camping and backpacking accessories, soldiers call TA-50. TA-50 is "loaned" to soldiers during their tour at each Army post. This small mountain of equipment comes from only one place: CIF.

CIF is always a great place when you first arrive on post. They give you all this neat, often new stuff to use. But come time to leave, CIF can be quite a hurdle to jump. The once friendly staff now transform into picky inquisitors looking for defects, dirt and damage in all that new gear you received. No need to argue either. If they say the piece of gear isn't good enough, then it isn't good enough. You'd better fix it or buy a new piece.

Some contrary souls dare to challenge the judgement of these civilians who man CIF. You overhear their pathetic excuses. "What do you mean my canteen cup is unacceptable? I spent two hours cleaning it!" "I don't see any stain." "It was issued to me that way and I never used it!" I pity them, for they are in danger of prolonging their CIF purgatory. Better to just go out and buy new stuff at the military clothing sales store on post.

In the large CIF building, the equipment turn-in area is normally a long counter with twenty or so stations and a final checker at the very end. My experience has often seen this checker at the end of the counter to be a husky, poker-faced lady. After much scrubbing and a couple of visits to CIF, you finally make it to her, anxious to learn whether you are worthy of parole. She carefully reviews the issue documents, the ever-important hand receipt. If I ever become the President of the United States, I'm going to hire these people to watch over the government's spending, so good are they at weeding out villainy. But this time the plump person is pleased, and grants you the stamp. As far as I am concerned, that is the final outprocessing point.

Free at last. Free at last. Thank CIF I'm free at last!

Memories

"Mankind owes to the child the best it has to give."
United Nation's Declaration

My custom is to always try and get a window seat when flying. My flight to the Middle East one late July afternoon was no exception. Another stint of duty without my family had begun.

Outside my window central Europe passed beneath a nearly cloudless summer sky. For now, as the plane flew over Germany, my mind wandered back to earlier times spent stationed in Europe where my children, now nearly all grown, had been toddlers and grade-schoolers. It was such a different time then, so much activity in our life. It was a magical time.

The picturesque countryside of Bavaria below gave way to the mountains of Austria. The lovely lake called Königsee came into view, all nestled in the Alps. The quaint villages, majestic mountains, manicured valleys, and serpentine roads near the lake could readily be seen. Even the lake's ferryboat launch was clearly visible, with a small boat heading out upon the green, glacier-fed lake water.

It was next to the ferryboat launch of Königsee that one of our most memorable family pictures was taken. It was a hot July day then too, as I recall, and we were on a small vacation. As we waited for the ferryboat, my wife and I, with four little children in tow, made our way to a small ice cream shop nearby. Those cold Italian ice cream delights were a welcome treat and diversion for our squad.

Each child made his or her selection and then found a small table to sit behind. Quite on their own they crowded themselves shoulder to shoulder on a small bench on the backside of one table, leaving the front two chairs on each side of the table free for mom and dad.

There they sat, youngest to oldest from right to left. Their flushed faces from the heat of the day forming the background for obvious joy as each tackled the cold ice cream cones before them. It was a Kodak moment, and we managed to snap a picture to freeze the scene for all time.

The lake slowly passed from view and I settled back into my seat. Tears welled up in my eyes. My daughter and three sons were much older now, and doing so well in their different pursuits. They too were becoming all they could be. Mom and I were very proud of them.

We are thankful to God and country that our lives in the Army allowed us the opportunity to give them the very best in our many travels, even Italian ice cream.

The Kapsa

"Dinner, a time when...one should eat wisely but not too well,
and talk well but not too wisely."
W. Somerset Maugham

Saudi Arabia is a difficult land to enter, but once inside the visitor is afforded many new and unique experiences. There are very interesting activities for U.S. military personnel assigned as advisors to the Arabs. Topping the list has to be a *Kapsa*.

A Kapsa is a communal feast and forms a key aspect of Arab hospitality. The meal originates in early Bedouin times where these travelers of the desert entertained strangers with the best they had to offer. For the Kapsa, the Arabs use a large circular serving platter, often three or more feet wide. Upon this platter they place a small mountain of specially made steamed rice, topped with a broiled lamb, goat, or, for those of great honor, a camel. Dinner guests sit on the floor around the platter with the soles of their feet carefully hidden or pointing to the rear, for it is offensive to Arabs to show the soles of your feet. There are no eating utensils, for one eats with the hand, but never with the left hand. Arabs use the left hand for bodily functions, so it is extremely impolite to eat with this hand.

Our group of four American officers enjoyed our first Kapsa provided by our Arab hosts. The conversation was polite over tea and coffee before the large Kapsa tray arrived. We avoided politically sensitive topics, but the conversation still flowed well back and forth, for our hosts were very fluent in English. When the main meal arrived, the Saudi's commenced to eating immediately and we hesitatingly followed. Our first efforts to eat with our fingers were comical and messy, but soon we got the hang of it. The Arabs became more relaxed as they saw our appetites begin to match our desire to learn their ways. We ate well enough, but the method of delivering the food to our mouths did blunt our appetites somewhat. Friendships were forged, however, for our presence and our willingness to share their ways honored them. We thereby learned to understand them much more.

Soon the meal and conversation ended. Arabs do not linger in small talk over a finished meal, preferring instead to get all the talk and visiting done beforehand over tea and coffee. When the business of eating is done it is then time to leave. As appetites are satisfied the main host rises, food is removed, hands are washed, and then our host bids his guests farewell.

Arab meals made us wiser. Arab opinions and food became for food for thought. A Kapsa was a chance to eat differently but well. It is wise to accept different ways, even in eating.

Prayer Lessons

"Prayer is the sum total of religion and morals."
The Duke of Wellington

My new job with the Saudi Arabian National Guard was exciting. Each day was filled with a variety of completely new experiences that can only be had in Arabia. I tackled the tasks and opportunities with gusto but sometimes my enthusiasm would get me into hot water.

Working at the Saudi military medical school, my office on the second floor of the administration building was just across the hall from the school Commandant. Having recently settled into my daily routine, I discovered that the Arabs were very particular about prayer and where it occurred. It is a very public event. The entire administrative staff would break at around noon each day for the communal prayer gathering around the only exit down from the second floor of the building.

As fate would have it, the day came when I just had to be at a meeting with my fellow American advisors who, being non-Moslems, didn't follow the prayer times. The Commandant had delayed me concerning some details and now I found myself blocked from exiting the building by the gathering of Arab soldiers at the large stairway landing. Barefoot and bowing towards Mecca, the prayer leaders' musical call echoed down the hall:

"Allah...Achbah...Allah...Achbah."

Since the major group prayer had not begun yet, I decided to gingerly make my way around the gathering faithful and their prayer carpets to the stairway and my escape. Thinking I was unnoticed, I quietly exited down the stairs and made my meeting on time in the finest Western tradition of never being late. But being on time this time would cost me dearly.

The new guy quickly learned how respected, powerful, and keenly alert the prayer leader was. Arriving early the next day loaded with good news for the Commandant on a number of issues, only one thing mattered to him. He made it clear that my impatience to leave had offended the faithful. I had violated the pious atmosphere so important to my allies.

No need for me to learn that lesson again. Many were the days when I simply missed meetings because of the roadblock of the devout. I had discovered the sum total of the Saudi Arabian religion and morals—the five-times a day prayer ritual. Respect it and all would be well. Ignore it and be considered worthless, no matter how valuable you might think you are.

Talkers

"After all is said and done, more is said than done."
Anonymous

I once knew an Army officer who didn't work much, but he loved to talk. You name the topic…anything…and the conversation could go on and on. His brilliant mind could bring forth ideas and perspectives you never thought about before. His eloquence was stimulating. His broad grasp of practically any subject was phenomenal. Because of his broad range of interests he was a likable sort of person too.

You wouldn't say this officer was a know-it-all. The opinions and offerings of others were important too. In fact, these served to engender more responses and conversation from him. Your input could actually influence his opinions and add further length to the overall topic, like adding wood to a warm fire. Find the right moment to introduce another subject and you had a self-sustaining talk show.

Time flies with good conversation. A good talk back and forth can be stimulating and mutually rewarding. You can learn. You can grow. You can also waste time.

Prognosticators in the workplace are notorious for low productivity. Everyone likes a good conversationalist. They are often hard to dislike. But they frequently fall short of real productive results from all their talking. The actual non-verbal aspects of work languish with these professional talkers. The making things happen with sweat, blood and tears seems foreign to them. They fail to see that it is productivity and results, and not just talking that makes the world go around. This soldier, sadly, numbered not among the movers and shakers. He numbered among the talkers.

The talkers are great when there is a party. They keep things moving. The conversation flows. Their often politically correct talents flourish in the verbal open season of a social gathering where each small crowd seems politely entranced by their parley as everyone mingles. Empires of words rise and fall in the back and forth discussion of which they are the center.

The doers on the other hand can be dull at a party, unless, of course, they know how to mix and talk. Often, however, they are not politically correct, more content with action rather than talk. If they talk at all is only to tell you like it really is.

Thank God many Army officers and NCOs number among the doers!

Life is not always a party. Sometimes we need to shut up and get to work. In the end there are two groups of people: those who make things happen and those who talk about it.

Adventure

"Better your allies do it tolerably than you do it perfectly.
It is their war, and you are here to help them, not win it for them."
T.E. Lawrence (*Arab Bulletin*, August, 1917)

Jeff Sloan is a great American from the farmlands of Illinois. We served together as advisors to the Saudi Arabian military. My memories of the Arabian Peninsula will always include Jeff and the adventures we were involved in over there.

T.E. Lawrence was another great man, an Englishman. Sent as an advisor to the same Army during World War I, his exploits were phenomenal. His adventures became, of course, the subject of an epic movie, *Lawrence of Arabia.*

One of our great adventures in Arabia occurred near the end of my one-year term with the Arabs. Jeff and I were determined to visit the famous Hijaz railway, where T.E. Lawrence led Arab attacks on the vital Turkish rail link to Medina during the Great War. With some time off and the freedom to travel unhindered all across the country, save the most holy cities, we headed out with two other buddies on a cross-desert trip in our four-wheel drive vehicles to see the lay of that historic land.

Saudi Arabia is not a country tourists visit. Though many faithful Muslim around the world make it a point to go to Medina or Mecca sometime in their lives, the Hijaz railway, now in ruins, is not on their "to see" list. For heathen Westerners, though, especially those who are history buffs, a trip to the Hijaz is a must.

Extending for hundreds of miles northward from Medina, the old railway path runs all the way into Jordan, the iron rails long since removed. Scattered along the route are old Turkish forts and destroyed or abandoned trains. Eighty years had passed and still these remains are clearly seen.

We had finished reconnoitering a good piece of the rail line when we hit upon the idea of getting a souvenir, a small piece of history there. All over the place were old, steel, Turkish railroad ties the Arabs were now using as fence posts. Eventually, Jeff and I were able to obtain one through a little bit of audacity, four bucks and muscle power. We managed to load the seven-foot, 150-pound behemoth into our Yukon and haul it hundreds of miles to our base in Riyadh.

Back in Riyadh we mounted the railroad tie on polished cherry wood and presented it as a gift to our advisory group, a not-so-small token of our time there. Perhaps today it hangs in some prominent place, a piece of T.E. Lawrence's spirit to serve as an inspiration to his not-so-famous successors.

293

Religion

"More things are wrought by prayer than this world dreams of.
Wherefore, let thy voice rise like a fountain for me night and day."
Alfred, Lord Tennyson

I grew up a heathen. Oh, there was the occasional effort of my mother to get me to Sunday school or vacation Bible school, but my spirit was like a nonstick frying pan. Even the loss of my father at a young age didn't drive me to religion. In general, the gods of my life were pagan ones and the golden rule was "If it feels good, do it."

My mother sure knew how to pray though. Eventually, in the latter part of my teenage years, I found a place for God in my life, probably because of those prayers. Not that I'm trying to proselytize anyone here, but for me the belief in something beyond myself became important. That belief still holds true, especially in a personal faith grounded in truth and not just some smooth-talking evangelist.

Apparently this religion business is important to many others as well, including a good number of soldiers. Though our religious beliefs come in many different varieties and wrappers, one cannot help but be struck by the interest in religion and not infrequent piety one encounters in the U.S. Army.

We had to eat fast during boot camp. Slam, bam, thank you Ma'am, it was eaten, and we were out the door. Despite the rush, there were those who would deliberately pause to render thanks for things the rest of us took for granted. Then there was this guy across from me before our first parachute jump. He wasn't napping. He was praying. One fellow in my squad always said, "Praise the Lord," when the platoon sergeant dismissed us for the day. Finally, I remember SFC Dan Massa kneeling to pray as we toured an ancient Christian church in Jordan. Yes, religion is a part of many soldiers.

Though it is true the foxhole makes many believers in God, I can truthfully testify that faith is alive and well in many soldiers of the United States Army. We should not forget that there is also a good crop of heathens in the ranks. And then there are others with a touch of religion, but who are really wolves in sheep's clothing. Between us all, you have a good mirror of American society.

The pessimists may bemoan the lack of faith in America today. Others say that religion is trying to usurp individual freedom. The glass is at best half empty to these people. The optimists, on the other hand, especially those who pray to the God of their own choosing, believe the glass is half full. It is my hope that the fountain of faith will keep us optimistic in the years to come. Optimism is the better bet when it comes to filling up the entire glass.

Mirror, Mirror

"Know thyself."
Anonymous

There is a group of people I will always envy. They possess something that will never come to me, for I haven't the time, determination, anatomy or patience to earn what they have. For me it is a bridge too far. What these people own are bodies that genetics and fitness centers have molded into muscular wonders. They are the body builders.

The weight lifter always stands out. His large chest supports a neck as wide as his head. Massive arms round out the upper body's imposing size, regardless of his height. His abdominal six-pack is in stark contrast to the bulge battle most of us are losing or have already lost. Large, flabless legs that look like finely sanded wood support the whole.

Body builders often walk in a smooth, almost deliberate manner. Like battleships gliding through a harbor full of tankers and tugboats, their movements slow and deliberate. Their style has been honed in response to numerous admirers and the dictates of their self-made anatomy. These people make me proud to be a human being. At least someone is out there to show the universe that we are not a bunch of weaklings and fatsoes.

There was a time or two when I made half-hearted attempts to improve my physique. The intimidating array of various body building machines in the weightlifting room are still a relative mystery to me. But the one thing about these centers of body improvement that impressed me most were the large number of strategically placed mirrors. Indeed, some exercise rooms have entire walls that are nothing but mirrors.

I believe the mirrors are what prevented me from sticking with my fledgling desire to be buff. Push, pump, and perspire all I'd like, the mirror would constantly remind me of the futility of my efforts. I was fighting against the laws of habit and genetics. It was not only an uphill fight, but I would also need rope and pitons to scale the obstacle of flab, flotsam and faithlessness.

The mirror on the wall always knew, as I now know, that I am not a hunk. There are things you cannot be. There is a frontier, a border beyond which only others can go. When you know your own limitations, you should look into the mirror again for other things—things you already are and realistically can become. The mirror knows there are other things at which you can be greatest. The trick is finding out what those things are. To be the greatest of all in one thing or another involves a good look now and again into the mirror of self-assessment.

Falafel

"The proof of the pudding is in the eating."
Henry Glapthorne

Without a doubt the best fast food sandwich in the world has got to be the Arab *falafel*. This is particularly true for falafels that are actually prepared in Middle Eastern countries. My love for this sandwich was so strong that in spite of increasing Arab displeasure towards Americans, I would still brave the stares, stress, and winds of war to obtain this delicacy.

My time in Saudi Arabia as a military advisor was punctuated by American bombings of Arab countries, notably the Sudan and Iraq. The Arabs of Riyadh, the capital of Saudi Arabia, were uneasy toward these scattered, easily recognizable Americans in their midst. One could palpate the tension in the air, but as of yet no public rallies or other overt anti-American activities had begun.

After my brief risk assessment, I decided that a trip for falafels warranted the risk. So, off I went downtown to probably the very best falafel restaurant on the entire planet, based on previous intelligence from my Palestinian translator and my boss.

I stood before the counter, watching the Lebanese chef prepare my three falafels. Nervous glances and stares from Arabs in the restaurant toward me were ignored. No sense trying to look incognito as a pale, redheaded, white guy in an Arab world. It did not matter anymore, for appetite can be stronger than protocol or common sense.

Specially prepared garbanzo-bean balls are deep-fried in a large vat of cooking oil. Warm Arabian pita bread is laid out to the side, awaiting these piping hot morsels, each about the size of a tennis ball. Pickles, green tomatoes, parsley, and a special sauce are added and the whole is wrapped together into a roll about the size of your average submarine sandwich.

The taste of the falafel is heavenly.

Now, I'm a big McDonald's fan. A Mickey D's establishment was even a few buildings down from this fine falafel restaurant. But this day, the cheeseburgers would take a backseat to this vegetarian delight. In short order I stuffed myself with two falafels and kept the third for my refrigerator and later enjoyment. An ice-cold mixed-fruit drink capped my ecstasy, made from real fruit there in the restaurant.

Certainly, the falafel is a vegetarian sandwich worth bragging about. You must try one someday. It is a culinary pleasure of the desert any Arab can be proud of. We can disagree over many things, but never over how good a falafel tastes.

Riff-Raff

"A great man stands on God.
A small man stands on a great man."
Ralph Waldo Emerson

Everybody likes to get ahead. One would be hard-pressed to find someone who turns down more rank or pay. For most people, if you can take it to the bank, it must be good.

Problems come when you meet people determined to get ahead at any cost. These dear souls are known to take no prisoners. Masters at maneuver and assassination, they will expend every effort to move up the so-called ladder of success by any route possible. The Army has a fair number of these people, often found close to important people. They enjoy being in their offices far removed from work that really makes a difference.

The Chairman of the Joint Chiefs came to visit our unit in Saudi Arabia. Well over six feet tall, he was a big, impressive man especially to us short people. The four black stars on each collar of his sharply pressed desert battle dress uniform complemented his size. We'd heard of him. Seen him on CNN. Now the great man was coming to see us.

As the General toured our area, I found it interesting how many followers, or straphangers, came with him. Some were his bodyguards, but most were senior officers and NCOs who normally didn't make time to see what troops did down in the trenches. They lived in their offices. All these desk leaders vied for the General's attention like pilgrims wanting to touch the garment of Jesus in order to be blessed.

The General would have none of their politicizing, their kissing up, or their brown nosing. Although he was patient with their pomp and maneuvering, it did not impress him. Nor did he allow this to distract him from seeing soldiers down where the work really gets done. You could sense that soldiers meant more to him than the political riff-raff or staff weenies.

The Army rewards patience and hard work. Sad to say the Army also rewards patience and little work. Promotions fall on soldiers that work hard and those who maneuver, make mountains out of molehills, and send too much e-mail. Accept this fact of Army life and you'll save yourself some antacid expense.

I'm convinced that the greater blessing comes to those who know they earned their rewards through hard, real work and not through the false and blasphemous worship of great men. My guess is that real soldiers sleep well. One wonders how the riff-raff can sleep at all.

Meetings

"Swift decisions are not sure."
Sophocles

A fascinating aspect of Arab culture is the distinct tendency of individual leaders to minimize personal risk in making decisions. Whereas successful Western leaders display a natural tendency to take chances, often at great personal or professional risk, successful Arab leaders will generally defer tough, politically sensitive issues for resolution or endorsement from a committee or group. This is particularly true when a leader hates to say no.

For American advisors to an Arabian Army, it takes some time to get accustomed to their unique decision making process. One may never fully understand it, but clearly the committee process is an interesting and informative lesson in how to deal with life's decisions, a process which had its origins within ancient tribal custom. Westerners raised in a freer, more individualistic society have difficulty understanding this time-tested Arabian custom.

The meeting ordeal begins with just getting all the key members together. This can be no small undertaking. It might take weeks, even with "urgent" issues. Eventually, the key players are brought together and the meeting is convened. After introductions, other pleasantries and tea, an agenda is established and a schedule is laid out.

A critical milestone is the pattern of this first meeting. If the issue at hand is indeed important, then all preliminary work towards a decision will have happened behind the scenes already. These include one on one contacts, phone calls, deals made, IOUs cashed in, issues and exceptions resolved. When the group comes together, the decision has already been made and the meeting is a mere formality that issues a recommendation endorsed by all. The leader will then proceed, knowing a consensus is struck. Responsibility for the decision will be shared.

On the other hand, if the intent of the leader is to have an issue die in committee, then the meeting will be entirely different. Particularly when leaders just cannot say no, they will employ the delay caused by unprepared committee meetings. This is their polite way of saying no. Many things die in a committee. An advisor who learns this early will do well.

American advisors to foreign armies need to be a group of the willing, picked from among the best to do the necessary. Those who are indeed best at what they do will have patience with the slower decision making process. But rest assured, slower decisions are often surer.

GPS

"A small rock holds back a great wave."
Homer

One of those devices we wondered how we ever managed to live without is the global positioning system, or GPS. One of the spin-off benefits of space exploration, GPS consists of a small, normally handheld, battery-operated device, which provides the user with an accurate reading of his exact location on earth. Through the use of satellite feedback, the receiver displays a numbered grid coordinate that corresponds to map locations, the accuracy of which is within ten meters or so.

My first real exposure to GPS was in Saudi Arabia. As a medical officer, I normally was not involved in much driving or navigating. In an advisor position, however, I had to learn to maneuver and survive in the desert wastes of the Middle East. A man I will always associate with my GPS knowledge was a former tank brigade commander. Compared to my stature, the Colonel was a massive man. When I stood next to him, it was like a jeep parked next to an Abrams tank. His chiseled features and bearing commanded respect, yet his eyes betrayed a genuine desire to take care of people. I have no doubt that man was the kind of commander who, in another time or place, would have broken through to save Custer's scalp at the Little Big Horn, beaten the Nazis at Kasserine Pass, or given Task Force Smith some needed "Hooaah!"

Joining the Colonel's group of tanker officers that night were a couple of us medical officers. Our nightlong exercise involved desert survival skills including learning how to use the GPS. After some opening remarks and basic instructions, the Colonel turned us loose. In addition to getting stuck in the sand and straining some muscles a couple of times, we tackled the task of maneuvering our trucks at night with headlights off. We were looking for special markers by using the GPS and our night-vision goggles.

Jeff Sloan and I must have been a sight as we navigated in our GMC 4WD truck over the dunes at a sometimes-thrilling speed. The pitch-black world outside was easy for us to see, thanks to the somewhat awkward binocular night-vision goggles (NVGs) on our faces. By the end of the course we were so good at both that we could find anything at night.

The Army will always need commanders like that Colonel. In the thick of battle, their stature and calm demeanor will steady the troops. Their 'can-do' aura is part of that command charisma. In the confusion of war when the world seems to be collapsing, I for one will be using my GPS to find commanders like the desert Colonel. In the storm of battle, it is best to anchor yourself to a rock.

Heather

"All the beauty of the world, tis but skin deep."
Ralph Venning

My thirty-day furlough from Saudi Arabia had just begun. Midway through the one-year tour in a land of totally covered women, I boarded planes that took me back to the Western world. That journey home presented to me one the starkest cultural contrasts of my life.

It was an uneventful flight. The Saudi government purchased our plane tickets, always in first or business class. For my final leg to Austin, Texas, I sat in a roomy business-class seat.

She boarded the plane after me, and immediately had the rapt attention of every male in the cabin. Probably in her early twenties, Heather was almost a carbon copy of Cindy Crawford, only somewhat more voluptuous. Her long, immaculately kept hair hung shoulder-length onto a tight blouse and short-shorts. The blouse was low cut in the front too. To this day, I cannot remember the color of her clothing, so distracted was I by her advertised anatomy. The empty seat next to mine was hers. I nervously shifted in my seat and said "Hello," as she stowed her bag and sat down. A waft of her unique perfume further blurred my senses.

The flight attendants completed their pre-flight briefings, and soon we were in the air. In time, Heather and I struck up a conversation. There were the usual questions about traveling, occupations, and final destinations. She immediately took a keen interest in what I did for a living, so different than her work in the entertainment industry.

Over peanuts and soda, I explained to her my work. To balance things out, I then quizzed her about her occupation. She was a model and had just finished posing as one of the upcoming-featured beauties in a national men's magazine. My traveling companion was a centerfold.

Heather had made good money from the centerfold photo session. Big money. She asked me for advice on how to use it. Never had I imagined giving financial advice to a nude model. Nervously, I haltingly said, "Invest and diversify your wealth," I went on to add, "for your beauty will fade and those $50,000 photo sessions will not last forever."

The flight eventually ended and good byes were said. As Heather deplaned, she created the usual distractions a provocatively dressed, beautiful woman does when she walks around. Another beautiful woman was waiting for me at the gate, my Irene, whom I hadn't seen for months. Somehow, I preferred to be married to a beautiful schoolteacher than a model that all would see. My investment in Irene's beauty will never fade.

Throwing Grenades

"An advisor is someone who speaks up if something is flawed—
who thinks out of the box—who throws a grenade if its necessary."
David Kay

For most people, throwing grenades is difficult to do, if not impossible. For a year I worked with the Saudi Arabian National Guard, a full-time, one hundred thousand-man defense force for the Kingdom of Saudi Arabia. I served with about one hundred or so other U.S. officers and senior NCOs posted as advisors there. It was in Arabia that I learned an important lesson on throwing grenades.

It was great duty. You worked with the best U.S. officers, stayed in nice billets, received your own GMC Yukon to drive, and could have just about anything you could justify needing to get the job done.

The downside of this duty was the significant downshifting of gears when it came to working with the Saudi Arabian military. As advisors, we found the greatest adjustment to be the slow pace, bureaucratic layers, and lack of command authority we were accustomed to in the American army. Brought up on the tempo of U.S. combat unit operations, we had to relearn our methods to succeed with our allies of the desert.

A successful tour with Saudi military is measured differently than an equivalent amount of time with a U.S. or European unit. For me, one success was working with the Saudi executive officer of the unit to which I was attached.

Western trained and fluent in English, the XO was the son of Bedouin nomads who, in the space of two generations, left their nomadic existence and became a part of the rising status of modern Saudi Arabia. To me this outstanding officer stood out from other officers, American or Saudi, in that he had a streak of aggressiveness.

The XO also talked straight, unlike a few officers I have known. There was no evidence of a forked tongue in him. You quickly knew his true opinions about something. He spoke up if something was flawed. He thought out of the box. He knew how to throw a grenade even with the best of plans, if he could sense some poorly appreciated, yet fatal flaw.

An advisor is supposed to teach, to guide, and to assist. We worked hard to do this. But the Saudi soldiers taught me a thing or two as well. Our western arrogance blinds us to the value of understanding peoples different from ourselves. Like the Romans of old, we should learn from all with whom we come into contact.

From that Arabian executive officer, I learned how to throw grenades and live to tell the tale.

Snake Lessons

"...that old serpent, called the Devil, and Satan,
which deceiveth the whole world..."
Revelation 12:9

Snakes are among the most fascinating and feared creatures on the face of the earth. It seems that every warm or hot area to which you travel has the fair prospect of having some serpents. The Middle East region is no exception, offering some of the most poisonous varieties to be found.

Near the King Fahad National Guard Army hospital in Riyadh, Saudi Arabia is one of the most important snake antivenin producing laboratories in the world. Established with the assistance of U.S. Army advisors, here you will find living examples of many venomous creatures including the cobra, the mamba, and the pit viper.

The laboratory snakes live a very pampered existence. They receive regular meals of white mice and live in a warm, safe, quiet and secluded environment. It is a comfortable life far removed from the wild habitats of where they once lived, before that night visit by a snake-hunting team.

These crawling devils are kept at the lab for only one reason—their venom. In return for all the care and attention they receive from a few dedicated and, I might add, brave workers, each snake must undergo a weekly handling session. During these exercises each snake is milked of its venom. The expensive antivenin produced is in high demand in the Middle East, where man and serpent frequently come into deadly contact.

One of the more interesting snakes at the lab is the horned viper. This creature could very well have been the inspiration for the visual images some have of the Devil. The viper's visage is one of evil incarnate. The sinister eyes are matched with two small horns on its head. Its methods are rather Satanic as well. It cleverly bores itself into the desert sands, leaving only a portion of its head exposed. The head looks like a half-buried pebble with an evil looking face. Victims are invariably ambushed unawares.

There are things that ambush us. Maybe it is the betrayal of a false friend, an unanticipated loss, or a drunk driver. Like a half-buried snake we step on them unwittingly and suffer the consequences. If we could only see these traps ahead of time! At times we may even be the serpent in the sand. It may be an uncontrolled temper, drug use, a poorly secured weapon, the reckless use of our body, or the neglect of some responsibility.

There are many dangers in life. They are as real as poisonous snakes. Frequently these dangers do far greater damage when they "bite" us. We do well to beware of these life-altering perils, these deceiving devils in disguise.

Coffee

"I have measured out my life with coffee spoons."
T.S. Eliot

There is nothing quite like the smell of freshly brewed coffee first thing in the morning. You wake up and there it is, a coffee aroma like incense, permeating the entire home or building. The smell will always remind me of the Army, and more specifically, the Arab Army.

A soldier's love of coffee is phenomenal. A common sight is a coffee mug on every desk, a brewing machine in every office, instant coffee packets in every MRE pouch. Coffee drinking can be a near-religious experience for soldiers and they expend every effort to get that daily dose. Others have perfected a near fanatical love for certain brands of coffee. Regardless of where they are located, significant effort is taken to find, ship in, or otherwise obtain that particularly desired brand.

Find ten soldiers and nine out of ten will immediately know what particular brand of coffee they enjoy: *Kona* coffee from Hawaii, *Folgers*, *Taster's Choice* or *Jacob's* coffee from Germany. Then there are the cappuccino varieties too. It seems like there are almost as many choices as there are soldiers.

Some soldiers, like me, never took a liking to drinking coffee. We've grown accustomed to the smell and some of us can appreciate the unique aroma. I suspect that there are many more of us out there, but they have learned to cream and sugar the black brew so that it is more palatable. Even with cream and sugar, I still prefer to just smell the stuff.

A posting to an Arab Army as an advisor cured me of my inability to drink coffee. The Arabs brew their coffee with unroasted coffee beans. The resulting coffee is light brown or even greenish in color. It packs a powerful caffeine punch and is therefore served in smaller quantities, not like the huge mugs found in Europe and North America. The circumstances of custom and the importance of not giving offense, force even a non-coffee drinker to accept the common Arab gesture of coffee. You drink it down and smile. A servant stands nearby, ready to top off the small cup again. A second cup brings a grin of approval from your host.

My preference is to still enjoy coffee from a distance. The smell is enough for me. Were I to be asked which coffee brand I would vote for, the answer would be strange to most soldiers who prefer their Starbucks or Nescafe. My reluctant vote would be for the light brown Arabian brew. For a year of my life was measured by those small cups of coffee in the interests of diplomacy, one difficult gulp at a time.

303

Eyes

"And say to the believing women…that they should not display their beauty
and ornaments…"
Koran (Surah 24:31)

The women of Saudi Arabia are unique among all the women of the
world. Theirs is a life shrouded in secrecy, a world within a world protected
by the dictates of religion, custom, family, and clothing. To the western eye,
nothing more dramatically illustrates this uniqueness than the black *abayah*,
or over garment.

Arriving in Saudi Arabia for the first time, a foreign traveler
immediately notices the fact that every woman is covered in black from head
to foot. As soon as the airplane lands, women on board begin the procedure
of draping themselves in these black garments, hiding their alluring beauty.
Some even wear black gloves to further hide their delicate hands. For most
Arabian women all that remains visible are their eyes, peeping through a slit
in the facial covering.

Coming from a comparatively liberal western country, one at first
wonders how these women cope. The abayah must be very hot in the heat of
the day, easily soiled, and surely it must constantly snag on furniture and
bushes. But wear it they must and wear it they do. Over time you sense that
these women, though covered, are also just as intensely interested in fashion
and beauty. The occasional breeze or sudden movement causes a momentary
gap in their abayah, exposing the glimmer of jewelry or the latest colorful,
western fashions beneath.

I never personally met any Saudi women in my year as a guest of their
country, though I saw thousands from an appropriate distance. No, my world
there was filled with Saudi soldiers who have an intense, jealous love and
respect for their ladies. Though forbidden by law and custom from making
contact with them, I nevertheless grew to appreciate their hidden beauty.

Returning to the United States, I found I had a deeper appreciation for
western women and their varied dress on display for all to see and enjoy.
Their God-given beauty and style are often taken for granted or exploited,
but no longer for me. There are worlds where men are denied the feast to be
had in seeing a woman's charms.

Often I am asked what I thought about the women of Saudi Arabia. At
first I didn't know what to say, but then I remembered an excellent quote
from a Saudi Commander I worked with. His answer was *ayuom gemila*.
They have beautiful eyes.

Ignorance is Bliss

"It is well to learn even from an enemy."
Ovid

We'd been driving all day long, just north of the city of Medina, Saudi Arabia. The mountainous desert terrain held a unique beauty and lots of dust. In fact, the dust was so great that my truck's fuel pump failed.

It was fortunate for me that another vehicle driven by fellow soldiers was along. With tow straps as a basic load for each truck, we were able to tow my ill truck some seventy miles into the city of Medina. There we looked for a repair station. Technically, non-Muslims were not allowed in Medina, but we had an emergency and managed to always stay on the outskirts of this important city. Our proverbial ox had fallen into a ditch of sorts.

We eventually found a GMC truck repair center and were especially happy to learn they had the necessary fuel pump part. For the next six hours or so, two very friendly African chaps set to work removing the gas tank and replacing the gummed-up fuel pump. They spoke no English, but between gestures, smiles, and our broken Arabic, we were able to communicate. It was tough and dirty work, removing the entire fuel tank and handling the gasoline. The energy and skill of these men, along with their remarkable friendliness towards us, left a deep impression upon me.

Eventually, the job was done and my truck cranked right up, running even better than before. We said our goodbyes to the always-smiling mechanics. We gave them each a liberal tip, for which they expressed great nonverbal appreciation in the form of wider smiles and deeper bows.

As we were about to leave, the Arabian shop manager, who spoke very good English, pulled us aside and said, "You know, my friends, those mechanics working on your truck are Sudanese." His point shocked us for a moment, because it reminded us that it was only a week prior when the United States had bombed the capital city of the Sudan in retaliation for the U.S. Embassy bombings in Kenya and Tanzania in 1998. We reflected on the irony of it all. We blew up their city and they fixed our truck.

I'm not sure if our mechanics knew we were American. It is hard to hide being an American in the Middle East, but perhaps they figured we were some well to do European business people. Whatever they thought, they did a great repair job on our truck without booby-trapping it. Our ignorance on how to repair things caused them some financial gain. As things turned out, our further ignorance of their nationality allowed them to do it. For both parties involved ignorance was bliss.

305

Cavities

"There is no sin but stupidity."
Oscar Wilde

I am not normally a tea drinker. Don't get me wrong, nothing beats a glass of my aunt's ice cold tea, specially prepared and readied in that fine manner of the deep American South. We do not drink tea at home, out of habit mainly, but partially to avoid a caffeine addiction. At any rate, an advisor assignment to an Arab army required a certain amount of tea drinking on my part for the sake of good international relations.

With the modernization of the Arab world in the second half of the 20th century, their long-standing tradition of hospitality underwent some refinement, including that key token of hospitality, liquid refreshment. Generally Moslem in belief, you will find no alcohol as an icebreaker for get-togethers involving Arabs. Instead, they have cultivated both the art of preparing and serving less stimulating drink, such as coffee or tea. They also have a love for that ubiquitous potion of American economic imperialism, the soft drink.

As an advisor, I was required to visit daily with several Arab officers. Each visit would begin with exchanged pleasantries and a dose of Arabian coffee, served in small cups. The light brown, bitter coffee one learned to tolerate. Following the coffee, my hosts would serve a sweet, hot Arabian tea in small, four-ounce glasses.

Now for me, the tea was good and I grew rather fond of it. As things turned out, I would be too fond of it. In fact, a normal day with four or five visits to different officers would see six or seven tea servings stimulating my palate. Under the auspices of enjoying the hospitality of my hosts, I actually looked forward to the coffee going away and the tea arriving.

Little did I know that there would be a price to be paid. After a year in the Arab world it was time to go home to a warm homecoming, women without black over garments, four wonderful children, and a dentist's chair. Yes, I was blessed with seven cavities! While I enjoyed the free, sweet tea, it had made itself at home with my teeth. In the end, the delicious tea was not free after all.

Lying in the dental chair for over four or five visits, staring up into that bright examination light above I had time to reflect on my folly. Deeper reflection and regret were assisted by the dentist's drill vibrating my head and the side of my face feeling like it was missing. It may not be a sin to drink sweet tea, but it is foolhardy, or at least painful, to forget to brush your teeth afterwards.

Secretaries

"I am the people – the mob – the crowd – the mass.
Do you not know that all the great work of the world is done through me?"
Carl Sandburg

Secretaries make the world go around. That is a fact. The important shadow of every big shot is their secretary. Without a shadow you might as well not exist. When the big person isn't there or available, it's the secretary that stands in, captures the important information and keeps things moving.

The first secretary the Army gave me was a wonderful person, a naturalized Armenian immigrant to the United States. She was the epitome of a talented and resourceful secretary. She was enthusiastic about her work and was easy to keep happy.

My secretaries all taught me important lessons. One very important lesson involved bureaucracy. Bureaucracy is notorious by reputation, layers and layers of "I'm going to make life hard for you" built in. If you want to oil the wheels of progress through the red tape, then take good care of the secretaries. Simply put, they can make things happen or stall them. Their networks and connections can help or hurt depending on what they think about you. Always remember that they are the true bureaucracy slayers.

Recognize the de facto power you give secretaries too, whether you like it or not. Also realize the trouble you can cause when you mistreat the secretaries of other people. There are powerful people and then there are the secretaries. Maybe your important message will get misplaced. Perhaps the secretary will put your information on the bottom of the "to read" pile.

I once had a senior sergeant who was a PA student wearing OCS rank. He didn't have time for an on the spot suggestion offered by a secretary. Two things happened: First, what the student needed from her was DOA. It was going nowhere. Second, his abrupt manner so ruffled her that she mentioned it to her boss, who happened to be the main man. It was not long before the student was back-pedaling to her office, seeking forgiveness.

Secretaries know how to call for fire. They have redundant communications too. They may seem harmless enough, but when you see one, remember they are potentially as dangerous as a solitary forward artillery observer with a good radio. Oh, how they can make or break your day with things that come out of nowhere to help or hurt you!

You want secretaries on your side. You need to remember their day every day, not just one day each year. If you ever wonder how things get done, it is a good bet that secretaries are the ones who really make things happen.

Integrity

"Chains of gold are stronger than chains of iron."
Thomas Fuller

Integrity is a very precious thing. It cannot be acquired with money or talent. It is an item we all start with but many lose. The loss is terrible and is felt even more acutely the higher up the chain of command it occurs.

When the President of the United States of America, William Jefferson Clinton, was caught lying about his relationship with Monica Lewinsky in 1998, his lack of integrity as Commander-in-Chief had a profound impact on the troops, particularly the officer corps. Already viewed by many soldiers with a jaundiced eye because of his lack of military experience, the lying by our Commander-in-Chief caused an even deeper drop in his esteem among the troops. Military leaders sworn to uphold good order and discipline within the ranks found themselves in an uncomfortable position of punishing soldiers for lying or adultery when the big guy seemed to be getting away.

At the helm of state when the dynamo of the American economy forged ahead to wonderful, new heights of prosperity, President Clinton's leadership and excellent choice of advisors contributed towards significant deficit reduction, paring down of welfare, and restoring the Social Security System to solvency. Internationally, his magic touch helped bring peace to Haiti, Yugoslavia and the Middle East, when his conservative opponents dogged every initiative, every attempt to make the world a better place for all. But despite all these remarkable achievements, he will forever remain soiled in the eyes of history and his countrymen over a breech of integrity.

All this was a pretty strong chain of accomplishments for one man with only one steamy, weak link. Those moments of passion were pounced upon by an evidence-starved independent counsel, desperate to find tangible results from the apparently fruitless and misdirected millions of taxpayer dollars spent in vain looking into a land-deal in Arkansas. The $40 million that Kenneth Starr consumed essentially produced a stained dress and a media soap opera at the expense of national honor.

The events of 1998 left a significantly weakened presidency and further erosion of American confidence in their elected officials. The wonder of the entire spectacle was the strength of our system, especially the military. The military chain of command was stronger than the sexual indiscretions of one very powerful member. The test, certainly of a very different sort, showed that the chain was stronger than its weakest link.

Duty, Honor, Country

"I am an American soldier—a protector of the greatest nation on earth—
sworn to uphold the Constitution of the United States."
Soldier's Code

I arrived for my one-year tour of duty as a military advisor in Saudi Arabia in January 1998, just a few days before the Monica Lewinsky matter first hit the news. As a military ambassador for the United States in the most sexually conservative nation in the world, it was an interesting year.

While the private life of our nation's commander in chief was flayed open for all to see, soldiers, sailors, airmen and marines continued to faithfully discharge their duties around the world. These people were not there out of loyalty to the President, the Congress, or the Supreme Court. No, they swore to support and defend the Constitution of the United States.

Service personnel are supposed to be apolitical, and for good reason. It keeps the peace within the ranks and helps prevent the military from ousting our elected representatives by force.

When turmoil strikes our government at home, I am reminded of the Continental Army's experience over two hundred years ago. Repeatedly neglected by the Congress and the colonies, this ragtag group of volunteers hung in there. Instead of marching on Philadelphia, they chose to defend an idea. That idea was not embodied in any branch of government. No, the idea they fought for and won, but just barely, became what is now our Constitution.

The U.S. military, scattered at thousands of outposts around the world, will continue the faithful duty of defending our idea. Those ideals are life, liberty, and the pursuit of happiness. These are freedoms that, yes, even the President is entitled to and something the world admires us for.

Meanwhile, scandals at home will always tarnish our image abroad. Those of us out in the world on picket duty get the red face. As part of the embarrassment, we are afforded a world-view of our country.

The United States government is made up of imperfect people who periodically provide good copy for the tabloid magazines. The turbulence caused in our leadership sometimes makes the world wonder if our democracy will self-destruct. I don't think so. The Constitution will survive and the U.S. military is sworn to see to that.

But scandals make good copy for our fourth branch of government, the press. And the drama of an investigation is apparently part of the fun. Meanwhile, nations abroad will stare in shock and U.S. soldiers, sailors, airmen, and marines will make do wherever they are.

Ambition

"Public life is regarded as the crown of a career,
and to young men it is the worthiest ambition.
Politics is still the greatest and most honorable adventure."
John Buchan

I was quite surprised when as a young man of seventeen, my high school classmates voted me, along with a redheaded girl in our class, as the two people 'most likely to succeed.' It was a hopeful year for redheads. And though life has taken me through some deep valleys, I have often been sustained by that high school vote of confidence.

Arriving at work the day the United States House of Representatives impeached President Clinton in 1998, I found a curious gift on my desk. It now hangs in my office, a constant reminder to me that someone out there shares the vote of my high school class. The framed gift was my very first campaign donation, totally unsolicited, but given nonetheless by two very special people in my life, Marieta and Onnick Boodaghians.

The Boodaghians have a very unique appreciation of the American dream. They are Armenian-Americans. They rose to success and prosperity out of poverty and prejudice, immigrating to the land that is still opportunity.

Sharing a dinner together one evening, we enjoyed the casual chitchat back and forth on many topics. Eventually the topic of politics came up. For these naturalized U.S. citizens, what goes on in Washington was very important. Their interest and ideas impressed me deeply. Would that more Americans realized the treasure democracy brings us all!

I shared with the Boodaghians my desire to continue in some sort of public service after the Army. There are great things to do entering into a new century and it would be important to be more than a bystander. A government by the people and for the people always benefits from fresh ideas. The ideas and abilities of former military people are an essential resource, well suited in the halls of our elected officials.

We need a good dose of idealism every now and again. There are still frontiers out there to push back: ignorance, crime, greed, and laziness. There is always much work to be done.

The dream of all Americans through the years is for something better. Immigrants like the Boodagians hold onto the dream sometimes more intensely than some of us who are native-born. In the great class of nations around the world and throughout recent history, these newcomers to our special land know that the United States is still most likely to succeed at making those dreams come true.

Bonnie and Clyde

"If you pick up a starving dog and make him prosperous, he will not bite
you. This is the principal difference between a man and his dog."
Mark Twain

The long year away from the family was coming to a close, and with
it came the need to fulfill a promise made to my daughter. At last it was
time to get some family dogs. Our family had wanted dogs for years, but
frequent moves overseas and busy lifestyles prevented it. But with the
winding down of a military career came the opportunity to finally get those
long-desired four-legged friends.

The entire family studied the issue of dogs for quite some time. There
were advantages and disadvantages with each breed. In the end, we settled
upon two Great American Pound dogs, one female and one male. We named
them Bonnie and Clyde.

The dogs were an instant hit with everyone. Their child-friendly
dispositions were well suited to the roughhouse play of the current children
and the grandchildren to come. They were a bit mischievous, just like their
namesakes. The dispositions of each dog complimented the other. Bonnie
was docile and quiet. Clyde was an alpha personality, salted with an
attention deficit disorder. I was struck with how Bonnie and Clyde reflected
attributes not unlike my wife and I. Even their fur matched our hair color.
Bonnie and Irene with their dark hair, and Clyde and I with a reddish color,
though Clyde certainly had more hair than me.

It was also a good time for dogs in our life, for our children were
beginning to leave home. The dogs could fill the gap, and in return, the dogs
could live out a quite comfortable life, far different from those poor canines
never chosen from the pound.

Very few people with important pedigrees join the Army. Most
soldiers who enter the Army see it as a much better opportunity than the
often pound-like experience of "back home." Little adventure there at home,
all caged up and living from hand to mouth. Clearly, the military offers
opportunities which rescue many people from being put into the permanent
sleep of a meaningless life.

Bonnie and Clyde live a prosperous existence. They also don't bite. I
have drawn some analogies from my dogs and the Army. The Army took
good care of me, and continues to take care of many other "Bonnie and
Clydes" out there. Overall I cannot say anything negative about my Army
experience. No need to bite the system for it was a darn good deal. That is
the principal similarity between my dogs and me.

Typing Fossil

"You can't teach an old dog new tricks."
Old Saying

Dominating the top of my office desk is a large computer monitor. Along with a keyboard and my "Darth Vader" mouse, this machine is a tool I wonder how I ever did without. This technological marvel cranks out memorandums, spreadsheets, briefing slides and gives me access to the information superhighway, all in a fraction of the time it used to take.

U.S. Army units began to enter the desktop computer world in the mid- to late 1980s. Before then, clerical work went at a snail's pace. Take, for instance, your basic memorandum, called a disposition form or "DF" in the Army back then. Before the advent of those first Zenith computers, the preparation of a DF could consume a fair chunk of time. Everybody needed triplicate copies, white out, and an IBM typewriter just to get started. After three or four attempts you finally had a passable copy the pencil neck geeks would accept.

Now we can crank out any form or letter lickety split through the clever use of saved files and laser printers. Change the name, date and a few details and, voila! You are done.

Back in high school and college, I bypassed the typing course. Too sissy for me back then. I mean, I didn't want to be a secretary, okay? But times have changed and now everybody needs to type. Most of us, thanks to this sweet PC on our desks, are now pretty much our own secretary.

So, here I sit with my own way of typing, pecking out a top speed of thirty words a minute. People who pass by my desk stop and giggle. It is fun to watch this freckle-faced fossil fiddle with a few fingers. Let them laugh, this old dog can type his own way, thank you very much.

My older sons have put me to shame over typing. Boy, can they type! Put them at a keyboard and they can tap out seventy words plus per minute and with no mistakes. These promising young men aren't even thinking about being secretaries either. With some luck and hard work, we'll have an airline pilot and a doctor in the family.

Dad will always plod along at his model-T typing speed. Whether at home or work, he'll stubbornly adhere to his old ways, preferring to do his own work at an ancient pace, never maximizing the potential of that incredibly powerful machine. The two-index finger-typing mode will undergo no upgrades. The version will remain the same.

Dad is definitely not the sharpest tool in the shed, at home, or at work. But he is still a tool nonetheless, albeit a two-finger one.

Fresh Eggs

"I like liquor—its taste and its effects—
and that is just the reason why I never drink it."
Thomas (Stonewall) Jackson

When man grew grain, made yeast and then prepared the two in certain ways, he discovered alcohol. Ever since that discovery, every culture has confronted the alcohol issue. Some societies cannot control it, some think they can control it, and others forbid its use outright.

The U.S. attempted to prohibit the manufacture, sale and consumption of alcohol early in the 20th century. But Prohibition had only limited success in reducing America's seemingly unquenchable desire for drink. The effort was, however, counterproductive in that it spawned an underworld of crime aimed at providing spirits to those that would always desire it—and were willing to pay dearly for it. So, in time, persistent demand caused the prohibition effort to fail.

American troops have always been fond of alcohol. Commanders always hope the fondness remains limited. When troops deploy abroad, sometimes they are forbidden drink because of the country they are in. For some troops this prohibition has a significant impact on morale.

Our Army advisory group was posted to such a country where alcohol was forbidden. Due to our diplomatic status, however, a limited amount of alcohol was brought in for morale purposes. The embassy's diplomatic immunity allowed a certain leeway with the local authorities. Camouflaged as "fresh eggs, please rush," the weekly shipment would arrive by air with other foodstuffs and supplies.

Jack Daniel's whiskey is famous in foreign circles. This Tennessee firewater is right up there with the finest French wines or German beers in foreign demand. For some reason, therefore, a fair supply of this powerful southern fluid would also find its way into our weekly airfreight.

An embarrassing moment for the U.S. embassy came one week as a shipment arrived. The air terminal workers, all local nationals, confronted a problem with the American food shipment. An urgent call came to the U.S. embassy. "Please hurry to the air cargo terminal," they said, "your eggs are leaking." It seemed the "eggs" from Tennessee were roughed up a bit during the flight and some had broken. Such a problem had to be handled with haste and diplomacy. So, the embassy dispatched a veteran mediator to handle the crisis, one that was particularly expert with ethanol issues. All ended well without further incident and I have on good authority that a few gift "eggs" alleviated the worries of those airport workers.

313

Fail-Safe Driver

"Times change and men deteriorate."
Unknown

I was once a safe, law-abiding driver. Conscientious and courteous, my driving would have made any drivers' education instructor from high school proud. By adulthood you would figure my habits would be so ingrained, that it would be difficult to change. But that was before tours of duty overseas.

Whether it was Paris or Cairo, Bangkok or Amman, Jerusalem or Rome, each place offered ever-increasing challenges to my abilities to survive in traffic. Add animals and bicycles to a mixture of near maniac drivers of trucks and cars in an urban environment and you have the ultimate driving experience. You grow tense behind the wheel. Adrenaline kicks in and you transform into one of the locals in order to survive.

To this day I marvel at how I was able to drive tens of thousands of miles in foreign countries without serious accident or injury. I've assembled a few unwritten rules that helped me to survive over there. These are apocryphal lessons. They are not in your standard American driver's education manual.

AVOID DOING THIS AT HOME
Lesson #1: When over there, drive as they do.
Lesson #2: Whoever is in front has the right of way.
Lesson #3: Speed can be good if your brakes work.
Lesson #4: Bigger cars get bigger results.
Lesson #5: Stop means yield; yield means go.
Lesson #6: Camels always have the right of way.
Lesson #7: You can be right and be dead, too.
Lesson #8: If your car fits there, then it is probably another lane.
Lesson #9: The least-educated people drive the biggest trucks.
Lesson #10: Seatbelts are good, even if locals refuse to wear them.
Lesson #11: Always remember that they have brakes, too.
Lesson #12: If they can't see you, then you are not there.

It is an adjustment to drive by the rules again when returning home to the United States after an overseas trip. But I caught on quickly, seeing how everyone else pretty much drives by the rules. I must confess, however, that my safe driving skills, though still present, are a bit corrupted. When I behold some character on American highways exhibiting less than acceptable driving behavior, I deteriorate once again.

Old Timers

"The only real officers are those with enough time in service
to retire as a captain."
Anonymous Army Sergeant Major

Every year in a hotel on the outskirts of Fayetteville, North Carolina hundreds of current and retired Army physician assistants get together. The Society of Army Physician Assistants (SAPA) sponsors this annual reunion and at the same time offers one of the most inexpensive medical continuing education conferences in the country. The PAs get a chance to see old friends, make new ones, pick up some new medical training, and get free pens from drug company representatives who are always present at medical conventions.

Most U.S. Army PAs are "home grown." By this I mean they rise up through the ranks by taking advantage of the Army's scholarship program for enlisted soldiers to train in the growing PA career field. Most of them started their careers as a private, gradually working their way up through the system. Very few Army PAs are direct accessions, that is, brought directly into the Army from the civilian sector.

Getting together with Army PAs is not your typical college reunion. These officers are mostly a self-made lot, no scions of the wealthy class among them. Each has a different background: former Special Forces people, airborne rangers, regular medics and even some grunts. They are people who the system has been good to. They have been all they could be.

There is always a bar at these conferences and a goodly number of these PAs congregate there. Though I do not drink, I'll sit there at the bar with my Seven-Up, visiting with old buddies and reminiscing on old times.

Mike Priest is usually there, one of the very first Army PAs I worked for as a medic. Bill Paterson often shows up—he saved my bacon as a young PA a few times. There were many others who influenced my years in the Army. Some of them included Jim McEvers, Charlie Solsbee, Polly Gross, Buddy Parrish, George Fisher, Lou Smith and Sherry Morrey. They are all good people. Real officers.

There are no officers with stars on their collars in this group. There probably never will be generals here either. For people who begin their Army careers as privates, Father Time and the Army Medical Department will pretty much keep PAs in the humbler officer ranks. But that doesn't matter. Despite the fact no generals number among them, there are those in the batch who wear stars in my book.

The Hundred Year's War

"And if there was ever a just war since the world began,
it is this in which America is now engaged."
Thomas Paine

It is a war of sorts, begun back at the turn of the twentieth century. While the century just gone by was punctuated by bloody international confrontations, there have been other smoldering struggles of a much less dreadful nature. This particular war is an on-going type of civil war. Already in progress for a hundred years, it is characterized by periodic skirmishes without strategic defeats and unconditional surrenders. Though there are casualties, prisoners are not taken. The Geneva Convention does not apply.

The United States Army expends a significant amount of time, personnel, material resources and funds on this war every year, all fully condoned by the United States Congress. Some of the Army's best soldiers and the latest equipment go into the battles of this war each year. The most brilliant Army minds plan the strategy and tactics, and the fruits of their labors often bring short-lived victories, but sadly never decisive peace.

Every general in the Army knows of this war and is committed to fighting it without any reservations. Though most are not directly involved with the troops in the conflict, they are certainly with them in spirit. With the arrival of television and battlefield reporting, everyone in the Army can stay abreast of each battle, the skirmishes, the victories, and the set backs.

This is a small, American-style Peloponesian War. One side dominates the land, the other the sea. The combatants speak the same language, worship similar gods, and follow familiar customs. But their multi-generational rivalry overcomes everything they may hold in common and brings them to a field of battle year after year.

Each hasty engagement's outcome has effects that are felt from the loneliest Army outpost in Alaska to the hottest Navy carrier deck in the Arabian Sea. Through the years, the balance of power has shifted back and forth between these brothers of a common land, engaged in a clash of bodies and spirits. It is a conflict without death, but by no means bloodless.

If there ever were a just war, then this is truly one, particularly when the United States Army is victorious. The war is, of course, the annual Army-Navy football game. By the year 2000, the final tally of the hundred year's war makes any soldier proud: United States Military Academy at West Point: 48 victories. United States Naval Academy at Annapolis: 45 victories. Seven tie-games round out the grand total. When your total war trophies outnumber those of your opponent, then one might say that the war is even more just. Hooaah!

Hail and Farewell

> "The cocktail party—a device for paying off obligations
> to people you don't want to invite to dinner."
> Charles Merrill Smith

Attending hail and farewells in the Army is the politically correct thing to do, especially if you are among the select few who are being either hailed or farewelled. But if given a choice of the two events, I would prefer to be farewelled.

For those who arrive into a new unit, being hailed can be, well, difficult. You don't know a soul and, in the case of my wife and I, we don't drink. So, as we arrive at whatever club where these affairs are held, we are just like fish out of water.

Now, even if some fish are out of water they still flop and jump around. Social butterflies. Drinks in hand they can drink like a fish and become a spectacle too. Not Irene and I. We sit off to the side somewhere, real quiet-like, sipping our Seven-ups. We love to mingle with folks we know, but otherwise, we are like deer staring into oncoming headlights when among strangers.

Sooner or later, and often later, the formal part of the get together begins. Eventually our names come up during the hailing phase and we're introduced to that crowd of strangers so that they can have a good look at us. We wave and nod politely, but inside we're somewhat embarrassed. We feel like fresh meat and we eagerly await the first kosher opportunity to exit.

Farewells on the other hand are splendid affairs for two reasons: First, we know most of the people there. We are fish in the water. We mingle. We reminisce and laugh about shared memories. We trade stories. Finally, we say public and private good-byes to people we've come to know and love. People we will remember forever. People we hope to see again.

The second reason farewells are cool is that we often go home with some memento or two, those keepsakes for the wall or shelf that really mean something. The token symbolized a part of our lives that we gave to the people and place we are departing. No doubt about it, farewells are better.

You meet some interesting people in a military career, and most people truly are wonderful. You come to accept and understand them as they do you. They are no longer strangers, but friends. They are people you'd invite to dinner despite their rank, accent, color, religion, gender or drinking status. You hate to say farewell to practically all of them. If the military life can teach each of us this kind of acceptance, then that is something I hope we never say farewell to.

Mothers

"The hand that rocks the cradle is the hand that rules the world."
William R. Wallace

"Army Evac two-three-eight-seven-zero, contact Houston Center one-three-four-point-two," the radio crackled. "Roger, one-three-four-point-two," the pilot responded. The chatter on the radio heard over my headset continued as we made our way through a cloudy sky toward Wilford Hall Medical Center in San Antonio, Texas. We were on another dustoff air evacuation mission, transferring a high-risk obstetric patient from Fort Hood, Texas, just north of Austin.

It was a Sunday morning in May. Mother's Day. While millions of Americans headed off to church, restaurants, or telephones to honor their mothers, we were transferring a soon to be mother. She lay quietly on the padded litter in front of me. Her young face betrayed a mixture of excitement and anxiety.

It was her first baby. It was also her first time as a patient in a hospital, the first intravenous line, and the first flight in a helicopter. It would also be her very first Mother's Day as a mother.

Over the noise of our Blackhawk helicopter, she forced a smile. I smiled back at her through the opening of my flight helmet and gently squeezed her arm that lay outside the blanket cocoon we had her bundled up in. She was going to be okay.

She moved her hand to her lower abdomen. Another contraction. Her son or daughter moved impatiently inside, wanting out. The problem was that it was ten weeks too soon. Her water had broken and soon that baby would indeed arrive anyway. That was why we were on our way to the medical center.

Our new mom had been through a great deal this Mother's Day. The staff of the Labor and Delivery Department of Darnall Army Hospital did a good job with her examination, medications, a Foley catheter, and various needle pokes and monitors. More was yet to come, but she was ready. She wanted this baby.

The one-hour flight went without a hitch and we arrived at the Air Force medical center. With what must have been a New Jersey accent, our patient thanked the flight medic and me for the flight as the nurses got her situated in the new room. We gathered our equipment to leave. Saying good-bye, I saw a look on her face I've seen so many times before. It was a peaceful look; a look mothers have when they know things are going to be all right. Hers was a look I vaguely remember from the time when a hand rocked my cradle.

Low Hanging Fruit

Carpe Diem
Latin for "Seize the day."

Like it or not, spend any amount of time in the Army and a good portion of it will be in meetings. These periodic gatherings of the faithful are designed to give the boss a chance to see everyone and to dispense wisdom and work from on high. In general, Army staff meetings for me tended to be boring affairs punctuated by those one or two minutes when the gods found interest in things medical before moving on to other, ostensibly more important, matters.

You can learn a great deal in staff meetings. I mean, if you have to be there anyway, then why not make the best of it? You cannot sleep and you had better pay attention. The Old Man may call on you at any moment. So, you give the august body your undivided attention. Over time an assimilation of information from other people occurs, some of it useful.

Take catchwords for instance. It is remarkable how the influence of ideas, as well as work and trouble, flow downhill in the Army. Some general somewhere goes to a special course, reads a new book on leadership, and comes to his next meeting all enthusiastic and pumped over a new word.

"Paradigm" is a classic example. Man, do I hate this word. For a few years, this was all we heard. Paradigm this, paradigm that. I must admit the word sounded interesting at first, like some sophisticated Ivy League words. But woe to the leader who laid this new word on the troops! I remember one soldier saying, "Hey, I'd rather have a pair of dollars than a *pair of dimes*."

One of my all-time favorite catchwords was "low-hanging fruit." Now here was something you could use constructively and the troops would understand. Using the symbolism of ripening fruit on a tree, low-hanging fruit meant goals or jobs most easily accomplished first.

Too many of us want what we think is the best fruit on the tree. Unfortunately, we find our choice to be the most difficult to reach, frequently at the top of the tree of our lives. We want to get rich quick, get promoted speedily, have the most beautiful spouse, or drive that fancy car. Some of us even fantasize about writing a best-selling book.

We just might eventually get to that fruit at the top of the tree. But first we need to take advantage of and enjoy that which lies close at hand, already ripe and ready to go. Army staff meetings were a good paradigm for this low hanging fruit idea. Learn from every experience and make the most of every opportunity. It will not hurt to go for the low hanging fruit first.

Carpe diem!

Cussing

"Languages are the pedigrees of nations."
Samuel Johnson

The language of Army life can be truly remarkable. I am not referring to technical terms, acronyms, or Army jargon. No, what is noteworthy are the colorful and creative, yet profane, ages-old ways soldiers communicate.

In the old Army days, using foul language publicly was widely accepted. Like General George Patton, Jr., leaders would get your attention or motivate you with carefully chosen words not necessarily found in the dictionary. Some soldiers could cuss so bad (or well) that I know even sailors would blush.

I knew public cussing in the Army was on its way out when a commander used the "F" word during a speech in front of mixed company. Someone complained, meetings were held behind closed doors, and the outcome of all this was that he had to apologize. Times have changed. Oh how the eloquent have fallen!

Though they might now be fewer in number, at least in public, it has long been my belief that cussers had a distinct advantage over the non-cussers. I mean, we non-cussers had to be pretty creative to make our points eloquently with the same punch as a four-letter word. "Take that damn hill" carries more weight than, "Take that good for nothing hill." No doubt about it, sometimes our use of creative words devoid of profanity drew some strange looks or snickers from the troops. Whereas a carefully chosen cuss word might be just the thing to get someone's attention and save a life.

As the 20th century ended, the U.S. Army had risen to a new level of eloquence, relatively free of the general use of public foul language. Leaders, standing before the troops, often had to dig deep down to find that acceptable word or phrase that conveyed that succinct idea, something otherwise easily contained in such exquisite vulgar utterances. Nothing was and is more humorous than a senior officer or sergeant struggling during an impromptu speech to find the proper word and then giving up in frustration by venting the taboo term amid laughter from his audience. Underneath, we are all Bohemian still.

In spite of the relative progress in cleaning up our language, we still have a long way to go until the King's English rules the Army. My bet is that we'll never get there. Maybe profanity is in our genes. Example will not get us there, at least not from our more eloquent British friends. In my career the all-time prize for using foul language went to the British soldiers with whom I have worked. In the pedigree of profane speech, the King's (or Queen's) soldiers remain top dog.

PA Joe

"Old soldiers never die; they just fade away!"
British Army Song

Joe Hatch was the best Army PA I ever knew. When I was a young, inexperienced warrant officer in my first assignment, it was the experienced, veteran Joe Hatch who treated me as an equal, without the indifference or condescension of other less noble souls. His wise advice kept me out of a lot of trouble.

The day I penned this story was the day I learned that Joe had passed on. His untimely death at the age of fifty-two came as a shock, but then again, Joe lived hard and enjoyed life to its fullest. Though he has gone, his spirit, enthusiasm, and the soldiers he mentored live on.

Douglas MacArthur once said that the American flag was the embodiment of our ideals and it teaches us not only how to live, but also how to die. Soldiers like Joe taught many of us how to live like soldiers, and when they die, a piece of ourselves dies too.

But Joe would not have us wallow in sadness over his death. No, I can hear him now, "Now Kay," in a voice that sounded like he was gargling gravel, "I don't want you fretting over my death. You get out there and make things better than they are."

And we do—every one of us who was touched by Joe Hatch, literally hundreds of Army field medical officers, physicians and physician assistants alike. Each is making the Army and this earth a better place than when we found it. A bit better now because we knew Joe. He was a man who could speak his mind about as plain as anyone from upstate New York could. Though he might seem gruff at first, the same man would shed tears over Kurdish refugee children he took care of during the Gulf War.

I refuse to accept the fact that Joe is gone. Sure, there was the loss of a great man that gray day in March in a veteran's hospital. But that was only the finite part of the man. The infinite part of Joe Hatch extends beyond the resting-place of his remains in the military cemetery at Fort Sam Houston, Texas. The infinite part comprises the people he touched. Many of the soldiers he mentored continue to touch others in a similar way.

At this moment if Joe were here he would say, "Okay, enough of this sad stuff, everybody back to work."

Right. That's how Joe would want it. Everybody back to work making a real difference, one patient or one soldier at a time. In this way the gift of Joe will go on and will never fade away.

Empathy

"God will not look you over for medals, degrees, or diplomas,
but for scars!"
Elbert Hubbard

Sustaining a laceration from some accident is not my idea of a good time. But there I was, struggling with the jack to my truck, changing a flat tire out in the middle of a backwoods excursion. Always one to immerse myself into the task at hand, perhaps I got in a little too close.

The jack turning ratchet suddenly kicked back and smacked me right across the front of my face. Stunned, I crouched over, covering my face with one hand. Recovering slightly, I pulled my hand away and saw some blood. My son Marlan, who was helping me, took one look at me and exclaimed, "Oh, no."

It would be a couple of hours until I arrived at the Army hospital emergency room. A good gash above my right eyebrow was a place I just couldn't sew up myself. So, on a late Saturday night and, as it would turn out, early into Sunday morning, I joined other injured and sick souls who had made the same pilgrimage as me.

We were a curious lot; thirty or so people patiently waiting to be seen. Some stupid cartoons on the TV provided background noise to our drama. In addition to this tomahawked medical officer, there were assorted other cases: the beat-up partygoer in a corner, complete with his own entourage of overly sympathetic, body-pierced comrades in need of a bath.

One lady looked as if her foot was broken. Another fellow, like me, had a laceration to his finger. I would have preferred a finger instead of my face. A young lady looked in a fair amount of rearside pain, finding the chairs a bit too uncomfortable. Maybe hemorrhoids, I thought. There were coughs, some occasional groans, and worried looks from others. Our motley group was rounded out with three or four small children, probably with ear infections or the croup, but not so ill as to prevent them from the usual mischief of toddlers in a public lobby.

It would be a few hours until the ER staff got to my triage number. I apologized for adding to their Saturday night, and now Sunday morning, workload. I was unable to fix my own booboo. In no time, my wound was closed, and I was on my way, scarred but strengthened from the experience.

Now, as I gaze into the mirror each day, that one-inch scar on my forehead, just above my right eyebrow, reminds me to be more careful. It also reminds me of what it feels like to sit in the lobby with all those patients, on the other side of the health care system of which I'm a part.

Paper Pushers

"To achieve great things, we must live
as though we are never going to die."
Vauvenargues

They say the appearance of a person's desktop is a fair idea of what things are like in their mind. Does an empty desk equal an empty mind? Or does a cluttered desk reveal a cluttered mind? One cannot be too sure, especially in my case, since my desk, depending on the time of day, can look empty or cluttered. More often than not though, my desk is cluttered. Given all the different things to do each day, taken as a whole the workday at my desk can seem overwhelming. The raw numbers for one of my days was:

132 pieces of paperwork
62 signatures
27 phone calls
14 pieces of mail
12 special problems
8 consultations
6 voice-mail messages
4 complaints
3 minor emergencies
2 meetings
And a partridge in a pear tree.

Fortunately, the Good Lord blesses us with only a certain amount of time each day and reminds us that "sufficient for the day is the trouble thereof." For paper pushers some days are more trouble than others are.

Thankfully there does come some slack time when you can begin to clear some of the piles, or in some cases mountains, off the top of your desk. You file papers or move them on to someone else's desk. Perhaps the piece of paper is now OBE and it goes into the circular file. Why, just moving paper to another location on your desk makes you feel better.

Move up in the Army and at some point you'll become a paper pusher. You become one of those folks you always spoke negatively about. Yeah, one of those people who have nothing better to do than to push paper. It might be an assignment in a plans and training office, a command position, or one of those cheesy Pentagon jobs. Whatever it is, it is likely to be a job that keeps the paper mills in business.

God did indeed put each of us here on earth for some purpose. One thing is for sure, the Army generates enough paperwork for those with the job title 'paper pusher' to achieve great things. It is an Army position so far behind that it will never go away.

Thanks

"I can live for two months on a good compliment."
Mark Twain

He stopped me in a hallway, as I was busily en route to some meeting. He looked vaguely familiar, but I couldn't place him. "Where had I seen him before?" I thought. "Captain Kay, you probably don't know me," he said, with a deep look of appreciation, "but I just wanted to thank you for probably saving my wife's life."

Wow, what a compliment! Imagine my reaction as he refreshed my memory with the details about what I had done. His wife, also a soldier, had sustained a heat injury while doing a forced road march. I had stopped by a field medical tent to check on one of my medics who was injured during the same march. I heard a commotion off in one corner of the tent. A couple of providers and medics were struggling with this soldier's wife. She was an obvious heat casualty, delirious and belligerent too.

I recognized her as one of the medical platoon lieutenants in our division, so I came over to the bed to see if I could render assistance. It did not take long to figure out that things were out of control with her inexperienced providers and that her condition was probably serious. She needed the right attention immediately.

I asked the medical officer caring for her if I could help. She gladly assented. We began getting a rectal temperature on the patient: 104.3° F. Could be heat stroke, I thought. We ordered a MEDEVAC helicopter and began to rapidly cool her down with fanning and cold water. An intravenous infusion was begun despite her resistance. In time, we evacuated her to an Army hospital and she was admitted into the intensive care unit for heat stroke.

Later, when she came to in the hospital, she had no memory of the heat injury, her resistance to care, or who took care of her. Over time the story was pieced together, enough to find out that I was involved in her treatments. The turbulence of time and place left no chance for our paths to cross until a couple of years later when her husband saw me in a hospital hallway.

Though I was glad to be of service to her, I had forgotten all about the episode. For medical folks this sort of thing is a part of our job. It is what we are trained to do. When people thank us for something about their care, it sure cancels out a lot of the grief and baloney we sometimes have to put up with. A good compliment is definitely something we can live on for a while.

Home Away From Home

"A man travels the world in search of what he needs
and returns home to find it."
George Moore

Army chaplains do wonderful work with the thousands of family members who accompany service personnel to their various assignments. Most of their service is non-denominational, embracing all faiths in outreach and social activities. In a way they are morale officers, bringing a piece of home and humanity into our lives.

From time to time, the chaplains get ambitious and organize mission trips to help the less fortunate. Early one spring I had the privilege to provide medical support to a chapel mission trip to Mexico. Approximately one hundred young people from Fort Hood, Texas, participated in the opportunity to build small homes for poor families in Neueve Progresso, a small town lying on the southern bank of the Rio Grande River. For most participants this would be their first exposure to the grinding poverty and need many Mexican people experience on a daily basis.

It was a memorable trip for everyone. We built nine small houses for people who essentially lived in shacks constructed out of garbage dump material. Each home cost approximately $900 to construct using concrete, cinder blocks, lumber and about a hundred hours of volunteer time. Imagine the look on each family's face as a new home on a modest plot of land was given to them at no charge. It was an invaluable lesson for every American boy and girl who participated in the effort.

Each evening we stayed in a camp just over the border in the United States. Though the lodgings were modest compared to home, they were much better than what our friends had across the border.

When we first arrived at the camp, our Army chaplain briefed us on the disposition of the two large cabins available. One would house the girls and the other the boys. He called us all into an open area near the cabins and said to us, "Now, everyone wait here for a moment while I decide which cabin will be male and which female." Amused by his remark I asked, "Now chaplain, how can you tell if a cabin is male or female?" "Simple," he said, "if the toilet seats are up, it's male."

By the end of the week I came to appreciate those toilet seats, running water, and a great many other things about the wonderful country we live in. There are many things we often take for granted. Sometimes we have to be apart from them in order to appreciate what we have. That is a round-trip home away from home everyone should experience.

325

Vulnerability

"Remember you are just a man."
A slave's Triumph counsel to ancient Roman Generals

Over the years of practicing medicine, doctors and other medical providers encounter some very ill soldiers. Particularly in the military, with all the traveling and exposure to the elements, it is a wonder we don't have even more soldiers with bizarre illnesses. Pneumonia, malaria, hepatitis, and tuberculosis are just some of the disease monsters out there, and confronting them head-on, complete with exposure to coughs, sneezes, and body fluids, is part of the doctor's job.

Sometimes, given enough exposure to disease without getting sick himself, a medical officer can almost think he is invincible, or at least equipped with one heck of an immune system. Mother Nature, or at least her diseased side, sometimes humbles these proud warriors of medicine.

Our youth group trip to Mexico was exciting. Building houses for poor Mexicans was a noble cause and one that the dozens of young people with us were very enthusiastic about. As their supporting medical officer, my job was to take care of their illnesses and injuries, and especially prevent them from getting the real bug down there—diarrhea. "Be careful with the food and water," I would admonish them.

They listened. No serious illnesses and certainly none of the bad diarrhea cases I had been warned about occurred. After ten days we were to leave for home, but first everyone had to do some local shopping.

One of the Army chaplains and I spent a good part of the shopping day together and were careful about what we ate and drank. Well, at least the chaplain was careful. As for me, I thoughtlessly grabbed a sample of green cactus to eat from a roadside vendor.

About eight hours later, as everyone slept snugly in his or her bed, Montezuma came to visit me with a vengeance. First the explosive diarrhea and nausea, then outright vomiting, followed by both ends of the digestive tract in full action. By dawn's early light I was a shadow of my former self. Never had I been so ill. Dehydrated and barely able to stand, I crawled into a van for the ride home as my charges wondered what happened to "Doc."

In time, my "invincible" immune system kicked in and things started looking up. The illness gave me time to really experience what being sick was all about. I had cause to reflect, to know that I too was vulnerable to the false sense of security around the diseases I see each day, and especially those maladies offered gratis in the cuisine of street vendors.

Army Brats

"Acorns are planted silently by some unnoticed breeze."
Thomas Carlyle

My son Marlan was born at Landstuhl Army Medical Center in Germany on a cold January morning in the early 1980s. It is hard for me to believe that he is in college now, doing quite well—Eagle Scout, near 4.0 GPA, and quite handsome too. Moreover, Marlan is a redhead like his father, for acorns never fall far from the tree.

Marlan is your classic Army brat. Born when I was a young enlisted medic, his growing years matched those of his father's growing military career. He has traveled all around the world and, like all Army kids, calls a grocery store the commissary and Walmart a civilian version of the PX.

Marlan has PCSd with the family, helped dad with a couple of DITY moves, knows how important an LES is, and even accompanied dad once on a TDY. Yes, he is also very familiar with Army acronyms.

Army children are very special people. They are our future. Through no choice of their own, their lives are filled with unique experiences within the military subculture. The Army experience provides them the potential for adventures and opportunities seldom afforded the children of civilians. They have seen what lies beyond the horizon.

I have no doubt the military has and will always be sincerely interested in Army families. Many efforts are in place to take care of families. Commanders know that a happy family makes a happy soldier, especially when perhaps fifty percent of soldiers in today's Army have families. I can attest that Uncle Sam took great care of my family.

Marlan will probably not join the military. His chosen path will be a different one. No need for him to join up really, since he has seen enough to know all about it and his talents are better suited for other areas. The Army will always be a part of him, though, wherever he may go.

Once a brat always a brat. Army kids are like acorns that grow into very strong trees. I believe they are trees of a stronger sort. I have no doubt, proud father that I am, that Marlan, and the thousands of Army brats like him, will grow into fine citizens of their great nation uniquely qualified to lead our future when the rest of us are spending our remaining days in pajamas in some old folks home.

It's good for our country that some civilian citizens, through either actual service or as family members of those who serve or have served, understand what the Army is really like, even if they're not listed on the TO&E.

327

Stupidity

"Life's a tough proposition, and the first hundred years are the hardest."
Wilson Mizner

He had eighteen years and six months of active federal service. A Sergeant First Class, he stood a good chance of making First Sergeant before twenty years in the Army. Excellent evaluations, dependable, a real go-getter—these were the attributes his superiors had given to him. He was on his way up.

Now he came to see me for a Chapter 14 physical exam. He was being kicked out of the Army for misconduct. His good record was trashed because of one indiscretion: a Saturday night fling with some woman and a puff or two on a marijuana cigarette to add to all the fun.

A few days after his adventuresome evening he reported to work to find that he was a part of a randomized monthly urine drug test group. Two weeks later his commander received the test results, read him his rights, and the rest is history. He had a promising Army career that literally went up in one smoke. With lost pay and retirement benefits over an average lifespan, it would be at least a $500,000 mistake.

As we went through the physical exam, I could tell he was struggling with the error he had made and the resulting consequences. Regret and anxiety about the future were written all over his face. He would be okay, he said, but it would take time. Somehow he would salvage his life and put it back together. Friends and counselors were helping him through.

Rules are important. Most of us are all for some regulation of our lives. But when rules are violated human beings with faces, families, and hopes not unlike our own pay the price. Most of us will never have to see the anguish on their faces, the suffering and loss their poor choices caused.

Most of us are all for rules as long as we are not the executioners. But there are people who do have to see the faces of those who mess up their lives. Judges, police personnel, lawyers, commanders and medical professionals do see their faces. These are the people who we appoint or elect to enforce the rules. Each day brings before them living examples of real people who messed up, who wish the clock could be turned back, who stepped out of bounds and got caught.

It is a great thing to be an outstanding soldier. Play by the rules and you'll go far. Soldiers who drink and drive, tell lies, smoke dope, abuse their spouse or child, or shoplift are a few examples of mistakes you don't want to make.

Being all you can be does not include being just plain stupid.

Retirement Thanks

"A man that fortune's buffets and rewards hast ta'en with equal thanks."
Shakespeare (*Hamlet*)

They would arrive at my clinic almost always with a smile on their face. Perhaps a bit nervous, but clearly they were glad to report for their final visit with the U.S. Army Medical Department. It was time for their retirement physical examination.

As officer in charge (OIC) of a soldier medical readiness center, the occasional retirement physicals I would perform were for the most part a joy. In addition to going over the necessary steps in completing the exam, I'd strike up brief conversations about their plans with life after the Army. Most of the soldiers were in their late 30s or early 40s, and were definitely setting their sights on a second career. For the first time in their modest lives, they were a free agent, able to choose from a wealth of opportunities. Their pensions gave them some freedom. Not much, mind you, but some.

Even the slightest query would get a quick response about what their plans were. "I'm going back to school." "I'll be taking a job with the post office." "I'm starting a business." "I'm going fishing." Almost to a person, these soldiers had a plan and were all fired up about it, too.

Eventually the physical would be completed and all necessary tests and referrals made. Many of these soon to be "retirees" were anxious to be going. They had more retirement outprocessing to do elsewhere. I would make it a point, however, to pause in the completion of their visit, reach out to shake their hand and say, "Hey, if nobody ever tells you this, thanks for your service." Oh, to capture the looks on their faces!

It costs nothing to say something kind to people. But oh, what a return for the small trouble of expressing thanks to some really great soldiers! What a personal joy it is for most soldiers when they bid an excited farewell to the United States Army and rejoin civilian life.

Retired soldiers return to the real world with pride too, for they have accomplished what very few achieve, especially those who complete twenty years or more of enlisted service. It is a small percentage of soldiers who go on, for many leave the service either honorably or dishonorably along the way. Though the rank and file is buffeted by losses through the years, there are rewards for the determined. The best reward is the heartfelt thanks of a grateful nation, a nation whose very existence depends upon the faithful service of soldiers.

We can do without many things, but a free country will always need soldiers.

The Bottom Half

"Do not imitate those unskilled physicians who profess the healing art
in the diseases of others, but are unable to cure themselves."
Sulpicius

Of the most honored professions, being a physician has got to be near
the top if not at the top of the list. Many aspire to this position, but few
attain it. This is partly because of the long academic path that leads to this
career. It is a journey to an important profession during which many fall by
the wayside and some others should have.

My assignment was being the physician assistant clinical coordinator
in an Army hospital. One day the Deputy Commander for Clinical Services
(DCCS) called me to his office. In charge of all physicians and physician
assistants, he called on me for help with a broken physician. He was
wrestling with how to keep a broken doctor gainfully employed who cannot
see patients anymore. Could we use the doctor to help train PA students?

How can you say no to your boss? I consented to help, but deep inside
there were reservations. Sure, we could use the doctor to train PAs, but do
we want to use a broken doctor to incubate new ones? The sarcastic adage
"Those who can't, teach," came to mind. I felt like we were putting the wolf
into the hen house.

Army PAs are by training some of the best clinicians you'll ever see
for medical care, not that I am impartial. Rising out of the ranks of the best
medics and soldiers in the Army, these people are generally smart, wise, and
empathetic. With this in mind, you can imagine that it did not take long for
the PA students to figure out that their new trainer was a broken doctor.

The students were good sports, though, and they made the best of the
situation. The "mentor" became an object lesson for them. They saw the
good and threw away the bad concerning the doctor's skills or lack thereof.
Meanwhile, the administrative discharge for the M.D. crawled its way
through the bureaucracy. Picking and choosing carefully, the PA students
learned what they needed and left the rest. The biggest take home lesson for
them was that there are good doctors and then there are broken ones.

They say leaders spend 80% of their time with the 20% who are a
problem. People problems can be especially frustrating. Overhearing my
disappointment about some medical officers once, a dentist friend asked me:
"What do you call a medical student who finishes last in his class?" "I don't
know," I said. "Doctor," he replied.

By the same token, what do I call the PAs taught by a broken
physician? Better PAs, even if those PAs are in the bottom half of their
class too.

Mistakes

"Wise men learn by other men's mistakes,
fools by their own."
H.G. Bohn

Back home in the mountains of North Carolina they call people who have a difficult time changing "hardheaded." I've encountered many such folks over my Army career. From time to time I have been hardheaded too.

They brought him into my office in handcuffs and leg irons. He was dressed in an orange prison garb and had two heavily armed military police guards as an escort. He was on his way to prison and my job was to do his confinement physical exam, identify any current or chronic medical needs, and clear him medically for his long years behind bars.

The former sergeant had had a good career so far. He had been a dependable, faithful, and reliable soldier. He had set a good example, but he had only one significant fault: his temper. Despite advice from friends, family, and supervisors, he couldn't control his outbursts of anger. He had trouble keeping cool when things upset him. The end result of his uncontrolled outbursts was an incident where he struck and injured an officer, subsequent assault charges, a felony conviction, and prison time.

The pain and agony were in his eyes, though outwardly he was calm and polite, just like anyone else. He was married and had children. That was the irony of it all. He was a good soldier, father, and husband. He had made one, and only one, terrible mistake. His mistake had seriously hurt someone and for that the book was thrown at him. There would be no second chance. No redo of the mistake. Only a bill paid for with time would suffice.

Life is a journey that can be a wonderful experience. It can also quickly become the pits if you make a wrong step. Our neat world we build for ourselves can be turned upside down because of some stupid mistake. A time comes when some have to feel the heat: the disrupted life, shattered plans, unfulfilled hopes, lost opportunities, and suddenly plenty of time on their hands to think about it all.

The physical exam was finished and cordial good-byes were said. He left shuffling out of my office with his guards, one in front and the other behind. The image is one you never forget. You cannot help but feel very sad for him and his family.

My hope was that I could learn from this soldier's sobering example. May I deal with the problems in my own life in such a manner that I always will see the light before having to feel any heat.

Hats

"Nothing fixes a thing so intensely in the memory
as the wish to forget it."
Michel de Montaigne

It is embarrassing. Here you are on your way to work and presto, you can't find your Army hat as you get out of the car. Now, I know I left my hat there yesterday. But, sure enough, it's nowhere to be found. So, you have to endure the stares and finger pointing from that crowd of soldiers you have to pass through to get to your office. You press on undaunted. They just have to understand that even captains can be out of uniform, too.

Military hats have a long, long history. Visualize a soldier from any era and there is headgear on that hairy or hairless head. Hats, helmets, scarves, or some sort of head covering adorns every soldier. Without it, you stand out. Without it, you aren't complete. Without it, you're out of uniform and in trouble.

The modern American Army is no different; though I must confess I wonder what purpose some Army hats serve. Take the garrison cap, for instance. This miniature pup tent that sits on our heads does little to shield its wearer from the sun, offers pathetic protection from rain, will not stop a bullet, and falls off easily.

When not wearing the hat, soldiers struggle with where to put it. Often on the move indoors, you have to keep it with you. The flimsy piece of cloth is too big for pockets, looks funny stuck under the belt, and Sergeant Majors oppose stowing it under the uniform epaulettes or anywhere else for that matter. Other than prominently displaying the fact that its wearer is in proper uniform or may be an officer, it escapes me to conjure up other reasons for the garrison cap's existence.

Whatever its true purpose and whether soldiers like it or not, a hat is part of being in proper uniform. The powers that be deem it to be so. Perhaps someday the Department of Defense will offer a contract for general bidding to produce a garrison cap that really has some specifications that mean something: protection, identification, and ease of wear and storage.

I hope someday Army hats will come equipped with a detachable cord to prevent accidental misplacement, the so-called "idiot cord." Yes, an idiot cord would be nice so that I wouldn't have to negotiate the looks and comments of the troops when their illustrious leader forgets his hat the next time.

Nothing fixes a hat so intensely on my head as my earnest wish to not forget it.

The Chapter Physical

"A failure is a man who has blundered
but is not able to cash in the experience."
Elbert Hubbard

Unfortunately, it is an all too common experience for medical officers: the chapter physical exam. Each year thousands of soldiers fail to complete their service obligation. From pregnancy to misconduct to being overweight, each has a different reason for leaving the Army, some honorable and some otherwise. Too often the term "chapter" is just another word for quitter and the quitters have to see "doc" before they can get out.

She sat in my office, the first patient of the day. I gave her a sincere "good morning," but she responded with something just above being mute and below a snarl. If looks could kill! Obviously unhappy, she was on her way out of the Army and was sent to see me for the chapter physical. Chapter 13—separation for unsatisfactory performance. Yes, the command obviously had picked the right one for her, for her performance so far this morning was already unsatisfactory.

Now the interesting thing about a fair number of folks being kicked out of the Army is how often they accumulate so many medical conditions in such a short period of time! This lady had been very busy. On her medical history form, over thirty blocks were checked "yes." Seventy-five year-olds seldom will have that many blocks checked. She was either very prone to illness and injury or merely thought she was and was looking for a free lunch, courtesy of Uncle Sam. My bet was on the latter.

Slowly, I worked through her story, sorting out the very few real things from those perceived. What emerged was an overweight soldier who refused to accept the fact that she might be the cause of her problems. That just maybe, she might be responsible for some of her trouble. To her, every-one else was to blame, including me, even if I had never seen her before.

Though not a perfect mirror of American society, the U.S. Army is only as good as the people America can provide. Just as the poor will always be with us, so will chapter physicals. There will always be those who cannot complete their commitment. That's okay. Army regulations allow for this. It is a part of dealing with imperfect human beings.

A bad attitude, however, is optional equipment. Everyone can have a bad day, but if a lousy spirit becomes a pattern you just might have an attitude problem. Fix the negative vibes and you will go places. Feed it and it will drag you down even further, whether you are in or out of the Army.

Recruiters

"If you tell the truth you don't have to remember anything."
Mark Twain

"So tell me, what is the Army like?" The soon-to-graduate physician assistant student at Emory University was looking at joining the Army as a PA. The loan forgiveness sign-on incentive looked good and so there he stood. In one hundred words or less, what do you say?

I am not a recruiter, but I couldn't turn down an opportunity for a trip to the national PA conference in Atlanta, Georgia. Never would I have envisioned my career involving recruiting duty, but a family emergency with the primary recruiter found me filling in. Expecting only a few interests from civilian PAs in joining the Army, I was pleasantly surprised to find dozens giving the idea some serious thought, especially those with significant debt as a result of their training programs.

So, what do I like about the Army? I explained that the pay was good, but you'll never get rich. The spirit of teamwork, the opportunities to travel, and the pride of serving one's country are unlike what most civilian jobs could offer. Vacation, federal holidays, and medical/dental care were awesome, again compared to what a civilian employer could offer. In return, though, you have to be physically and mentally prepared to go to war, something the country might eventually ask you to do. You'll get wet and cold, work long hours, and probably spend lots of time away from home. What am I saying? You <u>will</u> spend lots of time away from home!

My one week duty as a physician assistant recruiter would have me repeat the above message dozens of times to folks interested in joining the Army. You're never quite sure how you feel about something until you have to share it with someone, to answer their questions, to be as honest as you can be, even with the risk of scaring people off.

Sharing is verbal and nonverbal as I discovered while walking in my dress green uniform from the hotel to the PA convention center each day. Old soldiers on the street would greet me. They recognized the captain's rank and the badges on the uniform. One apparently homeless person even rendered his best effort at a salute, so long unused since the last time he wore a uniform. He smiled as I returned his salute and he also recognized my "hooaah" greeting. It felt very good to be in the Army.

Maybe a few of the civilian PAs I saw eventually signed up. With no recruiting quota required of me, there wouldn't be any feedback. But it was a good week well spent. It was a time to really share what it meant to serve our great country and to share it not sugar coated, but mainly as truth from personal experience.

The Examination

"There is nothing the body suffers which the soul may not profit from."
George Meredith

There are unpleasant things in life. Things we must face whether we like it or not. Fail to do so and there are consequences that are unacceptable. The medical world offers patients numerous examples of unpleasant treatments or procedures. Patients who experience these things and live to tell the tale, relate stories which to innocent ears sound like some form of medieval torture.

Even a routine physical examination has its challenges. For example, take the digital rectal examination, or DRE for short. Most of us over the years of our lives will get accustomed to shots and needles, even sitting half-naked in a paper gown on a cold examination table. Tubes or fingers inserted into our digestive tract, however, are things you just never get used to. Even the thought gives normal folks a chill. There is a feeling of violation when a doctor inserts a finger into our bottoms and I, from personal experience, can think of no more vulnerable moment in your life than this.

The DRE is an important test though. That's why we submit ourselves to it. Cancer, hemorrhoids, and hidden bleeding are just some of the things providers check for when doing this exam. But what about our dignity? Isn't there another way?

Sadly, there isn't, at least for now. But here is potential for someone to become a multi-millionaire. Simply invent a more comfortable, less embarrassing alternative to the DRE. People would pay big money for a more dignified, less intrusive way of checking our backsides.

Meanwhile, the ordeal remains before us, especially if you are over forty years old. We take comfort in the thought that even the President of the United States gets this exam. Our day comes and the indignity is administered, hopefully by a provider the same gender as us. You hope they will be gentle, use lots of lubricant, and get the job done fast. We reluctantly submit with a "let's get this over with" attitude. Once it is done and our abashment is swallowed, we clean up and, as my wife says, life goes on. We live to tell the tale.

They say there is a lesson in all that happens to us. Something we can profit from. Perhaps when your bottom has been examined, things can only go up from there. Clearly, the profit from this lesson lies in part with that perhaps yet unborn soul who will invent a less humiliating alternative to the DRE. Something more receiver friendly. I bless the day when this Thomas Edison of the digestive tract enters the world.

Soldiers with a Fortune

"Give me neither poverty nor riches, but give me contentment."
Helen Keller

There is a bumper sticker that reads, "He who dies with the most toys wins." That is certainly one way of looking at things, but when an entire country begins to believe in such a philosophy, then there will be few of its citizens who will become soldiers. If you are in life to accumulate things and wealth, then the United States Army, at least the way we know it, is not a career choice for you. Mercenaries can do tolerably well in amassing a fortune, if they survive, but soldiers of a democracy will not become rich.

I am the son of a truck driver and a convenience store worker. My father made a good living driving those big trucks all over the place and my mother got to know many people working at the local store. These were their chosen careers and, as you might guess, my family was not very well to do. A teamster and a cashier can have a very passionate love for each other, but in general don't expect millionaires out of the deal. They were common folk.

Most Americans come from very modest backgrounds and most soldiers hail from common stock. Abraham Lincoln once said, "God must love common folk, because He sure made a lot of them." If the most wealthy Americans are the top five percent of the population, then most of the other ninety-five percent obtain their living the old-fashioned way: they earn it.

A career in the military will make you neither rich nor poor, but it will provide ample opportunity to grow and excel. There are fringe benefits too like serving a great country and doing things that so many other people never get an opportunity to do. Sure, there are awful parts; but then again there are good parts too. In the end, you have a most excellent chance at being content. Perhaps Helen Keller is right—contentment is what we really need, not necessarily a lot of toys.

As my boys headed off to college we had that traditional father-son talk. You often wonder what to say to them as take off on their own. I dug back into my own experience in the Army to come up with something I hoped would be meaningful to them. I wanted to keep what I had to say simple so that they would remember it. The gist of it was this:

There are three things you want out of life: something to believe in, something to do, and someone to do it for.

Though the Army has its dark side, as anything else in life has, I found in the Army something beyond my own self to believe in, something really worthwhile to do with my life, and many, many people to do it for. This is the fortune of contentment available to every soldier.

Instant Winners

"Sorry, please try again."
Bottle Cap Message

The soft drink bottle sitting on my desk displayed a multi-colored label marked "Win Instant Cash." Now, here was my chance. I mean, who out there could not use some instant cash? In no time, the bottle's cap was unscrewed and a quick, excited glance underneath the cap revealed... "Sorry, please try again."

Sometimes I think the story of my life could be "Sorry, please try again." Indeed, every time I hope to get ahead by cutting corners or taking a shortcut, it usually leads back to the starting point. Please try again.

Most of us have to get money the old fashioned way. We earn it. Wealth for the vast majority of people doesn't fall out of the sky, grow on trees, come through lottery tickets, inheritances, or the underside of a soft drink cap. We get it by working and saving, something we need to do again, again, and again.

Rich people do not normally join the Army. Maybe a rare wealthy specimen will enter the military for a great adventure, especially during a war, but in general most of us come from very modest backgrounds. No silver spoons in our background checks. We have to work in order to eat. Heck, most of us had nothing much to our name when we signed up. In short, we traded our poverty and some minor freedoms in return for a faithful wage, job security, and education in the service of our country. Some of us even thought we'd get free lifetime healthcare if we stayed on.

Given time and smart choices, however, we just might win. But there is nothing instant about it. You have to crawl out of bed every day, be on time, get an education, play by the rules, walk the straight and narrow, and stick with it through thick and thin. You have to punch that time ticket. You have to put up with a lot of things and sometimes you will have to try again.

The time to leave the Army does eventually come. Those who are successful are the ones who retire or honorably end their term of service. They move on to others things, but often this is augmented by a small brown United States Government envelope that comes in the mail each month, or an electronic entry that magically appears on their bank statement. Open the envelope or look on that statement and they find a tidy dollar figure that's all theirs, kind of like instant cash. Instead of the message, "Sorry, please try again," the message from Uncle Sam sort of says,

Congratulations, you're an instant winner!

Listening

"It is good to speak to the future: the future will listen."
Ptahhotep

Enshrined within a climate-controlled glass case deep within the British Museum in London lies the Rosetta Stone. The stone is a fragment of what was a larger stone, but its importance is not in its size or lack of completeness, or even the meaning of its inscriptions. What makes this stone so special is that it presents three languages, side by side, all saying the same thing. This is a particularly important finding when one of the languages, Egyptian hieroglyphics, was untranslatable until the discovery of this stone by Napoleon's Army in Egypt during the early 1800s. The Rosetta Stone was the key that unlocked the code of a mysterious language and unknown history of Ancient Egypt. The stone spoke and the future listened.

In a not too dissimilar fashion, each generation needs to speak to the future, to write down things which might be important from the times that have passed, to communicate with those who are yet to be. Thoughts and things that seem trivial in our time, seemingly unimportant, become treasured keepsakes later. But one can never know for certain what the children of the future will consider valuable and what will be mundane. They who are yet to be will decide. It is merely up to us to communicate.

You don't fully appreciate the generational effect on the Army until you get near that fifteen-year mark. Until then, you seem a part of what appears to be a solid mass of young people, all speaking a similar language, desiring similar things, and living a similar experience. It's us versus them, "them" being those older soldiers, the lifers. They are different, from a different era, speaking a different language. They are the "old Army."

At about twelve or fifteen years of service, however, you begin to cross the generation gap. The Captain is now a Major. The Staff Sergeant becomes a Platoon Sergeant. All of a sudden you are one of "them," the "old Army." You start to think like they do and speak as they do. What caused this transformation? Maybe it was time, perhaps the promotion, or a combination of the two.

If you hang around you too will become something similar to what those old soldiers were before your time. You will take on the mantel of training and taking care of future soldiers, some of whom will follow in your footsteps as well. To them you are the Rosetta Stone that breaks the code on what to civilians and young soldiers is often difficult to understand in the United States Army. They will eagerly seek your wisdom. You will speak to this new generation of soldiers yet to be and they will listen.

338

Of Fruits and Fat

"Wherefore by their fruits ye shall know them."
Matthew 7:20

Get older and you get fatter. It's a law of maturity. Fond fans of fine food forever fear fat and forty. Soldiers are not exempt from being fat either, as evidenced by the career casualties of the U.S. Army's weight control program.

I used to be thin, well...okay... thinner than I am now. I honestly thought I was doing okay with my weight. Then the day arrived when a forgotten soul I was talking with about my weight actually poked their finger into my stomach. How rude! The Pillsbury Doughboy sign is a sure indicator that you're fatter.

Some of us have a keen appreciation for food. We can't help it. We go way back with this stuff, and generally cannot go long without it. We have difficulty empathizing with those picky eaters or anyone suffering from anorexia. We are the ones who always cleaned our plates because someone was starving in China.

My wife appreciates the fact that I'm not a finicky eater. If she'll cook it, I'll eat it. One year away from home cooking found me cooking for myself. The experience gave me an appreciation for food prepared by others.

I am devoted to Army food, too, especially around Thanksgiving or Christmas. You truly have not eaten well until you've tried the superb cuisine of U.S. Army cooks during the holidays. Chow is too demeaning a term for what these budding artists do with the basic ingredients and the often-crude tools the Federal Government provides for them.

There are many folks who are living proof that what goes in does not necessarily come out. In time, most of us will join their ranks, in one way, shape or form. Hopefully this is at a leisurely pace while still on active duty.

Perhaps too many Americans are obsessed with thinness. Their apathetic attitude towards food causes them to miss out on one of life's greatest pleasures. You miss out on the glow on my Aunt Marie's face as you sink your teeth into her homemade pecan pie. Or there is Ed's ecstasy as you sample some of his peppermint ice cream. And what about that mess hall sergeant's proud, beaming face, as you sincerely compliment him and his crew on a truly wonderful holiday repast.

Now a few extra pounds are okay. I needed new pants anyway. We moderates can get a little plump and not feel guilty about it, for we dare not starve ourselves of one of life's greatest pleasures. By their tummies you shall know who has and who has not discovered that some of the fruits of our labors are edible.

Military Hoboes

"The strongest of all warriors are these two – Time and Patience."
Leo Tolstoy

The Dover, Delaware Air Force base passenger terminal was crowded the 14th of July 1999. Dozens of active duty personnel on leave, as well as retirees on vacation, along with a healthy group of family members, were all trying to catch free rides in Air Force transport planes to Europe. It was and still is a great way to save money if, and that's a big if, you can catch a ride.

The process for getting on a "hop" seems very complicated, especially to the uninitiated. Stated in simple terms, you register by confirming your leave orders, military ID cards, and passports with terminal authorities. Then you wait. And wait. And wait. In time, flights show up and announcements of seats available for "hitchhikers" cause hopes to rise.

Scheduled flight times arrive and, more often than not, pass. There are delays and canceled flights for this and that: crew rest, spraying for bugs, mechanical problems, hazardous cargo restrictions, bad weather, you name it. The Air Force can be very creative. There are no guarantees.

In time, if you are patient enough, a plane releases seats and terminal personnel go through the formal process of picking who will fill them. Here the citizens of the "hop world" are divided into castes, or selection categories based on their time of registry and current relationship to the DOD (Active duty, retiree, family member, etc.). Each anxiously wonders if their name will be chosen next. You must be present to win.

Names are called, boarding passes issued, in-flight boxed meals ordered and bags checked in. But don't get too excited yet. A veteran retiree, with long experience in this "hop" hoboing experience, said to me, "Never get excited until you have actually arrived." I agree, it ain't over 'til the fat plane lands.

Never will you see disappointment greater than waiting for a flight, sometimes even for days, only to see them canceled or postponed. And you have no recourse, for beggars cannot be choosy.

For the patient, success eventually comes. After four days of waiting, our C-5 Galaxy transport plane touched down in jolly old England. We had finally arrived "over there." A spontaneous applause erupted from all the passengers as we taxied to the terminal. We could breathe a sigh of relief.

Though we now had a little less time for the vacation, we had more money because Murphy's Law and the Air Mobility Command finally gave some military hoboes a break.

Dyslexic Driving

"Fortune sides with him who dares."
Vergil

Travel overseas and eventually you will come to a country where people do things backwards, like drive on the left-hand side of the road. Stated in simpler terms, we Americans would say these people "drive on the wrong side of the road." The United Kingdom, Japan, Thailand, and Australia are examples of countries where this is the case. Naturally, the citizens of these countries probably feel that the rest of the world drives on the wrong side of the road too.

For years, I was intimidated by the thought of driving on the roads of these countries with their dyslexic drivers and traffic laws. Behind the wheel I would merely be an accident waiting to happen. Whenever I had to travel within one of these countries, it would always be by a taxi, bus, or train. Let the natives do the driving.

The time eventually came, though, when I had to attempt this ordeal of driving on the left side. With my huge family in Great Britain for a week, it was either rent a van or stay put, all other options being just too costly. So, I gathered my courage and rented a European seven-passenger van.

We traveled all over England and Scotland. What an experience! The steering wheel is on the right side of the car for starters, and, to complicate things, there were no automatic transmission models to be had, so shifting gears with the left hand would be the order of the day. It was good that the van at least had the floor pedals in proper sequence: clutch, brake, and gas.

My first foray into this opposite world of driving was nerve racking and fraught with errors. My wife was a champ, though, encouraging me and doing all the navigation from the left-hand front seat. It was all I could do to keep my eye on traffic. In the end, my left brain underwent a serious workout. Or was it my right side?

Despite the frequent dangers, close calls, narrow spaces, and traffic circles, I managed a week of driving fifteen hundred miles on those motor way marvels. I even got over the occasional obscene hand gesture and lips I could not read from concerned residents of the UK who probably wondered how I ever got a license to drive. In the end, the van was returned unscathed, my family unharmed by the experience, and the only marks I left were tracks on the road and rubber on the curbs. Meanwhile, the frontier of one man's driving experience was pushed back because fortune smiled upon him, even if it was backwards.

341

The Tower

"It is not a carol of joy or glee,
But a prayer that he sends from his heart's deep core...
I know why the caged bird sings!"
Paul Laurence Dunbar

The former East German outpost guard tower lay in a field of ripening wheat. Its gray, square concrete mass four stories high stood in stark contrast to the blue German summer sky and the golden grain below. Ugly graffiti decorated the outside walls of the lower floor, and the only windows, all on the fourth level, were shattered. The wall it was built to watch over was now gone. An overgrown old patrol road was all that remained of what was once the Iron Curtain.

My teenage children excitedly scampered up the narrow metal ladders inside the small, six-by-six foot, square tower. They had to see the view from above. Before long, they all stood on top of the tower where at one time communist soldiers watched for people trying to flee into West Germany.

From this very watchtower high above the fields some poor souls trying to flee were gunned down. When told of this, my children responded with puzzled looks. The looks led to questions. "Why did they want to keep people inside? Where were the minefields? Did the guards ever run?" My best answers only led to more questions.

The small, red-topped, white stakes marking the West German border were now gone, a border that for thousands of determined people meant freedom, a freedom hundreds died trying to reach. A small hiking path lay where the meter high stakes once stood, a path American and West German military patrols once walked, keeping watch on the frontier of freedom.

Climbing down from the tower, my children now played in fields once strewn with mines. What a contrast to the time when their father stood near here as a soldier! It had been a cold war then, where only the caged civilians of East Germany died. That was ended due to the combined might and determination of NATO, whose forces prevented a third world war and eventually brought the peaceful end of the Warsaw Pact.

It brought joy to my heart seeing my children stand beneath that gray tower. The frequent passage of modern cars nearby on a new road between the former East and West Germany meant freedom was there to stay. The cage of terror was now gone, with only this forlorn tower surviving, now merely a perch for happy birds and even happier people.

Hair

"A hair in the head is worth two in the brush."
Oliver Herford

My hair was something my wife found quite attractive about me as we were dating back in college in the mid 1970s. Fairly long and a sandy reddish color, she would fuss over it, especially the "cute" curls which grew just behind my ears. She liked other things about me, too, I assume, but the hair was definitely high on her list.

Not long after we married, I joined the Army and for the next twenty years my long hair was history. My wife has commented about missing my longer hair and has reluctantly grown accustomed to the sharp military haircut. But not so accustomed as to prefer short hair. Indeed, she readily recognizes when I've gotten a fresh haircut, almost lamenting the loss of even a modest two weeks' growth of new hair. After an extended leave and the inevitable visit to the barber, her reaction is even stronger.

Of particular frustration for Irene has been the varied quality of my military haircuts. Frequent moves, busy schedules, and plain laziness have prevented me from having a steady military barber. If only I could go in every time and get the same thing: "Just a light trim, taper in the back, and sharpen things up to last me another two weeks." But no, the result is as varied as the number of Army barbers out there.

Army barbers are an interesting group of folks. Some talk to you, others, especially those from Thailand, give you a post-haircut massage. Some constantly remind you to tilt your head this way or that. There are slow ones and fast ones, and some who manage to hurt you too. A few use scented tonic water and others, my all-time favorite, actually use shaving cream and a razor to give you that very sharp result.

Rare is an Army barber who cuts my hair in a manner acceptable to my CO at home. When I happen to find one, the extra wait and trip are worth the resulting satisfaction my wife expresses. It is a small consolation for her I suppose, putting up with the required short hair.

After twenty years of service this entire hair cut issue is overcome by events on two counts. First, my wife loves me for more than just my hair. She always has and that's good, because the aging process brings us to the second count: twenty years have left a mark on my scalp called "normal male pattern baldness."

I am hairier now than when I was twenty-one. But, to quote from George Bernard Shaw, I have a distribution problem. The new hair is in the wrong place.

Darlings

"We must march my darlings, we must bear the brunt of danger."
Walt Whitman

I do not know why the Army calls them "low little darlings." Though they are among the lowest forms of inflicting bodily pain, there is nothing darling about them. There you are, lying flat on your back looking up into the dawning sky. The crisp colors and the majestic expanse of that huge atmosphere above cannot be enjoyed just now. The shrill voice of the master fitness trainer sounds off: "The next exercise is the low little darlings." Moans rise up from the soldiers. "Starting position, move!"

So begins one of the most legal forms of persecution known to the Army. The moans quickly end as each of us grunt while raising our feet about twelve inches off the ground, keeping the remainder of our often pathetically out of shape bodies flat on the ground.

The sergeant bellows out, "In cadence, exercise!" At first things seem harmless enough. You follow the cadence count by moving your feet and legs about three or so feet apart and then bringing them back together again scissors-fashion, all the while maintaining your feet about a foot off the ground. At the end of the count, instead of four we sound off with the repetition count: One... two... three... ONE! One... two... three... TWO! and so forth. Along about FIFTEEN you truly begin to feel the effects.

Meanwhile the flab pack on our abdomens gets strained and drained. Over time, day after day, it begins to look like a six-pack. But oh how painful the process!

What makes this exercise so popular with sadistic types is how much discomfort it brings without causing permanent injury. Unlike the falls and trashed knees that occur with running and the messed-up shoulders and backs from push-ups and lifting, low little darlings provide pain and gain without getting lame. Army physical fitness instructors figured this out long ago, which explains their predilection to use this darling, little exercise.

There is a photo of me standing in the barracks during basic training with my shirt off. I have olive drab fatigue pants and bloused black boots on. There doesn't appear to be an ounce of fat on me, just hair and muscle. I looked good then. The six-pack on my abdomen has been super-sized over time, but my wife still fondly reminisces about the body shaping boot camp gave me, a shaping brought about in part by low little darlings.

I can think of nothing better to offset the effects of dangerous foods like Twinkies and Little Debbie's than to use exercises like torture and little darlings. Starting position, move!

344

Tenacity

Fulfill your obligations. Stick around. Be tenacious. Pretty easy things to say, but so much more difficult to do. Fulfilling one's obligations is one of the core values of the United States Army. In a world spilling over with broken promises and failures, it is a value that really stands out even more today when you encounter it.

I understand that the inspiration for Velcro came from pesky burr seeds that cling to your clothing when you are outdoors in the brush. They are troublesome little things, but we dutifully fulfill their purpose when we notice their presence, pick them off our clothing, and discard them to a new location far removed from where they started. Whether you believe in a divine creation or evolution, one cannot help being impressed with this cunning method of getting exactly what they want, the dissemination of their seed. It is also an excellent example of rewarded tenacity.

Sticking with something, especially over a long time, takes a lot of dedication and determination. It takes guts. To stick hard one needs a strong motivation, something that makes it all worthwhile. Goals.

There are many things in life that pay huge dividends if you hang on. Successful children, happy marriages, fulfilling jobs, promotions, and a comfortable retirement are some examples. Impatience or stupidity can rob you of the big payoff.

Often there is a direct relationship between what we want and how much we have to expend to get it. The expense may be time, a certain amount of freedom, money, or any number of other things. But if something is worth having, then you become willing to sacrifice to get it if you really, truly want it. I am reminded of the old pop song, *It Don't Come Easy*. If "it don't come easy" then we tend to really value something when it does finally come.

Things do happen if you stick with it. There are a lot of quitters out there. People who just plain give up. The losers. You do not have to number among them. The antonym of a quitter is a winner.

To succeed you don't have to necessarily be talented, a genius, the heir to some fortune, or beautiful. Just don't quit. The really successful people that inherit the future are the tenacious ones. They come, they see, and they do some serious sticking around. "Veni, vidi, *velcro*."

345

Need to Know Basis

"A secret is your slave if you keep it,
your master if you lose it."
Arabian Proverb

A friend of mine, who will of course remain nameless, worked for the Central Intelligence Agency. That's all I ever knew about his job, even after knowing him for many years. Though he was a super person and ready for a good laugh at the drop of a dime, he was also like some war veteran who was unwilling to talk about the horrors he had witnessed. He remained forever mum about details of his work. My intense curiosity was never satisfied.

He knew all about my work, though. The petty frustrations and the small triumphs, complete with every gory detail. But try and balance the scale with some token contribution on his part and you got a look that said, "If I tell you, I'll have to shoot you."

Have you ever wondered how you would react to torture? I have. Take away my food, bring in some isolation and loss of sleep, and presto, the chatter button gets pushed and I would probably spill the whole story. You're looking at a serious leak here. You know, the Army never did give me a top-secret clearance.

Some CIA types once debriefed me as I left a foreign country. There were some details they needed, even if I was a medical officer. They had a keen interest in what I had to say and so I gladly provided all the details they wanted. I basked in the attention, the interest they had in my every word. Bridges, buildings, people, you name it, and the blabbermouth mesmerized his audience. There lurks no tactful presidential spokesperson in my genes, fully prepared to dodge questions.

But my debriefing was a decidedly one-sided conversation. My questions at them were evaded like a fighter plane dodges surface to air missiles. All I got was chaff. Mind you, they were cordial enough, but they certainly were experts at this poker game of words. It was a one-way deal.

God bless the James and Jane Bond types out there. I envy their vows of secrecy, their loyalty to information that is power because so few people know it. These inside traders of details even the press can't get a sniff of.

National security will always need these secretive types who are in the know. They are good to have around, these deceiving bodyguards of the real deal. But be forewarned, getting to really know them will be strictly, as they say in the Army, on a need to know basis.

346

The Best Resume

Curriculum vitae
Latin for "the course of life."

Each time you see a soldier in his or her Class A uniform you will also see their resume, prominently displayed in the badges and ribbons on their chest and the rank on their sleeve or epaulettes. From the new recruit with an Army Service Ribbon and a marksmanship-shooting badge, to the seasoned veteran with rows upon rows of ribbons and a run of sleeve hash stripes, a soldier's uniform is a publicly displayed personnel file.

Civilians have a difficult time learning how to understand the varied badges, ribbons, and symbols on the uniforms of America's service personnel. The emblems and colors almost overwhelm the senses, especially on a highly decorated general or sergeant major. Just to figure out how to recognize the various ranks of the different services takes a good bit of effort. Trying to interpret the significance of each ribbon in the "fruit salad" rows above the left breast pocket requires even more dedication, almost equivalent to learning a foreign language. There are charts you can buy to help sort out all the different awards given to soldiers for various things. From peacekeeping duty to humanitarian service, from meritorious achievement to a joint service commendation, each ribbon symbolizes a formal recognition of some particular deed or service of that individual.

I once stood next to a Medal of Honor recipient, a veteran of the Iwo Jima campaign during World War II. His uniform was remarkably sharp and was the very same one he wore when President Harry S. Truman presented the nation's highest honor to him on the White House lawn over fifty years earlier. Despite my experience with learning various awards, there were ribbons on his chest I did not recognize, each one highlighting some aspect of his exceptional service during a most decisive war.

There were some awards in this hero's uniform I did recognize. A green and white-stripped ribbon signified an Army Commendation medal. Another purple ribbon with two oak-leaf clusters symbolized three awards of the Purple Heart. And then there was one more ribbon, a sky blue one with five small, white stars—the Congressional Medal of Honor.

Many people are powerful. They may make a lot of money, sit at the head of a boardroom table, play professional sports, or dominate the movie screen. But those who are truly deserving of this nation's praise and honor, who we should elevate to positions of power, who should be high on the endorsement and popularity lists, are those with the credentials of the soldier, sailor, airman, or marine. They are the best resume this nation possesses.

347

Plan B

"Men's plans should be regulated by the circumstances,
not circumstances by the plans."
Livy

One of the most curious systems in the modern world is the U.S. Army's promotion system. One would hope that given the expanse of time that lies before a new soldier in the Army, he or she could have a pretty good idea, given good behavior and duty performance, about when they would expect to be promoted. You would think that would be the case, the so-called 'Plan A.'

I had hoped to make Specialist (E-4) rank at about four months in the Army. It was eight months. Specialist Fifth Class (E-5) was also a few months delayed. In fact, most of my promotions were somewhat delayed, and I suspect this is true for most other troops as well.

The real promotion puzzle begins with advancements to more senior ranks. Take the promotion from Captain to Major. It seemed like that pair of bars on my collar, sometimes affectionately referred to as "railroad tracks," would remain permanently in place on my uniform. Year after year I waited for any chance to get 'looked at' for Major. The time finally came when I was in the 'primary zone,' that is, I was deemed qualified to have my file and photo looked at by a DA promotion board.

These unseen reviewers, usually full-bird colonels from various branches of the Army, go through stacks of records. They cull out the unfortunate ones deemed unfit to promote and finally come up with a list of names of people worthy to advance. Though you know when this board convenes to decide who gets promoted, the rest of the time line is unpredictable. First, 'the list' must be released, the official word that you were or were not selected for promotion. The list release generally takes months, depending on when Congress or bureaucrats finish reviewing it.

The average Joe would think that when that list gets released, you would 'pin on' the new rank right away. Not so. There is this little detail called sequence numbers. The lower your number, the better, but you still do not know for sure when you'll actually get the new rank. You comfort yourself with the 'promotable' business added to your Army title, but so far it will not impact your checking account in a positive manner.

Month by month, a certain number of officers actually pin on the new rank and get the pay too. Eventually your turn comes. Honest. You finally are happy, even though the promotion came IAW "plan B."

348

The Witch Which Wasn't

"This only is the witchcraft I have us'd."
Shakespeare

Over an extended period of time in any job you will go through different bosses. In the Army the overwhelming majority of my bosses have been men, since most of my assignments were with combat arms units. The occasional assignment to a school or hospital allowed four of my leaders to be female, two being physicians and two belonging to the Army Nurse Corps. Every Halloween reminds me of one nurse boss in particular.

Within the Army Medical Department you have certain spheres of influence. There are doctor, physician assistant, nurse, and administrative staff hierarchies, among many others. Generally, each group would rather do the business of bossing their own, but in the mid-1990s all that changed. The Army Medical Department leadership entered an enlightened era of putting people in charge based on ability and rank, not by branch or professional group.

LTC Diana Ruzicka was for me as a physician assistant the first nurse to be my boss. I was somewhat nervous about this, the nervousness made worse by negative warnings by fellow PAs and MDs. But their concerns were unfounded. LTC Ruzicka was extremely competent, energetic, capable, and readily sought help from subordinates when she bumped into the frontiers of her own knowledge and ability. Instead of building an empire, as so many Napoleonesque leaders do, she led with an uncharacteristic, even enviable selflessness. Her nurturing style made things grow and progress.

It was at Halloween when it dawned on me what a remarkable boss I had. She came to work dressed as a witch in keeping with others in the hospital dressing up that day. Her detailed costume included the traditional black garb, pointed black hat, a green face, stringy black hair, a couple of extra facial moles, and long fingernails. I could hardly recognize her as she sat at the head of the table during a staff meeting, trying to address the business of the day. I couldn't help but laugh inside.

Despite the garb and obvious attention to playing the role of a witch, I realized my boss was not the witch some had said she would be. LTC Ruzicka was no witch, even if she looked like one.

No sir, many employees mentally burn their leaders at the stake as the Salem colony leaders literally did to witches in times gone by. But I would not figuratively burn my boss, even if she looked like a witch. If anything, she was a good witch, one whose craft I would want to emulate.

Traveler

"Travel is fatal to prejudice, bigotry and narrow-mindedness."
Mark Twain

My time in college was probably the greatest time in my life. My application and nomination to the United States Military Academy at West Point was not approved, so I headed off to a small college with the most beautiful campus in the world near Chattanooga, Tennessee. Though I was disappointed at not getting into West Point, the loss was soon forgotten in a school where the girls outnumbered the guys two to one, and were beautiful too. No military service school could match those facts.

In college my lifelong commanding officer came into my life, but not until I had the opportunity to meet and date several lovely young ladies. Each acquaintance and each date helped me formulate exactly what type of woman was best for me. Also important was the further refinement of my own rough qualities during this dating around period. I had to be Mr. Right for her too.

When Irene entered the scene, I knew she was the one. It took her a while to reach the same conclusion about me, but she eventually found me to be a character she could put up with over the long haul. From the many to choose from, I clearly did well and definitely got the better end of the deal.

Deciding where to retire to from the Army is also like the dating process. Soldiers can travel around from assignment to assignment, which can be for some, including myself, quite often. Around the world and from coast to coast one gets to know and see many places, from Honolulu to Bangkok, San Antonio to Berlin, and all points in between.

Some moves and trips were by choice and others were involuntary. Every displacement though, afforded chances to make the most of getting to know new places and refine one's ultimate choice of where to eventually settle down.

Having grown up in the mountains of North Carolina, I thought it would be difficult to find places that were more appealing. Not so. Irene and I finally found and fell in love with what for us was the pick of the litter—northeastern Washington State. Yes, it is even better than western North Carolina.

Like people, there is no one place that's perfect, but one thing I've learned: there are many places and people you can be quite comfortable with. The travel an Army career offers, as well as various people one meets and works with, blesses us with an open mindedness. That openness can set you up for some really good choices. Few careers can boast such fringe benefits as these.

Sleeping Well

"Sometimes enduring peace can only be found on the other side of war."
Unknown / Army Staff Officer School Notes

As I neared my retirement from twenty years of service in the U.S. Army, I met a veteran of World War II. We had a short meeting, basically exchanging pleasantries, but he left me with one of the best compliments I have ever received. His was a compliment I will always remember.

In the small talk that strikes up when old soldiers meet, questions about one's service inevitably come up. He had served with the Army during World War II, seeing action against the Germans in Europe.

This veteran asked me what I had been doing in the Army. I explained that I had just returned from a tour of duty as a military advisor in Saudi Arabia. We talked a bit about the Iraqi problem and the interesting tour of duty I had with the Arabs. I added that I was looking forward to retiring from the service in a few months. He replied to my comment with a twinkle in his eye, "Well, now I understand why I have slept so well for the last twenty years." We both had a good laugh at that comment, but I truly took his remark as a compliment.

My older friend's service was during a great and terrible war. A war that cost many lives and forever changed so many more. There were some terrible devils in his earlier days. His generation knew well that the only way to achieve an enduring peace was through the deserts of North Africa, the beaches of Normandy, the sands of Iwo Jima, and a bomb the likes of which the world had never dreamed of. The Americans of Tom Brokaw's *The Greatest Generation* paid a price measured in lives.

By contrast my service was through twenty years of peace guaranteed by American military strength. That power was built by the people of my friend's time and has subsequently prevented the large wars seen during the first half of the 20th century. His generation bought the aircraft carriers and battle systems that projected American military might like no other country can. These extraordinary people created the *Pax Americana*. Their hard work and sacrifice are worthy of great honor from those of us who follow.

Our military service today continues to honor the greatest Americans ever and what they gave up so much for. The World War II generation of Americans paved the way to an enduring peace that is stamped with "Made in the U.S.A." Because of what my friend and millions of dedicated people like him did, I too have slept well and can continue to sleep easy for years to come.

Painful Promotions

"There is no gain without pain."
Anonymous

The adjutant reads out loud to the large formation of troops, "The Secretary of the Army has reposed great trust in…He is therefore promoted to the rank of…" It is a promotion ceremony. Selected soldiers will advance in rank this day. Along with a pay raise comes a raise in responsibility and prestige.

Any day you can get promoted is a good day. Normally it was a good day except for one small detail, now forbidden in the Army. There once was an honored tradition, a special rite with any promotion…*the blood pinning*.

The origin of this custom is obscure, probably a relic from ancient times where endurance of torture signified courage and fortitude. Or perhaps the ceremony is of more recent origin, part of an initiation to a military fraternity, or something harking back to the Indian warrior rites.

In its most recent form, blood pinning involved the placing of the new rank at the appropriate spot on a soldier's uniform, the collar or shoulder epaulettes. The two small spikes underneath the metal rank emblems are left unprotected. Once positioned, the pinning official deliberately hits each rank piece, driving it through the clothing and into the skin as the soldier stoically stands there, hopefully without even wincing. Hooaah!

Modern times and being more 'sensitive' have ended this custom, once quite common in U. S. Army promotion ceremonies, especially in units with high esprit de corps. But like most painful things an abuse or two led to complaints that in turn caused the abolishment of something considered to be barbaric by non-soldiers.

Indeed, when is war not barbaric? Highly civilized people send select members of their number great distances at large expense and hardship only for a chance at killing each other, usually for a cause started by non-soldiers. The blood pinning is child's play compared to what a bayonet or a smart bomb can do. Considering the justified horror that the military is prepared to execute, the abolishment of the blood pinning is a peacetime hypocrisy by those who might not be able to stomach the task of bringing down a Hitler.

A nation led by civilians who command our Armed Forces should well remember that without pain, there can be no gain. Certainly a case obviously can be made about certain rituals or customs being 'brutal,' but never forget that when diplomacy fails, we must then pursue, as Karl von Clausenwitz wrote, "political relations…by other means." When that time comes, as it most certainly will, do we wish to send in tough warriors or politically correct pansies?

The Aidbag

"We should pray for peace, but keep our powder dry."
Anonymous

The old, faded aidbag lies in the corner of my office now, still ready to bear lifesaving supplies for any contingency. It is one of the few pieces of military equipment that stayed with me through twenty years. From assignment to assignment, all around the world, that bag helped me to save life or soothe a hurt.

Though relatively small, about the size of a daypack, that bag held enough stuff to make a difference many a time. You can never be quite as good unless you had the Band-Aids, bandages, tubes, splints, and other things carried in a well-stocked medical kit. Head knowledge is one thing, but in life you've got to have the right tools too. The right equipment combined with the right training, enables you to be all you can be.

The aidbag was never far from me either. We saw each other practically every day. I was grateful it remained close at hand too, and I suppose others were thankful too—the injured Israeli hiker in the Sinai desert, that car accident victim in south Georgia, my daughter with her cut finger, or the soldier who collapsed during physical training.

We were always ready to go to war, that aidbag and I. Two or three times we almost went too, but in the end the Army did not require our services in combat during our twenty-year watch. We never saw the elephant. So, we made do with the business of helping sick and injured people outside of war, which is a fairly brisk business anyway.

There are a couple of stains on that old burlap exterior; the marks that time and service wrought. The bag has long since lost that newness smell that new Army equipment has. That's okay. Time and service leaves a mark on people and with age they lose their new smell too.

It is a tough old bag. Through mud and dust, rain and snow, use and reuse, the straps and even the zippers still work. The Army Medical Department spent its money well when they bought this bag. I hope I was like that bag too, tough and well worth the taxpayer's money.

Someday there will come another war. Big or small, mankind will always find reason or opportunity to shoot at each other. I hope we always stay ready for this sort of thing; especially those who choose to heal instead of kill. We should indeed pray for peace, but keep our soldiers ready and our aidbags well stocked. Someone has to survive the horror, the madness, the wounds, and the prices that will be paid in the future. Doc will be there and will be very important to the survivors, especially if he has that trusty aidbag at his side.

America

"We hold these truths to be self-evident; that all men are created equal; that they are endowed by their creator with certain unalienable rights."
Thomas Jefferson (*Declaration of Independence*)

Sometimes I just cannot be a conservative. Conservatism can be a good thing in many situations; with money, staying out of hassles, and keeping things stable. But sometimes it is good to be bold, to step forward with change, to be a radical.

America's forefathers were radicals. The Loyalist Tories of colonial America were the conservatives who wanted to preserve the status quo. Our revolution to free us from England was a quasi-civil war, the outcome of which was helped along by the providential intervention of France and the ineptitude of the British. In the view of George III, the activities of men like Washington, Jefferson, Franklin, and others were radically liberal. No doubt he had other, more colorful adjectives for these radicals as well.

It is hard to think of Abraham Lincoln as a radical too. But to Southern conservatives clinging to a dying institution, Mr. Lincoln was a radical. We should thank God that a "radical" was at the helm of state during its greatest ordeal. He not only held the whole together, but also purged it of a most foul evil, the inhumanity and hypocrisy of slavery.

Stability lovers wanted us to stay out of the 20th Century's world wars. Like law-abiding townspeople of an old western movie, they cowered under saloon tables while the bad guys were about to take over the town. Thank God, and the Japanese at Pearl Harbor, that we awoke to the threat and mustered the will to fight. Sometimes you have to fight if you're a man.

We Americans are proud of our nation. Blemishes and all, it is a most excellent deal. We can justly say that the 20th century was an American century partly because Divinity smiled upon us and we took chances that paid off handsomely. Our status going into the 21st century is a result of the leadership and risk taking of our forebears from the last century and before.

Like it or not, the whole world, including the bad guys, are still watching this great experiment in democracy. We are expected to lead and, quite frankly, we should. America is the senior officer present in a family of nations. Duty dictates that we assume a leadership role in world affairs. You cannot be proud and not accept morally lawful responsibilities as well.

The United States of America should be a conservative-liberal nation. As Teddy Roosevelt once said, "we should walk softly, but carry a big stick." We should always hope for peace, but kick butt if we have to, even if the butts are overseas. It is our duty and a truth we still hold to be self-evident.

Rank

"When an Englishman is totally incapable of doing any work whatsoever, he describes himself in the income-tax form as a *gentleman*."
Robert Lynd

Only a fraction of current Army officers rise to their positions out of the enlisted ranks, out of the so-called rank and file. Most gain their commissions through ROTC or West Point, and some through direct commissioning. Very few have been a private, sergeant, or warrant officer.

My military career began as a Private First Class or E-3. In basic, they called me "PFC Kay." A good rank in a world full of privates, but the drill sergeants coined a similar sounding title for me using a four letter vulgar word starting with "F." Basic is not a finishing school for gentlemen.

With time and effort the chevrons of the rank of sergeant found a place on my uniform. "Sergeant Kay" had a nice ring to it. Several years of being "Specialist Kay," or that irritating nickname "Special Kay," were over. In fact, buck sergeant was a great rank to hold. You gained some leverage.

In time I became an officer. Well, sort of. A warrant officer, actually. Now my rank was "Chief Kay." For seven years I went by the same title as the President...*Mister*. The nice thing about being a warrant officer was the work you were able to do and the people you could marshal together to do it. Warrant officers work hard as technicians in specific fields such as aviation, maintenance, or personnel. They are allowed to get dirty. And every now and again warrants can become fully commissioned officers.

My chance came in early 1992. The Army made physician assistants into fully commissioned officers. Finally, I was "LT Kay"—an RLO, or real live officer. With the rank came a nice pay raise but also the new and somewhat uncomfortable thought that you have to be a "gentleman." A captain once told me, officers don't work—they are there to make work. Probably true, but for me the work ethic was too ingrained as I began the journey up through officer ranks. I became a working gentleman.

When retirement came I became a mister again with a commissioned officer's retired pay. Looking back, the best title I ever had in the Army was "mister." I will never forget what a "mister" once told me. The crusty Chief Warrant Officer said, "When you commission something you merely place it into service. When you warrant something, you guarantee it will work."

Warrant Officer. Chief. Mister. Yep, best rank a gentleman could possibly want. You get to make work and do it too. And with RLO pay the benefits on the checking account were not too bad either.

Shaving

My Celtic and Viking ancestors would without any doubt be shocked at the appearance of their redheaded descendant. Though some of them would take exception to my shorter status, of greater concern would certainly be the clean-shaven face. The unshaven barbarians of yesteryear have given way to their future errant descendants who have surrendered to the modern custom of clean-shaven, "civilized" faces.

Before entering the Army, I sported a beard from time to time. Perhaps it improved my looks, but it certainly afforded the convenience of not having to torture the face each day with a razor. The Army changed that.

For twenty years the Roman custom of a clean-shaven face was for me an American 20th century requirement. Despite allied soldiers and US Navy personnel who are allowed to maintain beards, soldiers must shave.

There you stand, barely awake, each morning in front of the latrine mirror. The man you see is more wrinkled over the years. The facial stubble remains the same except for more white whiskers now. The five o'clock shadow of yesterday is now five a.m. sandpaper. Cream and razor magically transform the bum into a clean-shaven gentleman ready to take on the world.

Female soldiers of the American Army can keep their long hair, but male American soldiers will probably forever remain bound to short haircuts and a shaving razor, be it electric, twin bladed, or straight. The sharp haircuts and clean-shaven faces are an inseparable part of the American image of a modern soldier or marine.

Despite a man's extraordinary abilities and accomplishments, an unshaven face gives the opposite impression. On the other hand, a clean-shaven face buys the appearance of success for the owner, when underneath he might be a rotten failure or crook.

Ironically, the years of reluctantly shaving have caused me to willingly surrender to this Army-imposed habit. Claiming helplessness at being unable to do otherwise, I find the desire for a smooth face stronger than a beard. Besides, there are other incentives. I get more kisses from my wife with a clean-shaven face.

I'll probably flirt with wearing a beard from time to time, now that my Army days are over. But chances are I will probably one day join my Viking forefathers in honored burial with a habit courtesy of the United States Army, a smooth face provided by Schick, Norelco or Gillette.

Sunny Places

"Home, in one form or another, is the great object of life."
J.G. Holland

If you truly enjoy being in the Army, then it can be a difficult decision as the time comes when you are retirement eligible. This intensely personal choice, whether to stay in the Army or not, is influenced by many factors. Some of these include patriotism, job satisfaction, compensation, and family. A critical factor that weighs heavily on many soldiers who finally elect to retire is the prospect of finally settling down in one permanent location.

My children give people puzzled looks when they are asked, "Where are you from?" A strange question to ask Army brats. Do they state where they were born or the place where they lived the longest? For dad, this has been one of the sacrifices of military service: though my children have received a rich experience of travel and exposure to different cultures, they cannot comfortably state, "I am from Texas," or "I grew up in Seattle."

In the time of Rome, the faithful service of legionnaires sustained the prosperity and security of the empire. As each legionnaire completed their twenty to twenty-five years of often difficult and dangerous duty, the state recognized their service with a grant of land. They received a place to finish out their days, somewhere to call home.

Failing health strikes down many former soldiers and robs them of their well earned home. High blood pressure, heart disease, depression, and cancers are some of the robbers out there. How sad when such a well-deserved retirement is cut short by youthful habits carried over year after year. Smart soldiers stay away from the thieves of smoking, extra weight, drug abuse, a poor diet, or inability to cope with change. They will live longer to enjoy the fruits of their military labor.

A place to call home is a great longing of many career soldiers. There is no place like home. It is therefore natural for soldiers to search for where to live, perhaps many years before they are retirement eligible. They search and plan before it is too late to enjoy it. The modest pension from the US Government, smartly used, can guarantee its receiver a home.

As dedicated to the mission as many soldiers are, there comes a time, like it or not, when one has to move on. There will come a changing of the guard: a time to go home. You have no choice in the matter. Eventually you will be too old to stay a soldier. When you are finally called out of formation, step out proudly and take hold of your well-earned place in the sun!

Oz

"I'm really a very good man; but I'm a very bad wizard."
Lyman Frank Baum (The Wonderful *Wizard of Oz)*

It is perhaps a strange way to say good-bye to your wife in the morning—"Good-bye, honey, I'm off to see the Wizard." Its origin is obscured by years of getting out of bed, shaving, donning the green uniform and getting a bite to eat before heading out the door for another day in the Army. Days filled with change and adventure. Days often best described as living in the Land of Oz, a kingdom both strange and wonderful.

Why call it the Land of Oz? Well, maybe it is the Yellow Brick Road part, for no small portion of serving this great United States is the good living one gains by doing it. It might be the journey itself, a trip to places interesting and marvelous. It could also be the search for a brain, a heart, or some courage in a world so very different from home, no matter where you might come from.

Whatever the reason, that is how I would often leave the house each morning. Off to see the Wizard in a land that is the U.S. Army.

There certainly are many days when the Army does seem to be like the Land of Oz. There are interesting people, wicked witches, lost people looking for a way back home, or moments when you are attacked by flying apes. There are encounters with huffers and puffers trying to look and act bigger than they really are, but who are actually little people just like you and me. They too put their pants on one leg at a time. In the end, it's all a great odyssey full of smoke and mirrors, good and bad, and always rich with emotions and memories.

In time, my wife would hardly notice the curious farewell I'd give her each day. She too had been to Oz and sometimes marveled at the complexities of the Army subculture. She understood. As the years rolled by, she grew accustomed to the routine of military life, at first so completely foreign to her Canadian upbringing.

My wife especially rejoiced when her husband finally found a brain, a heart, and some courage. The brains to find a good career, the heart to do something good with his life, and the courage to say good-bye to the Army one day when that opportune time arrived.

Through much travel and many assignments we found our home. Around the world and from one end of the United States to the other, the United States Army's yellow brick road led us there.

The Wizard did well. There is indeed no place like home.

Rear Guard Action

"Every sweet hath its sour; every evil its good."
Emerson

In the fall of 1999, the U.S. Army gave me the task of preparing twelve-uncertified physician assistants in the Army for a final attempt to pass their national board examination. This was no ordinary group of medical officers. Out of over five hundred PAs in the Army, these were the bottom of the pile, the rear guard. They were all good people—professional, enthusiastic, with strong backgrounds of service to this country. They set themselves to the task of preparing for the exam with vigor, for they knew the Army's patience was running out. This was a critical juncture in their military and medical careers. Fail and they could no longer see patients.

We had four weeks to get ready. An intense program of study topics, readings, tests, and group drills would try to cover what normally is done in years of formal medical training. It was an uphill prospect, as each PA had already failed the exam an average of three times. By October they were as ready as we could get them and the "dirty dozen" sat for their exams. Though each felt more confident about how ready they were for the test, no one would know for sure until the results came eight weeks later.

The leadership of the Army medical department and other certified PAs were anxious for the results. We were already too short handed to lose twelve more, but the Army's overall effort to improve credentials and certifications on all medical officers led to moments like this, where doctors and PAs face the music for the last time. As the mentor of this special group, I was hoping for the best, but expecting to loose some nevertheless. Like Gregory Peck in the movie "*Twelve O'clock High*," I nervously awaited the return of "my bombers" from what many expected to be their last mission. The odds were against them.

On the 8th of December the results arrived. Symbolically, I was scanning the skies for any returns, hoping for some to make it even if their engines were on fire. Five PAs passed their boards and seven did not. The results were both sweet and sour.

From time to time the press may cast a negative eye toward military medicine. Funded by the taxpayers, military medicine is in a fishbowl of sorts. Coming from someone who shepherded a rear guard action with the last of the last, people need to know that there are standards in the practice of Army medicine. Those who are not to standard have to find another job. We can be proud of the healthcare the troops receive because it is delivered by the very best doctors, physician assistants and nurses in the country.

Toenails

"There is fungus among us."
Anonymous

It all began back during basic training. I joined the Army with good looking toenails and by the end of boot camp my left great toenail was getting yellow, thick, and brittle. All that time in humid boots and the stress on my immune system set me up for *onychomycosis*—the dreaded toenail fungus.

I remember my father having the same problem, only he had it on every toe. He had a textbook case. If he had been alive when I was stricken with the same malady, he probably would have said he originally got his case from the military also, albeit an Air Force variety. I remember how big and yellow his nails were and how he'd use a huge nail clipper to keep those monstrously thick nails under control.

I once reflected on what sort of disability claim I could conjure up from my personal medical history. All I could come up with was the long-term handicap associated with a single, brittle, thick, yellow, left, great toenail. Now surely here was a good claim for the Veteran's Administration!

Many people get disabilities while on active duty. It is interesting how many freeloaders out there try to get disability out of their service time. I mean, any ache or pain is a potential claim for these people. When it hurts they see dollar signs. Never mind that some pain comes with age. Normal wear and tear. Like a fungus to the taxpayers, there will always be folks with brittle ethics looking to thicken their wallets with their yellowish motives.

My teenage kids were always grossed out by my deformed toenail, my *hunchback of notre pedis*. My daughter in particular took a keen interest in the pathology of my condition and even felt sorry for me. If only I could get her onto the disability claims review board when my case came up.

The never ending wonders of pharmacological research finally produced a rather pricey medicine that did a good job of fixing people's toenail fungus problems without frying their liver at the same time. Why, even the Army eventually bought the wonder drug and I managed to get a prescription. In six or eight weeks I could see a big difference. After twenty years in the Army, the beast was turning into a beauty once again.

I went into retirement with a completely intact body. I had no pain, no missing limbs, no lost marbles, no toenail fungus, and, unfortunately (or fortunately) no disability either. I left the Army with the same good-looking toenails as before and proud to be seen in the common footwear of retirees: sandals.

Family Name

"Who serves his country well has no need of ancestors."
Voltaire

Although we are nine generations of Kay's removed, I am the namesake of another James Kay, a self-transplanted Yorkshireman who arrived in the New World in the year 1652. Settling in the Tidewater area of Virginia, my forefather established the first presence of Kay's on the American continent, well over one hundred years before the American Revolution. Since his arrival, the Kay family has flourished to the point that now his descendants number in the thousands, concentrated primarily in the American South, but also touching every state in the Union.

The family name Kay does not conjure up a lot of famous people. There are no kings, presidents, famous generals, popular singers or movie stars with the name Kay. Oh, there was a Danny Kaye, but he spelt the name with an extra "e" and Kaye wasn't even his real name. Kay's were primarily a hardy, common folk, building up this great nation like thousands of other regular families with names from Abel to Ziblinski.

The ranks of America's armies have seen a fair number of Kay's, mostly serving in the rank and file under the command of other outstanding people who would make their family name a household word: names like Washington, Jackson, Lee, Pershing, Patton, or Powell. The success and fame of a few families is built upon the bricks of many other families.

It is a good thing to trace your family tree. Many of us are naturally curious about our lineage and today it is not so difficult to trace your roots. You don't have to necessarily enter politics, as Mark Twain once wrote, to have someone trace your family tree for you. I once returned to my ancestral homelands in northern England and Scotland. From the picturesque dales of James Herriot's Yorkshire to the magnificent castle at Edinburgh, I found traces of Kay's who did not come to America. There were Kay's who stood in their kilts with Wellington against Napoleon, others who helped establish an empire upon which the sun did not set, and more recently some who dueled and died with Germans in the skies over Europe.

History will march on and will be written by the victors, sprinkled with the names of their now famous families. Only tomorrow will tell who those families will be. One thing is certain about Americans and their unique history: we generally detest dynasties. It is therefore highly probable that tomorrow's glories and accomplishments will highlight new family names, names that more than likely are sewn or attached to name tags prominently displayed on the uniforms of some of this great nation's soldiers today.

Daddy

"Old men are children for a second time."
Aristophanes

One thing I regret is that we do not have much film footage of our children growing up through my Army years. Of the many things we had to have, it seemed my income could never find room for a video camera until the children were much older. Too bad, for the few film segments we do have cause us to want to see more.

But that makes what we do have extra special. There were a couple of times when I rented or borrowed a camera and did some shots. Of the short clips we do have, some captured daddy on the floor with the kids.

I had forgotten just how much time I was on my hands and knees playing with my offspring. It was a great joy for daddy to leave the Army behind and go home to romp with the children. There were once huge battles in my home. My sons and I played with plastic toy soldiers and wooden blocks on the living room floor. Empires rose and fell in our make-believe world on the carpet. We also built sophisticated cities and space vehicles of tomorrow with the small fortune in *Lego's* that we had accumulated over the years. And toy cars! You haven't seen how many little cars three boys can amass while moving around in the Army.

In one film my auburn-haired daughter dominated most scenes. Stephanie was a toddler, maybe eighteen months old. She always got the biggest kick out of daddy being on all fours acting like a horse she could ride or some lion or other chasing after her. Running around the living room in her trademark pajama suit, I had forgotten her special grin and giggle the video brought back so vividly.

Children are a huge responsibility. Many people choose simply not to have children because of all the work and concern involved. I respect their choice, but frankly they miss out on a lot. Yeah, we'll have paid for the equivalent of ten or twelve new cars by the time they all finish college, but that's okay. Every now and again things happen which tell you it was a good decision to have kids and the inconveniences they bring are more than worth it. Those rare videotapes are such a reminder.

I reckon there will come more times when I can lie down on the floor again without fear of embarrassment. There will be new imaginary battles to fight. Toy cars will find use again. We'll dig out the same toys that entertained the parents of the next generation. Grandchildren afford old soldiers a legitimate chance to be a child again and get away with it without seeing a shrink. Grandma will want to make sure the video camera works.

Being Real

"Generally, by the time you are real,
most of your hair has been loved off,
and your eyes drop out
and you get loose in the joints and very shabby.
But these things don't matter at all,
because once you are real you can't be ugly,
except to people who don't understand."
Margery Williams (*The Velveteen Rabbit*)

Margery Williams probably was not thinking of soldiers when she penned the beautiful lines above, certainly the most memorable lines from a classic children's book. Even so, she was not far from the truth. Old soldiers were all young, new, and very energetic once. Starting out as privates or cadets, full of dreams and looking for that great adventure. They had more hair then too.

A military career consumes the prime of life for many of America's finest offspring. As their years in the Army roll by the roaring twenties flow into the thirty-somethings and on into their forties where, at least in the Army, you're an old man. By then, there are some bald spots on your head, your eyelids are starting to get baggy, the joints ache more with physical fitness training, and many begin to get flabby.

Mercifully, the United States Army understands this aging process and makes allowance for soldiers to gain a couple of extra pounds as they get older and also have a modest increase in the amount of time required to complete the obligatory, twice each year two-mile run. Not much, mind you, but at least it is a token acknowledgment that, yes, everyone cannot stay a jock forever. If you stay in the Army till your fifties, well, you are indeed very old then.

Most career soldiers bid farewell to the service in their forties. You've given twenty to twenty-five years to the country and it is still possible to get out and pursue another vocation. Drive a truck. Start a business. Write a book. Unless you have a good shot at general officer, it is a good time to go.

Younger soldiers in their lighter moments may poke fun at the older soldiers. You know, the ones upon whom father time is beginning to leave his mark—the slow runner, the portly appearance, the graying hair, the extra hair in wrong places. But these things don't matter at all. Because once you are a career soldier you can't be ugly, except to people who don't understand. By that time the rank you hold really does not matter a great deal either. What does matter is that you are real. You have been all you could be.

363

Clichés

"Even if you're on the right track,
you'll get run over if you just sit there."
Will Rogers

For practically my entire twenty-year Army career, the recruiting slogan for the Army was *Be All You Can Be.* Adopted just after I joined, it was the second most popular jingle of 20th century America, second only to McDonald's *You deserve a break today.*

Imagine my surprise when the U.S. Army decided to drop the once popular phrase in the very year my twenty-year career would end. In a sense, the change to a new slogan was a confirmation of the already decided title for this book, a work about a time when soldiers were indeed being all they could be. The end of a slogan, the end of a remarkable century, and the end of one man's military journey would all coincide. Indeed, we would all be history now.

History is the experience of others. Too bad that history is so boring to many people. Perhaps it is the way it is written. Maybe even now, as you read this book, the eyelids grow heavy. I hope not. Experience is for many people something they received long after they needed it most. History and experience teach us it is important to learn from others mistakes and short-comings beforehand, lest the same befall us in our time.

The next generation of soldiers will arrive and the Army will likely change to meet their needs. Past catchwords become outdated, passé, no longer as effective as before. Fresh, new ideas come forward, some clever phrase the government paid big bucks to an ad agency to conjure up.

A generation of soldiers passes on. Life is a process of moving on to something new and different. But I'm not sure just how much of the Army can ever be new and different. Old soldiers will chuckle at the new slogans and gimmicks.

Nothing is new except how things are arranged, someone once said. I wonder if that person had also been in the Army.

Yes, the new slogan will be just a new wrapper on the same loaf of bread. That loaf of bread can never change. You can do slick ads, make things look really cool, and even sweeten the deal with money, but the bottom line, what the United States Army will always need to be, will remain unchanged.

On their first day in the Army the new soldiers of tomorrow will learn very quickly that all is not what the recruiting ads tell them. The sergeants of the greatest Army in the world will see that they will be all they're supposed to be, or else.

Army Men

"Ability is trying all things; achieving what you can."
Herman Melville

As a child I always admired things military, a genetic hard wiring I suppose. Growing up surrounded by men who had fought during WWII and Korea, a young boy of the 1960s could easily gravitate towards the militaristic nature of American males at that time. John Wayne made it all cool. But the debacle of Vietnam, brought so vividly to everyone's attention by television in those days, began to erode some of my interest for all things martial.

The turbulence of that time led to the late 1970s, which found me as a young man unsure of what path to follow. Frankly, there were too many choices. I needed time to think and do some traveling too, so military ambitions resurfaced. Besides, the job market left something to be desired.

In the spring of 1979 I enlisted into the United States Army as a medical corpsman. I had always been interested in medical things, though my first love had been history and languages. With that enlistment began a journey that at the time I did not realize would last so long.

My life in the U.S. Army has been very much like that of tens of thousands of other people, yet on the other hand, somewhat different too. Seldom today do you meet soldiers who have had the opportunity of advancing through non-commissioned officer, warrant officer, and officer ranks. Also, not many Army personnel today have had the opportunity for assignment in such a variety of units: infantry, aviation, armor, cavalry, artillery, foreign advisor, peace-keeping force, hospitals and military schools. This and more were mine.

It was a great career. Joining up was a most excellent choice. By God's grace and the needs of the Army, I have been all I could be. The terrific journey leaves no regrets. My message to those who will follow is simple:

> To try and succeed is better
> Than to try and fail.
> To try and fail is better
> Than not trying.
> The true meaning of life
> Is to always try.
> And to not try is
> No good at all.

- David Kay

You are retired from active duty, released from assignment and duty, and on the date following, placed on the retired list. The people of the United States express their thanks and gratitude for your faithful service. Your contributions to the defense of the United States of America are greatly appreciated.

Opening statement to U.S. Army retirement orders

July, 1979

About the Author

Major James David Kay, USA-Ret. is a native of Asheville, North Carolina.
David enlisted in the United States Army as a medic in 1979.
His twenty-year career included assignments all around the world
and advancements through enlisted, warrant officer, and officer ranks.
He saw service as a physician assistant field medical officer in cavalry,
infantry, aviation, armor, foreign advisor and peacekeeping assignments.
His awards include the Legion of Merit and The Order of Military Medical
Merit. Major Kay and his wife Irene now reside in Spokane, Washington.
Their four children, all Army brats, are being all they can be too.

June, 2000
The Kay Family: Nathan, Irene, Stephanie, David, Marlan, Brian

Photos and Illustrations

Khaki, p. 14
Buddies at Medic
School, Fort Sam Houston,
Texas. (Fall, 1979)

The Volksmarch, p.33
Chaplain Workman and Family.
Irene, David and Nathan are to
the right. Note the yellow child
carrier/backpack.
(**Angels and Roots**, p. 39)

Top, p. 42
PFC Kay, Baumholder
Training Area.
Note the big mud holes.
(Winter, 1980) See also
Powerful Queens, p. 37.

The Gamma Goat, p. 60
Note the drip pan below
the engine section. (See
The Dubious Honor, p. 41
and **Leaks**, p. 135)

Boot Ornaments, p. 88
Fort Hood, Texas

Homesick, p. 102
Brian needs some attention.

Hover Button, p. 121
Fort Rucker, Alabama.
(Fall, 1987)

The Business Card, p. 137

Lo I beheld a pale rider astride
a **Blackhorse** and the rider's
name was **Death.**

REFORGER '88

West Germany

YOU
DIED
HERE

Compliments of 1st Squadron, 11th ACR
IRONHORSE

Caring People, p. 146. 1LT Mike Pankratz is on the far left.
SGT Kenneth Molbert (**Burgers**, p. 147 and **The Cough**, p. 163)
is crouched just to the left of the sign. Note the Iron Curtain
and guard tower in the background (**The Tower**, p.342).

High Tech Soldiers, p. 164
Here CW2 Kay is flanked by
an East German Colonel on
the left and a Soviet Union
Colonel on the right.

Working With the Best, p. 158
Pack 168, Fulda, Germany. (Spring, 1989)

Checkers, p. 190
Mount Sinai, Egypt.
(Fall, 1991)

Title Index

Title Index

Title Index

Title Index

Quotation Index

Quotation Index

Quotation Index